THE HISTORY OF
EUROPEAN LIBERALISM

The History of

EUROPEAN LIBERALISM

By Guido de Ruggiero

Translated by R. G. Collingwood

BEACON PRESS   BEACON HILL   BOSTON

First published by the Oxford University Press in 1927
First published as a Beacon Paperback in 1959

Printed in the United States of America

Library of Congress Catalog Card Number: 59-6394

Second printing, August 1961

IN THE NAME OF MY LITTLE
CORRADO
THIS BOOK IS DEDICATED
TO THE NEW GENERATION OF
ITALIANS

TRANSLATOR'S PREFACE

THE words *liberal* and *liberalism*, as used in this book, have a significance far wider than the platform or policy of any single party. They are used 'in their continental, not in their British, meaning. We borrowed them from abroad, and have used them to designate a party, or, rather, a particular section of a particular party. But "Liberalism" as used in its original home is a name for principles of constitutional liberty and representative government, which have long been the common property of all parties throughout the English-speaking portions of the world '. In these terms Lord Balfour explained his own use of the words in his introduction to the English translation of Treitschke's *Politics* ; and, with such authority, the present translator need not apologize for a severely literal rendering of his author's terms.

Liberalism, as Professor De Ruggiero understands it, begins with the recognition that men, do what we will, are free ; that a man's acts are his own, spring from his own personality, and cannot be coerced. But this freedom is not possessed at birth ; it is acquired by degrees as a man enters into the self-conscious possession of his personality through a life of discipline and moral progress. The aim of Liberalism is to assist the individual to discipline himself and achieve his own moral progress ; renouncing the two opposite errors of forcing upon him a development for which he is inwardly unprepared, and leaving him alone, depriving him of that aid to progress which a political system, wisely designed and wisely administered, can give.

These principles lead in practice to a policy that may be called, in the sense above defined, Liberal ; a policy which regards the State, not as the vehicle of a superhuman wisdom or a superhuman power, but as the organ by which a people expresses whatever of political ability it can find and breed and train within itself. This is not democracy, or the rule of the mere majority ; nor is it authoritarianism, or the irresponsible rule of those who, for whatever reason, hold power at a given moment. It is something between the two. Democratic in its respect for human liberty, it is authoritarian in the importance it attaches to the necessity for skilful and practised government. But it is no mere compromise; it has its own principles ; and not only are these superior in practice to the abstractions of democracy and authoritarianism, but, when properly understood, they reveal themselves as more logical.

The development of this conception, in the political theory and practice of the last hundred years and more, is the subject of this book. It is a subject of the utmost interest to-day, when from various sides, in various countries, the political systems that take their stand upon freedom are being attacked by powerful and dangerous enemies. Is political freedom a chimera, or is it the one lodestar of sound policy ? Is it destined to disappear, crushed between the opposing tyrannies of the majority and the minority, or has it the strength to outlive its opponents ? To these questions our author has here given a reasoned answer, and one to which no thoughtful student of politics can be indifferent.

The translator, by the author's wish, has modified a few sentences in the chapter on English Liberalism, where discussion with natives of this country has led him to be dissatisfied with certain details of his original statement. These passages are marked by foot-notes in square brackets; footnotes so distinguished being everywhere the translator's. In the rendering of certain phrases, the translator gratefully acknowledges the aid of Lt.-Col. A. S. L. Farquharson, Sig. Salvatore Breglia, and the author.

R. G. C.

STAPLETON'S CHANTRY,
    NORTH MORETON.
        March 1927.

CONTENTS

INTRODUCTION : THE EIGHTEENTH CENTURY

PART I

THE HISTORICAL FORMS OF LIBERALISM

I. ENGLISH LIBERALISM . . . 93–157

II. FRENCH LIBERALISM . . . 158–210

PART II

LIBERALISM IN ITS EUROPEAN SIGNIFICANCE

INTRODUCTION

THE EIGHTEENTH CENTURY

§ 1. FEUDAL LIBERTY

' IN France, liberty is ancient; despotism is modern.'
These words of Madame de Staël are not without historical truth. Liberty is an older thing than the absolutism
of modern monarchy, because it has its roots in feudal
society. Here it appears broken up and (so to speak) ato-
mized into a myriad of particular liberties, each enclosed in an
envelope which conceals but at the same time protects it : as
such, we know it under the name of privilege. Where the
force of the State is reduced to a mere appearance, this is the
only form in which liberty can exist. In the absence of a
superior and common safeguarding power, individual forces
try to preserve themselves by their own strength, uniting with
each other according to their closest affinities, and thus provide that minimum of security which is indispensable to the
development of their activity. Feudal aristocracy, urban and
rural communities, trade guilds, are privileged groups ; that
is to say, free each within its own sphere.

From this it follows that in the feudal world liberty arises
from a certain equality and from a certain security. Without
a relative equality of conditions inside each class or group, it
would be impossible to speak of liberty or right, but only of
conflict and force. Liberty or right, to have a meaning, must
imply recognition ; and this again implies a certain reciprocity. And we see that, in the development of medieval
society, the number of privileged individuals and groups increases as the circulation of life intensifies and creates wider
relations between man and man. A mere extension of privilege ultimately makes it possible to see the original source of
all privilege in the personality or nature of man.

The peculiar character of this privileged liberty is due to
the legal outlook which creates and maintains it. The Middle

Ages are the period of the exclusive dominion of private rights. There are no such things as independent public rights ; all the relations which we moderns are accustomed to comprise under that head are immediately rooted in property, contract, heredity, and the family. Here, too, is the legal source of liberties ; some of which are inherent in determinate situations relative to property and to the family, while others are derived from contracts or gifts. The fundamental distinction which we make to-day between civil liberty and political liberty is therefore foreign to medieval thought ; this is partly why, even in modern times, the distinction has not become familiar without a struggle.

Of course this does not mean that the Middle Ages knew no such thing as political liberties. It only means that they confused these with all others. The charters which sanction them are nothing but contracts between prince and people, where each contracting party is possessed of an exclusive right of his own, and exchanges it or tempers it with the right of the other party in view of their common interests. Political liberty is not claimed as something inseparable from human personality; it is bought and sold like a piece of property; and all institutions derived from this fundamental contract reveal an original nature which we might call, to use a juridical term, privatistic. Thus, for example, Estates General, Houses of Lords and Commons, and Diets, do not consist of representatives of the people, like modern parliamentary institutions; they consist rather of mandatories or persons deputed to safeguard the interests of particular classes and groups. Their function is wholly devoid of that character of universality which for us is the distinctive mark of public rights. Moreover, the contractual nature of political agreements not only implies the consent of all contracting parties to the object of the agreement, which deprives a mere majority of any value, but it also excludes all constitutional conflict, in the modern sense of the word, in cases of disagreement.

The survival of these conceptions during the eighteenth century, when modern liberalism was coming into existence, gave rise to many complicated legal and political problems :

for example, whether representation is a mandate; whether or no it has an imperative character; how voting ought to be carried out; and so forth. Even Rousseau, whose social contract, as we shall see, is radically different from that which we have been considering, is merely following in the footsteps of traditional contractualism when he demands a unanimous consent to the making of the social pact, and when he reserves to dissentients the right of denying all compulsory power to the pact and of withdrawing from the State.

This contractual character of the feudal state rests upon an original dualism between the contracting parties, the prince and the people, meaning by the people the privileged groups which form its active nuclei. This is the peculiar feature of the political ideas of the Germanic peoples, which in the West superimposed themselves upon the monistic Roman conception of the State.[1] Since the primary source of the prince's power is not different from that of the rest of the territorial aristocracy, but flows equally in either case from the property in which political sovereignty is inherent, it follows that their mutual relations are the relations of sovereign to sovereign, or, more strictly, of private person to private person, free man to free man. This original equality of rights, while creating the relations through which the feudal monarchy of the Middle Ages is organized, at the same time already contains within itself the living seeds of future conflict. Both sides soon begin to struggle for the preservation or expansion of their own power; the aristocracy striving to reinforce the régime of privilege, the monarchy to destroy it and to reduce its subjects to a dead level of subservience.

Modern liberalism, in its origins, is not connected exclusively with either party to this conflict, but with both at once, with the conflict itself. Without the effective resistance of particular privileged classes, the monarchy would have created nothing but a people of slaves; without the levelling effected by royal absolutism, the régime of privilege, however widely extended, would never have bridged the gulf which divides privilege from liberty in the proper sense of

[1] Jellinek, *Allgemeine Staatslehre*, Berlin, ed. 2, 1905, pp. 311 *seqq.*

the word—that liberty which universalizes privilege to the
point of annulling it as such. But the course of this struggle
and its ultimate consequences are so complicated and historically individualized that it is of little use to rest content
with this schematic and impersonal statement of the facts.
We must therefore descend, so far as possible, to the where,
the when, and the how.

§ 2. ARISTOCRACY AND MONARCHY

From this point of view the history of France differs fundamentally from that of Great Britain. Among the states of the
European continent, the kingdom of France, ever since the
dawn of the modern period, most clearly embodies the vital
needs of a continental policy. Hemmed in by two great
monarchies, Spain and the Empire, obliged to struggle incessantly for existence, she soon feels the need to concentrate
her strength and overcome the inner disunion that feudalism
implies. From Louis XI to Louis XIV this great work of
state concentration is going forward. But the monarchy
which is the author of this process, with the collaboration of
the *bourgeois* class, never formally attacks the constituent
principles of the ancient régime, but superimposes upon
them by degrees its own administrative activity, in such a
way as to swamp their empty but unimpaired form beneath
a new substance. It attacks the aristocracy only indirectly,
by depriving it of political power by means of its own in-
tendents; by reducing its economic strength, the source of
its independence and prestige; and by drawing it towards
the capital, away from its natural home and its sphere of
independent activity. The aristocracy, though still a privileged, becomes a parasitic and servile class. It loses the political capacity and talent which made it a governing class, and
while its economic situation becomes worse, and class prejudice
prevents it from restoring its fortunes by industry and trade,
it becomes dependent upon subsidies and salaries from the
Crown, and thus finds its privileges increased by the very
changes which make them harder to justify.

These privileges, in point of fact, were not at first a free gift. They implied a correlative service on the part of the aristocracy towards the community at large. Its tenure of land, its immunities, its franchises found a justification in the eyes of the people, the bearer of these burdens, in the task of protection, defence, and government. The aristocracy was the ' general class ' *par excellence*, exempt from the cares of daily life precisely in order that it might turn all its activities to the service of the common weal; and its monopoly of the land was justified by the fact that, being independent in the source of its power, it was able to form a real body politic, intermediate between the Crown and the people, a bulwark against all usurpation, whether from above or from below. Its pre-eminent military position was similarly explained by the organization of feudal armies, recruited, maintained, and officered as they were by feudatories.

But this spontaneous justification of privilege disappeared with the disappearance of the corresponding functions; and the immunities of the nobles became at last a dead weight upon the working classes, a burden the more odious as it was useless. In the eighteenth century a widespread feeling grew up not only of their injustice but, worse, of their moral degradation, so that, as a contemporary said, ' the same class of men could be loaded at once with honours and with infamy '.[1]

But the aristocracy was not the only privileged class upon which the action of absolute monarchy made itself felt. All classes and communities were subject to it, in varying degrees and with different results. The liberties of the communes were practically coeval with those of the nobility; and were all the more distasteful to the new monarchy as being more refractory to its discipline, as well as because of the antiquity and autonomy of their titles. Against these communal liberties the Crown adopted both a policy of gradual absorption through the expansion of its own administrative activities, and also the more radical and arbitrary expedient of confiscation, tempered by the practice of selling back these very privileges to their original possessors in moments of financial

[1] Montesquieu, *Esprit des lois*, xviii. 7.

stress; and this practice of alternate sale and confiscation prevailed so generally during the last two centuries of absolutism that the precarious character of these rights discredited their value more irreparably than mere suppression, however violent, could have done. Thus in the eighteenth century communal liberties may be considered as wholly extinct, even so far as traditional prestige is concerned; and this is one of the heaviest losses which modern liberalism will have to lament.

The trade guilds, the industrial and commercial classes, and in general the *bourgeoisie* possess privileges of a different kind. These were in great part created by the Crown itself. They have, further, a double character of burdens, as well as privileges, by which the State treasury benefits. These privileges correspond to a function beneficial to society at large, and in its social aspect not unlike that which once justified the privileges of the aristocracy; a clear sign that, even while the feudal system yet survives, the political and economic centre of society has shifted to the middle classes. The favour shown by the Crown towards the new class even extends to conferring titles and immunities proper to the nobility upon its chief members. In this way a social function fundamentally modern in character is consecrated, as it were, by ancient rites.

None the less the first signs of revolt against the régime of privilege come from this very class, a privileged class no less than the other, though privileged for a different reason. It grew up and acquired its strength at a time when its youthful energies required defence and assistance; but having now reached maturity, it feels that it can stand alone. The envelope which once protected it now becomes a burden. The restrictions upon industry and agriculture which at one time favoured the development of the *bourgeoisie* now become an obstacle to further expansion; and even if some of their own privileges are still of actual value, this is no compensation for the fact that they are compelled, by the solidarity of the system, to shoulder the entire burden of the vast privileges passively enjoyed by the nobles. This calculation of profit and loss forms the most cogent argument of the *bourgeoisie* in its controversy with the nobility at the meeting of the Estates General in 1614. To the request of the nobility for the abolition of the hereditary character of offices,[1] the Third Estate agrees; but desires that to this should be added the abolition of their sale, and on the other hand the abolition of pensions, which form an immense burden upon the treasury and are enjoyed exclusively by nobles.[2]

It was nearly two centuries before the controversy came to an end; and in that time it was to spread from a single point to the entire system of privileges; but this expression of opinion on the part of the French *bourgeoisie* already shows the character of its outlook.

What the Third Estate was beginning even at that date to demand was the reign of common rights, in which the equality of all individuals in the eyes of the law could place every one in a position to develop his own capacities, and the identity of men before the law might be the soil in which the differences of their individual activities should germinate. For the success of this demand it was fortunate that France was governed by an absolute monarchy, whose energetic levelling of its subjects permitted the introduction and diffusion of Roman law, a law applying equally to all *qua* subjects, in the place of a multiform customary law. Thus the new-born *bourgeois* liberalism had already acquired one formal and universal element, equality in the eyes of the law.

But what of the content of this form? We have just seen a new consciousness arising and consolidating itself in the struggle against the feudal régime; but it is still sheltering behind its strongest ally, the Crown, and turning the expansive power of absolutism into a means to the civil unification of the entire people. It will remain loyal to the monarchy until the revolution; that is to say, so long as it can hope that the monarchy will complete its work of reformation and liberate itself and the people from the last relics of feudalism.

---

[1] This request had been made against the Third Estate, which in its own interest succeeded in retaining offices in the holder's family.

[2] A. Thierry, *Essai sur l'histoire de la formation et des progrès du Tiers État*, Paris, 1864, ed. 4, pp. 163 *seqq.*

Mirabeau is to revive this hope for the last time in the very hall of the Constituent Assembly. But when the Crown reveals itself as wavering irresolutely between the new and the old, and more inclined to go back than forwards, then the *bourgeoisie* will turn against the Crown also; and, fighting its twofold battle by itself and for itself, will reveal once for all the physiognomy of its own mind.

In Britain the course of the struggle between the classes and the Crown was very different. Here, too, the power of the Crown asserted itself through the victory of one aristocratic family over the rest, and the political unification of the kingdom. But the vital motives of protection and defence against external enemies, which on the continent strengthened the State at the expense of individual liberty, had less weight with an island people naturally protected by the sea. The principal tool of oppression, armed force, was wanting; for on the one hand the fleet, Britain's chief defence, had an individualistic structure and, so to speak, a peripheric action, rendering it an ally of freedom rather than despotism; and on the other hand the army, almost always engaged in continental wars, was for that very reason useless for the work of enslavement at home.

Consequently absolutism, though asserting itself for a time, and attaining its apogee in the Tudor period, found itself confronted by powerful centres of resistance, which at last made common cause to destroy it.

The most striking fact in this connexion is the fundamental difference between the English aristocracy and the French. The former, like the latter, drew its power from landed property and from the public functions connected with its tenure; but its attachment to the soil was very much stronger, and the care with which it exercised the functions arising from that attachment very much greater and more vigilant. Between the greater and the lesser aristocracy there arose at an early date a definite division of political and administrative work. The former had its natural representative in the House of Lords, while the latter, its immediate offspring, fed the House of Commons, and (its most important function) formed the backbone of local administration and local justice. The very name of the ' gentry ', the lesser nobility of the country-side, is bound up with the characteristic English idea of self-government, the strongest protection against all encroachment on the part of the central administration.

Add to this, that while the French nobility formed an exclusive caste, the English had no definite limit to mark it off from the other classes of the people; and this fact, though it did not diminish the distance between the classes, made it less conspicuous and less unpopular. Further, nobility belonged only to eldest sons. Younger sons were absorbed into the middle class and shared in its industry and trade, thus replenishing the sources of family wealth.

Again, in contrast with the French system by which the poor man paid for the rich, here the rich man paid for the poor. Owners of property not only enjoyed no immunity from taxation, but they provided for the assistance of the poor and unemployed of their own parish. The poor-tax, which at the time of the industrial revolution was to be so bitterly opposed by the economists, really represents, under a narrowly feudal economic system, a measure of great political insight, calculated at once to increase the prestige of the richer classes and to protect society against the effects of famine, whose destructive onslaught has elsewhere grievously aggravated the diseases to which it is due.

The seventeenth and eighteenth centuries, which for the French aristocracy mark a period of decadence and economic ruin, were the age of greatest prosperity for the aristocracy of England. Its landed property underwent a striking extension, as it employed its political power to appropriate by legislative action the greater part of that uncultivated and unenclosed land, the residue of the communal property of the Middle Ages. The Enclosure Acts, suggested by the economic advantages of developing lands which the law and custom of the community had rendered infertile by excessive subdivision, turned to the exclusive profit of the great landowners; for their overwhelming influence permitted them not only to assign to themselves the greatest portion, but also to buy up those which fell to the lot of the small cultivators.[1]

The enclosures were the most revolutionary measure adopted for many centuries by this shrewdly conservative class. Their historical consequences were incalculable. It was through them that the independent cultivators were gradually destroyed, those yeomen who, as English historians are never tired of repeating, formed the glorious infantry of Crécy and Agincourt, and might in modern times have formed a solid economic and political nucleus able to counterbalance and consolidate the energies of the new industrialism. But the remnants of this class, dispersed and torn from the soil, were in fact destined themselves to become the industrial proletariate, and to bring with them into the factory, together with an unwearied diligence in labour, a great home-sickness for the land no less pregnant with consequences.

This exodus from the land was chiefly due to the fact that the aristocracy, when extending its estates, found it most useful and profitable to replace the small-scale cultivation of cereals by large-scale pasture and even large-scale sporting estates requiring a small amount of labour. What was the use of the small-scale farming of yesterday? It could do nothing but multiply population, the most useless of products, as a great agriculturist of the eighteenth century described it.[2] Crops of human beings had their value in the darkest ages of feudalism, when the fief was primarily a human farm for supporting soldiers; but the English aristocracy had by now undergone profound changes, and, although it preserved the forms of feudalism for the sake of the advantages that they still offered, it was working hard to supply them with a utilitarian and bourgeois content. Through the agricultural developments of the eighteenth century, large estates became the form best adapted to the introduction of large-scale cultivation of an industrial type; and if a contemporary had repeated Sir Thomas More's complaint that the sheep devoured the men

---

[1] Paul Mantoux, *La révolution industrielle au xviiie siècle*, Paris, 1906, pp. 132 *seqq.*   [2] A. Young, *Political Arithmetic*, i. 47.

it would have been replied that they served to feed the woollen mills that were multiplying in the land.

Thus the agricultural development, which on the continent could only take place after a revolution, came about in England by imperceptible changes in the old system of landed property. Without requiring to destroy any of the great institutions of the feudal period, Great Britain at the end of the eighteenth century was, in the unanimous opinion of the best judges, in the forefront of agricultural progress and a model to all continental nations.

Against this aristocracy, economically so strong, so zealous in the performance of its public duties, so uninfluenced by the attractions of the court and the capital, the weapons of monarchical absolutism soon spent themselves in vain. By means of parliament, its genuine expression, it defended at once its own and the people's privileges from invasion by the Crown. It took the upper hand in the time of the Stuarts, and, after a short interlude represented by the Caesarism of Cromwell, reaffirmed its ascendancy over the restored monarchy, and at once extended and consecrated this ascendency by an explicit recognition of its rights following upon the second revolution, which placed a foreign dynasty upon the throne to the general satisfaction. The monarchy of 1689 was precisely that moderate power, more apparent than real, which was best to the liking of the noble lords, because beneath the specious cloak of a mixed government, in which all the forces of the nation were proportionately represented, it concealed the substance of an oligarchical power.

This apparent equilibrium of powers deceived even the sagacious eye of Montesquieu, inclined as it was to an unduly rationalistic view of things. He conceived, from the partly illusory example of England, the idea of a formal division of powers and a system of mutual checks and balances: *felix culpa*, if indeed we must call it a fault, because, instead of an historical model, Montesquieu offered to posterity an ideal model, capable of expressing the clarity and rationalistic precision of the new political outlook. But other students of the eighteenth century, led by his example to the study of the English model, very soon discovered its real essence. The so-called mixed monarchy was nothing but an aristocratic republic.

This does not alter the fact that the English Constitution of the period had, for its time, a definitely liberal aspect. The liberties of the individual, especially security of person and property, were solidly assured. Administration was decentralized and autonomous. The judiciary bodies were wholly independent of the central government. The prerogatives of the Crown were closely restricted; indeed, the predominance of the Whig Party after the revolution of 1688 tended to destroy them altogether and to concentrate political power in the hands of parliament. What similar spectacle could the continent offer? At the very end of the eighteenth century, when, in the fever of revolution, men on the continent felt and proclaimed themselves free, two acute English observers, very different from one another in mentality, agreed in regarding this liberty as an illusion.[1] Judging by the experience of their country, they asserted that without an aristocratic body liberty was impossible, because there was no barrier against absolutism. And France was to learn, at her own cost, that between the despotism of monarchy and that of democracy there is little to choose, at least so far as servitude is concerned.

But the eighteenth century was not called upon to choose between aristocratic liberty and democratic liberty. Between the aristocracy and the Crown a third term intervened : the *bourgeoisie*; which complicated the situation and turned the original antithesis in an unexpected direction. In France, allied at first to the Crown in its struggle against feudal privilege, the *bourgeoisie* ended by turning against the Crown and bringing into being a kind of *bourgeois* aristocracy, in which many marks of the old feudal system reappeared. In England, the action of the *bourgeoisie* was the precise opposite. It joined forces with the nobility in its struggle against the Crown and its effort to consolidate its traditional aristocratic liberties; profiting in its turn not only by

[1] Burke, *French Revolution*; Young, *Travels during the Years 1787-94*, cf. esp. i. 613.

the general benefits of security for person and property, but also by the special protection given to its trade and industries. But it, too, in the nineteenth century, ended by turning against its old ally and attacking the territorial privilege of the aristocracy.

In this way we find in the nineteenth century a curious reciprocal influence between English and continental liberalism. Each tends to reproduce in itself the phase which the other was manifesting in the preceding century. English liberalism tends to model itself on the rationalistic and democratic attitude of continental, while the latter in its turn draws inspiration from the traditional forms and privileges of the former. The final result will be an interpenetration giving rise to a genuinely European liberalism.

§ 3. THE SPIRITUAL FORCES OF LIBERALISM

We have spoken hitherto of liberty in its most rudimentary and particularized forms, which are also the forms most remote from ourselves. We have seen them founded upon tradition, upon property, upon contract, but not upon the spiritual personality of man; and yet without this ultimate foundation we can never explain how even the most general and widespread privilege could give place to a true affirmation of liberty properly so called. Between empirical generality and a universal value there is a gulf only to be bridged by a consciousness that grasps the intimacy of that value. If man does not feel himself free, all the conditions favourable to freedom are of no avail. If he does feel himself free, he is truly free, even in the most oppressive subjection; and it is not long before he breaks his chains and creates for himself an outer life consonant with his inner will. Liberty is consciousness of oneself, of one's own infinite spiritual value; and the same recognition in the case of other people follows naturally from this immediate revelation. Only one who is conscious of himself as free is capable of recognizing the freedom of others. There is here, in this subjective kernel of freedom, a force at once of diffusion and of organization which penetrates and vitalizes the whole social and political structure by degrees, only to return at last to its centre and enrich its initial liberty through the liberation of an entire world. This is the true development of liberalism, and the soul of whatever other development it may have.

Let us try to catch sight of this soul at the moment of its birth. Its first appearance in modern civilization comes about with the Protestant Reformation. Here the revolt against an age-long religious tradition takes place not because of any need or impulse detached in some way from the personality of man, but from this personality itself. No yearning after external goods, but the love of that which is good in itself, drives the Protestants to their struggle against the Church and against her secular arm. Two spiritual forces inspire and support them: faith and examination. Faith is an unlimited trust in God; but it is at the same time trust in oneself as a servant of the true God. Examination means the free study and interpretation of the Holy Scriptures; but it is at the same time the study and interpretation of one's own faculties and states of mind. Armed with these two weapons, the Protestants came forward to create a spiritual world of their own, after destroying that which they had received from their elders. What matters it if, in their excessive individualism, they presumed too much upon their own strength? Sometimes they discovered truths already possessed by tradition; but these truths, precisely because newly discovered, were really new. They were, as Milton said in a sculpturesque phrase, ' their own heresy '. Sometimes they erred; but even these errors were of their own making: painful, but not useless, attempts to find the road of truth. On its impetuous current, faith carried much lumber of the past: predestination, original sin, the denial of free will, grace from on high; but these ideas it transfigured and shaped anew, and from their very servitude drew the means of escape.

This transvaluation of values was most perceptible precisely in that branch of the Reformation which most strongly emphasized the aspect of human servitude, that is to say, in Calvinism. While the Lutheran reform stopped half-way along the path of negation, and coming early under the control of political interests ended by consecrating a half-servile political consciousness, Calvinism on the contrary pushed its negation to the point at which the extreme subjection of the individual turned into its opposite.[1] The follower of Calvin believed in the most fatalistic predestination; but in so far as he was bound to offer proofs of his own election by divine grace he acted with energy and self-control. His very preoccupation with the 'beyond' became the means to discipline his whole earthly life. He denied all saving efficacy to works and relied upon faith alone ; but from the firmness of his faith sprang new works, which, if not means and vehicles of grace, were its signs and witnesses. His God was a distant God ; no Church could come near him; but the worshipper's very isolation, far from depressing him, strengthened him and gave him a sense of high responsibility towards the Deity and towards himself.

Thus Calvinism became an education of the will and the character. It worked for conscientiousness and rectitude. It gave a systematic direction to the development of the individual's activities. As such, it was an immense expansive power in the modern world. While Lutheranism remained the national and State religion of numerous German principalities, Calvinism invaded the whole of Europe and imparted its energy to the majority of the dissident sects, Baptists, Quakers, Independents, Puritans. Even the great Methodist movement of the eighteenth century was a derivative of Calvinism.

This internal energy was strengthened by all the accidents of its historical life and the particular forms which it was compelled to assume in its struggle with a hostile environment. The Calvinists, except in their primitive home, Geneva, were everywhere in a minority, and this fact led them to defend their rights against an unfriendly majority with the greater zeal. The chief merit of Cromwell is that

[1] V. Max Weber, *Gesammelte Aufsätze zur Religionssoziologie*, Tübingen, 1920, i. 93 *seqq.*; Schulze-Gaevernitz, *Britischer Imperialismus*, Leipzig, 1906, pp. 27 *seqq.*; Troeltsch, *Soziallehre der christlichen Kirchen*, Berlin, 1917.

he supported the freedom of conscience of a Puritan minority with extreme vigour against an overwhelming orthodox majority. Enemies of every ecclesiastical hierarchy, they set themselves up as opponents of a whole world of hierarchies and privileges; and hence their Church organization could never hope for external assistance and support, but was based entirely upon their own strength and mutual aid. But this unfavourable situation gave birth to the first free and autonomous societies, societies based on self-help, self-administration, self-government. All future social and political organizations had their roots in these early communities, and might have inherited from them the proud liberal device, *Dieu et mon droit*.

The equality of members within these communities was an incentive to discussion and criticism. It favoured the spontaneous emergence of the best talents; and since the ministers of religion were consecrated not by investiture from above but by selection from below, there arose a new way of looking at authority and government, as a function rather than as a transcendent law. Here was a whole democratic view of life in embryo. These men, while dreaming of a mystical theocratic state, were in fact creating an earthly state, bound together by nothing but the cohesive force of individuals. Each contributed the sum of those personal and inalienable rights which the consciousness of his inmost manhood had proclaimed; and the equality of his position in the eyes of the law to that of every other man made the compact of their union a perfectly reciprocal compact. In these first covenants of the Calvinistic communities the germs of Rousseau's *Contrat social* are already present; but they contain something more: a livelier feeling for the rights of the contracting individuals, anticipating in this the American and French *Declarations*.

If we examine these sects, thus organized, at work upon their proselytizing task, face to face with the Churches ready formed and consecrated by long tradition, we shall soon see that struggle or competition is the very law of their existence. They must create their own prestige out of nothing. They must practise upon themselves a constant selection. They must multiply in every possible way the means of propaganda and attraction. This is also and especially true of their relations to one another. Competition is nowhere more keen and nowhere demands more vigilance or more energy than between the groups that are most akin to one another and working under similar conditions. Here, too, the anticipations of political liberalism already visible at its source are many and striking.

From the presence and conflict of diverse and hostile religions springs the first great affirmation of modern liberalism : religious freedom. This has sometimes been said to spring from the conflict of two equally pernicious fanaticisms, each cancelling out the other. This would be a true description of religious freedom as we find it in the legal formulae of the numerous treatises and edicts on peace and toleration. But a liberty so understood, though not without justification as a purely formal and outward expression, would be even from this point of view a complete destruction of all the living and spiritual content of religious struggles. The cancelling-out of two fanaticisms represents nothing but the triumph of scepticism and unbelief. If that has been the only outcome of an age-long torment of conscience, we might well strike out religious freedom from the roll of modern liberties.

Happily, the truth is better than that. Beside the barren liberty of scepticism there is another liberty, the need for which is based on a profound faith and a respect for the intimacy of man's consciousness ; and this respect implies, or in the long run comes to imply, full reciprocity. If the Churches continued to attack each other, as their mutual exclusiveness compelled them to do, within the consciousness of believers there took place by degrees a higher synthesis of the motives peculiar to each separate Church, in virtue of which, even in the apparent discord of words and acts, a substantial unity in devotion and love came to be recognized. That which, seen from below, through human eyes, was multiplicity and discord, was concord when seen from above, in the eyes of God.

This truer conception of religious liberty was grasped by Milton, and gradually made headway in Protestant circles. Henry Vane,[1] a contemporary of Cromwell, formulated it as a universal tolerance based not upon general indifference towards all religions but upon the conviction of the sanctity of reason, divine even if fallen, which could not be constrained by anything less divine than itself. The policy of toleration made further progress through the Quakers, even though these represented Calvinistic rigorism in its most orthodox form.

In the sequel, owing to the infiltration of a free-thinking rationalism and an easy-going Catholicism, the principle of toleration was perverted into a kind of appendix to the opposite principle of intolerance; and it is now that we find the most precise conception of religious freedom taking shape. At the end of the eighteenth century the distinction between toleration and liberty was so far common ground as to form a subject of discussion in a political assembly.

' I am not going to preach toleration,' said Mirabeau, in a session of the Constituent Assembly. ' The most unlimited freedom of religion is in my eyes a right so sacred that the word toleration, intended to express it, seems to me to convey a suggestion of tyranny. In fact, the existence of any authority which has the power to tolerate is an encroachment upon the liberty of thought, precisely because it tolerates and therefore has the power not to tolerate.' [2]

These words were echoed in England by Tom Paine, who regarded it as a high merit in the French Constitution that it renounced both toleration and intolerance, and established full liberty of conscience. For him, too,

' toleration is not the *opposite* of intolerance but is the *counterfeit* of it. Both are despotisms. The one assumes to itself the right of withholding Liberty of conscience, and the other of granting it. The one is the Pope armed with fire and faggot, and the other is the Pope selling or granting indulgences. The former is Church and State, and the latter is Church and traffic. But Toleration

---

[1] T. Hill Green, *Four Lectures on the English Revolution : Works*, iii. 296.
[2] *Discours et opinions de Mirabeau*, Paris, 1820, i. 328.

may be viewed in a much stronger light. Man worships not himself but his Maker ; and the liberty of conscience, which he claims,
is not for the service of himself, but of his God.' [1]

Seen thus at its source, freedom of conscience is purely
a Protestant claim, and implies the denial of any ecclesiastical
authority superior to the conscience of the individual. Does
this mean that religious freedom is irrevocably denied to
Catholic peoples? Doubtless it is made harder for them by
the position taken up by the Church of Rome towards the
individual conscience ; but the fertility of a principle is not
exhausted by the limited sphere in which it originally
appeared. It propagates itself, and finds other ways of
penetrating. Through philosophical and scientific rationalism, through historical criticism, through moral convictions,
the soul of the Reformation diffuses itself through the whole of
modern society and triumphs over all confessional obstacles.
But, in addition to this, the Catholic Church, notwithstanding
its monarchical authoritarianism, shows a secondary and peculiar tendency towards religious liberty, and one destined to
produce a great effect upon the structure and history of liberalism. Ever since the feudal period, and with renewed vigour
in the age of absolute monarchy, the Catholic Church has
fought against State supremacy ; and the very fact of this conflict between two great powers has been an effectual safeguard
for individuals against the peril of utter enslavement to either.
If the Western peoples have succeeded in saving themselves
from the stagnant theocracy of the East, it has been because
of the age-long rivalry of Church and State, rooted ultimately
in the fact that both Church and State were self-contained
and self-sufficient institutions forming in fact two separate
and independent states.

At the beginning of the modern period the conflict reached
an extreme point, because the new monarchies were no
longer hampered in their work of consolidation by all those
obstacles which impeded and arrested the activity of the
medieval Empire. In their efforts to set themselves free from

[1] Thomas Paine, *Rights of Man*, Fr. tr., Paris, 1793, i. 110–11 ; [ed. 1,
London, 1791, p. 74.]

Rome, they demanded in the name of liberty the control of the various national Churches in their respective realms. But this control, from the point of Rome, is servitude. The liberty of the Church means her own right to supreme control over all Catholic communities. These are two half-freedoms, each concealing a half-servitude. Thus, on the one hand, we find Anglican liberties and Gallican liberties bitterly opposed by the Pope; and, on the other hand, assertions of liberal principles on the part of the Catholic circles most attached to Rome, to which we must not deny the merit of having effectively opposed the despotism of the State, even if they did so with an *arrière-pensée* directed towards absolutism. And it was precisely the stoutest champions of Papal monarchy, the Jesuits, whom no one would suspect of liberalism, that made the first and fiercest onslaughts upon the autonomy of the new sovereigns' rights, and most explicitly affirmed the rights of popular sovereignty, and even the justification of regicide.

These are manifestations of a liberty *sui generis*, to be taken at their proper value, but not to be set aside as valueless. We shall see that in the course of the nineteenth century they will reappear, mingled with other manifestations of a truer liberalism, assisting in its triumph, but bringing with them a dangerous confusion of ideas and the shadow of an ambiguity which will often distort the pure image of true liberty.

In the principle of free examination we have pointed out the source not only of religious liberty but of all modern liberalism. No interpreter to come between man and the scriptures; no ecclesiastical mediation to come between the believer and God. From the very solitude of his consciousness the individual gains an intimate sense of trust and responsibility. This same attitude is found in modern philosophy, rejecting as it does all authority and tradition interposed between reason and the proper object of its speculation, and reconstructing its own ideal world for itself.

The doctrine which first and most strikingly (a matter of considerable exoteric importance) professed free examina-

tion, and swept away the lumber of scholastic and dogmatic tradition, was Cartesianism. This philosophy achieved
truth and certitude by the very same process by which the
religious consciousness of the Reformation attained to its
God : by an extreme rationalistic simplification and clarification, eliminating all opinions and intermediate beliefs which
obscure while they appear to illuminate the object of the
intellect; thus it created the conditions favourable to an
immediate revelation and apprehension by consciousness.
It was a kind of lay Methodism, far more radical in its application than religious Methodism, because it never stopped
short at any dogma, or at any rate it postulated an unlimited possibility of progress along the road of criticism.
Descartes himself may have cut his criticism short too soon,
and forgone it altogether in questions of social morality,
religion, and politics; but Cartesianism, without departing
from its master's method—on the contrary, while merely
applying this method more completely—could invade even
these privileged domains of the old intellectual feudalism.

To the Cartesian school belong almost all the exponents
of the higher and middle culture of the eighteenth century :
the scientists, attempting to unveil the true face of nature;
the social reformers, drawing up their indictment against
history as a museum of irrational uses and abuses, and en-
deavouring to reconstruct the whole social system ; the jurists,
in whose eyes law is and must be a system deducible from
a few and universal and self-evident principles; the economists, conceiving the play of economic forces as a human
mechanics, in which the individuality of the particular
action is nothing more than a perturbing element; and the
politicians, who imagine that with a little clever legislation
they can correct all the faults of the past. The new *bourgeoisie*
in general may be called, in a popular sense of the word,
Cartesian, in its cult of common sense, which is nothing but
la raison in small change. A middle class, distinguished by
the absence of extremes in its virtues and its habits, educated
in the levelling school of absolute monarchy, finds its natural
intellectual expression in an illuministic philosophy, speaking

in clear and persuasive language, making *tabula rasa* of all the subtleties and obscurities of ancient doctrine, and veiling the personality of its exponents beneath the veneer of a self-evident and universal ratiocinating intellect Not only Voltaire, but all the illuminists, the men of the *Aufklärung*, may be said to represent *Monsieur tout-monde* ; and this constitutes their immense strength ; for no obstacle could oppose the diffusion of their thoughts, granted the perfect homogeneity of the medium in which they were to propagate themselves.

In speaking of Cartesianism we are not here referring to the strictly speculative and technical part of that system, which few were able to understand or to develop, but rather to its illuministic aspect, apparent not only in the schools of thought directly inspired by Descartes, but no less in different and even hostile schools, animated by the same purpose of revealing under its manifold and diverse aspects the presence of the one sound human reason. From this point of view we may regard rationalism properly so called, and the naturalism, materialism, and sensationalism so prominent in eighteenth-century philosophy, as all on the same footing.

What indeed is materialism but an attempt to convert human reason *en bloc* into matter, and compel it to organize, explain, and in a sense justify itself at the scientist's bidding? Naturalism, again, gives Nature so human a face that man comes to love her with filial piety, and dreams of returning to her as a homesick man turns to his mother. Sensationalism, while it claims to make intelligence a mere reflection of sense, in reality invests sensation with intelligence, and creates an empirical rationalism, of dubious speculative validity but of great practical value, being as it is the model for all attempts to co-ordinate and systematize the diverse experience which forms the theatre of human activity.

This philosophy, accessible as it is to a widespread audience, easily becomes the property of every one ; every one collaborates in it, because the reason which creates it is his own reason. Here lies its intimately liberal character, and the psychological motive of what is called freedom of thought. That which is free is simply that which is one's own, the fruit of one's own activity or the object of one's own choice, in contradistinction to that which one owes to the authority of dogma or the passivity of tradition. Freedom of thought, the subject of so many declamations and so much rhetoric, has been called either a contradiction in terms or an empty tautology, because thought can never be anything but free. This is true, if we take our stand upon purely speculative ground. But we must reflect that the phrase 'liberty of thought', like all modern liberties, has a polemical meaning and purpose; that is to say, it expresses not a mental category but a declaration of war against the tyranny of schools, Churches, States, and customs, over conscience; and from this point of view, in spite of its rhetorical degradations, which often vindicate nothing but the liberty *not* to think, it has an historical importance no less than that of religious liberty. Both equally serve to create that inviolable stronghold of consciousness in which all human liberties have their birth and their growth.

It is this liberal attitude of the modern man, this sense of the inviolability of his person and his freedom, which will provide the material for the Kantian and post-Kantian conception of liberty, by far the greatest contribution made by philosophy to the history of liberalism; yet not so great as to deprive of all importance the manifestations of popular illuminism.

§ 4. NATURAL RIGHTS

From the same source arises the great modern movement known by the name of jusnaturalism. Granted that there is an intangible sphere of individual activity which forms the individual's natural liberty, this is also the sphere of the individual's rights. Liberty and rights are correlative terms, in the sense that one expresses the immediate expansion of a living content, the other the form of this content, that is, its self-creation as an autonomous unity, demanding that it shall not be disturbed in its self-creation by other unities which in their own sphere possess the same claims to independence. This right on the part of the individual is asserted directly, in virtue of an inherent self-evidence : an assertion which is merely the formal recognition of an undeniable fact, the ultimate value of human consciousness. Here, too, all intermediary activities and functions are repudiated, whether those of a State or a Church or any other sanctioning authority. Jusnaturalism is thus a kind of legal Protestantism.

In the phrase ' natural rights ', the adjective ' natural ' expresses a twofold polemical attitude towards a pre-existing historical situation. Customary rights, as we know, were nothing but the privileged rights belonging to man not as man but as living and acting under determinate historical conditions. Natural right, on the contrary, is the utter negation of privilege, merely because it appeals to the most ancient and inalienable of all privileges, that of being a man. In this apparent naturalism there is, therefore, an infinity of spiritual value, however inadequate its formulation and however childish its regret for a vanished golden age.

But natural rights implied not only this opposition to the medieval world, but also another and directer opposition to the new monarchical State. In effect jusnaturalism maintained that the rights belonging to the individual were, in origin, independent of the State ; which, far from creating them, could do nothing but recognize them. In accordance with the abstractly rationalistic outlook of the time, it asserted that the individual was prior to the State, both temporally and logically ; and this assertion, however crude regarded as history, succeeded in overthrowing the very foundations of the existing political system. First the individual, then the relations between man and man, the political organism ; which therefore cannot destroy or oppress its own creator, but must on the contrary serve his ends as a means designed to consolidate and increase his powers.

The riper historical and scientific consciousness of the nineteenth century will successfully attack the abstract crudity of this doctrine, and will show that the State comes into being not *after* the individual but *within* him; and having, as it has, a spiritual structure identical with his, cannot be his irreconcilable enemy. But those who would turn these truths into an attack upon jusnaturalism fall into a grave error: the error of thinking that the despotic State, against which jusnaturalism was contending for the priority of the individual, is the same State as that which comes into being by the organic development of spiritual individuality. They are using as a weapon against jusnaturalism a political conception derived from it and based upon it.

In its struggle against the despotic State which claims to reduce its subjects to the level of chattels and docile instruments of its higher purpose, jusnaturalism sees in the individual not only a limit and a safeguard, but a positive principle of political organization. It is in embryo the modern State based on liberty itself, whose aim is to harmonize the rights of each with the rights of all others. The least adequate part of this conception is the atomistic view of the constituent elements, and therefore of the State, which is made to consist of a mutual cancellation of numberless individual wills, in the form, familiar to the legal mind, of a contract.

It is in fact a conception of the State still too much influenced by the anti-State frame of mind that called it into being. The love of rationalistic simplification, strengthened and reinforced by the practice of absolute government, and destroying all intermediate political bodies in its zeal for reducing its subjects to a dead level, brings the individual and the State into direct contact, in a purely legal and formal relation. Such a contact is pregnant with the danger of revolution; it leads people to think that in the mere technicalities of law they possess the means and the power to effect unlimited changes in their political system, and believe themselves absolute masters of the State, so long as the State, purely for the sake of the private interests and compacts which sanction it, continues to exist.

The eighteenth century is rich in illusions of this kind, cherished by lawyers who imagine that, by drafting new constitutions and laws, they can begin the work of history all over again, and know nothing of the force of traditions, habits, associations, and institutions. Bitter experience alone will reveal this sluggish but tenacious force in all its fullness ; and even then it will not discharge itself directly into the river-bed of the State, but will reach that channel by a roundabout path, by the insensible interposition between the individual and the State of a third term, namely, Society, in which the political mind of the nineteenth century will see a mighty reservoir of political energy.

But notwithstanding its anti-historical attitude jusnaturalism contains at least the germ of this further progress ; for it taps the source of this progress, the personality of man. This becomes clear if we compare it with the Roman conception of natural law, the reflected and continued expression of a law whose centre lies not in the man but in the citizen. The Stoic philosophy which inspired this conception does indeed contain the idea of a liberty, and therefore the idea of a right, belonging to man as man ; but its formulation of these rights is negative and barren. Goods, relations between man and man, family life, even of his own body : none of these are at the free and autonomous command of the man himself. To enter into himself, the individual must sacrifice himself to the point of becoming a ghost. Such is the corrosive liberalism of an Epictetus or a Marcus Aurelius.

Modern jusnaturalism, on the contrary, has an expansive force which radiates from the individual, but tends by degrees to enlarge the sphere of his liberty and rights, as it includes elements and contributions from an ever-widening experience. At first, freedom of conscience is considered essential to his personality ; this implies religious liberty and liberty of thought. Later is added all that concerns his relations to other individuals : freedom to express and communicate his own thought, personal security against all oppression, free movement, economic liberty, juridical equality, and property.

Thus little by little we enter upon a sphere in which the mere expansion of natural rights profoundly alters their original aspect. This is especially clear in the origin of the right of property, which is of very great importance for the history of liberalism. For the moment, let us confine ourselves to its purely legal aspect. The right of property, as a right of nature, has its pseudo-historical justification (conformably with the peculiar rationalistic use of history) in the ancient institutions of occupation in the case of a *res nullius*, and military conquest. But this reminiscence of Roman and feudal law here serves only as a starting-point, a traditional theme for a new variation, a deeper rationalistic theory of property running as follows: Property is a natural right of the individual, independent of the State, because it represents his most immediate field of action without which his formal independence and autonomy would be wholly empty. Only so far as he is an owner of property is he self-sufficient and able to resist encroachment by other individuals and by the State.

This justification of property is common to all jurists, and through them to all publicists, in the eighteenth century; so that the right of property stands in the forefront of all revolutionary declarations of the rights of man, not only those of 1791 and 1795 but also of the more radical declaration of 1793. Jacobins, Girondins, reactionaries, all unite in the defence of property.

But from the conception of property as a natural right follow certain unexpected consequences, which undermine the foundations of that conception. If property is essential to the development of man's natural liberty, it ought not to be enjoyed exclusively by a few, as an odious privilege; all ought to be owners of property. Thus the same theory of natural rights which consecrated individual property, and for its sake demolished the castle of feudalism, issued in the opposite conception, namely communism. The eighteenth-century sense of the word communism, unlike its current sense in the following century, is essentially agrarian; its associations are legalistic and individualistic; this is clearly visible in the works of Mably, Morelly, Brissot, and their followers.[1] Its purpose is to demonstrate that, if all men have

[1] See Mably, *De la législation, ou Principes des lois*, Lausanne, 1777, 2 vols; Morelly, *Code de la nature*. In a short work by Brissot, the future

a right to own property, the individual property of the few, by inflicting loss upon the many, is a wrongful appropriation; in the words of Brissot, a theft; and this property ought to be confiscated for the benefit of all. Thus the utter negation of individualism proceeds by a logical development from the conception of individuality.

But even apart from these extreme consequences, which for the moment produced little effect in the field of history (even Brissot felt it necessary to recant them as an error committed in a youthful essay), the right of property, conceived as we have described it, gives occasion for other and more important legal developments. The thought of the eighteenth century began of its own accord to doubt whether property is a natural right, independent of Society and the State, or whether it implies the co-operation of these bodies. Roman law handed down, almost with the authority of a dogma, the idea of *ius in re*; by which it meant that property is a purely immediate relation between the individual and the object, excluding all intervention by other parties. But is there any such thing as a real right with this title? Can there be a legal relation between an individual and a physical object? is it not essential to the idea of such a relation that its terms should be individual human beings? To state a doubt is to begin the work of resolving it; and to resolve it implies detaching the right by degrees from the material things concerned, and recognizing that, arising as it does from personality, it can exist only in relation to other personalities; and that therefore the right of property, though exercised upon physical objects, has its being in the sphere of human relations and in the last resort implies as its constitutive elements Society and the State.

Traces of this idea are to be found in Blackstone, who, though considering property as a natural right, adds that, even if this is its fundamental character, the modifications of it now in existence, the modes of acquiring and transmitting property, are wholly derived from Society, and represent those

Girondin, occurs the famous exclamation, ' la propriété c'est le vol ', which by its paradoxical form confirms the remarks in the text.

civil advantages for the sake of which the individual has in exchange given up some part of his natural liberty.[1]

In a far more developed and complex form, the doctrine reappears in Kant. He, too, begins with natural rights; but he very soon recognizes that in nature there can only be a provisional *meum* and *tuum*, there can be possession but not property. It is impossible that any external object should be absolutely one's own, except in a state of law, that is, of Society. If the empirical title of acquisition is provided by physical possession, founded upon the primitive community of land, the rational title of acquisition can only be found in the universal will, because an individual will cannot impose upon others an obligation which otherwise would not have lain upon them.

This means that property is not a right *in re* but is a right as against another person; and this necessarily implies the presence of a superior will which can create obligations and give to every one his own.[2]

KANT

The importance of this conception for liberalism is obvious. Society and the State become necessary complements of natural liberty as originally conceived. Instead of instruments of despotism they reveal themselves as instruments of legal liberty. But their presence implies a limitation upon the individual's activity, which at first appears all the more serious because it is imposed not by an external power but by the internal dialectical demands of individualism itself. Granted the social basis of property, it follows that Society can and must intervene to restrict the powers of the owner, which in the abstract are unlimited, for the sake of the common welfare.

The French Revolution drew this conclusion logically in its measures of expropriation and its new laws of inheritance.[3]

---

[1] Blackstone, *Commentaries on the Laws of England*, 16th ed., 1825 (the first lectures out of which this great work developed date from 1753), i. 131, 138.

[2] Kant, *Rechtslehre*, §§ viii, xv.

[3] The same point had already been made by Turgot, who wrote: 'A right does not go beyond the title upon which it is founded, because

It confiscated the property of the *émigrés* and the Church, and sold it to the people, with the double consequence of attaching the new owners to itself and of demonstrating in a practical manner the social utility of the confiscation. It is characteristic that the dispossessed and their partisans protested against this revolutionary act by alleging in their favour, not the old traditional right, but the pure jusnaturalism of Article II of the *Declaration of the Rights of Man*, which made property an inviolable right. By confiscating property, the Revolution was formally contradicting itself; but it was the contradiction of to-day with yesterday, the real name of which is ' development '.

The other social limitation of quiritarian property was concerned with inheritance. We find the main points vigorously formulated in Mirabeau's last great speech of the 2nd of April 1791.[1] Property, we read, is not natural, but is a social creation. The law is not limited to its protection and preservation, but in some manner creates it, determines it, and gives it its place and its importance in the rights of the citizen. Society therefore has the right to refuse to its members, in particular cases, the power of arbitrarily disposing of their own fortunes.

' Perhaps it is time for us, after bowing so long to the authority of Roman Law, to subject this law itself to the authority of our reason ; to be its judges after being its slaves. Perhaps it is time for us to see in this law the genius of a people which never knew the true principles of civil legislation, and was more occupied in ruling abroad than in creating a reign of equality and well-being at home. Perhaps it is time for Frenchmen not to go to school to ancient Rome any more than to modern Rome.'

Is it not enough, he adds, for Society to endure the caprices

the effect is always proportional to its cause. The right of property is founded upon general utility. It is therefore subordinate to it ; and the legislative power has the right to watch over the use which every man makes of his lands.' But he also added that equity, and public interest itself, prescribed that the interest of the individual should be damaged as little as possible.—Turgot, *Œuvres*, Paris, Alcan, 1913, i. 439.

[1] Not delivered by Mirabeau, who died on the previous day ; it was read by Talleyrand, and is printed in vol. iii of Mirabeau's *Discours*, *op cit.*

and passions of the living? Must it also submit to the caprices
and passions of those who are no more?[1] Hence the legal
principle of equal division, applied to an intestate person's
estate, and of the legitimate quota in testamentary disposition,
based upon the social end of a more equal distribution of
goods, so as to bring Society nearer to the new jusnaturalistic
idea that every individual should own property.

Thus we see coming about the gradual interposition of
Society between the individual and the State, to which we
have already referred; and thus the relation between the
state of nature and the social state is profoundly modified.
At first the state of nature was considered the ideal state, and
Society an evil, a perversion of man's original nature. But
in the sequel this relation underwent a change amounting
finally to a complete reversal. The stages of this transition
are visible in the thought of Rousseau himself. The Genevan
certainly looks with admiration and regret at the state of
nature; yet the *Contrat social* is an attempt at a transition
from the state of nature to a state of Society, an attempt (as
his follower Tom Paine [2] expressively put it) to ' exchange '
natural rights for corresponding civil rights. Now the purpose of an exchange is not to lose, but to gain; and if by the
social contract men gain nothing as regards the extension of
their rights—in this respect they lose—they gain in the
security with which they exercise these rights, and the gain
outweighs the loss. And this advantage will appear progressively greater as the security of rights, with the advancing
reorganization of Society and the State on the new individualistic basis, acquires a greater prestige relatively to the precarious and insecure life which the state of nature presents
to the deluded fancy.

Let us translate these legal conceptions into the more
familiar terms of liberalism. The publicists began by exalting
liberty as a natural right in contrast with human society.
They placed freedom at the dawn of human history, in a

---

[1] *Op. cit.*, pp. 482, 486, 490.

[2] *Rights of Man, op. cit.*, French ed., p. 74 [1st ed., p. 50: every civil right
. . . is a natural right exchanged].

state of complete independence and anarchy. But was this a real freedom? In the first place, it was not a right; for the very idea of a right implies recognition on the part of other individuals, and hence subordination to a superior power, which, by definition, is impossible. It was therefore a mere datum of fact, devoid of all stability and certainty, because the caprice of individuals themselves, the niggardliness of nature, and a thousand other factors might perpetually undermine and destroy it. In the state of nature men are not free, but slaves of nature. Men are not born free; they become free by means of Society and the State, which, while limiting the claims of individuals, in reality bestow upon these claims an effectual recognition and sanction, and elevate them from precarious facts to rights whose fulfilment can be confidently demanded. That is the real gain which the individual makes when he exchanges the uncertainty of natural liberty for civil liberty.

This is the great distinction between the liberal conceptions of the eighteenth and nineteenth centuries. The one places liberty at the beginning, the other at the end, of the historical process. But we must also recognize that the first conception did much to open up the way to the second.

§ 5. ECONOMIC FREEDOM

We shall consider agricultural freedom and industrial freedom separately, since the two corresponding forms of modern economic activity present certain remarkable differences.

The first liberal demand, in the order of time, comes on behalf of agriculture. This is easy to explain, partly through the prevailingly agricultural character of European economic life throughout the eighteenth century, partly because the limited character of industry during this period makes the fetters of the traditional régime tolerable and even beneficial.

We have already studied the legal aspect of the emancipation of land, while examining the development of natural rights. We must now complete our examination by considering the economic expansion implied in the transformation of land tenure. If property is a natural right, in contrast with rights derived from privileges, this implies that the proprietor has full liberty to dispose of his property; and this again implies the abolition of all those restrictions and obstacles which an age-long tradition had interposed between him and this liberty.

These obstacles were of many and various kinds: primogeniture and trusts, excluding large numbers of persons from the land and hampering its transference; estates in mortmain, likewise withdrawn from free purchase and sale; distinctions between noble and non-noble estates, requiring different methods of legal treatment; communal estates whose produce was dispersed over a multitude of particular rights; feudal privileges and customs implying a network of relations between the lord, the peasant, and the soil; government restrictions on traffic in agricultural produce in the interest, often the misunderstood interest, of the population that was to subsist upon it. This ancient system of land-tenure might have lasted, and even performed a useful conservative function, through many centuries of stagnant medieval life; but upon the rapidly progressing economic life of the modern world it soon appeared as an intolerable burden. The absence of any circulation of property prevented the employment of the capital necessary to introduce intensive cultivation; the dispersion of produce among many hands all having a claim on it paralyses the efforts of the cultivator. The impossibility of disposing freely of the crops, or those portions of them which belong to the agriculturist, owing to government restrictions, glutted the market in a year of abundance and led to a shortage in the following year.

These evils, resulting from feudalism and the absence of free trade, appeared increasingly oppressive and irritating, in proportion as men felt, with the awakening of modern individualism, the profound injustice of a barbarous legislation separating the produce of labour from labour itself, human personality from something now recognized as an integral part of it.

But the reaction against feudalism asserted itself differently in different countries, according to their several historical situations. We have seen that in England the great landed proprietors themselves led the way in sweeping aside the more irksome relics of feudalism, by enlarging their estates and modernizing agriculture on their own initiative. And when, as happened in England too, a consciousness of the rights of man superimposed itself upon the traditional conception of liberty, the aspirations of the people were for the moment turned away from the land toward industry, so that the feudal character of land-tenure was able to remain intact.

Conditions in France were very different. Here the great aristocrats, absentees from their own estates, never dreamed of engaging personally in the task of promoting agricultural progress; while the minor country nobility, weak and in debt, lived on the margin of agriculture by levying dues and imposts upon the peasants. Here the dead weight of feudalism was heavily felt, not only by the producing classes, the peasants and the *bourgeoisie*, but even by the aristocracy itself; which, though it had lost all affection for its land, could not by getting rid of it confer on the nation those benefits that might have resulted from the concentration and free transmission of all the rights attaching to property.

France was therefore the scene of the great anti-feudal reaction whose epilogue, the Revolution, was to be the means of spreading it over all Europe. The merit of promoting and guiding this reaction, and giving it a definitely liberal character, belongs to the physiocrats. The forerunners of this school, Vauban and Boisguilbert, drew public attention to the decay of agriculture and the means of reviving it as early as the time of Louis XIV; but its real leader was Quesnay, who by his writings and propaganda promoted a lively and widespread agitation in the country, and employed a number of enthusiastic helpers, such as the elder Mirabeau, Turgot, Herbert, Condorcet, Condillac, Dupont de Nemours, and many others.

Quesnay regards property as a right of nature; but the social state for him represents, not a perversion, but a consolidation and development, of the state of nature. Men put themselves under the protection of positive laws made by a protecting power, and thus extend their capacity for owning property; in this way they enlarge their natural right instead of restricting it. This means that law, provided it is good law, does not limit man's liberty, but is manifestly the object of liberty's best choice; and the individual cannot reasonably refuse to obey it. If he did, his liberty would be hurtful to himself and others, instead of beneficial.[1]

But what is the legitimate aim and object of good law? The legislator must above all be convinced that agriculture is the sole true source of a nation's wealth, because its produce not only repays the cost of production but in addition provides a clear rent. Industry and commerce on the other hand are sterile, since they do nothing but transform or transport the fruits of the earth, leaving their quantity unchanged.

These premisses once laid down, the first task of legislation is to liberate real property from all the encumbrances which feudal policy had by degrees accumulated round it, influenced as it was by the desire to make it the foundation of the military power of feudal lords. In modern times it is recognized that the same end is far better served by the indirect means of promoting the nation's economic prosperity, since wealth multiplies population, than by all the curiosities of feudal law.[2]

Now in order to secure the greatest possible yield from the soil, the law must provide for the concentration in the owner's hands of all those rights and powers which feudalism dissipated; must convert the onerous personal service, which distracted the peasant from his own work, into money payments; must make the agriculturist the sole judge of his own interest in everything that concerns the choice and management of crops; must favour active trade in agricultural produce, between different provinces and states, so that where this is abundant it may not glut the market, and where it is scarce there should not be a dearth ruinous to the productive efficiency of the people; and must even promote the passive commerce in manufactured goods, that is, their

---

[1] Quesnay, *Droit naturel* (*Physiocrates*, Paris, 1846), i. 41, 51, 55.
[2] Id., *Analyse du tableau économique, op. cit.*, p. 68.

exchange against surplus agricultural produce, so that a nation able to export should not lose the profit of this natural advantage.[1] All these rules can be summed up in one single rule, *laissez faire.* Let the individual be the judge of his own economic interest, no less than of his own religious conscience. The State cannot artificially bring about that harmonious distribution of activities and riches which only nature can create. And, since the State is not the enemy of nature, but is working along natural lines, what it can usefully do is to facilitate free development by removing those obstacles which misunderstood self-interest has scattered broadcast over the course of history.

To the riper economic science of the following century this conception of Quesnay seemed too abstract to be sound. It naïvely relies on the Cartesian self-evidence by which it ascribes to land the miraculous power of providing a net profit or surplus, as opposed to manufacture ; thus converting into a mark of abundance that rent in which Ricardo, more truly, saw a mark of nature's niggardliness. The degradation of industry and trade to the level of barren functions savours of a naïve materialism, as if changes of form, in time, and in space, were not equally productive of value, and as if agriculture itself were not at bottom a case of such changes. And from the very beginning Quesnay and his contemporaries were entangled in the curious paradox which compelled them to place the often idle landowner among the productive classes, and the hard-working artisan among the unproductive.

But with all its deficiencies, the physiocratic system had the merit of interpreting the vital needs of an essentially agricultural country like France, and of indicating with a sure hand the faults and abuses that must be stamped out. Even its abstract rationalism furthered the rapid diffusion of its programme of reform ; the more so that this programme was in practice wholly dissociated from any idea of political revolution. Indeed, Quesnay expressly makes economic freedom one of the fundamental tasks of an enlightened despotism, and many of his followers found a butt for their

---

[1] Quesnay, *Maximes générales de gouvernement, op. cit., passim.*

wit in the abstract fantasies of the ' advocates ' of political liberalism.

How social liberty can exist without political liberty is a problem which we shall consider in its own place : here it is sufficient to observe that this separation, temporary and transient though it was, made it possible for the powers of the State to support the programme of the economists so long as the absolute monarchy endured. Beneath the protection of authority numerous agricultural societies took root and grew ; sweeping inquiries were made into the agricultural condition of the various provinces ; prize competitions were inaugurated for the best essay on this or that controversial point in agriculture. One of the most indefatigable pioneers of agricultural progress in France was De Gournay. In Turgot's life of his predecessor he is placed among the ' economists ', a name applied at that time to the physiocrats, not because he had the temperament of a doctrinaire, but because he regarded the principles of the *système nouveau* as mere maxims of elementary good sense, all reducible to this : that a man knows his own interest better than another man to whom this interest is entirely indifferent. From this he inferred that where the interest of the individual coincides with that of the community every man should be left free to pursue his interest in the way he likes best.

Is there any fear that this may give rise to abuses? None whatever. It is not true that dishonesty is to the interest of a trader, unless he enjoys a monopoly. If the government limits the number of vendors by granting monopolies, the consumer will certainly be injured ; the vendor, certain of doing business, will compel him to buy bad goods at a high price. Universal liberty to buy and sell is the only way of assuring the seller a price able to encourage competition, and the consumer the best goods at the lowest prices. There will always be a few vendors who are *fripons* and a few buyers who are *dupes*; but competition itself tends to minimize this possibility.

De Gournay, his biographer adds, was astonished to find that governments acted in a manner utterly opposed to these maxims of common sense. He thought that every industrious citizen deserved the gratitude of the public ; but on the contrary, experience showed that a citizen could neither produce goods nor sell them without first buying the right to do so, and having himself enrolled at considerable expense in a guild. He thought it inconceivable that a piece of cloth, because it did not conform to certain regulations, should be liable to fines capable of ruining an entire family, and that a workman, in making, for example, a piece of cloth, should expose himself to risks and expenses from which an idle man was exempt. He would never have dreamed that in a kingdom ruled by a single monarch every province and town could regard itself as an enemy of all the rest and arrogate to itself the right to prevent other Frenchmen from working within its own boundaries, under the name of foreigners, and oppose the export of its own goods for sale in a neighbouring district. He was no less surprised to see the government occupied in regulating the production of different commodities, forbidding one kind of crop in order to encourage another, and putting countless obstacles in the way of the sale of the most ordinary necessaries of life.

In 1753 De Gournay undertook a great journey throughout France, to examine its resources and requirements at first hand. In 1756, in Brittany, he founded the first society for the improvement of agriculture. The result of his varied experiments confirmed the principles already suggested by common sense, and was summarized in a programme of reforms directed towards introducing full freedom of trade, and encouraging the labour of every member of the community so as to heighten competition, while providing at the same time a sufficiency of consumers to employ this increased number of competitors and opening all possible markets to the sale of produce.[1]

We have spoken at some length of De Gournay, because we also intend to speak of his greater follower Turgot, who devoted his life to the realization of this programme. Turgot likewise was an economist, but without the narrow and dogmatic outlook of his masters : indeed, his distaste for the

[1] *Éloge de Vincent de Gournay:* Turgot, *Œuvres*, Alcan, 1913, i. 600 *seqq.*

sectarian spirit of the school kept him at a distance from all its collective expressions. Unable though he was as yet to dispel the fallacy upon which the physiocrats had based their distinction between a productive and an unproductive class, he nevertheless saw, with his greater openness of mind, how paradoxical it was to describe manufacture and trade as unproductive ; and he substituted for this description the phrase ' salaried class ', a less degrading but not less inaccurate title.

Apart from this and certain other corrections in the doctrine of the school, it is Turgot's chief merit that he was able to gather together the most positive and realistic elements of the physiocrats' proposed reforms, and to attempt to carry them out, first as intendent of Limoges and later as minister of Louis XVI.

Thus, chiefly through the work and initiative of Turgot, the physiocratic principles began to work upon legislation affecting landed property. The new economic rationalism began to transform the venerable usages and customs which had reduced the old agricultural society to its complex and stagnant condition. The innovations essentially consisted of simplifications. The complicated and unremunerative personal *corvées* were replaced by rents proportional to the value of the holdings ; the tolls, the burdensome tithes, the infinity of feudal dues, by proportional levies upon the yield. The physiocratic school had propounded the theory of the single tax upon land, which so acute an observer as Arthur Young regarded as an absurdity ; yet in spite of exaggeration it contained a new and fertile principle, the principle of direct taxation ; far more conducive to liberty, as was later recognized, than that of indirect taxation.[1]

Of more immediate importance were the State regulations making for free trade, which were conceived in the new spirit and expressed in the very language of the economists. A

[1] But this advantage could not be clearly perceived. In fact, as Turgot himself observed, such a law would deprive the English parliament of all its influence, which depended upon voting taxes, and the king would become as absolute in England as in France (*op. cit.* ii. 306).

first edict by the king, on the 21st of May 1763, permits within certain limits the free circulation of grain all over France; a later edict in 1764 extends this faculty to international trade, while fixing a maximum price of grain above which all exportation outside the kingdom was forbidden. These edicts were abrogated in 1770, reinstated by Turgot in 1774, and again abolished by Necker in 1777.

These vacillations show that the physiocratic principles were stubbornly opposed by the old world of tradition which they were intended to destroy. Even in educated circles their triumph was by no means unopposed. The Abbé Galiani thought that freedom of trade was in theory a profound truth, but might in practice give rise to even greater evils than its opposite; nor did he share the physiocrats' view of agriculture, which to him seemed a mere game of chance, the farmer putting down his stake while nature and the treacherous elements held the bank. This was a profound truth paradoxically expressed, and was destined later to lead to valuable reflections on the necessity of connecting agricultural and industrial production so as to introduce stability and equilibrium into the national sources of wealth. Grimm was deeply sceptical as to the physiocrats' hopes; Necker brought to the work of government a policy opposed to theirs. The one point in their programme which seemed unassailable, the abolition of the *corvée*, aroused the opposition of Rousseau, who thought the *corvée* less prejudicial to freedom than taxation, because in a truly free State the citizens did everything with their own hands and nothing by means of money; far from paying in order to be excused their proper duties, they would pay in order to carry out these duties in person.[1]

The classes chiefly interested, the feudal proprietors and the peasants, opposed the new principles far more resolutely. The landowners, or those of them who did not yet understand the drift of the reforms, feared a gradual confiscation of their rights; the peasants instinctively recognized the

[1] Rousseau, *Contrat social*, iii. 15; *Gouvernement de Pologne*, 11. *Contra*, Turgot, *Œuvres*, ii. 295.

danger of the concentration of property, which deprived them without recompense of numerous feudal customs which they had for centuries enjoyed. This was the period at which the struggle of the poorer rustic population against *bourgeois* liberalism first began; that liberalism which, under colour of emancipating all citizens, really advanced the interest of property owners, and, while bestowing on the rest an empty form of liberty, left them actually at the mercy of the rich. The most stubborn conservatives always found in the peasant class numerous recruits to assist them in their attack on the liberal position; though this alliance involved for themselves the serious consequence of liberating undisciplined and half-civilized masses anxious to appropriate the land not for their masters but for themselves.

These resistances, though at first hardly perceptible, delayed the carrying out of the physiocratic programme. Turgot fell into disgrace and was succeeded in office by Necker. But the Revolution, by destroying the power of the nobility and by selling their confiscated estates, satisfied, at least for the time, the land-hunger of the agricultural classes, and marked the triumph of Turgot. But the unsolved and insoluble problem of fully satisfying this hunger will again, in the nineteenth century, bring the land-owning *bourgeois* face to face with the peasant, with important consequences for the history of liberalism.

We have spoken of the land-owning *bourgeois*; and this phrase precisely expresses the result of the physiocrats' liberal system. *Bourgeois* property is property by common right as opposed to property by privileged right; the land is no longer in bondage, no longer indivisible, but may form the object of free contract and partition; it appertains to the personality of its owner, who may cultivate it as he thinks fit, employ whatever labour he pleases, and dispose of its crops however he thinks best. But the appropriation of the land produces not only these economic consequences, but also political consequences reacting upon the former. In the feudal period the land, in addition to maintaining the population, provided a ruling class in the shape of its proprietors. *Bourgeois* property, in a predominantly agricultural country, alters the form of the problem but not its substance, and indeed makes it more difficult of solution. Quesnay looked upon the new proprietors as the class destined by nature for the service of the community. Turgot, completing and correcting his master's *tableau économique*, saw Society divided into three classes : the productive class, consisting of agriculturists actually working the land; the salaried class of artisans and employees; and the landowning class, which, not being tied to the task of earning its living, could be employed in the service of Society and the State, government, justice, administration, and war, which for this reason he called the ' disponible ' class.[1] But the question was too complicated to be solved by a classification. The old feudal régime provided a truly disponible class, because primogeniture and the indivisibility of estates ensured the economic and political independence of some individuals, however few. But *bourgeois* property, hereditary division, and the democratic tendency to increase the number of landowners, resulted in so minute a subdivision of the land that not only did agriculture suffer but the landowning class itself tended to disappear. The owner of a very small plot of land is not a disponible man at the service of the State. He needs a subsidiary occupation, which often becomes his principal source of income. In this case his land becomes a mere appendix in his livelihood, and exercises only a marginal influence upon his economic and political outlook. Thus, even in agricultural countries, the political importance of the land has diminished as its economic value has increased. The consequences of this fact for Liberalism have been very serious. With the diminution of the class of independent landowners, able to discharge the functions of local government and political representation without payment and without servility towards the State, have come its replacement by the bureaucracy, the modern unwanted general class, and the illicit intrusion of business into public life through the plutocracy. Moreover, even where the land

---

[1] Turgot, *Réflexions sur la formation et la distribution des richesses*, ii. 541.

has not lost all its political influence, it has often been able to exercise it only in an indirect manner through the medium of the so-called liberal professions, to which landowners and their sons have been able to devote themselves thanks to their comparative economic independence; to this is due the invasion of the political stage by the lawyers.

§ 6. THE INDUSTRIAL REVOLUTION

Industrial freedom is another child of modern individualism; its favourite child. It is a commonplace of Protestant literature that industrialism has reached its highest development in the countries most affected by the Reformation; from which it is inferred that the expansion of modern industry is due to the spirit of conscientiousness and responsibility characteristic of Protestantism. Catholic countries, these writers admit, have not entirely failed to develop this branch of human activity; but even here, it is pointed out, the strictly industrial regions are those which have directly or indirectly felt the influence of the Reformation. In any case, it is added, the spirit of self-dependence, initiative, and organization, characteristic of great industries, is absent from a truly strictly Catholic mentality. The latter has produced the artisan system and Colbertism, but not the Industrial Revolution. Finally it is observed that, while the science of economics, originally based, at least in part, upon industrialism, arises in England, the French system of the physiocrats denies all value to industry; though from this negation it draws an unexpected liberal corollary: that since industry is unproductive its burden upon the life of the country ought not to be increased by grants and subsidies from the State.

The importance of the problem of industrial freedom begins to be generally felt in England in the second half of the eighteenth century. Hitherto industry had confined itself to a narrow and secondary sphere of action, to which the traditional guild system was well enough adapted. Production was regulated by local consumption; labour was decentralized; the capital employed was small, and labour was for the most part highly specialized; the artisans, masters, and apprentices had clearly defined mutual rights and duties; they were separated by no class distinction, for after an apprenticeship of greater or less length every one became a master; the State guaranteed the guilds a monopoly of production, and secured the interests of the consumer by requiring all products to pass certain standard tests.

But this patriarchal state of things suddenly gave way before a movement which, because of its obviously revolutionary character, has been justly called the Industrial Revolution.[1] In the second half of the eighteenth century a series of technical inventions—mechanical spinning and weaving, the steam-engine, the utilization of coal for the extraction and working of iron—entirely transformed the old sedentary industries; machinery displaced, at least for the time being, the specialized skill already acquired by the labourer, and rendered possible a vast influx of new labour; this necessitated the concentration of labour in factories, vastly increased the fixed capital of a business, put an end to the old relations between master and man, and increased production to such an extent that local consumption was no longer equal to the supply, thus necessitating the discovery of wider markets and the extension of the chain of middlemen linking the producer to the consumer.[2]

To these gigantic changes the guild system soon showed itself inadequate. Here, as in the transformation of agriculture, the most serious opposition came both from above and from below : from the manufacturers whose fortunes were already made, especially the woollen manufacturers, and from the poorest artisans, who were unable to face the competition of machinery. But the advantages of a free manufacturing system soon made themselves indirectly felt, through the

[1] The phrase was perhaps used for the first time by Toynbee, *Lectures on the Industrial Revolution in England*, 1884, uncompleted at the author's death.

[2] Space forbids more than the briefest reference to this complex movement. The reader who wishes to go farther may consult Toynbee, *op. cit.* ; Mantoux, *La révolution industrielle*, Paris, 1906 ; or Schulze-Gaevernitz, *La grande intrapresa* (Ital. tr., *Bibl. degli Economisti*, ser. v).

growth of a completely new industry which because of its newness was unprotected by the old system. This was the cotton industry, which arose in England by a curious reaction against the protectionism of the woollen manufacturers, and in a few years attained a prodigious development, through being able to make unhampered use of the rapid improvements in manufacture, and to introduce labour devoid of any guild organization and largely recruited from the peasants whom the enclosures carried out by the landed aristocracy had set free for employment in the factories.

The contrast between the protected and unprogressive woollen industry and the free and progressive cotton industry must soon have forced itself upon the notice of the manufacturing class, whose excessive protectionism had been rebuked by Adam Smith as early as 1776. And in fact, with the increase in number and power of the free employers, implying as it did the increase of their political influence in government circles, the old restrictions, the old monopolies, the old regulations as to the quality and quantity of products, began by degrees to disappear. Artificial and external compromises between the various interests were no longer needed. To assure the production of good wares, it was no longer necessary to provide State control; the interests of the producers themselves, prompted by mutual competition, were enough. Indeed this competition was the consumer's best defence, serving as it did to reduce prices, sharpen the manufacturers' wits, and compel them to improve their machines, increase production, and cut down the cost of production to a minimum.

In this school of initiative and self-criticism, under the normal discipline of an habitual self-dependence, urged by an ever-present necessity for progress and growth with ruin as the only alternative, grew up the stalwart industrial middle class which in the nineteenth century was to form the backbone of the new English Liberalism. Compared with the landed middle class which formed the chief source of continental Liberalism, it was remarkable for its individualistic character. It had no sense of duty towards the

State, which it might well have addressed in the contemptuous words of the philosopher, ' Get out of my sunlight '.
No privilege, no monopoly had gone to the making of its
fortune; such a parasitic life it despised no less than the
indolence of the *rentier*. Its nature was forged and tempered
in the factory, whose individuality was in perfect harmony
with the individuality of its creator.

Unlike the manufacturer, the landowner cannot call himself at once the father and the son of his work. He owes his
rights to the State and to Society; Liberal though he is, he
enjoys a privilege, a monopoly, since the total quantity of
land is limited. He can gather its fruits without having
lavished upon it his labour. His consciousness of his own
individuality is therefore less quick and lively; his spirit of
initiative meets with difficulties harder to surmount; competition is less direct, and less stimulating in its effect upon
his personality.

Hence arises a new difference, very visible in the nineteenth century, between English and continental Liberalism;
a difference of temper, of attitude, of activity, vividly
reflected in their respective histories. But industrial Liberalism has its own defect. In a different way, but no less
seriously, it feels the difficulty of creating a governing class.
In the most heroic period of its life, the time of Peel and
Cobden, it gave its best children to the service of politics;
but later, absorption in their own business, and their traditional antipathy towards the State, surviving like an inherited characteristic even when the State had passed into
their own hands, drew them away from the work of government, which they handed over to their dependants, or tried
to effect in underground and indirect ways.

Even more serious are the social consequences of this form
of Liberalism. We have seen that the freedom of the soil,
by depriving the peasants of their customary rights, put
them at the mercy of their masters, and drove them to
agitations wavering between the two extremes of reaction
and revolution. The same phenomenon appears far more
frequently and more intensely in industry, on account of its

greater concentration and mobility. The employers agree in regarding liberty as a principle of universal application; but equality of rights between employers and employed, where their conditions are markedly unequal, appears a mere mockery of equality.

This state of things was a stimulus to the manufacturers in their mutual relations; but what of the workmen? Formerly these were protected by the statutes of their guilds, assuring them at least permanence of labour and livelihood: this defence gone, they were exposed to every caprice of their masters at the very moment when the use of machinery and the need for cutting down the cost of production drove the new captains of industry to the most relentless exploitation of their men. The labourer had been proclaimed free; to prevent the reconstitution of the old guilds the law forbade all associations between working men; but this freedom, so valuable to the middle class, was for him, deprived as he was of means of subsistence and the tools of labour, merely the freedom to sell himself into slavery. Thus it was precisely at the period of intensest industrial growth that the condition of the labourer changed for the worse. Hours of labour multiplied out of all measure; the employment of women and children in factories lowered wages: the keen competition between the workmen themselves, no longer tied to their parishes but free to travel and congregate where they were most in demand, further cheapened the labour they placed on the market: numerous and frequent industrial crises, inevitable at a period of growth, when population and consumption are not yet stabilized, swelled from time to time the ranks of the unemployed, the reserves in the army of starvation.

These were at least the first-fruits of liberty for working men, who now began to form a class sharply distinct from that of the middle-class manufacturers, and soon sharply opposed to it. It is characteristic that the first economist to note these immediate consequences of industrialism was a physiocrat, Turgot, who observes that freedom of contract tends to reduce wages to the level of bare subsistence.[1] But

[1] Turgot, *Œuvres*, ii. 537.

from this observation he did not draw the pessimistic inferences later drawn by Ricardo and his socialistic followers.

We thus see, beginning in the closing years of the eighteenth century, the growth of a distinction between the
working and middle classes, and the rise of an opposition
between bourgeois freedom and an egalitarian principle
tending towards a substantial, not only a formal, equality
of conditions between man and man. The antagonism which
formerly arose between the *bourgeoisie* and the aristocracy
now begins to assert itself by degrees between the proletariate and the *bourgeoisie*. Beneath the veil of a universal
Liberalism, the *bourgeoisie* disguised a privilege similar to that
once flaunted by the aristocracy : and thus the proletariate's
efforts to overthrow the new privilege, though anti-liberal in
appearance, were in reality to bring into existence a wider
Liberalism.

For us, therefore, it will be necessary to follow the course
of the working-class movement not only in its self-contained
and revolutionary manifestations, but also in those which seem
most remote from any such goal. We refer to the alliances,
of which the nineteenth century offers conspicuous examples,
between the working classes and the conservative landowners, against industrial Liberalism. These alliances have an
indirectly Liberal significance because, resulting as they do in
the protection and defence of labour (in England social legislation dates from 1802), they serve to broaden the basis of
Liberalism as originally understood.

While the reformed economic life of agriculture found
expression in the system of the physiocrats, that of industry
was modelled upon the doctrines of Adam Smith. The
reader of his great work on *The Wealth of Nations* may at
first fail to realize the enormous distance that separates it
from the writings of the physiocrats. Smith, like them,
affirms the primacy of agricultural economy, and makes no
secret of his dislike for manufacturers and traders. But these
antipathies are accidental, and are chiefly due to the protectionist attitude of these two classes in his own day. The
main fact is that Adam Smith justifies their functions by

recognizing them as productive of social utilities. But the peculiar feature of Smith's conception lies not so much here, as in the fact that he shifted the centre of gravity in economics from the estate—a hybrid mixture of legal and economic elements—to the business, whether industrial or agricultural. Thus the new science declares its independence of the ancient family and social institutions, repudiates the static hierarchy of classes which the physiocrats had perpetuated, in a word follows and to some degree anticipates the transformation gradually coming about in modern industrial society, the sweeping redistribution of its classes and functions.

This is Adam Smith's true modernity : and his followers, developing these aspects of his doctrine under the guidance of experience itself, have done much to clear away whatever features in his work have, in the narrower sense of the phrase, a merely agricultural or rural character.

The ultimate cell of modern economic society is not the family with its property, but the business ; a spontaneous division of labour distributes the task of production among the various businesses ; exchange causes the product to circulate and equates it with the demands of consumption. The whole of society thus assumes the aspect of an autonomous and self-sufficing organism. The one law which effectually controls its internal relations is freedom ; freedom in the creation of businesses, in the division of social labour, in exchange. In these relations there is no place for the action of the State, which would in vain, or worse than in vain, attempt to replace the spontaneous organization of nature by an artificial and ephemeral organization of its own. To the State belongs only the external task of providing a security and defence which may permit the free play of the organic forces ; and solely on behalf of this task Smith grudgingly allows certain restrictions on commercial freedom and the survival of a few ancient privileges.[1]

[1] e.g. the Navigation Act (iv. 7). At the time of the free-trade agitation the conservatives quoted passages from Adam Smith in favour of their own position ; they found no lack of these, but failed to convince the public that they represented the real spirit of the book.

At bottom, this conception is obviously individualistic: its motive force is self-interest. But it is an individualism which spreads out so as to cover the whole of society, in virtue of a naïvely optimistic feeling that the general interest was nothing but the sum or resultant of private interests. This applied not only to the relations between the economic forces acting within a single State, but also to the relations between State and State; the well-being of each was a condition or means to the well-being of all the rest. In these rudimentary economic principles we can see a new view of international politics.

But are the interests of individuals really harmonious? When Adam Smith published his work in 1776 the Industrial Revolution was hardly begun; no serious conflict had as yet broken out between the agricultural and industrial classes, and his optimism seemed justified. This enabled him to paint an idyllic picture of a society in which town and country mutually supplied each other's needs, the former offering to the latter its industrial products, to receive the produce of agriculture in return, so that the economic forces of the nation balanced one another; where the profits of industry automatically tended, through competition and the well-being of the nation at large, to diminish, and wages to rise; where the position of the landed proprietor living on rent could be justified from the point of view of the general interest of society.[1] But the Industrial Revolution, the conflict of capital and labour, the clash between the agricultural and manufacturing classes, very soon dispelled these illusions; so that the picture of economic society as drawn by Adam Smith's followers, though still preserving the fundamental lines laid down by the master, was painted in darker colours and expressed a more pessimistic outlook.

§ 7. CIVIL AND POLITICAL LIBERTY

We have seen the new freedom germinate in the modern consciousness as a contrast to the privileges of feudalism. This gave rise to a new mentality growing up as it were in-

---

[1] i. 9; ii. 4; iv. 9; &c.

voluntarily before our eyes : the mentality of a new bour-geois class, in which this modern consciousness is incarnate. This *Homo novus* repudiates all ecclesiastical mediation in the service of his unworldly interests, and extends this intolerance to the organization of his worldly life. He will be his own critic, his own judge, his own advocate, his own adminis-trator, his own ruler. And since in the intimacy of con-science, where all social barriers are swept away, he recog-nizes himself the equal of all other men, his freedom appears to him as a right capable of extension to all, a primordial right common to all men as men. Liberalism, as we have said, regarded as a universal and widespread historical con-sciousness, implies not only the feeling of liberty but the idea of equality. This feeling and this idea develop together ; but from their very triumph new conflicts between them arise, the effect of which will be to create a democracy dis-tinct from Liberalism and often in opposition to it, yet imply-ing a perpetually renewed demand for a higher unity.

Now the liberties of which we have spoken are not discon-nected each from the rest ; they form a system, which is the very system of human personality in its progressive organiza-tion. Their most appropriate and original name is the liberties of the individual. And yet, by the mere fact that they imply no privileges on the part of one man as against others, but proceed from a root common to all individuals, and because their practical application can only take place in human society, they may also be called, and have actually been called, civil liberties. This name, of course, contains no suggestion of any privilege belonging to the *civis* as opposed to the mere *homo*. They are civil liberties because they are human liberties, because humanity is essentially social, and in its most developed form constitutes precisely what is called civil society. The civil quality of this liberty, far from absorbing wholly into itself the original quality of individuality, serves only to emphasize it ; so much so, that when society threatens to tyrannize over the individual the individualistic energy of this freedom asserts itself and turns against society.

This element of social unity we have seen gradually growing up in the evolution of individualism. And this leads us to consider the two terms, individual and society, as, within certain limits, synonymous, in spite of their latent antithesis. In the eighteenth century the individual and the new society that springs from him have a common enemy, the despotic State, against which they learn to direct their energies, united by the optimistic feeling that the action of the individual must fully harmonize with the action of society.

Thus freedom, whether we call it individual or civil freedom, stands in opposition to the State. The State has no right to control religious belief, to direct thought, to intervene in the private economic life of the citizen ; it meets with an insuperable barrier in the conscience of the individual and in everything that immediately proceeds from this conscience. Freedom, then, means freedom *from* the State, the right of the individual *as against* the State.

But what is the value of freedom without recognition, of right without sanction? What if the State, in spite of the individual's claim to the contrary, intervenes and attacks his inviolable prerogatives? While the State subsists on its own account, independent of the individual, the individual's rights are always in danger of violation : the only safeguard is that the individual should appropriate the State.

This idea of appropriation comes into being by degrees, after many unsuccessful attempts at compromise. Between crude despotism and the Revolution intervenes a period commonly called the period of enlightened despotism, to which the *bourgeoisie* entrusts its hopes of freedom. If the monarchy has already in part destroyed feudalism, why should it not complete its work of reformation? The physiocrats, convinced of the mathematical self-evidence of their liberal principles, look for their realization to no other power ; to solve a mathematical problem, a single individual, furnished with reason, is surely sufficient. The same view is shared by illuminism as a whole ; granted the strictly rationalistic manner in which it conceives its reforms, it is inevitable that their execution should be entrusted to a single individual.

A legislative assembly, with its conflicting passions and interests, could only produce chaos. And how could anybody who remembered the recent history of legislative assemblies maintain the opposite view? The Estates Generàl had not been convened since 1614; the parliaments which claimed partly at least to supersede them had made the worst possible impression, showing themselves more reactionary than the Crown, and had finally been suppressed amid universal satisfaction.

The confidence in monarchy was so strong throughout the eighteenth century that it even survived the first shocks of the Revolution. In 1789, not only Mirabeau and Sieyès but Robespierre and Danton were monarchists. None the less, monarchy had done everything in its power to destroy this faith, whenever after each crisis of disillusionment and despair it had once more been set on its feet. It irritated the nobles while it paid their pensions; it taxed its allies the *bourgeois* to pay for the luxury and waste of its court; it created a sense of the precarious and insecure character of all rights, and turned reactionary whenever it seemed to have desired a decisive advance; and by yielding tamely to its own subjects' commands it demonstrated its impotence even while asserting its omnipotence. This vacillating and inconsistent conduct created by degrees in the minds of citizens the demand for a more secure guarantee of their own civil rights, which should place them beyond the power of arbitrary infraction. Thus arose the idea of political liberty as an addition to civil liberty, as a safeguard against the State and the Crown. This conception had originally the same anti-State character which marked the substantial rights it was intended to protect.

The idea of this guarantee, in the sense here defined, is modern; but in a broader sense it is connected with the medieval institutions which tempered feudal monarchy in the interest, not of individuals, but of privileged groups: the representation of orders or classes. Fallen into abeyance in France, these institutions survived in England, and there showed their vitality by producing two victorious revolutions and providing an effectual check upon the Crown. This gave reason to suppose that they were still capable of discharging a political function in the modern world.

The writer who more than any other preserved the memory and renewed the prestige of these institutions was Montesquieu, in his famous *Esprit des lois*. Montesquieu is a rationalist, but at the same time a scholar, a combination far from rare in the age of Leibniz and Mabillon. His scholarly tastes led him to particularize, and thus to qualify his abstract affirmations of freedom by setting forth the conditions of time, place, and manner in which freedom had actually been achieved. In him therefore we find a spontaneous approach to what the French call guarantism,[1] that is, the conception of substituting guarantees of freedom for formal and often ineffectual declarations of its ideal essence.

From the work of Montesquieu an interesting anthology of liberal expressions could be collected. That freedom which abstract rationalists treated as innate right reveals itself to the author's eye as depending on many circumstances, and in its turn producing many effects, not to be deduced from any *a priori* conception. It has its roots in the soil; in fertile plains the movement towards despotism is only arrested with difficulty; in an inaccessible mountain district liberty is easier of attainment. The same is true of islands as compared with continents. Lands are cultivated not in proportion to their fertility but in proportion to their freedom. If we mentally divide a country, we are astounded to see wastes in those parts of it that are naturally most fertile, and dense populations where the soil appears to refuse all wealth. The reason for this is that the barrenness of the soil makes men industrious, sober, hard-working, and courageous; develops, we should say, their individuality. As a general rule, heavier taxes can be raised in proportion as the subject enjoys more liberty; as liberty decreases taxes must be diminished. In free States heavy taxes are counterbalanced by liberty; in despotic States the lightness of the

[1] [*Garantisme*, a system designed to protect the individual's rights against encroachment by the State.]

taxes is a compensation for the loss of liberty. In a republic the citizen will pay most heavily, because he believes he is paying himself. Industry on a large scale is more appropriate to a republic than to a monarchy; because in the former the greater security of property makes every one willing to invest his capital and take risks. Freedom of trade does not consist in allowing traders to do what they like; that would be rather slavery. A restriction upon traders is not necessarily a restriction on trade; indeed, it is precisely in free countries that the trader finds himself most hedged about by restrictions, while he is nowhere less subject to restrictions than in countries devoid of freedom. In general, freedom does not consist in doing whatever one wants, but, in a society ruled by laws, it consists in being able to do what one ought to want. The forms of justice are necessary to liberty; but if they are too numerous they end by frustrating the very purpose of the law. Some people contrast the disquietude which accompanies freedom unfavourably with the tranquillity at which despotic government aims; but this is not real peace, it is the silence of a city occupied by the enemy.[1]

This is the spirit in which Montesquieu approaches the problem of political freedom. It is not, for him, separable from civil freedom, but is complementary to it, connected by the fact remarked above, that it stands between the forms of government and the liberties of the people. What is political liberty? It is that tranquillity of mind which comes from every man's conviction of his own security;[2] as such, it is the condition of civil liberty. The conviction of one's own security in its turn can only arise from a Constitution which sets definite and inviolable limits upon the action of the State. Of the practical working of such a Constitution England offers a highly suggestive example and model. Here, of the three constitutive powers of the State, the legislative, the executive, and the judiciary, the first corresponds to the liberal principle that each man must be able to govern himself; but since the mere expansion of territory

---

[1] *Esprit des lois*, v. 14; xi. 3; xviii. 3, 5, 12; xx. 4, 12; xxxix. 1.

[2] *Op. cit.* xi. 6.

makes it impossible for the whole people to have legislative power, popular representatives have been introduced, renewable from time to time, so that the citizens represented may carry their aspirations to a new parliament when they have been disappointed by the old.

The legislative body which forms the strictly political power consists of three parts : king, lords, and commons, each independent of the rest, but connected with the rest in such a way that each is able to check and hinder the action of the others. Thus the House of Commons can check the House of Lords and vice versa ; the king, and through him the executive, opens and closes the sessions and may dissolve the Houses, but cannot give any edict the force of law without their consent. Now it might be thought that these mutual checks would result in complete inactivity ; but since the inevitable movement of events necessitates an advance, the three are compelled to move together. This is the so-called system of checks and balances.

But political liberty is not considered only from the standpoint of the Constitution, but also from the standpoint of the citizen. The Constitution may be free and the citizen not. That the citizen may be free, there must be good general laws and an independent power to apply them. Where the judiciary depends on the executive, or is confused with it, there can be no guarantee that the law will be impartially applied. Hence arises another and broader conception of the separation and equilibrium of the general powers of the State.

It has been stated, not without truth, that this construction is wholly unlike its supposed model. Montesquieu's descriptions of the functions of the English Houses and the special attributes of the executive and judiciary powers are sometimes correct ; but the sharp separation and equilibrium of powers upon which he so strongly insists are foreign to the political system of eighteenth-century England. If anything, the opposite principle of the confusion of powers was actually at work. The best observers and inquirers have regarded the England of that age as a mixture of oligarchy

[1] *Op. cit.*, Book XI, *passim*.

and anarchy, at any rate in its outward political aspect, but inwardly as a country steeped in a strong consciousness of its traditional privileges and rights, and able for this very reason to triumph over the disintegrating influence of its anarchism. It is easy to understand how Montesquieu's rationalistic and legal mind left the inner and more organic aspect of English political life unplumbed, and confined itself to its formal and outward elements, even exaggerating the formalism of its distinction. His sincerely liberal spirit must have been struck by an observation which even to-day seems undoubtedly correct, that the central executive power was extremely weak; and since the true explanation of this fact escaped him (as we shall see, this could only be grasped by the mature historical thought of the nineteenth century) he invented an ingenious mechanism of checks and balances to provide it with a rationalistic justification.

The most curious thing is that his explanation was widely accepted in eighteenth-century England. The Englishmen of the day, rationalists no less than himself, understood little of their own history, and were easily led astray by the architectonic appearance of his picture. Montesquieu's inspiration thus affected Blackstone's epoch-making *Commentaries on the Laws of England*, which were to be the Bible of political liberalism. In Blackstone we again find the notion of three independent powers, king, lords, and commons; a mixed government composed of monarchy, aristocracy, and democracy, uniting in itself all the advantages which Montesquieu had already ascribed to each of the three forms. The prerogatives of the various powers are enumerated with a thoroughly English precision and detail; the complex interplay of their functions is lucidly described; and the whole complex of political guarantees summed up in this system appears as directed to the supreme end of defending and safeguarding the rights of individuals, divided into two categories: absolute or natural, and relative or social.[1] These

[1] It may be thought that Blackstone's distinction of the three powers does not exactly coincide with that of Montesquieu. But it must be remembered that in Montesquieu there are two separate distinctions:

conceptions were popularized later on the continent by De Lolme.

The work of Blackstone, impeccable in its form, shares with that of Montesquieu the fault of emphasizing the purely external aspect of the constitutional machinery, and ignoring the inner forces by which this machinery was moved and animated. This fact produced two opposite consequences in England and on the continent respectively. It helped the English to give to their own political thought a somewhat rationalistic character which assimilated it to that of the continent. On the continent, for a time at least, it created the dangerous illusion that this well-constructed machinery had only to be transplanted into another country in order to function as perfectly there as in its place of origin. The ignoring of the internal motive forces produced in the latter case the most disastrous consequences: the separation of powers led revolutionary France to the absurd exclusion of the king's ministers from the political assembly, and this contributed to the breach between the Crown and the people. Still worse, the search for the best constitution or perfect political machine occupied people's minds all through the nineteenth century, and produced hopes of a millennium that were foredoomed to disappointment.

But a form, though it is not everything, is always something; and the imitators of the English tradition certainly did not go away empty-handed. The numerous failures to apply the form of the English Constitution on the continent ended by making it clear that its success required a further explanation, a deeper understanding of the English Constitution; which led to the discovery of the content of this form in the shape of local self-government. With its feet upon this new road, continental Liberalism has since endeavoured to stimulate the languid vitality of its communes, in order to

that between the legislative, executive, and judiciary powers, and, within the legislative, that between king, lords, and commons. The double position of the king as head both of the legislative and of the executive gives rise in Montesquieu's conception to a certain equivocation and interference between the two distinctions.

render its copy an adequate representation of the English original.

At the time of which we are speaking, all this still lay in the distant future. We have anticipated, in this case as in others, in order that the development and connexion of historical problems may appear in a clearer light. History never improvises, and, like nature, *non facit saltum*.

Returning to Montesquieu, we must observe that the influence of his work, uncontested in the first few decades after its publication in 1748, began by degrees to be counteracted by other influences of very different origin and character. One thing especially strikes us in the continental writers, French and Italian, of the second half of the eighteenth century: an increasing dislike of England. To the formation of this new feeling many political accidents contributed, including renewed national rivalries and hatreds; but this does not explain why the feeling of dislike for England was reinforced by a profound lack of confidence in her future. She now appears as a nation far gone in decay: corruption and anarchy within and without, an impotence soon to be demonstrated by the loss of America. In the minds of political writers on the continent, one central doubt begins to take shape: whether the much admired English Constitution may not itself be the true cause of the incipient downfall.[1] The doubt grew stronger as the English Constitution was known better—or rather worse, because the rationalistic spirit in which its students examined it led them to see nothing but confusion and anarchy in a complex of institutions formed and consolidated by a tradition many centuries old. And its practical working seemed to reinforce this judgement. Beneath the cloak of a mixed government, could one not detect, as the only political force actually at work, a tyrannical, selfish, and greedy aristocracy? Was not the executive power, which ought to have been held in check by the system of balances, neutralized in fact by

[1] See, for example, D'Argenson, *Considérations sur le gouvernement ancien et présent de la France*, Amsterdam, 1764, but written several years earlier, pp. 36–43.

corruption? Was it not the king, who ought to have been able to do nothing by himself, that took the initiative in a disastrous war with America? As for property, which had been pronounced as inviolable right, had it not been violated through the enclosure, sanctioned by parliament, of the open fields? These and similar observations seemed to many writers to justify the assertion that the political guarantees offered to its citizens by the British Constitution were illusory and deceptive, and induced them to follow another path toward the goal of a firmly established political freedom.

The path suggested by the English or their interpreters was guarantism, or political liberty conceived as the freedom of the individual from the State and in face of the State. The new path which to Reason and her radical admirers appeared more satisfactory consisted in the rational reconstruction of the State in accordance with the indefeasible demands of the individual. Only so could security be attained against every revival of aggression on the part of the old powers and traditional classes. The individual would be truly free in his own State. And liberty would now consist not in being independent of the State but in taking active part in it; in the government of the State regarded as the self-government of the individual. This is the aspiration which we have already expressed in the formula that the individual, in order to make himself secure against the dangers arising from the State, must appropriate the State.

This idea was not absent from the English system; one need only think of the institution of popular representation; but its operation was only indirect, because the traditional function of parliament was not so much to govern as to guarantee and to check, to refuse and to grant. This explains why the new doctrine draws its inspiration not from England but from Greece and Rome. Political liberty in fact, for the peoples of classical antiquity, consisted in the citizen's right to a share in the work of government.

But a Liberalism so understood has other names more familiar to memory: democracy, republicanism. Montesquieu, in his review of the forms of government, spoke at length of the republic, taking examples from the States of antiquity; and, while not concealing his preference for a mixed government, bestowed on the republic an impartial and even benevolent glance. This form of government thus continued to attract attention, even if in a certain sense it was now regarded as out of date.

To this movement of Liberalism, which we may call democratic, belong almost all the political constructions of the eighteenth century, including those of a communistic character, which are based no less than the rest on the republics of antiquity. If we had at command a little historical leisure we might here have given some account of them; but a long journey awaits us, and we must confine ourselves to an analysis of the most important system of this period, the *Contrat social* of Rousseau, which exercised an immense influence on European political history.

What is the social contract? It is not a compact of subjection or of government, by which the individuals of a community agree to submit themselves to a master; it is no reminiscence of those medieval contracts between prince and people of which we have already spoken. It is connected with the free covenants of the Calvinistic communities; and Rousseau's Genevan origin confirms this derivation. It is a contract between equals, between men naturally free, intended to establish the rules of their common political life. The contracting parties surrender their natural liberty to the community, to receive civil liberty in exchange, so that, since each surrenders himself entirely to the whole, conditions are equal for all; and since every one obeys the general will which springs from the compact of union, he is in reality obeying himself.

This contract might be called by the more usual name of a Constitution; though in that case it should be observed that, unlike the medieval constitutions, it is a voluntary act whose title is founded upon the express consent of the contracting parties, not on the recognition of a pre-existing custom or right; and unlike the greater part of modern constitutions, which are one-sided acts of concession on the part of a monarch or compacts between a monarch and his subjects, it is a self-constitutive act in which the power constituting and the power constituted reside in the same community. The privatistic nature of this contract, from a legal point of view, lies in the fact that the source of all public or State right is the individual.

The conception of the sovereignty of the people follows inevitably from the principles already stated, and is developed by Rousseau with relentless logic. Granted the identity and continuity of the constituting power with the constituted power, sovereignty rests permanently with the people. It cannot be represented, or the people would be sovereign only at the moment of choosing their representatives, and would relapse into slavery as soon as their members of parliament were elected, which actually happens in the case of England. The people cannot have representatives, but only commissaries; that is, delegates responsible to the people and not authorized to conclude anything definite without popular ratification. Sovereignty is moreover inalienable; it cannot be sold or ceded to a prince or ruler of any kind. It has already been said that the act by which the people gives itself a government is not a contract; it is a law, that is to say an act of sovereignty; thus government is a function, and rulers are functionaries, of the sovereign people. Lastly, sovereignty is indivisible in virtue of its very conception; since to divide it would be to create two or more sovereigns, and this is the negation of sovereignty.

These attributes are the exact opposite of the principles of guarantism as derived from the English Constitution. Indivisibility is the antithesis of the separation of powers and the systems of balances; inalienability tends to destroy the prerogative of the Crown and turn the monarch into a magistrate; the impossibility of representation tends to destroy the prerogative of parliament. But now that the opposition has been thus pushed to extremity, can we say that the rights of the individual are more effectively safeguarded? Can we say that freedom by means of the State, as Rousseau established it, is more secure than the traditional freedom from the State?

To answer this question is enough to follow Rousseau's conception in its later development. His thought took as its starting-point the natural liberty of the individual, and converted this by means of the social contract into so-called civil liberty. But the very fact that all individuals wholly and unreservedly surrendered themselves to the community created a gigantic and tyrannical collective power ; a monarchy in the style of Louis XIV, all the stronger and more concentrated because it had more radically levelled the individual by reducing him to the limit of bare human nature, and because, instead of a monarch distinct from the people, against whom the people could at any rate make claims on its own behalf, it set up as sovereign a general will against which no one could raise his voice.

The new monarchy aggravated the slavery of absolutism by making it more intimate, by transferring its seat to the conscience, on whose threshold the most unbridled despotism stopped short. As compared with the old monarchy of Louis XIV, the new was soon to find for itself a far more dreaded name : that of Convention.

Rousseau has as yet no presentiment of such a power. Faithful to the ancient tripartition of the forms of government, he asserts the principle that taxes become heavier as the distance between people and government increases : thus in a democracy the people is least burdened, more so in aristocracy, and most of all in monarchy. Thus monarchy is suitable to rich nations, democracy to small and poor nations, aristocracy in intermediate cases.[1] These are reminiscences of the past ; the new democracy which he created was a very different thing.

But if Rousseau, who at this point shows himself inferior to Montesquieu, fails to realize the concentration of force that can be effected in a democratic government, he nevertheless worked to prepare for this event. What was said of Richelieu may be said of Rousseau, that despotism was in his brain if not in his heart. It is enough to reflect on the power which he gives the sovereign to impose a State religion on the

[1] *Contrat social*, iii. 8.

citizens and to treat its articles of faith not as religious dogmas but as sentiments of sociability without which they can be neither good citizens nor faithful subjects. True, the sovereign cannot compel any one to believe them; but he may banish from the State any one who does not. The citizens' liberty of religion is nothing but the liberty to withdraw from the State. But worse is to follow. If any one, after having publicly subscribed to these articles of faith, acts as if he did not believe them, he is to be punished with death. He has committed the greatest of crimes; he has lied against the law.[1]

In these conceptions what relics can be discovered of the natural rights of man as an individual? Rousseau continues to distinguish the rights of the citizen and the sovereign from the natural rights which the former must enjoy merely as man. The individual does not by the social contract alienate his whole self to the community, but only that part which the community requires to employ; but (and this reservation is important) the sovereign is the sole judge of its requirements.[2] This means that the idea of natural right disappears, in the very act of its apparent recognition, as soon as the State power is permitted to determine its limits.

But the primary and inexhaustible source of democratic despotism lies in the conception, which Rousseau also enunciates, that the general will cannot err, that it is always *droite* and always directed towards the public interest. It is therefore an infallible and irresistible power, against which the individual can neither rebel nor appeal. How can he rebel against himself, and to whom can he appeal against the truth?

Here we seem to find actually in being the state of things foreseen by the prudent Montesquieu, against which his constitutionalism was intended to protect the individual: a State rendered free by its constitution while its citizens are slaves. The latter seem to exhaust their initial freedom in the act of fastening their own chains.

But what was the use of the State's being free when the individuals are not? The first experiments in democratic despotism were to create in a renewed and livelier form that

---

[1] *Op. cit.* iv. 8.   [2] *Op. cit.* ii. 4.

demand for security for the rights of individuals which first arose as a protest against monarchical despotism. Freedom from the State, instead of being rendered unnecessary by the individual's appropriation of the State, became more necessary and more urgent, but at the same time more difficult. Protection against oneself is a more difficult thing to achieve than protection against another; especially when an illusory security against all external aggression has encouraged the individual to raze his defences to the ground and forgo all the safeguards which he has gradually accumulated in the course of history, leaving him reduced to the state of nature, naked and unarmed.

The problem of simultaneously establishing both kinds of political liberty, arising as it did from the bitter experience of the Revolution, became overwhelming in the nineteenth century. Each made a demand that could not be suppressed, or whose suppression, resulting in the exclusive reign of the other, would at least imply sheer slavery.

But is their combination possible? Without for the present engaging upon a premature discussion of all the relations between Liberalism and democracy, we may here confine ourselves to the points at issue between Montesquieu and Rousseau. We have seen how Rousseau conceived the attributes of sovereignty. The demand expressed in his conception is undoubtedly just. As against the atomistic subdivision of powers, he affirms the indivisible unity of sovereignty. As against a political representation by which the representatives once elected lose all contact with the people, he affirms that the popular power cannot be represented. As against the autonomous prerogatives of the Crown, he affirms that this same power cannot be alienated, and that in comparison with it the prince is no more than a functionary. But if these just demands are isolated from the opposite demands contained in the other thesis the result is an immense concentration of power and a demagogic liberation of popular caprice. To avoid these excesses, power, though one at its source, must be divided in its application; sovereignty must remain with the people, not in the sense that the crowd may impose itself by mob violence upon its degraded and servile representatives, but in the sense that the assembly of representatives is itself the people politically organized, and that an active circulation of public opinion may raise to the level of a substantial truth the legal fiction by which every citizen is present and active in the assembly. The government has no independent prerogatives but only a function; yet it is in no sense like a mere employee, to be dismissed at will; it is the organ of sovereignty.

A combination, then, is possible ; and we shall see how the political consciousness in its development travels towards its achievement.

§ 8. THE DECLARATION OF THE RIGHTS OF MAN

All that has hitherto been said is a mere introduction and historical commentary to the famous *Principles* of 1789, the *Declaration of Rights* preceding the first French Constitution of 1791. Seen as we have tried to see them, these principles are neither the empty generalizations, nor the transcendent truths, nor the deceptive mirage, which many writers and publicists of various political opinions have thought them, reading into them their own partisan passions rather than studying them with an open and candid mind.

Let us begin by reading them ; a thing which very few people, however much they talk about them, are in the habit of doing.

' The National Assembly recognizes and declares, in the sight and under the auspices of the Supreme Being, the following rights of the man and the citizen :

' Art. I. Men are born and live free and equal as regards their rights. Social distinctions can be based only on the common interest.

' Art. II. The end of every political association is the conservation of the natural and imprescriptible rights of man. These rights are liberty, property, security, and resistance to oppression.

' Art. III. The principle of all sovereignty resides essentially in the nation. No office and no individual can exercise an authority not expressly emanating from it.

' Art. IV. Liberty consists essentially in being able to do whatever is not harmful to others; thus the exercise of the natural rights of each individual has no limits, except those which ensure to other members of society the enjoyment of these same rights. These limits can be determined only by the law.

' Art. V. The law has the right to prohibit actions harmful to society. Whatever is not forbidden by the law cannot be prevented, and no one can be constrained to do what the law does not command.

' Art. VI. The law is the expression of the general will. All citizens have the right to take part, either personally or through their representatives, in its formation.

' The law must be equal for all, whether it protects or punishes. Since all citizens are equal before it, all are equally admissible to all dignities, offices, and public employments, according to their capacities and without any other distinction but those of virtue and intellect.

' Art. VII. No man may be accused, arrested, or detained, except in cases contemplated by the law and according to the forms which it prescribes. Those who promote, transmit, carry out, or cause others to carry out arbitrary orders must be punished; but every citizen summoned or arrested in pursuance of the law must instantly obey. In resisting he renders himself culpable.

' Art. VIII. The law must only establish penalties strictly and obviously necessary; and no one must be punished except in pursuance of a law passed and promulgated previously to the offence and legally applied.

' Art. IX. Since every one is presumed innocent until he has been declared guilty, if it is considered necessary to arrest him, all severity except what is necessary in order to secure his person must be repressed by the law in the most determined manner.

' Art. X. No one must be disturbed in his opinions, whether religious or other, provided their expression does not disturb the public order established by law.

' Art. XI. The free communication of thought and opinion is one of the most precious rights of man. Every citizen may accordingly speak, write, and publish freely, except that he shall be answerable for the abuse of this freedom in cases contemplated by the law.

' Art. XII. To guarantee the rights of the man and the citizen, public force is necessary; this is therefore instituted for the advantage of all, and not for the private interest of those to whom it is entrusted.

'Art. XIII. For the maintenance of the public force, and for the expenses of administration, a general contribution is indispensable. It ought to be divided among all citizens in proportion to their wealth.

'Art. XIV. All citizens have the right to examine for themselves, through their representatives, the necessity of the public contribution, to consent freely to its imposition, to watch over its employment, and to determine its amount, its distribution, its exaction, and its duration.

'Art. XV. Society has the right to demand from every public official an account of his administration.

'Art. XVI. Any society in which rights are not securely guaranteed, and the separation of powers is not determined, has no constitution.

'Art. XVII. Property, being an inviolable and sacred right, can in no case be taken away except where public necessity, legally determined, clearly demands it, and always on condition of a preceding indemnity.'

In these brief articles is summarized the charter, an historical document like all charters, of modern Liberalism. They are in great part translated, as Jellinek has shown by a textual comparison, from the American Bill of Rights of 1776, and through these they attach themselves to the covenants of the Puritan communities and in the last instance to the spirit of Calvinism. This derivation is already familiar to the reader, and we will not dwell upon it.

The Declaration is concerned with the rights of man, not the rights of the citizen. This is just, because it is intended to sanction no privileges of citizenship, but universal human rights, the fruits of a slowly effected revolution centred in the consciousness of man. From the new man will in time spring the new citizen, not *vice versa*. The accusation brought against the articles by the thought of the nineteenth century, to the effect that they put the man, an abstract term, before the citizen, a concrete reality, becomes in this light nothing but the eternal indictment of every son against his father: the accusation of having been born earlier than himself.

In appearance, the tone of the Declaration is abstract; but the reader who examines the various liberties with the eye of an historian easily recognizes that each represents a point of controversy and opposition with a definite aspect of the society of the time and place; and thus discovers a confirmation of Mirabeau's saying, that the revolutionaries meant to draw up not so much an abstract declaration of rights as a declaration of war against tyrants. And these revolutionaries were so little befogged by abstractions, whether verbal or substantial, that they were careful to omit from their table of liberties the liberty of association. They had not forgotten the lately destroyed guilds, and they thought of all associations as something coercive; and later, when confronted with the spontaneous revival of workmen's societies, they felt it necessary expressly to forbid them. This prohibition, the result no doubt of inexperience, was to be maintained for more than half a century through class interest.

The juridical form of the Declaration is borrowed from jusnaturalism; and that is the aspect of least permanent value. It speaks of natural rights anterior to the State, as if there could be rights where as yet there is no State; it places liberty and equality in an original condition of man, whereas these are in fact values progressively realized in social life. But, if the legal form is transitory, it enshrines an imperishable demand, which will find the means of creating for itself more adequate legal and political expressions: that there should be a limit, even if only a shifting historical limit, set up by the individual conscience, and not to be transgressed by the State on pain of destroying the sources of personality and moral energy, and thus degrading and impoverishing its own life. When the State was still an external power, as it was in the eighteenth century, this limit took the form of an almost material barrier; when the State learns to base itself on the conscience of the individual, this limit also will be shifted, and will become a more intimate thing, a limit laid down by the mind itself; but it will always exist, and will be re-established as often as an attempt is made to remove it. The modern consciousness which creates the new State will never resign itself to be the slave of its own creature; it feels profoundly, even if confusedly, that once so enslaved its vital energy would be for ever stilled, all fresh creative activity precluded, and nothing left but a stagnant theocracy. The true immortality of the principles of 1789 lies in the fact that they express, even though in a contingent and imperfect form, the inner conflict between the individual and the State: a conflict perpetually revived by every compromise and every synthesis, because the creator is always more than the creature; he is the germ of new creatures.

It would be wrong to regard the opposition between the individual and the State as the absurd antithesis of heterogeneous and incommensurable entities, which on a superficial inspection it might seem to be: an antithesis like that between the atom and the material universe. It is in fact an antithesis between two dialectical terms, the creator and the creature, the State *in fieri* and the State *in esse*, the ideal and the real. Hence the vital importance of vindicating the rights of the individual, even from the strictly political point of view, in the interest of the progress and development of the State.

On a closer view of the Declaration we find two elements, of diverse origin and inspiration, juxtaposed and to some extent confused: on the one hand, the freedom of a pre-political condition; on the other, the individual's participation in the formation of the State. As we already know, there are two different forms of political freedom. In Art. II we find a statement about the natural and imprescriptible rights of man, liberty, property, security, and resistance to oppression; in Art. III a statement of the principle of popular sovereignty. The reader who knows how the Declaration was composed, by a highly eclectic process of compilation, and by compromises voted by closure between the formulae of the various leaders, will not be surprised to see the two conceptions side by side; though logically they are incompatible, because, once Rousseau had given currency to the principle of popular sovereignty, any idea of individual right as against the State, or of resistance to oppression, became impossible.

Yet this conjunction served a useful purpose, since the development of the Revolution was very soon to reveal the danger of one-sided doctrinal formulae, and the necessity for compromise. The inexperience of the authors of the Declaration left a loophole for experiments in various directions without overstepping the bounds of the Constitution. Montesquieu and Rousseau, the English and the democratic types of Liberalism, were left face to face: the one offered a freedom conceived as the power to do whatever does not harm others; the other a freedom understood as the sovereignty of the people; the one a chamber of representatives, the other a body of popular commissaries; the one the separation of powers, the others their indivisibility. But both were agreed in interpreting liberty and equality as purely formal and legal principles, whose aim was to sanction and not to annul the actual differences between individuals: men ought to be free within the sphere of their own rights and equal only in the eyes of the law. An essential complement of this formalism was the defence of the institution of property, that is to say, the explicit recognition of the economic and social differences which emerge through the identity of men in the eyes of the law. All this was doubtless in agreement with the spirit of modern individualism, which aims at developing human personality in the greatest possible richness and variety of faculties, not reducing it to undifferentiated atoms; and equality in the eyes of the law is simply the necessary formal condition which makes possible the free development of the individual's powers.

But though this legal conception arose in contrast with the régime of privilege, which aggravated natural and spontaneous differences by adding to them differences artificially imposed by law, does it exhaust all the possibilities of modern individualism? Does it not rather consecrate a new privilege, the privilege of property, of wealth; a new artificial difference, likewise created by law, added to the differences created by nature and distorting or preventing their free development? While analysing the new conception of property, we pointed out that it is understood as closely attached to personality; it is precisely for this reason that all men demand the right of owning property. Now so long as property belongs to the few, it represents a privilege of the few as compared with the many, whose injustice is the more strongly felt according as it is based upon a principle common to the few and the many, which thus divides where it ought to unite. Those who do not own property can hardly regard themselves as protected by the law in exactly the same manner as those who do; and what do they gain by a formal identity of conditions if they cannot develop their own personality? It only serves to sanction their misery and their oppression, to convert that which ought to be a bond into a fetter. The profound sense of social justice and injustice is a purely modern thing. The Middle Ages had their revolts due to hunger, and their explosions of social hatred; but they never knew of claims made in the name of justice, precisely because there was no point of contact between the privileged and unprivileged, and the rights of the former, being based on a title peculiar to themselves, could not excite jealousy and rancour. Conditions in the modern world are wholly different. Here the privileges which arise from the consciousness of the liberty and equality of individuals bear upon them the visible signs of injustice and abuse; and thus they generate a sense of injury which is the source of social conflict.

In this way we see in the *Declaration of Rights* the source of a new interpretation of liberty and equality, contrasting with the legal formalism of the Liberals and democrats, and concerned with the substance of rights instead of their form. Against the liberty to starve, it appeals to the right to a fair share of the moral and economic wealth of the community; against the mere equality in the eyes of the law, it demands social equality.

Thus the *Declaration of Rights* contains the germs of three revolutions: a Liberal revolution in the strict sense of the term, a democratic revolution, and a social revolution: but these three only represent the progressive expansion of one and the same individualistic spirit developed to the extreme point of socialism ; hence they all equally figure in the history of the Liberal mind. But in order to see these three revolutions at work, and not merely in effigy, we must widen the scope of our inquiry and look not merely at constitutional formulae but at the men who were their effective champions.

§ 9. THE REVOLUTION

The protagonist of the French Revolution at its commencement was the Third Estate. What is the Third Estate? asked Sieyès in 1789. It is the body of citizens belonging to the common or unprivileged class ; but it is at the same time a complete nation. What is required in order that a nation may live and prosper? A productive activity, and a complex of public functions ; the first, which falls into the sub-species of agriculture, industry, trade, and the liberal professions, belongs wholly to the Third Estate. As for public functions, their entire burden falls upon the Third Estate ; while their lucrative and honourable positions are occupied by members of the privileged class.[1]

But if the Third Estate is a complete nation, it can subsist by itself, without the privileged class, and even in defiance of it ; annulling its privileges, and framing for itself general laws. Practical consequences of these principles are seen in the oath of the Tennis Court and the night of the Fourth of August. By this overture to the Revolution, the Third Estate constituted itself politically a nation, and set on foot the gradual absorption of the other classes. Its aspiration was to set up a limited monarchical government under the eye of its own representatives, in which the division of powers should hold the government in check and guarantee the impartial application of common laws, while the system of checks and balances prevented the defeated but not routed feudal classes from returning to the attack. In the nineteenth century this régime was to be called constitutional government *par excellence*. The representatives of the people

[1] Ed. Sieyès, *Qu'est-ce que le Tiers État ? précédé de l'Essai sur les privilèges* (*éd. crit.*, Paris, 1888), pp. 28, 29, 33.

legislate, vote taxes, exercise a function of criticism, but do not directly govern; indeed, they are formally precluded from nomination as ministers of the Crown. Mirabeau was to protest in vain against this consequence of the rigid separation of powers, as prejudicial to the political unity of the nation; only later, when democracy was in full swing, was Sieyès to work out a compromise between the two systems, according to which the constituting power was one and indivisible and the constituted powers alone were divided. But this compromise had a merely transitory effect and chiefly served to open the way to the Convention.

But the very triumph of the Third Estate reopened a question which seemed closed: did it represent the entire nation? So long as two other orders, the nobility and the clergy, confronted it, the Third Estate, the only other class which made itself heard, could be regarded as representing the whole of the nameless multitude thronging behind its back. But once victorious, it began to delimit its own permanent boundaries; and these, granted its peculiar character as we have already observed it, were not the material barriers of the privileged classes, but ideal legal limitations, more insidious than their predecessors, because *de iure* they could be crossed by any one, while *de facto* they were crossed by very few. The Third Estate was the legal nation,[1] that is to say, that part of the nation whose economic circumstances enabled it to actualize the theoretically universal capacity of enjoying civil and political rights. The new division thus introduced into the citizen body was based upon property; a property by common right, and therefore accessible to all, but in fact confined to a limited number of individuals, thus serving to isolate a body of property-holders possessed of active citizenship from the great mass of the proletariate to which this active citizenship was denied.

We can now understand why this ' legal nation ' warmly advocated a moderate constitutionalism which, by the divi-

---

[1] The name legal nation, or legal country, originated in 1830 and served to characterize the régime of Louis-Philippe; but, if the name is modern, the thing was older.

sion of powers and parliamentary control, tended rather to
limit than to appropriate the action of the State and the
government. It instinctively realized that to confine the
power of the State to an external function, as defender and
guarantor of rights, was a good way of maintaining its own
position as a holder of property; while any increase of this
power might involve applications of the principle of popular
sovereignty leading to dangerous interferences and even more
dangerous social redistributions. The State is a dangerous
weapon to handle; once set in action, it goes its own way,
heedless of the intentions of those who would treat it as their
monopoly.

But the ever-present possibility that the State might
correct social injustice and help the weak against the strong
was recognized no less by the great mass of exiles from the
ranks of the legal nation. Three centuries of absolute
monarchy had accustomed the people to count on the omnipotence of the State. Now the *bourgeois* revolution, by
setting in motion increasing masses of the people, led on with
promises of wealth as soon as the decisive action had taken
place and then disappointed of their expectations, provoked
a reaction in the shape of a second and more violent wave of
democracy, finally overwhelming all the obstacles with which
the Liberal *bourgeoisie* tried to stem it. The strength of the
democracy lay in the fact that it turned against the Liberals
of yesterday their own weapons. Its motto was liberty, not
degraded into a privilege of the propertied classes but
extended to all citizens. With the abolition of the property
qualification and the coming of universal suffrage, democracy could rely directly upon the State, without requiring
to stop short at a prudent constitutionalism; for it recognized
that its overwhelming numerical force enabled it to appropriate the power of the State and use it to checkmate the
bourgeois minority. Hence arose the unification and concentration of all the powers which the Liberals endeavoured
to divide; hence the omnipotence of the Convention, uniting
in itself the functions of legislative, executive, and judiciary.

But the democracy in its turn soon broke in two. If we

examine the composition of the first democratic groups, we shall find that they consist essentially of *bourgeois* elements which interpret the passions of the people, but bring to this interpretation the legal spirit of their own class. They believe that the popular revolution may be successfully effected through the purely political means of universal suffrage and the conquest of the State. In their opinion a further social revolution, unexpectedly subverting property and law, would mean anarchy and disaster; the redistribution of the wealth of society can best be secured by the gradual and legal action of the State. This democratic spirit inspired the Constitution of 1793, resembling its predecessors in its respect for property and differing from it by the greater scope which it gave to the functions of the State and to popular sovereignty.

But the stream of democracy included another more turbid and tortuous current, whose sources lay in the lowest strata of society. Merely in order to understand its nature, we may venture to apply to it the name of Socialism, while bearing in mind that the name came into being at least thirty years later, and that, at the time we are considering, no one had conceived the idea of anything like an organized socialistic system, because there was as yet no factory proletariate and the peasants had hardly emerged from the state of feudal serfdom.

But there was in fact an attempt at the violent expropriation of the property of the rich, nobles or commons, on the part of the town and country masses, eager to gather for themselves some positive fruits of revolution. To this proletariate, what good was the vast and sudden extension of political rights, if unaccompanied by more tangible gains capable of alleviating its misery? Side by side with these acts of summary popular justice attempts were made to justify and legalize them. The ideology of the eighteenth century had included a strain of communism, which might here be of assistance; and the keener democrats of the capital did not omit to employ it, and to assert, as against the new privileges of the *bourgeoisie*, the universal validity of the claims made by the proletariate. The people, says a writer in the *Révolutions de Paris*, has entered upon its rights; now it must enter into its property, and expel the latest usurpers. A Conventional, Rabaut de Saint-Étienne, writing in the *Chronique de Paris*, expresses himself even more clearly. The poor, says he, feel that political equality is impaired by inequality of fortune; and since equality is independence, that is, liberty, they are exasperated against those whose dependants they are. The laws must therefore provide for a more equal division of fortune, and guard against future inequality. The legislator must establish the maximum of property which a man may possess.[1]

These claims, not merely political but social in character, find an echo in the project of a Constitution compiled by Robespierre in 1793, when the proletarian revolution was at its height. In this project, property is still recognized, but at its side there now appears the doctrine of progressive taxation as a means of gradually equalizing possessions. There is also a statement of the right to work, in virtue of the principle ' that society is obliged to provide for the subsistence of all its members, whether by procuring them work or by ensuring the means of livelihood to those who are unable to work '. The right to work was to be the motto of the proletariate in the revolution of 1848. A far more radical socialism inspired the so-called Conspiracy of Equals, led by Bateuf; but it came to a head when the *bourgeois* reaction had already set in, and was quickly drowned in blood.

In the brief space between 1789 and 1793 three revolutions took place successively, each at once the complement and the antithesis of the last. They contain by anticipation and in a condensed form the whole course of the political and social struggles of the nineteenth century.

At the period which we are considering, only one of these three revolutions reached maturity: the Liberal *bourgeois* revolution. This revolution was to survive its temporary eclipse by the Terror and build the structure of its civil liberties during the period of Caesarism. Its political liberties it was gradually to regain at the Restoration. Its

[1] Aulard, *Histoire politique de la Révolution française*, Paris, 1901, p. 449.

sphere of action widened so as to include every continental country in which an active and industrious property-owning *bourgeoisie* either existed or was coming to exist. Belgium, Western and Southern Germany, and Italy were its first conquests; its influence spread more slowly over countries in which the roots of feudalism were still strong. The other two revolutions were immature or premature. They stand out illuminated by a glare of unexpected and sinister light, and pass at once into the shadow.

§ 10. THE COUNTER-REVOLUTION

The first counter-revolutionary movement comes from England, a country traditionally regarded as Liberal; it thus serves to bring out the differences between the two historical forms of Liberalism, the insular and the continental.

The French Revolution, at its beginnings, had zealous partisans in England. Not only did the Whig opposition, led by Fox and Sheridan, applaud its first successes, but even Pitt followed it with sympathy. In London Francophile clubs grew up, the Revolutionary Society and the Constitution Society. Members and ministers of nonconformist sects were its principal partisans; and Price, speaking in 1789, compares the French Revolution with the English Revolution of the century before, and points out their close similarity.

Public opinion was soon to undergo a sudden change, thanks to one of the leaders of Liberalism, Edmund Burke. At the time of the American secession Burke had been a keen champion of colonial independence, since in the loss of the colonists' liberties he had seen a threat of danger to English freedom; but now, amid general surprise, he declared decisively against the new Revolution in his famous *Reflections on the French Revolution* in 1790.

He took as his text Price's attempted identification of the two revolutionary movements, and pointed out its inconsistency. In seventeenth-century England, he observed, it was not the people but the Crown that had been, in the French sense of the term, revolutionary; for the Crown had claimed to change or abolish national customs, traditions, and beliefs in virtue of the abstract metaphysical principles of monarchical right. The English, in overthrowing the Stuarts, had merely upheld their traditions. The Revolution was essentially conservative. When and where had the English ever conceived a so-called right of choosing their own rulers, banishing them for misconduct, and choosing others? The very idea of manufacturing a new government, he added, was enough to fill the mind with disgust and horror. At the date of our Revolution we wished, and still wish, to derive all our possessions from the inheritance handed down to us by our fathers. All the reforms which we have made spring from the principle of appeal to antiquity. Magna Carta itself only sanctions a still more ancient custom. Thus we have a hereditary crown, a hereditary peerage, a House of Commons, and a people which has inherited privileges, franchises, and liberties from a long series of predecessors. Here lies a sound conservative principle in no way excluding the possibility of improvements.[1]

What were the French doing? Overthrowing all their institutions and customs to establish natural and metaphysical rights. They did not reflect that these rights, though certainly not devoid of foundation, when they entered the sphere of everyday life underwent a refraction from the straight line, like a ray of light passing through a dense medium. So, in the vast complex mass of human passions and relations, the primitive rights of man underwent such a variety of refractions and reflections that it was absurd to speak as if they maintained the simplicity of their original direction.[2]

Grant, he continues, that society is a contract. Even so, it is not a combination of selfish interests, each existing merely for the moment and capable of being detached from the rest. The State is not a compact like that which may be made for the purpose of trading in pepper or tobacco. It must be regarded with far more respect, since it is not a contract aimed merely at those things which serve the material existence of an ephemeral and perishable nature;

[1] Burke, *French Revolution* (in *Selections*, Nelson, pp. 217–36).
[2] *Op. cit.*, p. 267.

it is a collaboration in every art, every science, every virtue, every perfection. It unites not only the present generation but the past and the future.[1]

The freedom of the revolutionaries, devoid of all historical foundation, is merely a stimulant, an irritant ; their equality is a levelling based not on creation but on destruction. The Third Estate, which claims to be a complete nation, is in fact represented in the Assembly by men of letters, advocates, whom he calls the ' mechanics of profession ', and bankers ; some, lovers of wordy abstractions, others of hazardous enterprises. What the English call the natural landed interest of the country is absent, or present only in the smallest traces. Ability prevails over property ; the former is an active and vigorous principle, the latter an inert and timid principle, which cannot protect itself against the invasions of the former unless it enjoys a predominant representation. This disproportion, with an excessive love of equality and the triumph of mere numbers, is leading France inevitably towards democracy, that is, a government in many respects similar to tyranny.[2]

Upon a framework of doctrines whose main lines are as above, Burke builds up a detailed, bitter, and petulant criticism, whose exaggerated character is clear enough when we consider that the reflections date from 1790, and are the result not of direct observation but of second-hand information. More balanced and sober are the notes which Arthur Young was making at the same time, in the course of his long journey, province by province, through revolutionary France. He noticed the dangers into which unskilful destruction and creation were leading ; but he also bore witness to his clear conviction, arising from all that he saw and heard, that the happiness of the people absolutely demanded changes limiting the authority of the King, restricting the feudal tyranny of the nobles, reducing the clergy to a level of ordinary citizens, redressing financial abuses, and purifying the administration of justice. In a note added later in 1792, he began

---

[1] *Op. cit.*, p. 306.   [2] *Op. cit.*, p. 338.

to recognize the benefits accruing from the innovations in land-tenure that the Revolution was bringing about.[1]

The work of Burke, expressing as it did the heart of the English political consciousness, for which the deceptive similarity of external constitutional forms was stripped of its apparent value, revealed the profound contrast between the two Liberal systems. The authentic English Liberalism of the eighteenth century did not consist merely in the ingenious machinery of powers and institutions described by Blackstone and Montesquieu; it consisted also, and more truly, in the spirit which moved this machinery, and turned the apparent anarchy of political and social powers towards the end of conservation and order. It was the age-old spirit of the nation, which had built up its work piece by piece without ever destroying what had once been built, but basing upon it every new departure. Thus it had added institution to institution, privilege to privilege, and insensibly adapted ancient traditions to modern needs. It had instinctively recoiled from all abstract proclamation of principles and rights; its liberties had arisen from keenly felt needs, and had been paid for by sacrifices; every class had gained its share and justified its gains by the discharge of its functions. The result of these unceasing efforts was a narrow, aristocratic, tenacious Liberalism, whose inner meaning had escaped the eyes of the abstract illuminists of the seventeenth and eighteenth centuries, and was now for the first time revealed by Burke in the new self-consciousness which he bestowed upon the native pride of his fellow-countrymen.

This Liberalism was now confronted by the new Liberalism of France; genuinely new, because, instead of basing itself upon the privileged liberties of the Middle Ages, it arose from their ashes. It was far more akin in spirit to the absolute monarchy which had already begun to destroy the old feudal world and had given to its subjects the feeling of equality. The new Liberalism, like the monarchy, was egalitarian; but its egalitarianism was inspired and ennobled

[1] A. Young, *Travels during the Years 1787–1788–1789*, London, 1794, i. 617, 621.

by a broader rationalistic consciousness attributing to all
men one identical spiritual and human value. But the love
of equality which gave its peculiar tone to the new freedom
was so overwhelming that it ended by overthrowing and
crushing it. In its logical development, it was impelled
to level and thus suppress all singularities and differences,
everything based upon private and individual initiative;
everything, in other words, based upon freedom. Democracy
and Liberalism are two inseparable but opposed terms, whose
conflicts and treaties of peace will occupy the political thought
of the nineteenth century and our own.

In the course of the French Revolution, the Liberalism of
1789 was stifled by the democracy of 1793. This was the
second reason for the triumph of Burke, whose work, though
exaggerated when it was written, seemed to his contemporaries nothing less than prophetic in its relation to the
later phases of the Revolution, and became the *credo* of the
European counter-revolution.

The democracy of 1793 was a true butcher of liberties;
it was that tyranny which Burke, following Aristotle, had
described. In order to maintain itself it was compelled to
suppress one by one all the liberties previously proclaimed:
freedom of thought, freedom of the Press, property, at any
rate for those who did not share ideas of the new dictators,
personal security, and freedom of worship. The individual
was completely at the mercy of the crushing power of the
Convention. And the Convention in its turn, after making the world tremble, itself trembled before Robespierre;
political omnipotence, as usual, went hand in hand with
impotence, because where all power is concentrated at one
point all becomes equally contingent and precarious. With
Robespierre comes Caesarism, the necessary complement of
a levelling and concentrated democracy. It is a maxim of
classical wisdom that the tyranny of the many breeds the
tyranny of one. Anti-Liberalism has run its course to the pre-
destined end.

But the Counter-revolution was already in motion. It was
not confined to the old dispossessed classes, whose relics were

wandering through the courts of Europe, offering to the
world a wretched spectacle of moral bankruptcy, or awaiting
in the Vendée a glorious but fruitless death. The real and
effective counter-revolution was that of the revolutionaries
of yesterday, the Liberal *bourgeoisie*.

Its first presentiment was the Girondins' effort at federalism, designed to set up a federation of all the French provinces to oppose the tyranny of the Commune of Paris, and
thus restrict Paris to that eighty-third share of power in the
councils of the nation which properly belonged to her. For
the moment the attempt failed; and for more than a year
Paris continued to usurp the whole power of the nation.

But the reaction in the provinces, slow as it necessarily
was, had nevertheless begun. Its strength was provided by
the entire *bourgeoisie*, liberated by the Revolution from the
burden of feudalism; especially the numerous small *bourgeoisie* of the country districts, which, by acquiring the
national property at the moderate cost of *assignats*, had
realized its desire for the possession of land. This class feared
two opposite dangers: the restoration of the old régime,
which would deprive it of its property, and revolutionary
excesses, equally prejudicial to the security of its gains by
exciting the cupidity of the landless masses. Its aspirations
were naturally moderate, opposed to all extremes, at any
rate in internal politics. In external politics it favoured war
à outrance as a means to new gains, and, even more important,
a simple outlet for the unruly masses of the unemployed.

The slow but stubborn action of this class reveals itself in
all the counter-revolutionary incidents, from the reaction of
Thermidor to the Constitution of the year III and the
government of the Directoire. But its deepest aspiration
is expressed in the resolution to sanction and definitely conclude the work of the Revolution. So long as political agitation and rivalry between factions subsisted, there was always
a danger of *coups de main* and changes of government, which
might endanger everything that had been won, and overthrow peace and public order. These dangers were inherent
in political freedom, which the *bourgeoisie*, already disgusted

by an excess of licence and democratic tyranny, was by now ready to give up in exchange for civil liberty or security of person and property. That was why it calmly accepted the Caesarism of Napoleon.

Napoleon's Caesarism served at least for a time to unite and combine all the forces which had hitherto waged war each against the rest. Into this channel flows the new and immature democracy, which sees the realization of its desire for a strong concentrated government and an immediate and unitary expression of the will of the vast majority, free from the fictions of representation. The old monarchical feeling finds satisfaction in the renewed prestige of the army and the court; Napoleon reinstates that *honneur* in which Montesquieu placed the might and symbol of monarchy. And the Liberal *bourgeoisie* sees in the civil code, the code of property based on common right, the recognition of all its baffled aspirations towards liberty.

A permanent agreement seems to have been reached; but it is only a temporary compromise. It depends upon the precarious support of a single life, and the presumed infallibility of one man entitled to think for all. Caesarism is only a counterfeit democracy, in which the sovereignty of the people conceals their real servitude. It is a monarchy without predecessors and without heirs; that is, it is, strictly speaking, a tyranny; it is a degraded Liberalism which satisfies material interests but oppresses conscience and annihilates personality. Napoleon disappears from the stage of politics; and all the forces which seemed united find themselves once more in conflict, with their different needs, their various demands, their diversities of structure; and the problem of their mutual relations reappears in the very same form in which it had been originally stated.

§ 11. THE RESTORATION

The name Restoration covers not only the Congress of Vienna, the Holy Alliance, and all the political events connected with them, but also, in the intellectual sphere, the reactionary thought of De Maistre, De Bonald, De Lamennais, Ballanche, and Haller. Yet in all this there is nothing to which the word 'restoration' in its proper sense can be applied. It is rather a continuation of the same revolution, showing a new side of itself. How much of the ancient world did the mystics who founded the Holy Alliance restore? When did the religion upon which they called ever serve as the common protection of a league of States, or the justification for the universalistic claims of a few kings, self-proclaimed the divine instruments for the union of all peoples into one flock?

The monarchies of the modern period really arose from the break-up of the religious universalism of the Middle Ages, and devoted their strength to the differentiation of worship in their respective realms, either by making use of the Protestant secession, or by claiming partial freedom from Rome. In this respect the French Revolution attached itself to the old European tradition; its Jansenist legislators, in establishing the civil position of the clergy, were only developing the old Gallican liberties, and the Concordat of 1801, which sanctioned the principle of an agreement between Church and State, was equally consonant with the traditional legal mentality of the eighteenth century.

The religious universalism of the Holy Alliance is therefore wholly unconnected with tradition; it is aimed against the *Declaration of the Rights of Man*, and is itself no less revolutionary in character. Though profoundly perverted in practice, it is at the outset the declaration of the rights of God.

De Bonald, to whom we owe this energetic affirmation, by making it, in 1802, marked the end and completion of the French Revolution.[1] His predecessor Joseph de Maistre had already brought the Revolution within the plan of Providence, and shown that it was no fruitless subversion of the divine scheme; it was certainly the work of Satan, but Satan himself was the instrument of God. The hand of God had never so clearly shown itself in the affairs of man; it was necessary that the great work of purification should be done in a way striking to all eyes; it was necessary that the metal

[1] De Bonald, *Législation primitive*, Paris, 1802, i. 184.

of France, purged of dross, should come pure and malleable into the hands of the future king, the servant of God. In fact, granted the revolutionary movement, France and the monarchy could not be saved but through Jacobinism. The Terror on the one hand, immorality and extravagance on the other, had produced the precise effect which might have been anticipated by a consummate and prophetic wisdom. The horror of the shambles drove the citizen to the frontiers. All power was in the hands of the revolutionary government, that monster of force, drunk with blood and success, a frightful phenomenon never seen before and never to be seen again, which was nevertheless at once a terrible chastisement for Frenchmen and the only means to the salvation of France, which the Royalists wished to entrust to the hands of foreigners. The innocent no doubt had suffered for the guilty; but was not that the fundamental principle of Christianity? [1]

De Maistre's *Considérations sur la France* were published in 1797, and already show in their tone a national particularism which the author was further to emphasize in later works. De Bonald's *Législation primitive*, written in 1802, shows more of the universalistic spirit of the Revolution. Its author shares with the revolutionaries the desire to base law upon *Les seules lumières de la raison*, to draw up a Declaration of Rights and reduce sovereignty to a formula. Sovereignty belongs not to the people but to God, in whom alone it can rest with perfect stability. But De Bonald does not draw from his premises all their possible theocratic conclusions; he merely refers to them in passing, showing how Europe ever since the Peace of Westphalia has been moving towards general revolution because revolution is merely the effort of society to pass from a transitory and unnatural condition to a stable and therefore natural condition. It will end when Europe returns to religious unity.[2] But the vague goal of De Bonald takes a more precise shape, as a rigid theocratic

[1] J. de Maistre, *Considérations sur la France*, Paris, ed. 3, 1821 (after the first Basle ed. of 1797), pp. 21, 24, 25, 54.

[2] *Op. cit.* iii. 368, 379.

system, in De Maistre's later work *Du Pape*, in which the Pope is regarded as the natural head, the most powerful agent, the great demiurge of universal civilization ; and the Catholic Church is described as the perfect monarchy, uniting infallibility in the spiritual order with sovereignty in the temporal : two perfectly synonymous terms.[1] Even in its obvious exaggeration, this work is a characteristic expression of the intense mysticism of the post-revolutionary period, and at the same time the last statement of the rationalistic universalism of the eighteenth century, pushed home to the point of glaring contradiction with history.

In the writings just quoted may be seen, side by side with an expression of the most rigid transcendence, a timid attempt on the part of the mind to return upon itself and reaffirm historical values. To offer a justification of the Revolution, even if only in the service of a counter-revolutionary ideal, is the first stage in this movement ; because, once on the firm ground of concrete reality, thought must keep its feet in order to grasp the essential features of the country, and restrain the impulse to fly back into the clouds of abstraction.

Thus De Maistre's *Considérations* contain critical remarks of great importance from the point of view of the political thought of the nineteenth century. The abstract character of the idea of popular sovereignty, at least in the form in which the Revolution had tried to bring it into being, is pointed out in all its main features. Nor does he spare Constitutionalism. A Constitution, he says, is never the result of express deliberation. There has never been a free nation which has not had germs of liberty in its natural constitution coeval with itself. Here De Maistre is treading in the footsteps of Burke, and translating into language more comprehensible to the continental mind the Liberal experience of England, emphasizing the importance of the traditions and customs which the Revolution had violently negated. His dislike for the fever of legislation, which had infected the whole revolutionary period, has the same origin and the same

[1] J. de Maistre, *Du Pape*, ed. of 1821 (first publ. 1808), pp. 2, 3, 344.

significance; the more people write about an institution, he says, the weaker it becomes. Laws are no more than declarations of rights, and rights are only declared when some one attacks them; and therefore a multiplicity of written constitutional laws only proves the multiplicity and destructiveness of the attacks upon the Constitution. Every true legislation has its Sabbath, and intermittency is its distinctive characteristic. The Constitution of 1795, like its predecessors, is made for man; but there is no such thing as man, there are only particular men. A Constitution fit for all nations is fit for none.[1]

A few years later the same ideas were re-expressed by a liberal, Vincenzo Cuoco, in his *Historical Essay on the Neapolitan Revolution*. But whereas for the reactionary De Maistre they constituted a definite attack upon Constitutionalism, for the Liberal writer they became merely the negative and critical aspect of a renewed Liberalism in which constitutional formulae were to be reinforced by historical and traditional institutions.

Similar features can be observed in De Bonald. Here, side by side with dogmatic abstractions, are found many living problems bequeathed by the Revolution to posterity. Behind the ideal of a patriarchal and feudal society, one hears the voice of the physiocrats, from whom De Bonald derives his dislike of trade, which he says has been wrongly considered as a universal bond of the human race by people who mistake bodily propinquity for spiritual union. Far greater is the value of agriculture, in which every one without competition or deception profits by the liberality of nature; so that one may say that trade, which peoples towns, brings men together without uniting them, while agriculture, isolating them in the country, unites them while keeping them apart. The main thing for France is therefore her agricultural and continental system, her commercial and maritime system being a mere accessory.[2]

More original and interesting are De Bonald's references

---

[1] J. de Maistre, *Considérations &c.*, pp. 94 *seqq.*
[2] De Bonald, *op. cit.*, iii. 395 *seqq.*

to the naturalism of the preceding generation. Like De
Maistre, he looks for a return to nature, as interpreter and
minister of God. But nature as he conceives it is not the
nature of the illuminists ; it is the nature of Vico : an historical reality and the source of history. Nature is in process of
creation ; a being is born for an end and with the means of
attaining it ; this end and these means together make up its
nature. Thus man at first lived in domestic society, and
therefore the nature which existed for him was a purely
domestic nature. Natural rights, natural laws, natural
religion, were therefore the rights, the laws, and the religion
of this early domestic or family condition of man. But human
history did not stop at this point ; that is the error of the
philosophers who, setting out from the correct idea that the
nature of a thing is its perfection, ascribed every perfection
to the native and original condition of society. The true
nature of society is to be found in its ultimate development :
that is, political society. Through failure to observe this
truth, necessary laws and institutions have fallen into discredit and hatred.[1]

Here are the accents of a new outlook, in curious contrast
with the futile home-sickness for a remote age of feudalism
and the programme of anachronistic return to the past.
This new outlook is the real Restoration ; for the name
cannot be correctly applied to the movement which, in the
name of loyalty to a distant past, would make a clean sweep
of the recent past, that is, of the Revolution, which has now
taken its place in the historical consciousness of peoples ;
for this movement unconsciously repeats the same error
which was committed by the revolutionaries.

From this point of view, the true Restoration is not contained in the territorial system of the Treaty of Vienna, nor
yet in the policy of the Holy Alliance, but comes about by
degrees in the history of the European nations in which
tradition and revolution, reactionaries and Jacobins, collaborate in opposite ways in a common work of restoring
equilibrium and effecting a fusion of the old and the new.

[1] *Op. cit.* i. 169 *seqq.*

The Revolution has imparted a vigorous momentum to the life of Europe; but this impulse, single at its source, is refracted, as Burke has already put it, by the dense medium through which it is travelling; the different reactivities of individual nations receive it in varying degrees and in different manners, so that in the final result it multiplies and individualizes itself while yet preserving the unity of its original direction. From the one Revolution arise the manifold national histories, which flow in parallel paths in the circulation that forms the unity of the European mind.

To study the Liberalism of the nineteenth century, in the diversity of its national forms and the unity of its historical organism, is the task of the present volume.

PART I

THE HISTORICAL FORMS OF LIBERALISM

I

ENGLISH LIBERALISM

§ 1. RADICALISM

THE first effect of the French Revolution upon England was to stiffen it in its isolation and its traditional pride. Against the nascent democracy of the European continent, the aristocratic consciousness of English Liberalism as expressed by Burke, uniting Whigs and Tories in spite of their external differences, asserted itself. The party conflict became a harmless parliamentary duel between the leaders of two parties, both based upon a single aristocratic tradition and grounded in the same privileges of birth.

This substantial unity was further reinforced by the war. To the conservative position the war gave the highest patriotic sanction; the continental blockade compelled the landed aristocracy to live in its own castles year after year and to forgo all contact with Europe; and by raising the price of corn immensely swelled the rents and with them the power and prestige of the governing class.

But the same barriers which separated England from the Revolution saved her also from the excesses of continental reaction. If nothing was changed, what was there to react against? Castlereagh in 1815 could excuse himself from sending the text of the proposed Holy Alliance to his government, although it was his official duty to do so, calling it ' a mixture of mysticism and sublime folly '. The mystical universalism of the crowned heads of Europe was no better received than the rationalistic universalism of the revolutionaries by a people whose special position safeguarded it equally against both these opposite aberrations.

The absence of any grudgingly reactionary spirit was the condition most favourable to the normal development of the forces of the country, once they had begun to move after the congestion due to the war. As we saw in the Introduction, the Industrial Revolution had during the eighteenth century created a large class of manufacturers, which increased in numbers and wealth during the war owing to the monopoly indirectly secured by the blockade, the provision of military supplies, and trade in contraband goods. But the war over, and relations with the continent re-established, causes of discontent began to appear. The blockade, while favourable for the time being to English industry, had induced the continent to set up industries of its own; so that when contact was once more established the English found themselves faced by new competitors. And if their industries were now sufficiently developed to combat this competition triumphantly, there was yet a fact which threatened to frustrate all their efforts: the high cost of living, which raised wages to a level far above that of the continent.

What was the cause of this fact? During the war, as has been said, the price of corn naturally increased; but at the same time the price of manufactured goods also increased, because the same cause acted upon both. After the war, a fall of prices ought to have taken place in both branches of production; but in 1815 the landowners, in order to keep up the price of corn, imposed high protective tariffs on imported grain, so that the benefits which they had reaped from the war were still secured in time of peace. They were able to effect this artificial correction of the natural course of things because they had a monopoly of political power.

The manufacturers on the other hand were defenceless. A newly formed class, they found themselves confronted by an ancient political system in which they had no place. Not only was the House of Lords monopolized by the landed aristocracy, but the House of Commons was in the same condition; for its representatives were for the most part nominated by electoral bodies entirely subservient to the great landowners.[1] On the one hand stood the counties and

[1] A minute examination of the peculiar method by which political representatives were elected has been made by Halévy, *Histoire du peuple anglais*, 1913, i. 110 *seqq.*

boroughs, formed by a few scores of electors depending upon a landowner and voting publicly under his eye; on the other, the new industrial centres, either unrepresented or possessing privileged representations like those of other electoral bodies, which emphasized still farther the contrast between the actual forces of the country and the few possessors of political rights.

The manufacturing classes, being unable immediately to alter the political situation in their own favour, first attempted to recoup themselves at the cost of their dependent labourers; to compensate for the high price of corn by merciless exploitation of their employees. From 1815 the condition of the English proletariate became progressively worse. Factory life became harder and harder; the hours of labour rose to fifteen and seventeen a day; the employment of women and children increased in the most inhuman manner; the competition for employment kept wages down to bare subsistence level, and the truck system contributed still farther to their reduction. These evils were increased by the extreme instability of a newly established industrial system. New works sprang up without regulation on every hand; crises of so-called over-production, due in reality to ill-regulated and ill-distributed production, were frequent; hence bankruptcies and times of scarcity were common. All this reacted disastrously upon the working class, incapable as yet of uniting in its own defence, and compelled to wander from place to place at the call of the demand for labour, constantly threatened by unemployment, and prevented by law from uniting in order to obtain better conditions. The great increase of the poor-tax in these later years is a sure index of the great misery of the working class during this period of industrial progress. Foreign visitors like Sismondi were deeply struck by the strange contrast between the condition of industry and that of the working man, and were tempted to invent explanations for it, and to find the cause of the widespread social malady in machinery, competition, or the arbitrary freedom of the manufacturer. Thus they raised the instinctive hatred of the workmen against machinery, their visible and tangible enemy, to the level of a theory. It was the god of steam that had made his country a prison for his most industrious children; and against this sinister deity the operatives rose in revolt, breaking machines and looting workshops in unforeseen outbursts of despair.

But the continual unrest of the working class, while making the condition of industry more unstable and precarious, was bound to produce by reaction a corresponding sense of enmity in the minds of the manufacturers against the land-owners, to whose greed, rather than their own, they attri-buted the diseases of society. Thus no sooner was peace con-cluded than a conflict began between two classes; the landed class entrenching itself in its monopolies and determined to fight tooth and nail to defend them, the industrial class summoning its forces to destroy the enemy's position.

This struggle in many ways resembled that which the continental *bourgeoisie* had victoriously undertaken, in the course of the preceding century, against feudalism. The fundamental difference, which accounts for the difference in result, consists in this: that the continental *bourgeoisie* was a landed middle class, bent on destroying the feudal régime from within; in other words, on the liberation of the soil; the English was an industrial *bourgeoisie*, little concerned, at any rate at this early period, with the system of land-tenure, and anxious only to neutralize the economic and political power of the land so far as it conflicted with their own interest. To secure for themselves adequate representation, and to abolish agricultural protection in order to reduce the cost of living and therefore the level of wages: these were the main points of their programme.

But in spite of these differences the resemblances were many, and such as by the force of insensible suggestion to apply to the new manufacturing class many experiences and ideas long familiar to the continental *bourgeoisie*. In both cases an unprivileged class existed for whom the absence of privilege was a source of strength and pride (as in the case of the cotton manufacturers and iron-masters) no less than their success in overthrowing the possessors of privilege through the proved superiority of a free economic system. Its hostility was directed against a privileged class which, though not a mere passive burden, like that of the continent, showed indirectly a certain parasitic character. To what did it owe the great recent increase in its rents? Not to itself, but to the work of the manufacturers. By exploiting mineral wealth these had created mineral royalties; by forming vast urban and suburban populations they had increased ground rents; through their mills they had enriched the owners of large sheep runs; by increasing the population they had increased the demand for, and the price of, corn. The work of the one class had in great part enriched the other, without any collaboration on the latter's part. Was not this a parallel situation, even if only indirectly parallel, to that which had exhausted the patience of the continental *bourgeoisie*? In both cases alike the new claims were directed towards the universal abolition of privilege and the reign of common rights, at least in the mutual relations between class and class.

Further, the English manufacturing class knew nothing of the cult of tradition, custom, and heredity which Burke described as characteristic of the Liberal landed aristocracy. On the contrary, it had acquired in practice an opposite attitude of mind. In its eyes the cult of tradition meant the old régime of trade guilds, the negation of freedom of management, and the perpetuation of technical routine. All this had been swept away by their own act; no less decisively than the continental revolutionaries, they had determined to begin again from the beginning and to base their fortunes upon themselves alone.[1] These manufacturers were true rationalists of industry and business; accustomed to weigh every act, to co-ordinate each act with the rest, and to subordinate it to their chosen end, they form a complete contrast with their predecessors who were content with a servile imitation of their fathers. Modern industry, like everything modern, is the child of rationalism; its expansion is a living

[1] We have already tried to describe the fundamental character of this mentality in section 5 of the Introduction; here we shall add an account of certain elements not previously discussed.

logic, which, from the simplest premisses, through an ever-growing series of middle terms, attains the complexity, if we may use the phrase, of a real discourse, closely articulated in its connexions and forming an organic and harmonious whole.

There is thus in the industrial mentality an inherent tendency towards clear and self-evident reasoning, of the kind favoured by the illuminism of the eighteenth century, and an equal hatred for all dogmatic obscurities, for the useless curiosities of history and the medieval lumber of tradition.

But there is also something different: a love of the particular and the concrete, and a wholly English dislike of abstract general principles. A combination of these two attitudes is only possible if the experiences of rationalism are translated into realistic terms; if the cogency of its logic is demonstrated by bringing into relief the logic immanent in business and self-interest. In this way alone can a kind of Liberalism grow up on English soil with an unmistakable character of its own and yet forming part of the general political life of Europe.

This interpretation was the work of Jeremy Bentham. Bentham has the typical eighteenth-century mind of the social reformer. A stranger to political problems almost to the end of his days, he passed most of his life inventing reforms and systems of penal and civil law which have given him greater fame among the peoples of Central America than in his own country. This *idée fixe* is a curious thing by itself, in a country like England, which has never felt the need of codifying its laws, and whose experience provided Savigny with many of the grounds for his hostility to codification as such. But to Bentham's ratiocinative mind Savigny's historicism is mere nonsense. If you want, he says, to apply the favourite method of Savigny and his school, you must abolish your army and fleet, and substitute the history of your country's wars; instead of ordering dinner from your cook, you must send him your bailiff's complete accounts for the last few years.[1]

[1] Halévy, *op. cit.* i. 553.

Codes of law, then, we must have; and their principal merit will lie in the greatest possible clarity of the regulations and the extreme simplicity of the relations between them. Bentham's mind, intent on clarity and simplification, recoils from all complicated forms of procedure, in which he sees nothing but incentives to fraud; here, again, he opposes himself to the traditional point of view expressed, for example, by Burke, which found the distinctive mark of liberty in the complexity of institutions and saw in simplification a danger of tyranny, whether exercised by one man or many. But Bentham cares for none of these things; he even throws over the classical jury, and would prefer a single judge capable of feeling the responsibility of his own decisions; for the complications of legal procedure which necessitate an army of lawyers he would substitute summary jurisdiction, in which man could defend his own case. ' Every man his own lawyer ': [1] that is the motto of his individualism, which is closely connected with the formulae, already examined, of religious, economic, and political individualism.

But this admirer of French rationalism, with which he shares the worship of enlightened despotism, does not believe in the power of laws to work miracles; and here he differs profoundly from his models. All law is for him an evil, because an infraction of the liberty of the individual; and, in general, every function of government is an evil. Since these are necessary evils, they must be reduced to a minimum. Of two evils the less must be chosen.[2] This principle is the clue to his legislative programme, which aims precisely at eliminating, so far as possible, artificial and unnecessary aggravations of the evils inherent in law. Thus Bentham's projects of reform, though demanding considerable activity on the part of the State, do not and are not meant to contradict the principles of individualism, but only give them a necessary complement. The limitations of freedom cannot be altogether abolished; it is impossible to create rights,

[1] Halévy, *Le radicalisme philosophique*, Paris, Alcan, 1904, iii. 129.
[2] Bentham, *Principes de législation*, *Œuvres*, Bruxelles, ed. 3, 1840, i. 32 [*Works*, ed. Bowring, 1843, i. 32].

impose obligations, or protect person, life, reputation, property, subsistence, and even liberty, except by a sacrifice of liberty. Let us content ourselves with making this sacrifice as bearable as we can, by making good laws satisfying the two essential conditions of guaranteeing liberty and equality. And if a conflict arises, as it often does arise, between security, which is the same thing as civil liberty, and equality, the principle of choosing the lesser evil requires us to sacrifice the second to the first, which is the foundation of life itself. In this case the true reconciler of conflicting interests is time. Do you wish to follow the counsels of equality, without contravening those of security? Await the natural time which puts an end to hopes and fears, the time of death. When estates have become vacant by the death of their owners, the law can take in hand the work of redistribution, by limiting the power of testamentary disposition or by turning the succession to egalitarian ends.[1]

This explicit adhesion to two leading principles of the French Revolution would lead us to expect a complete acceptance of the *Declaration of Rights*. But no. For Bentham, the Declaration belongs to the category of political fallacies. It is not true that all men are born free. On the contrary, they are born in a state of subjection. There are no imprescriptible natural rights anterior to the State; every right presupposes a sanctioning authority; to speak of natural rights is to commit a *petitio principii*; if there were ready-made laws, why should any one make new ones? The supposed natural rights are liberty, property, security, and resistance to oppression; but if liberty is natural, it is unlimited; hence there can be no other rights, because there cannot be a right without a corresponding obligation, which would be a limitation of liberty. And how can the right of resistance coexist with the obligation—a strange feature in a declaration of rights—sanctioned by Article VII, of instant obedience when summoned in the name of the law? If the law is oppressive, am I committing a crime in resisting it? And how can the

---

[1] Bentham, *Principes du code civil*, *Œuvres*, i. 55 *seqq.*, 66 *seqq.* [*Works*, ed. Bowring, 1843, i. 302-3, 312-13].

sacred and inviolable character of property be combined with equality? If property is a natural right, all should have their share; in that case, how can it be said that no landowner shall be deprived of an inch of land?

The attribution of the origin of government to a voluntary compact is in fact a false hypothesis. The separation of powers required by Article XVI is a fallacious and confused idea; separate and independent powers could never be combined into a single whole, and a government so constituted could not govern. There must be a supreme power to which every branch of the administration is subordinate; but in that case there is no separation of powers, but only a distinction of functions, because a power exercised according to regulations laid down by a superior is a branch of this superior power, not a separate power.[1]

Bentham's criticisms, while intended to demonstrate the derivative character of all rights, do not exclude the possibility of a legitimate search for something that is not derivative: something not due to the action of society and government but lying at their very foundation. This principle, which proceeds from human nature itself, is for Bentham self-interest. The cell of moral and political society is for him not man as the possessor of rights but *homo oeconomicus*. If we translate the abstract legal formulae of the Declaration into the language of economics, we shall see the entire structure of society arising upon a secure foundation.

Self-interest is an individual and independent force, whose development requires no external assistance; every man is the best judge of his own interest and is best able to secure and provide for it. But the co-existence of different men with different interests spontaneously creates the problem of a reconciliation. This problem is solved by the logic of self-interest itself, which demonstrates in concrete facts that the interests of individuals so harmonize with each other that each man, in attending to his own business, creates one element in a common utility, the sum of particular utilities.

[1] Bentham, *Traité des sophismes politiques et des sophismes anarchiques, Œuvres*, i. 509 *seqq.* [*Anarchical Fallacies, Works*, ed. Bowring, 1843, ii. 491 *seqq.*].

Granted this natural and spontaneous harmony between individual utilities, and granted their contribution towards a common good, there is nothing left in society for a government to do. But in fact the individual does not always develop the logic of his own interests with perfect consistency; sometimes he follows what he falsely believes to be his interest, thereby infringing the interests of others and in the last resort his own. Here lies the opportunity for the work of government, which represents the logic of truth as against the anti-logic of error, and draws its inspiration from the interest of the greatest number, as against a narrowly selfish interest falsely so called. Hence all institutions, economic, social, juridical, and political, and all the mutual interests of individuals and classes, must be judged by this simple and universal test: do they answer to the interest of the greatest number or not? If not, the law must destroy them for the sake of the well-being not only of society in general but of the individuals themselves.

This was clearly a criterion no less revolutionary than that derived from abstract rationalism, and capable of creating a democratic tyranny no less overwhelming than that of the Jacobins. Further, it had the merit of being fully intelligible and convincing to business men, the manufacturing class, who soon adopted it as a weapon against the selfishness of the landowners. It is easy to imagine what a vast amount of dross could be purged away by the working of an implacably Benthamite mentality, with its abstract and radical logic, once it had been set in contact with the traditional British world dear to Burke. There was an enormous mass of prejudice to sweep away, an enormous number of customary and legal curiosities to be fused into a new unity, of privileges to be destroyed; the whole administrative organism, dispersed as it was round the margin of society, had to be rebuilt; ancient political divisions had to be made afresh; public education, the Church, the magistracy, the government, the colonial system, and many other things, had to be entirely transformed.

Bentham himself made a few attempts to describe the

work that was to be done. After 1808, his interest in strictly political problems, which at first was lukewarm and secondary, began to take the leading place in his mind ; he threw himself into the preparation of schemes of reform, which later, in 1820, he proposed to condense into a Constitutional Code in three volumes. The first alone was published during his life in 1827 ; the rest saw the light much later. The problem propounded for solution in this Code was how to place every member of political society in such circumstances that his private interest might coincide with the general interest. This amounts to demanding a synthesis of Liberalism and democracy, such that the government may be as much concentrated as possible, and at the same time as little of an evil as possible to the individual.

We need not describe in detail these dreams of reform, which transfer so-called concrete interests into a world of nebulous unrealities. The historically important thing is the principle that inspired Bentham's radicalism, which very soon, owing to the work of less visionary and fantastic minds, developed into more realistic programmes and efforts at reform. Bentham's fate was a strange one; he lived in solitude, unheard and almost a stranger in his own country, until the closing years of his life; and afterwards met with a degree of recognition and admiration which would have been inexplicable had they depended wholly on his intellectual qualities. The fact is that very few of his so-called followers and admirers were really acquainted with his chaotic works ; what interested them and answered to their actual historical needs was the intellectual motive, not the monotonous and wearisome applications of it. Any one could adopt the principle of utility as his own weapon without bestowing another thought upon the old *maître d'armes* who had taught him to use it.

Bentham's one pupil, in the strictest sense of the word, was James Mill. The others, John Stuart Mill, Macaulay, Grote, Molesworth, Roebuck, Villiers, and Hume, owed to him only a certain mental stimulus to which, in the case of the first three, their own richer and more complex personalities gave a new shape; the rest, who belonged to the sphere of practical politics, used it for their particular narrow ends.

But if the group of rising men gathered round Bentham, who were to revolutionize English politics, was no Benthamite school in the traditional sense of that word, the word can be used with justice as the name of the nucleus of a political party: the germ of the Radical party.

In 1823 James Mill and his friends founded the *Westminster Review* in order to expound and defend their political opinions. Mill inaugurated the review with an article analysing the English Constitution from the Radical point of view. He displayed its aristocratic character; he showed that political representation was a mere appanage of landed property; and he pointed out that Whigs and Tories, for all their apparent antagonism, were equally interested supporters of the *status quo*. With these criticisms arose the problem of political reform based on a more truly popular representation.

The importance of this problem was soon to force itself on the consciousness of the country, already obscurely aware of the evil consequences of an unequal distribution of political power, an inequality perpetually increasing through the decline of the agricultural class and the simultaneous growth of the industrial population. The entry of the first Radicals into the old parliament brought matters to a head; and the political writers emphasized the main points at issue. Grote not only advocated a redistribution of seats based on the numbers of the population, but even went so far as to demand the introduction of the ballot, without which a popular suffrage would be ineffectual. Macaulay pointed out that the working-class riots were not in fact, as on the surface they appeared to be, symptoms of a conflict between rich and poor drawing its motive from the perennial fount of servile envy; the true protagonists, he maintained, were the middle class and the landed aristocracy: the former composing the main body of an army officered by the flower of the English aristocracy, of which the flower of the working class made up the rearguard.

From the political writers and parliamentary speakers, the agitation spread rapidly to the hustings, with that steady expansive motion characteristic of English propaganda. Little by little it began to make headway among the best elements of the governing class, recently enriched by new recruits from the middle classes, like Peel and Canning. Signs of a political reformation were soon visible. In 1824 and 1825 the laws against associations of workmen were repealed; in 1829 parliament voted Catholic Emancipation; and in 1832 the great Reform Bill became law. The Reform Bill, a concession painfully wrung from the conservatives, represents a compromise between the Radical programme and the traditional régime. It left intact the principle according to which the vote was a privilege of the counties, boroughs, universities, and propertied classes; it confirmed septennial parliaments, public scrutiny, relative majorities without ballot, and the fixed number of members. But it suppressed some glaring inequalities by a redistribution of seats giving representation to the new industrial centres and regulating the roll of electors in a uniform manner. The importance of the reform was that it permitted a large influx of new elements into parliament, able to bring pressure to bear on the conservative classes and bring about a gradual transformation of the political atmosphere. Thus it was not the end but the beginning of a phase in the evolution of Great Britain.

Radicalism naturally did not rest content with its first success. Its electoral programme, as laid down by Bentham, included as its main points universal suffrage and annual parliaments; and it was two Benthamites, Cartwright and Place, who later became the leaders of the Chartist movement. It was a group of Radicals, Grote, Molesworth, Joseph Hume, and Roebuck, who in 1826 founded in London the first society for opposing the Corn Laws; and it was a Radical, Bowring, who two years after the failure of this attempt made another and more successful attempt in the same direction at Manchester.[1] The Colonization Society

[1] Halévy, *Le Radicalisme philosophique, op. cit.*, pp. 383, 386.

founded by Grote, Molesworth, and John Stuart Mill for the reformation of colonial government was based on strictly radical principles, and the first projects of public State education emanated from the same source.

Radicalism was a ferment pervading the whole fabric of the nation; it was the French Revolution working at a distance and disguised beneath the features of John Bull. It completed the task taken in hand by the first English revolutionaries, Priestley, Paine, Price, and Godwin, the task of transforming the system of custom and tradition by means of reason and justice; a task which national pride alone had for a time arrested and delayed. Radicalism is a complex and turbid phenomenon containing in itself germs of liberalism, democracy, and socialism. The principle of utility or self-interest was strictly individualistic and liberal in its character; it implied freedom of initiative and universal self-help. It was held in check by the opposing principle of the interest of the greatest number, conceived though this was as a mere sum of private activities. In practice, however, the second principle could assert itself only artificially, through the authority of a State, impersonating in itself the needs of the majority, and ensuring their prevalence over the selfishness of individuals. Here we have the substance of an authoritarian democracy from which could spring not only the purely political claims of Chartism but also the social claims of a working class awaking to a consciousness of its own true interests.

Radical universalism did not stop short at national frontiers, any more than the universalism of the French Revolutionaries. Interests, like individual rights, know no nationality, since their object is human nature. ' I should reject with horror ', says Bentham, ' the name of patriot, if in order to be a friend to my own country I must be an enemy of the human race.' Happily, interests were harmonious; and the cosmopolitan ideal of the Radicals therefore did not require the renunciation of one's own country, and even acquired that somewhat vague and mystical tone generally recognized in a nation which has a right to call itself cosmopolitan without overstepping its own frontiers, because it has actually peopled the world. This tone was to reappear in the Liberals, the Conservatives, the Labour Party, and even the Imperialists.

The agreement of Radicalism with the revolutionary cast of mind extends to its religious policy. In a work on the Church of England, Bentham propounds a plan of ecclesiastical reform on a democratic basis, according to which the clergy are to be elected by the parish and paid out of the taxes, and the Church is to be at any rate in part disendowed. At bottom the temperament of Bentham was irreligious. The fanaticism of St. Paul exasperated him, and the only thing that he liked in Jesus was his humanitarianism. His ideal was a civil religion, without dogma and without ritual, a kind of sentimental reflection of the gospel of self-interest. His lack of religion was not unusual in English society at the time. Many Radicals followed James Mill in calling themselves Freethinkers; Robert Owen, the famous reformer, was an unbeliever, and even the romanticists, Byron, Shelley, and Keats, were pagans by choice.

But political, economic, and religious society in England offered an immovable resistance to Radicalism in its extreme forms, wearing down its revolutionary spirit and permitting free play only to those impulses which could act through processes of gradual reform. We shall later study the operation of the various social factors which preserved the continuity of English historical life and by their opposition to the Radical movement created that equilibrium between new and old, conservatism and revolution, which is characteristic of modern England; but in the inner structure of Radicalism we can already discern the causes which, by acting upon the minds of its partisans, checked the rush of their onset and brought about a fruitful inner conflict. The principle of self-interest, while giving great persuasive power to Benthamism, marks at the same time its limitations. Its narrowness and logical barrenness could never arouse the enthusiasm and passion which lead to revolutions. Confronted by the danger of a great upheaval, the pupil of

Bentham is led to consider the pros and cons ; and this means deserting his party even before his mind is made up ; for the habit of calculation is in itself anti-revolutionary. Utilitarianism, moreover, shows its spiritual barrenness by reducing all activity and every value to the level of self-interest, and thus deadening and degrading the life of the soul. No sooner had the first flush of the conflict against opposing forces, which could give utilitarianism an appearance of vitality and fruitfulness, passed away, than it appeared petty and mean. Such at least was the impression made on the mind of John Stuart Mill immediately after the Radical victory, when he saw the victors of yesterday naked and stripped of the halo that had transfigured them.

Thus the best followers of Benthamism felt keenly the need to escape from the confines of the school and breathe a freer air. John Stuart Mill escaped from the watchful eye of his father and made friends with the romantics, Maurice, Sterling, and later Carlyle. Grote and Macaulay found in the study of history a natural antidote to the historical obtuseness of their master ; Macaulay, indeed, did not hesitate to criticize sharply the abstract and schematic political conceptions of James Mill, and to expound a political method more respectful towards the historical facts of human development. The economists found in economic phenomena a complexity far greater than anything imagined by Bentham when he outlined his facile scheme for the identification of private and public interests. Other Radicals found means of asserting their loyalty to a wider and more human reality than that which had been summed up in the gospel of self-interest. From every side the Radical mind acquired new elements, at once enriching it and impeding the rapidity of its motion ; with the passage of time and the process of gradual absorption, the possibility of sudden and violent action dwindled, and Radicalism by degrees lost its Jacobin attitude and the character of an exclusive political party. Henceforth its function was limited to the fertilization of the new political life of England.

§ 2. THE ECONOMISTS

The economists form for the greater part a somewhat separate branch of English Radicalism. Though belonging to the Benthamite group, they remembered that their father was not Bentham but Adam Smith. In practical politics, they were ready to identify themselves with the Radicals, with whom they shared a hatred for State protectionism and the monopoly of land; but as scientists, they found no support in the facile schemes of Benthamism. Their *homo oeconomicus* was a reasoning and calculating creature; but they kept him in the laboratory, like a piece of apparatus, and did not send him out into the street like a man of flesh and blood to make laws for his fellow men.

This difference of mental attitude produced a very different outlook on the problems of social life. Where the Radicals had only seen generic interests, with neither name nor class nor content, co-operating in an idyllic harmony, the economists saw highly differentiated and individualized interests in violent mutual opposition. Malthus, the most akin in temperament and in spirit to Adam Smith, and the most alien to the mentality of the Radicals, emphasized the first of these conflicts in his famous *Essay on Population*. The eighteenth century had uncritically accepted from feudalism the idea that a large population is a heaven-sent blessing; though even then a few voices were raised in protest. When the Enclosure Acts were depopulating the English countryside, an agriculturist already quoted raised the question, What is the use of a dense population? But the men who were disappearing from the country-side were not annihilated; they drifted into the towns and factories, and their immense number, their poverty, and their frequent unemployment, raised the same question with a new urgency: What is the use of all this population?

Malthus was disturbed by the spectacle of the industrial world, whose grave condition was in his opinion essentially a crisis of over-population. This belief he raised to the rank of a theory by the doctrine, which in its strict mathematical form is highly disputable, that the increase of production and yield from land is far less rapid than the simultaneous increase of population. The warning note sounded by his work, in spite of his vaguely philanthropic intentions, had a remorselessly conservative significance. Your misery, he seemed to say to the working class, is your own fault. Your improvidence and lack of self-control has led you to multiply to the point of murderous mutual competition. You are wrong in blaming your masters, who share the ill-effects of your fault; for what is the poor-tax but the contribution paid by the rich to assist the improvidence of the poor, and to give a new incentive to the increase of population? [1]

Malthus's originality is all in the *Essay*; his remaining economic works merely mark a passing phase of the transition from the agricultural to the industrial system, and from protectionism to free trade. A more authentic exponent of the new movement of thought is Ricardo, one of the first Radical members of the House of Commons, and the first economist to give the science of Adam Smith a decisive turn towards industrialism. Ricardo's view of the economic world in which he lives, and which he analyses with cool lucidity, is no more optimistic than that of Malthus. He is deeply impressed by the *Essay on Population* and draws from it a highly indirect inference far more important than the original premiss: the theory of rent. For Smith and Malthus, the rent of land is a gift of nature. The landlord, comforted by this scientific benediction, could sleep soundly in the knowledge that he had not unjustly usurped anything, but owed his wealth to God alone. This naïve confidence was dispelled by Ricardo. Rent was not a gift of nature; it

---

[1] The argument of Malthus is not stated in this stern manner; but this is its inner significance. To convince himself, let the reader turn to the passages in the *Essay* in which the author criticizes Godwin's *Social Justice* (p. 329 of the French translation, Paris, 1845), those in which he opposes the democratic ideal (pp. 341 *seqq.*), those in which he criticizes the claim that the reward of labour ought to serve for the maintenance of an entire family and that work should be provided for all who demand it (p. 372), or the bitter criticism of the Poor Laws (p. 365, &c.) [ed. 1, 1798, chs. v, x–xv].

arose from the fact that the fertility of the soil differs in degree, and that the necessity of cultivating the less fertile areas confers a privilege upon those who own the best land. But what is the cause of this necessity for cultivating less and less fertile areas? The increase of population. Thus in the last resort the supposed bounty of nature is nothing but the avarice of nature; and the benefit of the rich depends wholly on the misery of a superabundant and hungry population; it grows as this by its increase necessitates the cultivation of the worst and heaviest soils of a country. The Radical Ricardo comes to the same conclusion as the conservative Malthus.

It is easy to see what a powerful weapon this doctrine might become in the hands of the manufacturers, in their struggle with the landed proprietors. The theory of rent had not yet been extended to industry, and thus it was impossible to turn the weapon against its users by pointing out that they too enjoyed the unjust privilege of monopoly. The landowners appeared as the sole usurpers of goods created by society at large, which ought to belong to society in order to serve the needs of its poorest members. The industrial *bourgeoisie*, it is true, did not draw this final inference from the theory of rent, and confined itself to emphasizing the negative and polemical side of the theory; but the deduction of a positive programme of expropriation finds a solid foundation in Ricardo's theory, and was in the future to be the basis of democratic and proletarian claims. All projects for the nationalization of land, from that of Henry George to that of Wallace and the English miners of the present day, are connected with Ricardo's theory.

Thus a new conflict arose between economic theory and Bentham's postulate of the harmony of private and public interests. The interests of the landed class were opposed to those of every other class; their condition was never so favourable as when food-stuffs were scarce and dear. But even dismissing property, and considering only the internal structure of industrial life, the eye was met by other conflicts. The two chief factors in production, the employer and the workman, had opposite interests: the rise of wages tended to diminish profits and vice versa. But if the improvement of the labouring classes was desired by the 'friends of humanity' in general, it was no less true that in the natural progress of society wages would tend to sink as long as they were regulated by supply and demand; the number of workmen would continue to increase more rapidly than the demand for labour.[1] It seemed the inevitable fate of the workman to be crushed between two opposing forces, the employer and the landowner: the former reducing his wages, the latter reducing his purchasing power by raising the price of corn. The conclusion was the principle later to be called the brazen law of wages: that their tendency is to sink to the minimum indispensable for the subsistence of the workman.

Like Malthus, Ricardo has before his eyes a picture of desolation and misery, which he attempts to fix and render permanent by an appeal to laws of nature. His *bourgeois* industrial mentality is incapable of dissociating the idea of social welfare from that of employers' profits; any attempt on the part of the workmen to alter the situation arbitrarily in their own favour seems to him disastrous; the determination of wages must be left to the free competition of the market, which must never be hindered by the intervention of government;[2] which means, for the workman, the freedom to let himself be exploited. The only possible means to alleviate social pressure are indirect: the improvement of methods of production, the reduction of the birth-rate, as Malthus has suggested, and a reduction in the price of corn. Thus Ricardo provides the manufacturers with a new argument against the protectionism of the landlords, and the alliance, in their struggle with the landed interests, of their own employees, of whose interests they are apparently the natural protectors.

But here too, as in the doctrine of rent, the logic of the argument transcends the private ends of the class that employs it. The working men soon rejected the proffered alliance and quoted Ricardo against Ricardo. The lowered

---

[1] Ricardo, *Principes de l'économie politique*, *Œuvres*, Paris, 1847, ch. v, pp. 72-3.   [2] *Op. cit.*, p. 80.

price of corn would be an illusory gain, because the play of the labour market would once more tend inevitably to lower wages to the level of the new cost of living. They fully accepted the principle laid down by Ricardo, but converted it from a sentence of doom into a banner of revolt. To Marx and Lassalle the brazen law of wages appeared an irrefutable fact not of nature but of history : the inevitable consequence of capitalistic exploitation. And they attempted to use the class warfare implied in Ricardo's clash of interests between employers and workmen as a means to the expropriation of the capitalist and the liberation of the working man from the slavery of wages. But as the final phase of the struggle was deferred it was seen to have produced more immediate partial consequences, equally remote from the purpose of both conflicting parties. The workmen, united by means of trade unions in a common rebellion against the law of wages, obtained better conditions without transcending the status of wage-earners ; the employers and capitalists did not find their profits annihilated by the increase of wages, because the greater productivity of a better-paid working class permitted new progress and a greater development of business. Thus in the last resort the conflict between wages and profits, and the class conflict to which it gave rise, while retaining their importance as necessary stimulants to economic development, are seen, even while discharging this function, to obey the law of a higher solidarity. The brazen law of wages is at once confirmed and repealed : confirmed as the historical expression of an early stage in the organization of industry, and a powerful incentive to the association of workmen ; repealed as the statement of an inevitable natural necessity and a complete summary of the ultimate effects of industrialism.

How could so dramatic a view as Ricardo's of the oppositions which spring up within the bosom of economic society coexist with the naïve and facile optimism of the Radicals? For it must be remembered that Ricardo was a supporter of the Benthamite programme and the authoritative spokesman of the Radical group.

There is one way in which the two opposed views may be reconciled, by appeal to that fundamental optimism which, in spite of everything, marked the growth of English industrialism. Ricardo trusts in the future of industry, which he expects to be far richer than that of agriculture, impeded as the latter is by the natural limits of productivity and the diminishing returns of the soil. The relation between the two forms of production asserted by the physiocrats, and to some extent endorsed by Adam Smith, was exactly reversed; it is not industry but land that is sterile, or at any rate unequal to the task of reacting adequately to man's attempts to exploit it. Here again, Ricardo's abstract assertion is merely an accurate historical expression of the gradual reversal of the relations between agriculture and industry that was going on before his eyes.

His faith in industry is essentially a faith in the will, initiative, and freedom of its directors, as capable of nourishing an increasingly complex organism, purifying and improving it through competition and developing it beyond the limits of individual nations by an international division of labour. If this complex structure contains elements of friction and resistance, they are merely a stimulus to the renewal of efforts to prosecute the struggle for the removal of the causes of social distress. Ricardo's conflicts thus form a subordinate element in his scheme of radical optimism; the spontaneous development of industry was bound to overwhelm the artificial barriers placed in its path by the selfishness of the landowners; the expansion of capitalism would heal the wounds which capitalism itself in its earlier phases inflicted upon the working class. Is it not a Radical dogma that only liberty can cure the evils that liberty has created?

This optimistic feeling intensified itself in Ricardo's followers, MacCulloch, Senior, and John Stuart Mill, either through increasing failure to face the opposite point of view, or through a strong conviction, made possible by the progress of industrialism, that the labour problem could be fairly stated in Ricardo's narrow and rigid terms. The idea that wages were necessarily restricted to the level of bare subsistence, and the more moderate but not fundamentally different theory of a wage fund beyond which it was impossible for the employer to go, were by degrees abandoned by Senior and Mill. In their place arose the idea of high wages as a condition of industrial development, and of the tendency of profits to decrease through this development in such a way that the employer, owing to increase of output, suffers no loss.

This optimistic doctrine absorbed into itself the Malthusian theory of population.

' Malthus's population principle,' says Mill, ' was quite as much a banner, and point of union among us, as any opinion specially belonging to Bentham. This great doctrine, originally brought forward as an argument against the indefinite improvability of human affairs, we took up with ardent zeal in the contrary sense, as indicating the sole means of realizing that improvability by securing full employment at high wages to the whole labouring population through a voluntary restriction of the increase of their numbers.' [1]

The best contribution made to Radical optimism by classical economics consisted in the universal and scientific form into which its propositions were thrown. At bottom, as we have seen, the supposed laws of Malthus and Ricardo were nothing more than shrewd observations of contingent and changing facts; but expressed in general forms valid for all times and for all places, they gained an unprecedented prestige, and were able to supply an adequate content to a Radical ideology rising superior to the course of historical facts. Thus it came about that the classical free trade doctrine, the accurate expression of the industrial evolution of an exporting country like England, was so firmly united to the general body of the Liberal ideology as to become practically synonymous with Liberalism.

We shall consider the influence of the combined forces of the Radicals and the economists upon English political life after completing our historical review with a study of religious development.

[1] J. S. Mill *Autobiography*, [ed. 1908, p. 60], Fr. tr., Paris, 1874, p. 100.

§ 3. RELIGIOUS DEVELOPMENT

The subject to which we now turn is highly complex, uniting as it does a large number of discordant elements. From the religious point of view, England was divided into Anglicans, Nonconformists, and Catholics. But over and above these confessional divisions a Methodist movement and an Evangelical movement were going forward, and characteristic tendencies were at work approximating Nonconformity towards Anglicanism, and Anglicanism towards Catholicism.

As Gladstone remarked—and the fact is generally recognized—Nonconformity was the backbone of British Liberalism.[1] We already know why.[2] The dissenting sects were free communities animated by a Calvinistic spirit whose very existence depended upon individual initiative, propaganda, and competition. In organization they were congregational, that is, organized into independent groups each with its own belief, its own ritual, and its own administration. They were recruited from the great mass of the middle classes, and the *élite*, now gradually taking shape, of the working classes ; and they attained their greatest strength in the new industrial centres. In these sects a process of selection and training for administrative, political, and organizing work was always going on. But their extremely individualistic religious outlook and interpretation of the Scriptures exposed them in the eighteenth century to an illuministic deism and threatened them with the loss of all their ecclesiastical coherence. During the French Revolution they were drawn into the revolutionary current, and ran some danger of being overwhelmed by the conservative and nationalistic reaction.

But at the same time a ferment of new life was working within them, which by degrees was to bring them back to the source of their original inspiration. In 1739 Wesley and Whitfield set on foot a Methodist movement which attempted to renew the Calvinistic spirit in defiance of all sectarian

---

[1] Gladstone, *Gleanings of Past Years, 1843–76*, London, 1879, 7 vols., i. 158.   [2] Introduction, § 3.

differences; though its Calvinism was somewhat attenuated by the abandonment of the dogma of predestination. Wesley's preaching was at first received with hostility, because of its moral and religious rigorism, which appeared to mark a regression to a narrow and obsolete attitude of mind. But the zeal of an ever-increasing crowd of indomitable propagandists by degrees overcame all opposition, and established the new spirit within the old body of Dissent. Nonconformity thus regained that dogmatic precisianism and cohesive force which alone could save it from disintegration. Moreover Methodism, transcending as it did sectarian distinctions, served to temper the exclusive particularism of the sects, and to direct their attention towards common ideals and common ends without infringing their respective identities. It must be borne in mind that, recruited as they mostly were from the middle classes, they found in the Methodist view of religious and moral conformity an efficacious means of uniting the forces of this new class by distracting it at first from a mystical doctrine of election, with all its revolutionary suggestions, and later from the narrowness and inhuman selfishness of utilitarianism.

So it came about that in the nineteenth century the revived forces of the nonconformist sects joined hands with Radicalism and served to correct its one-sidedness. The great humanitarian, philanthropic, social, and anti-slavery movements of industrial and commercial England in the nineteenth century were largely inspired by Methodism. This combination of selfishness and sentiment has always provided satirical critics of the English temperament with pleasant occupation. The eccentric Member of Parliament, Cobbett, already found in it a subject for his bitterest diatribes. But it must not be forgotten that this combination works with extraordinary power and a kind of unconscious cunning in the cause of stability. Nothing else could have tempered and made tolerable the social pressure produced by industrialism; and by playing on the religious and humanitarian feelings of the new ruling classes it led them to a higher and more scientific conception of their own interests, which were in reality furthered and not impeded by a fraternal interest in the welfare of other classes.

Face to face with the nonconformist sects stood the great official Church of England. At the beginning of the nineteenth century the old distinction between High Church and Low Church had lost its earlier significance, and the ferments of Evangelical and Tractarian thought had not yet troubled the placid face of ecclesiastical life. The high dignitaries of the Church were either members or clients of the feudal aristocracy, living on princely stipends, out of touch with the religious life of the country, and seeing in the outward forms of religion little more than official duties to be perfunctorily discharged. Even the parish clergy were largely pluralists and absentees, whose interest in their parish was the interest of a sportsman in the land over which he hunts. The Church of this period was a religious toryism, hierarchic, traditional, an integral part of the structure of the State which nourished it and lent it the weight of its own authority.[1]

This state of things was broken up by a movement of new life parallel to that which inspired Nonconformity. Methodism was followed by the Evangelical movement, promoted by Wilberforce, resembling Methodism in many points and distinguished from it principally by the fact that it attempted to work upon the Church of England from within, and to lead it along the path of Protestantism. Its activity, not sharply distinguishable from that of Methodism, produced moral and social results of the same kind; in the classes of the population which it chiefly affected it aroused the same desire for order, loyalty towards the public powers, mutual aid and organization, which Methodism had aroused in the industrial classes.

This impulse from below finally overcame even the indifference and apathy of the higher clergy. The contrast between the exemplary life and sincere evangelical labours of the newer school of clergy and the extravagant and self-indulgent lives of the old-fashioned fox-hunting parsons and

---

[1] [This paragraph has been modified by the translator; so, in a few points, have the two following.]

absentee rectors prepared the way for a real revival in the religious and moral life of the Anglican Church. Hence when at Oxford, the stronghold of rigid orthodox clericalism, signs of a religious crisis began to appear about 1830, the eyes of all who were interested in religion turned anxiously towards the venerable university.

The so-called Oxford movement had a forerunner in John Keble, author of the *Christian Year*, a volume of poems steeped in Christian mysticism which inspired with religious fervour a group of university students whose leaders in 1827 were Newman, Pusey, Gladstone, Froude, and later Manning. At first its character was indefinite; the religious awakening seemed likely to emphasize the separation of the Anglican Church from Catholicism. When in 1829 Sir John Peel, after supporting Catholic emancipation, stood for election as a Member for the University, the younger generation mobilized their forces and defeated him. But the inner significance of the movement was to appear indirectly somewhat later. In 1833, after Newman's eventful visit to Italy, members of the University began to publish a series of *Tracts for the Times*, detached anonymous essays laying before a wide public their authors' views on various questions. This was a form of propaganda of which political parties were in future to make extensive use.

The intention of the Tractarians was to emphasize and consolidate those elements in Anglicanism which distinguished it from Nonconformity. Anglicanism, they contended, was not a sect but a genuine religion; it was Christianity itself, and went back directly to the resources of Christianity through an uninterrupted apostolic tradition. This differentiating mark was no mere formality, but carried with it momentous consequences; if Anglicanism was a Church, or rather *the* Church, it had a mediating function between the believer and God which no sect has or can have. Ordination, ritual, worship, ceremonies, and hierarchies acquired a fundamental importance which might be called Catholic; and the Oxford Tractarians used the term Catholic to distinguish the Church of England even from that of Rome.

From these premisses an important political conclusion was drawn. If the privileges of Anglicanism were derived from the Apostolic Succession, it needed no support from the State; and ought in fact to reconsider the separatistic and sectarian character originally given to it by Henry VIII and Elizabeth. Disestablishment, separation of the Church from the State, was the watchword of this new other-worldly clerical Radicalism, which yet in its practical consequences was akin to liberal Radicalism. Gladstone's conversion to disestablishment is unmistakable evidence of the influence of his Tractarian friends upon his mind. Separation from the State, Catholicism, ritualism, formalism : do not these indicate a move in the direction of Rome? The Oxford Tractarians were anxious at all costs to avoid this inevitable inference; their curious problem of conscience lay in the fact that whereas, in order to resist the attractions of Popery, they wished to restore to Anglicanism its inner religious energy, in order to carry out this programme they were compelled to reinstate all the traditional values upon which Roman Catholicism is built.

In the end, the logic of actions prevailed over the logic of intentions. Conversion to Roman Catholicism, long deferred in great tribulations of conscience, as Newman's famous *Apologia* shows, came about at last : first in isolated cases, sensational owing to the public position of the converts, men like Newman and Manning; later with a frequency surprising and disconcerting to the public and the government. English Catholicism, lately readmitted into the circle of public life, and skilfully directed by Cardinal Wiseman, gained immensely in strength from its new recruits. Manning, appointed Cardinal in succession to Wiseman, showed in the discharge of his duties the uncompromising zeal of a convert, which served to close the ranks of the Catholic party; later, in the council of 1870, he was one of the strongest supporters of Papal infallibility. Newman, a mystical and lonely spirit, also received the purple as a reward of his great achievements as a preacher; and in a monastic solitude wrote works which, re-read and pondered upon some decades later, were to stir up the Modernist movement.

But the very intransigence of the English Catholics, working as it did in a land torn by sectarian differences, helped indirectly to strengthen the idea and love of religious freedom. These Catholics might be slaves of Rome, but they demanded full freedom in relation to the State; they demanded abolition of the privileges of the Church of England, especially its detested Irish branch, whose maintenance was so grievous a burden upon the Catholic peasantry.

Even within the Church of England, the spiritual crisis which had led to the apostasy of Froude, Newman, and Manning aroused a sense of increased respect for its adversaries' opinions and thus produced a higher consciousness of religious freedom in its true sense, of different paths leading to the same goal. This consciousness is especially visible in Gladstone, who though parting from his old friends in order to remain true to Anglicanism shows in the later development of his ecclesiastical policy a broader and more humane liberality of spirit.

Among those who did not go over to Rome was one of the leaders of the Oxford movement, Pusey, whom Pius IX jestingly compared to a bell ringing to call the faithful to church but remaining outside itself.[1] But in spite of this equivocal position, and marked out by the strictures of the Church and the hostility of churchmen, Pusey continued to exercise, with a small group of friends, an important function of publicity and consolidation. The Catholic movement was no isolated phenomenon; it answered to one of the English Church's most deeply seated needs; and, the crisis of apostasy once passed, we see it reaffirming itself within the High Church and continuing down to the present to inspire the annual Lambeth Conferences of Bishops, each of which displays a timid but definite tendency towards a reconciliation with Rome and a reunion of the two main branches of the one Catholic Church.

This, at bottom, is an expression of the same universalistic attitude which inspired Methodism in its attempt to tran-

[1] Thureau Dangin, *La Renaissance catholique en Angleterre*, ed. 2, 1899, 3 vols., iii. 66.

scend the divisions of the Nonconformist sects. Outside the
sphere of religious activity the same spirit appears as the
universalism of the Radicals, economists, and Liberals; it is
the impulse to break down the isolation imposed by the pride
of past generations and to take part in the circulation of
European life. Perhaps the most striking characteristic of
nineteenth-century England is this tendency to Europeanize
itself, which in combination with the simultaneous tendency
on the part of continental countries to study and imitate
England results in a fuller understanding, a reciprocal
adaptation and a mutual assimilation of problems, attitudes
of mind, feelings, and institutions.

A general survey at this point of religious beliefs, in their
distribution and circulation, reveals an ordered hierarchy of
forms corresponding to the order of social classes. The mass
of the rural population belongs to the Anglican Church;
the transition from agriculture to industry leads to the growth
of the nonconformist sects, recruited especially from the
middle classes of society; the aristocracy finds its religious
symbol in the Established Church. This hierarchy is not a
static system of castes, but a mobile and loose formation, in
constant change. The individuals whose personal efforts
raise them above the masses in ability and wealth tend
to leave the Church and to join the sects of middle-class
nonconformity; those of the upper middle class who aspire
to an aristocratic position generally move in the opposite
direction and join the Church of England. This is due to the
fact that Anglicanism is everywhere the religion of the landed
gentry; and members of the industrial classes who join the
ranks of the landed gentry on making their fortunes tend to
pass over from ' chapel ' to ' church '. In a progressive industrial society the transition from a middle-class nonconformist to an upper-class Anglican point of view is easy and
rapid.[1]

Religion thus acquires the function of a powerful stimulant
to the circulation of social energy, and a bond uniting class
to class. In its hierarchical distribution, no less than in the

[1] [This paragraph has been modified by the translator.]

special characteristics of its individual forms, it makes at once for stability and for progress, and contributes in a remarkable manner to the steady development of English life.

§ 4. THE MANCHESTER SCHOOL

The political reforms of 1832 were only the beginning of a series of economic claims which, in their turn, reacted upon the political organism, so as to place the new industrial class at the head of affairs.

We have already seen this class, taught by the economists and stimulated by Radical propaganda, preparing for war with the landowners.

In 1820 appears the first historical expression of the mentality of this class : the Petition of Merchants presented to the House of Commons and drawn up in the form of an economic catechism. It is a lesson in elementary political economy, read by the English merchants to Parliament, in order to serve as a guide in its legislative work. It states that foreign trade is what promotes the wealth of the country ; that freedom from all constraint can alone give the fullest extension to trade and the best employment of the country's capital and manufactures ; that the maxim ' buy in the cheapest market and sell in the dearest ', upon which every merchant acts in the conduct of his private business, is rigorously applicable to the trade of the nation as a whole. It proceeds to demonstrate that the general prejudice in favour of a protectionist system is due to the false belief that every importation of foreign goods diminishes and discourages production at home. These restrictions really do very little for the class in whose interests they were at first imposed, in comparison with the loss which they inflict on all other classes. In the long run, the most liberal attitude will in practice prove the most politic. The free trade merchants, in attacking agricultural protectionism, profess themselves in no way opposed to the maintenance of import duties for the benefit of the treasury. They do not wish to curtail the customs of the Crown, but only to abolish those duties which are imposed in a protectionist and prohibitionist spirit in favour of the landowners.

But the Conservative majority would not attend to the lesson. Very different arguments were required to win their consent. From 1820 to 1836 free trade propaganda confined itself to sporadic and isolated manifestations, which had a certain echo in parliament after the entry of the first Radical members. In 1836 the first anti-protectionist society was formed in London, with little success; the following year another unsuccessful attempt was made in Liverpool. In 1838 the failure of the harvest and the high price of corn led to much popular excitement, especially in the industrial centres, where the population was densest; during the autumn a few manufacturers met at the Manchester Chamber of Commerce and decided to create a third society, which was founded in the spring of 1839 under the name of the Anti-Corn-Law League.

This time the attempt was successful, thanks to the support and encouragement of a man of strong character, Richard Cobden. Cobden was a manufacturer, but he had already shown unusual power as a writer and political controversialist in a work published a few years before, in 1835, called *England, Ireland, and America*. In this work the contrast between the old English mentality and the new appears in a forcible manner. For the quarrelsome policy based on fancied prestige and national pride Cobden proposes to substitute the essentially pacific policy of self-interest. His opponents maintain that we must arm ourselves to fight for our trade; but the requirements of trade are incompatible with force and coercion; trade implies international solidarity, and the dependence of the welfare of one nation upon the welfare of others. Statistics show clearly that even the Napoleonic blockade did no real harm to English commerce; what then is the use of making war to defend a trade which is so well able to escape, unaided, the attacks of all its enemies?

Protectionism is only another, and no less harmful, kind of war. Thus, England has attempted to promote her own interests and those of her Canadian colonists by granting a monopoly in the home market to exporters of Canadian timber. All they have done is to inflict loss upon two parties:

the colonists, by diverting to the dwindling lumber industry capital which might have been more profitably invested in agriculture; and the English themselves, by compelling them to use worse and dearer timber than they could have bought in the open market.

England boasts of being a free country. But it is not the military and protectionist attitude of mind that can make the people of a country fitter to enjoy constitutional freedom. During a reign of terror, when minds are under the influence of an extremity of hope and fear, there cannot be that progress of thought and education which fits men for freedom. And the example of a genuinely liberal England will do more for the emancipation of Europe than any intervention undertaken in the name of freedom.[1]

To the Anti-Corn-Law League Cobden imparted all the fervour of a convinced believer in the industrial system. He soon gathered around him numerous supporters of free trade, the chief of whom was John Bright, a characteristic nonconformist Radical. The League resolved to promote a lively agitation all over the country in favour of free trade by means of tracts and lectures explaining to all classes of society, in language adapted to each, the *casus belli* against agricultural protectionism. The whole country was divided up by degrees into districts, each entrusted to an economic missionary;[2] and the leaders of the League travelled constantly from district to district in order to keep them in touch with one another and to speak on subjects of the most general importance. Methodist and Evangelical propaganda had already set the example of such organization, and had created an environment favourable to its success.

The success of the new missionaries varied according to their public. The manufacturing class was easily converted; all they had to do was to become conscious of their own elementary interests. The lower middle classes also listened with favour to the League's proposals, which harmonized

---

[1] Cobden, *England, Ireland, America* (in F. W. Hirst, *Free Trade and other Fundamental Doctrines of the Manchester School*, London, 1903, pp. 3 *seqq.*).   [2] Morley, *Life of Cobden*, London, 1882, p. 19.

with the general interests of consumers. This class in especial was impressed by the plea of justice as against the injustice of monopoly; by the advisability of so redistributing the work of agriculture and industry that a fall in the price of corn should lead to a larger and cheaper production of manufactured goods with a double benefit to the consumer; and by the individual's natural right to demand that the harbours created by providence should not be closed by the act of man.

The farmers and factory hands were harder to convince. To the former the League tried to demonstrate that agricultural protection benefited only the landlord and damaged the actual cultivator. But the farmers instinctively realized that it was in their interest to sell their corn at a high price, and that their interests were therefore identical with those of the landlords. As for the factory hands, the League approached them as consumers, and showed them the attractive picture of a great industrial development, made possible by free trade, whose benefit they would be the first to reap; it tried to work upon their pride and love of independence. The monopoly of the landlords deprived the community of a part of the fruit of its own labour; by means of high prices it created unemployment, and then tried to alleviate the misery which it had caused by a degrading and servile system of poor-relief. We ask, said Cobden to the labourers, not for charity, but for justice.

' [I do not] partake of that spurious humanity,' he said in a vigorous passage, ' which would indulge in an unreasoning kind of philanthropy at the expense of the great bulk of the community. Mine is that masculine species of charity, which would lead me to inculcate in the minds of the labouring classes the love of independence, the privilege of self-respect, the disdain of being patronized or petted, the desire to accumulate, and the ambition to rise. I know it has been found easier to please the people by holding out flattering and delusive prospects of cheap benefits to be derived from Parliament rather than by urging them to a course of self-reliance; but, while I will not be the sycophant of the great, I cannot become the parasite of the poor.' [1]

[1] Hirst, *Free Trade and other Fundamental Doctrines of the Manchester School*, *cit.*, p. xii.

Yet—so strong is class prejudice even in the most independent mind—the same Cobden who demanded freedom for the working man opposed the reduction of the number of hours in the factories; and even if this opposition cannot be explained by his hostility to the intervention of parliament in the labour contract, it is impossible to reconcile his demand for freedom with his profound hatred and contempt for workmen's associations. Trade unions are for him based upon the principle of brutal tyranny and monopoly; even Morley, his most faithful follower, accuses Cobden of here betraying the narrow spirit of an employer.[1]

With these implications, it is easy to see why the League utterly failed to convert the working man. Beneath the disguise of a missionary, the labourer saw the master whom he hated and whose treachery he feared; in especial, he feared the danger pointed out by the skilful Conservative counter-propagandists, that the abolition of the corn-laws would only be an excuse for the reduction of wages. This was a fallacious argument, because the diminution of nominal wages does not imply a diminution of real wages; and in any case, even if the working class gained nothing by the change, it would always gain by the industrial progress inevitably following the reduction of expenses. But the working class at this time was at once dominated by hatred and unable to form a policy. It rejected the League, and built all its hopes upon the Radical movement known as Chartism, in the naïve confidence that universal suffrage, annual parliaments, and the other merely political claims contained in the People's Charter would suffice to satisfy its economic needs.

The contrast between these two contemporary movements is highly significant, because it indicates the point of divergence between the political action of the two classes; but it is also a paradoxical contrast, when we consider that, while the Liberal *bourgeoisie* was fighting on economic ground, the social democracy was demanding political rights; thus the situation was the exact opposite of the respective claims which the two parties were to make in the future. This is why

[1] Morley, *op. cit.*, p. 42.

Chartism, instead of being a movement inspired by clear and conscious motives, appeared as a chaotic ferment; and its ultimate emphatic failure served greatly to clarify the confused minds of its supporters.

With its failure to embrace the labourers and farmers, the Manchester League acquired a strictly middle-class appearance. For the old traditional division of Whigs and Tories it began to substitute a new division, based on class interest. Both Whigs and Tories included large landowners, and also many individuals, attached to their respective parties by force of habit rather than by conscious recognition of their interests, to whom the League now gave an opportunity of considering their position afresh. By cutting across the traditional political divisions, the League, formed as it was for an object which at first appeared merely contingent and temporary, could gain recruits from Whigs and Tories alike. Thus, little by little, the old Conservative majority broke up and its component parts underwent a process of redistribution; many Tories, drawn like Peel from the manufacturing class, or like Gladstone from the educated middle class, attached themselves to the policy of the League and went to form the parliamentary majority which in 1846, after seven years of unremitting work and varying success, voted the abolition of the Corn Laws and launched English politics upon the path of free trade.

On its attainment of its end, the Manchester League was dissolved; but in this very dissolution it began a new life, not now as a particular association with a particular end, but as a new political attitude of mind, which, having taken shape in the course of a sustained effort directed to the solution of a special problem, could extend itself and apply its sharply differentiated point of view to other political problems. It became the Manchester School, the fountain-head of the new Liberal Party.

This new phase only began to appear after the victory had been won. Peel and his followers, who had left the ranks of the old Conservatism in order to vote for abolition, seemed condemned by the animosity of the landowners whose power they had defied to live in a kind of political limbo; and the position of the growing party was made worse by Peel's premature death. The traditional parliamentary system seemed unable to admit by the side of the Whig and Tory parties a third not reducible to either. But in time the more active and vital mentality of the free trade party drew the antiquated Liberalism of the Whigs into its own orbit and so restored the old two-party system, though giving its form a new content. Yet between the Whigs and the Manchester School there remains a fundamental difference, clearly discernible in the case of Gladstone. A Whig is born; a Liberal is made. This process of making was so rapid and continuous that the old privilege of birth was soon absorbed into the growing organism of the party.

After 1846, much more than after 1832, a new spirit appears to pervade and dominate English politics. The abolition of the corn duty was followed by several other economic reforms, together initiating a system of free trade. But the other branches of political activity were also undergoing profound changes. During the life of Palmerston, with his quarrelsome and punctilious Liberalism, international relations were dominated by the Whig spirit; but not without increasing protests from the Manchester school. The new Liberals owed to their economic principles the idea of an international solidarity destroying the rivalries and vanities of States and demanding a peaceful policy calculated to favour trade and an international division of labour. Defying the infatuation of the public, they opposed the Crimean War; and their opposition, though for a time ineffectual, finally aroused a well-founded doubt whether the traditional friendship for Turkey might not be an error and a danger to English policy. Greater positive importance attached to the Liberals' moral support of national claims in Europe, especially those of Italy.

But the mark of the political maturity of Liberalism in international affairs was the attitude of England during the American Civil War. Appearances were deceptive. The South demanded its independence, and this led Liberals to support it. The solidarity of principle was reinforced by a solidarity of interest; it was the South that contained the great cotton plantations which supplied all the English mills.

At first the Liberals were deceived. Cobden wavered; Gladstone, less prudent, at least so far as his official attitude as a Minister went, declared for the South, and very nearly provoked an outbreak of hostilities between England and America.[1] But Bright opened his friends' eyes. The freedom demanded by the South was only the freedom to retain slavery which the North wished to abolish. It was therefore a false liberty with which English Liberalism must have nothing to do. Nor was there any reason for fear on behalf of the cotton planters; any one who believed in liberty must believe that the substitution of free for slave labour in the plantations would increase, not diminish, their productivity. Thus the two Liberal arguments in favour of the secessionist South turned into more genuinely Liberal arguments in favour of the unionist North. In the end, Bright carried the day; and the event of the war proved him unmistakably right.

Liberal pacifism demands that war be replaced by peaceful compromise between conflicting interests through arbitration: and when this method was first successfully applied, in the case of the *Alabama*, between England and America, it was hailed as a great victory, in spite of the large indemnity which England was condemned to pay. But the perils of war were to be exorcised most effectually by the remedies proceeding from a strictly economical financial policy. If you want peaceful governments, said Ricardo, reduce their budgets. And by accepting this Radical maxim the lover of peace killed two birds with one stone; for he gratified his Liberal distrust of the State, which, trusting as he did in spontaneous private initiative and organization, he wished to reduce to a minimum of governmental and bureaucratic interference. As for the more technical side of financial policy, Liberalism showed itself in a taste for the simplification of taxation and a preference for direct taxes, which as compared

[1] Morley, *Life of Gladstone*, 2 vols., London, 1905-7, i. 972 *seqq.* [1st ed. in 3 vols., ii. 70 *seqq.*].

with indirect have the advantages of being easier to collect, more just in their incidence, and more educational both for the taxpayer and for the rulers, because, emphasizing as they do the sacrifices made by the citizen for the community, they also emphasize the question whether the public services form an adequate repayment for these sacrifices. From this point of view, Gladstone's budgets are famous in the history of finance.

Colonial politics were also profoundly modified by Liberalism. Under the old régime, colonies were regarded as fields for economic exploitation or political domination by their British rulers. It was in great part the younger sons of the aristocracy, with their predominating position in the army and in colonial government, and the merchants, with their monopoly of trade, who served to keep alive the connexion between these distant offshoots and the aristocratic system of the mother country. But the secession of the American colonies inflicted a severe blow on this colonial régime in the eighteenth century; and it received other blows, more constant though not so serious, through the economic losses due to protection. The Liberal thought of this period was pessimistic as to the future of the colonies and the Empire. The subjection of English peoples, to whom self-government was a right and a duty, outraged its inmost sense of liberty; and the economic fetters which turned their activities and products from the path traced by nature seemed prejudicial to its own interests. These feelings gave rise to a policy which at first sight seems wholly negative and pessimistic: to allow the colonies to organize and administer themselves, and make them the sole arbiters of their own destinies. Secession was inevitable, because it was natural that sons when grown up should part from their parents; one might at least hope that the separation would be peaceful, and that the continuation of merely private friendly and business relations might make it possible to save so much of the great wealth of the colonies as did not conflict with the order of nature.

But this Liberalism of expediency produced consequences which even its partisans never suspected or hoped. The freedom which they bestowed on the colonies in order to facilitate their separation proved the best bond for consolidating their union with the mother country. It created the spiritual union of the British Commonwealth, which coercion, domination, and exploitation would have rendered impossible. Only freedom could have given to every citizen of the British Empire the consciousness of a single race, language, and tradition, and to all its scattered communities the proud sense of being governed by one law and forming one family of nations, equal in rights and duties.

In its religious policy, Manchester Liberalism, as compared with the Radicalism of Bentham and James Mill, shows signs of a livelier religious feeling. Cobden regarded himself as fortunate in possessing, together with a strictly logical mind, a width of religious sympathies which enabled him to co-operate with men of different beliefs.[1]

Bright was a man of strictly Puritan temperament; Gladstone something of a theologian. In the latter's personality, which in its gradual development exhibits all the phases of Liberal evolution, one observes the emergence of a new ecclesiastical policy out of a narrowly conservative religious attitude. In 1832 Gladstone holds the orthodox Anglican doctrine of the unity of the State and the Church, the ' State conscience ' and the maintenance of the Irish Establishment; from this position he gradually moves away first by embracing the policy of Catholic and Jewish emancipation, and then by forming the plan of Church disestablishment. For so intimately religious a mind, disestablishment does not mean State atheism, any more than freedom means a sceptical indifference : it means the recognition that the whole value of religion lies in freedom of conscience, and is destroyed by State coercion and a compulsory and hypocritical conformity.

'Away with the servile doctrine,' he writes, ' that religion cannot live but by the aid of parliaments. When the State has ceased to bear a definite and full religious character, it is our interest and our duty alike to maintain a full religious freedom. It is this plenary religious freedom that brings out into full vigour the internal energies of each communion. Of all civil calamities the

[1] Morley, *Life of Cobden*, p. 26.

greatest is the mutilation, under the seal of civil authority, of the Christian religion itself.' [1]

In fields where it is impossible to trust entirely to individual initiative without the support of the State, the Liberal policy was less successful. Here the ever-present warnings against the State and against the perils of bureaucracy led to a neglect of the value of State intervention, even when this would appear most obvious. Thus classical Liberalism had no public educational policy; and it was only at a late date, after the rise of democracy and of the new Toryism, that a Liberal Minister, Forster, was to feel the necessity of framing an educational scheme. Even more serious were the defects of its social policy; a pedantic reverence for freedom of contract, often a mere disguise for the interests of the masters, led the Liberals to oppose the Factory Acts and every kind of State protection for labour. Here again, increasing pressure from the working classes led to a profound crisis in the generation of Liberals succeeding that of the original Manchester School.

Of this Liberal outlook, individualism was at once the strength and the weakness. Its religious convictions, its economic training, its Radical origin, all combined to inspire it with confidence in human spontaneity and the purely private activity of individuals. In freedom it saw the means to the awakening of all the individual's faculties, and at the same time the development of a sense of responsibility and self-criticism; but it also saw the immanent end of social and political life, as consisting in a harmonious union of strong and self-conscious personalities inspired by mutual respect and capable of arranging their mutual relations upon their own responsibility. Freedom was the means and the end, the path and the goal; freedom alone could make men fit for freedom. In these striking words Gladstone sums up the idea of the completely circular and self-contained character of the Liberal experience.

[1] Morley, *Gladstone, cit.*, i. 384. Cf. Gladstone, *Gleanings*, vii. 145 *seqq.*, where disestablishment is expounded in a less radical form than by Macaulay.

From these premisses the necessary conclusion was an implacable hostility towards all unnecessary State interference, which might set the individual free from the struggle to assert himself by his own efforts, and provide for him through a legislative providence, weakening his character and corrupting it by the servile habit of awaiting and soliciting help from above. But is it true that State interference is always of this kind, and always has this corrupting influence? Are there not cases in which the State represents a higher development of individuality itself, and can achieve tasks for which mere private enterprise is insufficient? May it not be a means for aiding the development of individualities as yet immature, which unassisted would be overwhelmed in their struggle with other individualities, more mature and more aggressive? May it not even be the expression of a higher justice, equalizing the conditions in which the struggle is carried on, and thus rendering it fairer and more human? Classical Liberalism, though not without some presentiment of these questions, was intoxicated by the exuberant vigour of its individualism, which stifled any pangs of conscience it may have felt for the misery and wretchedness which the irresistible expansion of the individual forces of a new class left in its train. There were still strong traces of the employer's selfishness and the Benthamites' narrow utilitarianism.

Nevertheless Liberalism had made great progress from the Radical point of view of the twenties. Its naïve revolutionary confidence was a thing of the past. With it had vanished the dream of making a clean sweep of history, and reconstructing the political world on the plans of Bentham. Liberalism had taken its place in the traditional life of England ; and, once in contact with facts, had learned to do justice to the forces in its environment making for resistance and stability. It had destroyed the protectionism of the landlords, but had been compelled to leave the monopoly of the aristocrats standing, though deprived of part of its economic and political strength, and therefore part of its influence and prestige. It had given a new content to the Whig Party, but it had preserved its old form and accepted the two-party system and the function of a constitutional opposition. It had extended the franchise to members of the industrial class, but had preserved its privileged character. Its very respect for freedom and self-government, strengthened by its hostility to State action, contributed to the preservation and consolidation of local government, the strictest preserve of the old landed aristocracy.

In this English Liberalism new and old were indissolubly united ; the revolution came about with no break in the continuity of traditional historical life. This synthetic character will reappear in the later development of its outlook and policy. By the mere fact that the Liberal Party became a governing party, it was forced to give its programme a wider aspect and transcend all mere class interest. As early as the days of the Manchester League, it showed an increasing desire to represent free trade as a claim put forward in the interest of all classes alike ; and if the industrial interest preponderated, that did not render insignificant the universalistic aspiration which was already a symptom of political maturity ; for the capacity of a party to govern is measured by its capacity to see from its own particular point of view the interests of the entire community. And as the party gained new members it exhibited a similar effort to overcome class boundaries by welcoming elements drawn both from the old Whig Party and from the new aristocracy of labour. Here in politics we find once more the fertilizing mutual interaction of classes already observed in religious life.

But English Liberalism was not confined to the Liberal Party. It found a complementary expression in the Conservative Party, which, as we shall see, took on a new shape from contact with its opponent, and actually realized certain Liberal principles which the other, through its tendency to perpetuate class prejudice, was in danger of obscuring. In the last instance, the full expression of English Liberalism is to be found in the party struggle, developing freely within a single State, which is not only undamaged by this internal opposition but actually draws nourishment from it.[1]

[1] This wider aspect of Liberalism will be considered at length in Part II of the present work.

§ 5. THE CONSERVATIVE REACTION

Toryism, as we have seen, emerged from its struggle against the Liberal middle classes weakened, but not, like the continental aristocracy, defeated. It retained not only its property, but, more important, the political talent which the long practice of government had formed and strengthened. Instead of abandoning itself to vain recriminations, it accepted the new situation and at once tried to orientate itself, in its capacity as the opposition party, in accordance with the motives and demands arising from the establishment of the industrial class at the head of affairs.

The middle-class tendency towards a more active exchange of relations with the continent had resulted in the introduction not only of continental liberalism but also of the ideas of the Restoration. Through the work of Coleridge and his followers, the writings of the German romanticists had begun to find a public in England. They offered an organic conception of social life, in contrast with atomistic individualism, and a mystical view of the State as an earthly god uniting in itself all the spiritual forces of individuals and directing them to a higher national and moral end. Here again, what a contrast with the Liberal State, understood as a necessary evil to be reduced to a minimum and made as harmless as possible !

The German doctrines found favour with the Conservative classes because they connected themselves with a native tradition. A main point in the Tory programme had always been the defence of the prerogatives of the Crown against the parliamentarianism of the Whigs ; and now, in accordance with the change of environment, this defence, though remaining at bottom identical, transferred itself from the Crown to the State. It was the State whose importance and prestige were to be reasserted. The State was to be regarded not as a compromise between opposing self-interests but as what Burke had called it—a living communion of minds.

For this reason the Conservatives recognized the need of broadening the basis of the State and building it not upon the tower of privilege but upon the humble yet solid platform of the feelings and interests of the whole people. The old Toryism had created an oligarchical government: but was not the Liberal government an oligarchy, less entitled to rule because based solely upon wealth detached from birth and from the privileges of an ancient tradition?

Why, asked the Conservatives, did Liberalism wish to weaken the State? The answer was easy. It wanted to allow free play to the strongest forces in competition with the weakest, and full power to exploit the defenceless masses, which were the victims and not the protagonists of the struggle, by destroying all power superior to individuals and able to exercise upon them a moderating and equalizing function. The school of Sismondi illustrated for the benefit of the English, from whom indeed it borrowed the greater part of its facts, the disastrous consequences of the vaunted principle of competition, a kind of maleficent god upon whose altars innumerable human victims were sacrificed. Morality and religion were deeply moved by the documented account of the cruelties and legalized crimes taking place in the factories beneath the disguise of freedom of contract. A Christian Socialist movement sprang up, led by Charles Kingsley, to fight against the pretended Liberalism of the employers by means of books and propaganda and to help the working classes by works of charity and compassion.

To the doctrine of competition was opposed that of solidarity, collaboration, mutual help, whose highest and most comprehensive form was the State. Robert Owen had already set the example of a more humane conception of the relation between masters and men, and had elevated his attempts at associationism into universal laws for the relations between the members of the community. But as a factory owner he attempted in vain to arouse the humanitarian spirit and kindly interest of the other masters. His attempt was an isolated one; to become effectual, it ought to have been undertaken from below, by the spontaneous combination of the labourers. And in fact trade unionism and the co-operative movement throve vigorously after the rise of

the Liberal Party, and in spite of this rise; but the Conservatives, watching their rise with a friendly eye, favoured
their growth, and before long tried to draw them into the
orbit of their own party.

The echoes of this social movement were soon heard in
political life. Liberalism had fought the aristocracy in the
name of the general interest. But its actions showed itself
attached to its own interest alone; and in its worship of freedom it permitted the unopposed development of the industrial system to result in the formation of an impassable gulf
between masters and men. Here too the Conservatives oppor-
tunely realized the danger to political stability and security
that lay in this division between two classes, compelled to
live together and day by day accumulating grounds of
mutual hatred and envy. A young writer who was later to
lead the Conservative Party, Disraeli, expressed his uneasy
recognition of the menace hanging over the English people
in novels dealing with social questions. Beneath the apparent
national unity there were in reality two peoples, each foreign
and hostile to the other, with different customs, different
traditions, even different languages; how long would they
walk side by side before their latent enmity broke out? There
was only one remedy. The nation richest in wealth, morality,
and culture, must approach the other, understand it, and
unite with it. The Liberal motto ' trust the people ' became
with greater truth the watchword of the Conservatives.

In a distorted and eccentric form, but a form at once in-
cisive and impressive, the same new demands were set forth
by Thomas Carlyle. *Past and Present* dates from 1843; but
it already sketches the main features of the two historical
periods that followed. The period that was drawing to a
close believed in the gospel of dilettantism—it was the age of
privilege and aristocratic idleness; the new age believed in
the gospel of mammonism—it was the age of brutal and
rapacious money-making. The new age was certainly better
than the old. ' Thank heaven that there is even a Mammonism, anything we are in earnest about ! Idleness is worst,
idleness alone is without hope : work earnestly at anything,

you will by degrees learn to work at almost all things. There is endless hope in work, were it even work at making money.'[1]

But profit is not everything ; it is not even all profit. ' Men ask on free-trade platforms, how can the indomitable spirit of Englishmen be kept up without plenty of bacon? We shall become a ruined nation !—Surely, my friends, plenty of bacon is good and indispensable : but, I doubt, you will never get even bacon by aiming only at that.'[2]

There is an inhuman profit which dries up others' sources of profit and draws its wealth from others' misery. Such is the profit of the landlords' protectionism, which lays up for itself a store of indignation in the heart of every just Englishman. But such is also the profit of the greedy manufacturers, who defraud the working class of ' a fair day's wages for a fair day's work '.[3] We look calmly on at the valiant sons of toil, who have conquered everything for us, herded and deadened by the million in their bastilles created by the Poor Law, as if the Poor Law were a law of nature ; and we repeat the various formulae *laissez faire*, supply and demand, exchange, as if there were not in reality a God of labour, as if divine labour and brutish mammonism were identical !

No, this is not freedom ; it is at least not the whole of freedom. The right of each one of us to resist oppression at our brother's hands, indispensable though it is, is one of the most insignificant fragments of human freedom. A new definition of this is still to seek.

Carlyle is a Conservative, like John Bull, like all (as he himself says) who are conscious that they belong to a great nation. His conception of the State is derived from German romanticism and from Burke. He sees in the rehabilitation of labour the means of consolidating national unity, and in opposition to a narrow utilitarianism a polemical motive necessary for leading the national consciousness towards a higher goal of imperial civilization and culture. Great honour, says he, to him whose epic is a melodious *Iliad* in hexameters : but greater honour to him whose epic is an

[1] [Carlyle, *Past and Present*, iii, ch. ii, ed. 1, p. 198.]
[2] [*Ibid*. iii, ch. iv, p. 208.]   [3] [*Ibid*. i, ch. i ; iii, ch. xii.]

empire slowly formed, a mighty series of heroic actions, a great victory over chaos. The indifference of Liberals towards the Empire is a grave injustice towards history, towards the real greatness of John Bull. The Empire is the State as a mission ; it is the great theatre for the doing of duty, as Fichte had foretold.

But the conception of this empire in the minds of Carlyle and his Conservative followers is far from illiberal. The epic written by John Bull in gigantic letters on the face of our planet was made up of roads, railways, canals, embankments, factories, in a word all the industrious labour of that middle class that had summarized and symbolized its efforts in the one word ' freedom ' ; which had made distant colonies into new nations and bound them together in a common Liberal bond. Liberalism was an integral part of the Empire ; this express recognition was to be made by the Conservative Disraeli in his famous programme of 1872 ; but Liberalism as absorbed into a Conservative point of view was to be understood merely as a means, a path, a discipline, in the service of a higher end, Empire.

From 1850 to 1870 the Conservative party worked to reorganize itself on this new basis. Disraeli's intention was to create a popular and democratic Toryism, rejecting all relics of the old aristocratic régime, and by taking the working class under its patronage strengthening the fabric of the State to turn its now concentrated forces to the realization of a vast imperial design. The reluctance of Liberalism to grant the petition of the trade unions and embark upon the path of labour-legislation was cleverly exploited by the Tories, who succeeded in gaining for some time the confidence of the working class and profiting by the second electoral reform of 1867 to defeat Gladstone's cabinet in 1874 and come into power.

But a democratic Toryism is only an attenuated Caesarism without a Caesar or a Napoleon; aggravated by the presence of the unchanged aristocratic outlook beneath the mask of democracy, and threatened by the menace of a Liberalism defeated for the moment but quick to rally its forces. If

Disraeli, *homo novus* and converted Jew, could dream of a Radical Toryism, the born aristocracy was incapable of following his lead; in social legislation it saw only a means of revenge upon the captains of industry, not a fertile principle for the reconstruction of its political system; and its gesture of sympathy towards the working class can only be understood as an attempt to lessen a gulf too wide to be crossed, and at best a mere act of benevolence or protection, devoid of any sincerely democratic spirit, and capable only of inspiring the policy of a condescending paternalism.

Nevertheless, the Conservative attempt to capture the working class, which did not form a party of its own till the closing years of the nineteenth century, was significant and was soon to be imitated by the Liberals. Even if one cannot acquit it of demagogism, its positive results—progressive extension of the franchise, increase of State interference, improvement of the economic, social, and political condition of the proletariate—transcend the intentions of its authors, hasten the democratization of English public life, and enrich with new demands and new problems the two parties that still hold the field.

§ 6. THE DEVELOPMENT OF LIBERALISM

The changed attitude of the Conservative opposition soon produced its effect upon Liberalism itself. The beginning of an internal crisis may be seen even in the generation of Cobden. The Manchester School, his contemporaries, were not all bitterly hostile to social legislation. The economists began to reckon up the economic advantages which might accrue to production from a higher standard of working-class life. And if many manufacturers continued to emphasize the danger which high cost of production might cause to the supremacy of English industries, Macaulay turned against them in a remarkable passage, in which he declared that a supremacy purchased by the wretchedness of the people did not deserve to be maintained. ' If we must yield the first place among manufacturing nations ', he adds, ' we shall yield it not to a race of degenerate beings but to

a people stronger than ourselves in body and mind.' At the
same time the idea grew up that associations of workmen, far
from representing a spirit of monopoly and tyranny, as
Cobden maintained, had a doubly Liberal character, because
of the spontaneous and free formation of such bodies by the
workmen themselves, and because of their purpose of equalizing the conditions of masters and men and thus permitting
competition on equal terms. With the recognition of the
right of association, Liberal individualism emerges from its
first anarchical and atomistic phase and enters upon a more
organic phase; in this way it came to support the development of industry which by now was concentrating businesses
originally isolated and scattered, so that both capital and
labour were now concentrating and combining their forces.

The work of the State, too, now begins to appear as something more than merely negative and barren. If the State can
restrict the freedom of employers by factory legislation, it can
also extend it, by a commercial policy opening new markets
to trade and permitting an outlet for a production now no
longer regulated by supply but anticipating it, soliciting it,
and claiming to regulate it.

The Manchester School's hostility to the State expressed
the needs of an industry as yet little developed, for which
competition was a purely internal and domestic phenomenon. Large-scale industry creates an international competition carried on not by isolated manufacturers but by
States as expressing and furthering the productivity of whole
nations. It was in fact as representative of the British State
that Richard Cobden in 1860 negotiated a famous commercial treaty with France. But in other ways also the democratic attitude, with its policy of State intervention, made
itself felt within Liberalism. Education could not be left at
the mercy of private individuals; great public works, banks,
shipping companies, railways, all the businesses which fulfil
the functions of public services, must be either carried on, or
at least directed, controlled, and promoted, by the State.
Even private property was not a matter of indifference to the
community. The Manchester School had contented itself

with abolishing agricultural protection, and had left the feudal privileges of the aristocracy untouched. But with the progress of industrialism the necessity of feeding an urban population of ever-increasing density forced itself progressively upon the attention of the new governing class. The landed aristocracy washed its hands of the problem; it did not hold itself to blame if, now that the culture of cereals no longer paid, owing to the abolition of the Corn Laws and the entry of foreign wheat, it was compelled to leave the land uncultivated or convert it into pasture, parks, and sporting estates. In the eyes of its opponents, however, it was guilty of the one cardinal crime of holding a monopoly of land, a thing repugnant to the new Liberal and democratic principles.

At the end of his life, Cobden confessed that he had never been enough of a Radical in his conduct of the struggle against the landowners. Had he been younger, said he, he would have taken his Adam Smith in his hand and undertaken to preach free trade in land; in other words, the full emancipation of landed property from the bondage of aristocracy and feudalism.

But what Cobden could no longer do, his followers did. Some pushed their Radicalism to the point of proposing to confiscate rent and nationalize land; others, more moderate, tried to increase the prosperity and independence of the farmer and encourage the labourers to take up small holdings of arable land. Gladstone attempted to put the two more moderate proposals into practice, the first in connexion with the Irish peasantry, the second by adopting it into his electoral programme of 1885. But even a redistribution of this kind demanded further powers of intervention on the part of the State.

This tendency toward the democratization of Liberalism is documented in an important manner by the works of John Stuart Mill. The son of James Mill, and trained rigidly in the school of Bentham and his followers, he soon became aware of his teachers' limitations. His friendship with Maurice and Sterling, the followers of Coleridge, and later with Carlyle, the study of De Tocqueville and the influence of Saint-

Simon, by degrees enlarged his mental horizon until his original and tenacious individualism absorbed into itself the ideals of democracy and Socialism.[1] But attracted though he was by the new social outlook, his horror of despotism made him alive to the dangers attaching no less to democratic and socialist government than to the old absolute monarchy.

Under a despotic government, the nation as a whole and the individuals composing it have no influence upon their own destinies. A will not their own, which they cannot without committing a crime disobey, decides everything for them. What kind of human beings can grow up under such a system? That a man should have no duty toward his own country is a sufficient reason for his losing interest in it altogether: under a despotism there can at most be one patriot, the despot himself. All the other best energies are compelled to divert their activity from the public interest and devote themselves to private cares, luxury, and the embellishment of life; but this means that the hour of decay has struck for the people as a whole; a sluggish and static tranquillity replaces the unrest and vital motion characteristic of the reign of liberty. Now of the two kinds of men which represent these opposed systems, the passive and the active, we are inclined to sympathize with the first: we may admire energetic characters, but peaceful and subservient characters are preferred by the majority of people. Yet all progress in human affairs is the work of the active, restless, and discontented characters. The forces which improve human life are those which fight against natural tendencies, not those which give way to them; individuality is the triumph of mind over nature and therefore the source of all progress.

Individuality means freedom. The value of Liberalism is that under its rule government cannot set aside the spirit of the individual and improve his conditions without improving himself. If it were possible for a people to be well governed in spite of itself, this government would only last so long as the independence of a people lasts when it is due wholly to the arms of foreigners. Evil for evil, a good despotism, in

[1] Cf. Mill's *Autobiography*.

a country at all advanced in civilization, is more noxious than a bad one; for it is far more relaxing and enervating to the thoughts, feelings, and energies of individuals.[1]

Now the political condition most favourable to the formation of active and energetic individualities is that provided by democratic governments. Here there may be as many independent centres of progress as there are individuals; and here man learns to feel himself part of the public and to identify the common interest with his own. But democracy presents two kinds of dangers, which only a watchful liberal attitude can effectively counteract. The first is a political danger, and consists of the fact that the citizens as a whole may be oppressed by the tyranny of a majority, often a fictitious majority, swayed by the interests of a class or, worse, of a few demagogues. Against this danger Liberalism must put forward all the defences contained in representative and parliamentary government. Above all, it must restrain the action of the universal suffrage of the democracy by means of the proportional system expounded by Hare, which assures to the minority a representation and a voice in affairs. It is also necessary to set up a second chamber, not hereditary and privileged like the Lords, but formed of the best technical and intellectual minds, as a counterpoise to the lower elective House. Finally, an important function belongs to local sub-parliaments for deciding questions of local importance and fostering the political abilities of the governing class.[2]

Less obvious and more insidious is the tyranny of Society itself, whose weapons are not political laws, but traditions, customs, routine, and public opinion. It was a prejudice of the early democrats that when the governing class was identical with the people, and its interest one with the interest of the nation, individuals would have no further need of protection, because no one need fear to be oppressed by himself.

[1] Mill, *Representative Government*, Fr. tr., Paris, 1862, 2 vols., i. 51–82 [ed. Everyman, pp. 202–7].

[2] *Op. cit.* ii. 155 *seqq.*, 206, 287, 325, &c. [ed. Everyman, pp. 256–75, 324 *seqq.*, 346 *seqq.*, &c.].

But phrases like these, we can now see, did not express the facts. The people which exercises power is not the same people over which power is exercised; what is called self-government is not the government of each by himself, but the government of each by every one else. Society has no need of political power and executive functions in order to become tyrannical; it has the means in education, religious conformity, associations, and newspapers. In other days the various ranks, trades, and professions lived each in a world by itself; to-day all live in the same world. Men read the same things, hear the same things, live in the same places, hope and fear the same objects; they have the same rights, the same liberties, and the same ways of asserting them. Thus democracy is always at work levelling men down and reducing them to an identical mediocrity, a kind of anonymous and collective tyranny which reduces every prominence, smooths away every angle, and stifles every living voice. This is the greatest danger for individuality and human progress, a danger which no legal safeguard and no economic foresight can counteract. There is no escape except within conscience itself, which demands the rights of personality and affirms them in the face of everything, and rebels against the tyranny of Society wherever the inviolable sphere of the self is concerned. Social slavery can only be opposed by moral freedom. But in order to determine this higher liberty, the empiricist Mill required a speculative gift which he did not possess. He remains standing upon its threshold, with nothing but a presentiment or promise of it; had he gone farther, he would perhaps have exchanged the substance, liberty, for the shadow, mere eccentricity.[1]

Another road towards a combination of Liberal and democratic ideas is followed by a thinker of the Hegelian school, Thomas Hill Green. His essay on *Freedom of Contract*, written in 1880, contains a frontal attack on the entire social problem, and is of capital importance for the development of English Liberalism.

[1] See Mill's book *On Liberty*; suggestive, but unsatisfactory; losing its inspiration as it proceeds, and finally ending on a note of dissatisfaction.

We are told, says Green, that the workman must be left to make his own terms in the contract of labour. If the law protects him, it destroys his freedom and degrades him; that is the position of the Liberals of Cobden's generation. But our times present us with new problems, which cannot be solved without interfering with the liberty of contract.

To the spirit of our fathers' love of liberty, says Green, we still adhere; but for that very reason we are compelled to depart from its letter. What is freedom? We do not understand it as a mere absence of restriction; still less do we think that one man may enjoy freedom at the expense of others. When we speak of freedom as something to be highly prized, we mean a positive power or capacity of doing or enjoying something worth doing or enjoying, which we do or enjoy in common with others. When we measure the progress of a society by its growth in freedom, we measure it by the increasing development of all those powers which constitute social well-being. But the mere removal of restrictions is not by itself a contribution to true freedom. In a sense no one is so free to do what he likes as the savage; yet we do not count him truly free, because his freedom is not strength but weakness; he is not the slave of man, but he is the slave of nature. Even in the ancient civilization to which we owe so much, the extraordinary efflorescence of the privileged class was accompanied and conditioned by the slavery of the multitude, and therefore the freedom of the ancients was short-lived because partial and exceptional.

If this is the true conception of freedom, not formal and negative but substantial, freedom of contract must be regarded as a means to this end. No one has any right to do what he likes with his own in such a way as to contravene freedom. He only owns his property because Society secures it to him, and this security is based upon a common interest which limits and controls the activities of individuals. Hence one man cannot be the property of another; and a contract by which one man undertakes to enslave himself to another is for us null and void. This is a limitation of freedom of contract which every one recognizes as just. But are there not contracts which amount to the same thing, less obviously indeed, but not less really? Let us consider contracts relating to labour. As the economists tell us, labour is a commodity that can be bought and sold like any other. In a sense that is true; but it is a commodity peculiarly bound up with human personality; and therefore Society is within its rights when it limits the freedom of contracts for the sale of labour. Similar considerations apply to education, health, and so forth. If it is contended that enlightened self-interest or individual benevolence, working in a system of unlimited freedom of contract, can fulfil these demands spontaneously, the answer is plain: left to itself, or to the operation of a casual benevolence, a population becomes more and more degraded. State intervention is therefore inevitable.[1]

Another problem attacked by Green is that of natural rights. Bentham had tried to deny their existence, and replace them by the principle of self-interest; but the jurists like Austin, who followed him, extracted once more from the formula of self-interest the idea of individual and primordial rights; and in the theory of Manchester Liberalism the antithesis between the individual and the State had finally come to express itself in the very terminology of eighteenth-century jusnaturalism. For Green, too, the idea of natural rights as representing the demands of spiritual autonomy in the face of State despotism has an indestructible substratum. But the naive idea of a right antecedent to Society, which is implied in the phrase natural right, is false; rights only arise within social life; and only between persons, in the ethical sense of the word, can there be legal relations. Natural rights may, however, be defended, regarded as ends inherent in Society itself, ideals whose realization is the work of social life. Such an idea does not contradict the modern doctrine, accepted by Green, of the ethical state; for its ethical character does not consist in its directly promoting or creating the good, but in its promoting the conditions of life in which morality is possible. Thus Green can accept Hegel's view of freedom as

[1] T. H. Green, 'Lecture on Liberal Legislation and the Freedom of Contract', in *Works*, iii. 365 *seqq.*

realizing itself in the State, with the qualification that the freedom of the individual is freedom only so far as it is recognized by the State.[1]

This conversion of Liberalism to a programme of State intervention did not take place without opposition in the name of the old Manchester spirit. What is the difference, asked Spencer in 1884, between Toryism and Liberalism? If the latter gives up the freedom of contract and voluntary co-operation, which differentiate it from the type of Society based on coercive military organization, it becomes a kind of Toryism. Indeed, it is far more dangerous than the old Tory system, because the new worship of the State by its democratic character implies a general slavery, not military but bureaucratic in character, in the interest not of a small class but of an anonymous abstraction. Granted the modern tendencies of Liberalism, its inevitable future is a socialistic slavery.

But to return is impossible. Is not even Bentham's Liberalism authoritarian and democratic and therefore illiberal? We have, however, a new means of restoring life to individualistic Liberalism : the Darwinian theory, which transfers to the world of biology, where no economic accidents can impair its working, the law of competition and natural selection.[2]

But does this law apply, asks an acute writer, Montague, in the spiritual world? Free competition may strengthen the strong, but it leaves the weak helpless ; and the weakest are not necessarily the worst ; indeed, in contrast to what happens in the world of nature, they do not disappear from the struggle, but continue to form a dead weight upon Society. Would it not be better to help them to raise themselves, instead of condemning them to a degradation harmful to the rest of Society? The doctrine of self-help, adds Montague, satisfies only our animal nature : hunger, lust, and vanity are strong enough to provide for their own satisfaction ; but

[1] T. H. Green, ' Lectures on the Principles of Political Obligation ', *Works*, ii. 6, 33, 39, 44, 47.

[2] Spencer, *The Man versus the State*, 1884, Fr. tr., pp. 1 *seqq.*, 25 *seqq.*, 102.

with social life the case is different. Here *laissez-faire* and the law of supply and demand are not enough. Men forget that the supply of anything good is proportionate not to our real need but to our consciousness of our need. The more ignorant a man is, the less he demands instruction. The less refined he is, the more he is satisfied with a vulgar existence. In the social world the principle of mutual aid and defence holds good ; Society consists of a judicious mixture of freedom and coercion ; Society is most free when it is organized for the attainment of the highest ends.

People speak of individuality, Montague adds, as if it were something existing by itself out of all relation to the life of Society. But on close observation can we say that a single feature, a single glance, a single word, a single thought of our own, is our own unaided creation? What is there in the individual that is really individual?

At bottom, individuality and universality are only two aspects of the same thing. What is the distinctive quality which renders a prominent person moral? A quality which leads him to egotistic self-assertion, or a quality which leads him to self-abnegation? Or a combination of the two? How far is it developed by freedom, and how far by discipline? Does it owe more to tradition or to criticism?

Experience shows that the strongest and most complete individuality appears in the most civilized and advanced Society. We hear, it is true, that as Society grows stronger the individual grows weaker, and men sink to a dead level of uniformity. It is truer to say that in a socialized life individuality does not cease to exist but withdraws into itself and becomes less visible. Beneath the varied and picturesque exterior of the Middle Ages, a keen eye might discover a widespread monotony. The peasant, the citizen, and the knight differed more in clothing and demeanour than in their inner life. Perhaps none of the three could read or had ever travelled. To-day men are more alike in externals ; but a metaphysician, a biologist, a poet, and an historian differ far more than the same number of ignorant men separated by rigid barriers of class. Nevertheless, it is true that we too are in danger of becoming machines, and the special source of our danger is our overwhelming interest in gain : the reason why we have so few really great men to-day is not that Society is too badly organized to leave individuals a sufficiency of freedom, but that Society is organized to make money, and disorganized for all other purposes.

This assertion of the value of Society, which Montague pushes to the point of condemning the Reformation for detaching the individual from the social world, is at the same time an assertion of the value of the State, to which he ascribes an educational function in the broadest sense of the word and a great part of the credit for the strong and well-differentiated individuality of its citizens.[1]

§ 7. CRISIS AND RECONSTRUCTION

The distinction between Liberalism and Toryism in the last decades of the nineteenth century, adhering as they did to a common policy of State intervention, was that, as Chamberlain put it, intervention for the Tories is an act of ' patronage ', while the Liberal principle is that ' all people shall be assisted to govern themselves '. In practice, the difference was often very slight ; and the underlying motive of the Liberal policy was ultimately overwhelmed by the flood of democracy.

This can be seen in the reconstruction of the Liberal Party after 1876, intended to adapt it to the new requirements of social organization and democratic ideas. While in the past the individualism of political and economic doctrines had been reflected in the autonomy of various electoral districts and units, it was now desired to emphasize the unity of the party by giving all candidates a common platform and all voters a common watchword. Chamberlain took the lead in reorganizing Liberalism on this basis ; and the formation which took its rise from him borrowed from the American

[1] F. C. Montague, *The Limits of Individual Liberty*, 1884 (Ital. tr. by Orlando, in Brunialti's *Bibl. di scienza polit.*, ser. i, vol. 5).

democrats the name of Caucus.[1] But what becomes of the freedom of the voter, if a central committee imposes its candidate upon him? ' Vote as you are told,' replies the Caucus in 1876 and subsequently.

This is not the only danger arising from the anti-Liberal tendencies of the new organization; the danger extends over the whole of modern life, as it now takes shape after transcending the individualistic phase of the early nineteenth century. It extends to industry, where the initiative of the individual employer goes down before the syndicate, the combine, and the trust; to finance, which frees itself from all connexion with merely national production and cherishes imperialistic ambitions; to the working class, which organizes itself and imposes upon itself a working-class mentality; to the diffusion of a uniform culture; to the ethical convictions of the new society, the gigantic increase in the importance of the State, the gradual penetration of every branch of public activity by the bureaucracy, and even the government of the Liberal Party itself, whose active Liberalism is blunted by the habitual exercise of administrative power.

It is not every year that a Mill or a Green arises, able to revive that consciousness of oppositions and antitheses which practical life deadens and blunts. The average mind regarded the mutual concessions of Conservatism and Liberalism, and the conservative practice of government, as symptoms that the two parties were coming together and that their conflict was drawing to a close. In the midst of Gladstone and Disraeli's oratorical duels, public opinion began to believe that the violent opposition between the two parties had had its day and that it was now watching not a bombardment but a display of fireworks. Gladstone, dominating the political stage all through the second half of the nineteenth century, in vain became more and more Radical; the years of his most emphatic Liberalism, from 1876 to 1885, were the years in which his influence declined. At last he was overwhelmed by his great Irish campaign, which was

[1] Cf. the important work of Ostrogorski, *La Démocratie et la formation des partis politiques*, 2 vols., Paris, 1903.

intended to bring about a revival of the Liberal Party and in fact marked the gravest crisis in its history.

The man who provoked this crisis and aggravated it by his very prestige was a Radical : the Liberal exponent of social democracy, Chamberlain, whom we have seen organizing the Caucus. His political conversion is the clearest proof of the democratic peril pointed by Mill and Spencer.

Down to 1885 he was one of the most influential and extreme members of the Liberal Party. In the election of that year he went beyond the programme laid down in the party manifesto and drew up an unauthorized programme of his own, demanding among other things the freedom of land and the complete separation of Church and State. He was elected and included in Gladstone's Cabinet ; but three months later he refused to accept the Home Rule policy, resigned, and split the party.

In reality the Home Rule question was a mere pretext, or at least a mere opportunity. The change that had taken place in his mind went deeper, and arose from a democratic outlook out of sympathy with the compromises and perplexities that hampered Liberalism in its movement towards State concentration and a social policy. To such a mind, Gladstone's Home Rule could only appear a fruitless dissipation of political energy, directing it away from the goal upon which, as laid down in his own programme, it ought to be concentrated.

His alliance with the Conservatives, however paradoxical it might appear, was the logical consequence of this change of front. Lord Salisbury accepted his plan of social legislation, in which, like an able Conservative, he saw a useful means for the consolidation of the State and of his party, and in exchange asked Chamberlain to give up his religious and agricultural proposals. It would be enough to give the people small allotments of land, the famous ' three acres and a cow ' ; a trivial sacrifice for the great landowners, and perhaps a means to a subtler and less obvious exploitation— ' dwarf exploitation ', as it was clearly described by an economist at a later date.

Thus the Conservative Party and the friends and followers

of Chamberlain together formed a new party known as the Unionist Party, which, profiting by the public hostility towards Home Rule, a measure for which public opinion was not yet ripe, succeeded in wresting the power from Gladstone and the Liberals.

But State unionism was for Chamberlain only the starting-point of a larger and more ambitious scheme which matured in his mind during the Boer War. This was imperialism : the conception of a national State, broadened and concentrated by a great accession of democratic energy, as the centre and support of a vast network of states.

But even imperialism contained liberal elements. Freedom and self-government were the traditional bonds between the colonies and the mother country. Neither Disraeli nor Chamberlain nor any other imperialist ever tried to deny this fact; indeed Chamberlain himself, at the end of the Boer War, favoured the grant of autonomy to the new Dominion and lived to see its success. But if the feelings and rights of individuals, whether men or peoples, must be respected, their interests are inseparable; and the colonies themselves, of their own accord, demanded more and more emphatically the protection of imperial interests, that is, the abandonment of free trade and the adoption of tariffs providing full economic reciprocity for all members of the Commonwealth, to the exclusion of foreign nations, which were to be separated from the Empire by a wall of protective tariffs. Imperial preference and protection were Chamberlain's watchwords in the struggle which, like the Manchester School, but with the opposite aim, he carried on during the three years following the conclusion of peace with the Transvaal, and whose conclusion was cut short by his death.[1]

This struggle culminated in the two electoral campaigns in 1906 and 1923, in both of which the Liberals entered the

---

[1] Space forbids us to discuss the details of the imperialistic doctrines. The reader may consult Chamberlain's *Speeches*, 2 vols., London, 1914; Schulze Gaevernitz, *Britischer Imperialismus*, and my own works : *L'Impero britannico dopo la guerra* (Florence, Vallecchi, 1921), and *La formazione dell' Impero britannico* (Brescia, 1925).

lists to defend their traditional free-trade policy and won decisive victories. But during this period the political situation was profoundly changed by the intervention of a third element, the Labour Party, which, founded in 1891, made rapid progress in uniting under its banner the working class and part of the lower middle class, and thus disturbed the normal balance of the two existing parties.

In its origin the Labour Party shows many traces of the environment in which it grew up. It falls into two conflicting elements : a Fabian element, democratic, advocating State interference, and a guild element more definitely liberal in character, basing itself upon the autonomous and decentralized action of the trade unions, and opposing the State, in whose patronage of social interests it sees a danger for the working class very like that already pointed out by Cobden— the danger of parasitism, of trusting to others instead of to oneself, and thus suffering a loss of vital energy. Both elements are influenced by the analogous currents of continental Socialism, the social democracy of Germany and the libertarian syndicalism of France ; influences whose value lies in the fact that they give the new party an opportunity of emerging from its isolation and taking part in the general movement which is uniting England to the continent.

In the struggle against imperialism the Labour Party joined hands with the Liberals, thereby showing that their internal differences do not obscure their common industrial origin and their attachment to the system of free trade which created the greatness of English industry. By this alliance the Liberal Party lost its position of sole opponent to imperialism ; but it gained by the reconciliation of the mass of its own members to the new social policy laid down by Mill, Green, and Arnold Toynbee. At the same time it created the need for a more accurate definition of its own political principles, in order to differentiate it not only from the Conservatives but also from the Labour Party.

The best formulation of the new English Liberalism of the twentieth century is in our opinion that of Hobhouse. Here we find the teaching of Mill and Green in a modernized form.

Freedom is based upon the idea of growth and development. The individual is what he makes himself; he makes himself by assimilating his environment, and assimilates in proportion as he affirms himself by reacting to it. Liberalism is the belief that Society can be constructed upon this self-directive power of personality; and that in virtue of this power there are no limits to the extension of this construction. Liberty thus becomes not so much an individual right as a social necessity. It rests not upon A's right to be left alone by B, but on B's duty to treat A as a rational being. It is not the right of crime and error to go unmolested; it is the duty of treating the criminal and the erring or ignorant man as beings capable of justice and truth, and raising them up instead of letting them lie. Based upon personality, it demands free scope for the personal development of every member of the community. It is not enough to proclaim in its name equal rights in the eyes of the law; it demands also equality of opportunity, the *égalité de chance* of the French democrats.

Coercion is the destruction of a growing personality; for personality is shaped not from without but from within, and the function of the external order is not to create it but to provide the best conditions for its development. Progress is not a mechanical process but the liberation of living spiritual energy.

This implies that the function of the Liberal State is not to oppose the freedom of personality, but to realize it in practice. The State does not supply its members with food or other material commodities; it supplies the normal man, healthy in mind and in body, with the opportunity to provide for himself by useful work. The right to work and the right to a living wage are as real as the right to person and property. The labouring man who is unemployed or underpaid owing to bad economic organization is a reproach not to the charity but to the justice of Society.

This, it may be said, is not Liberalism but Socialism. But Socialism is a word with many meanings; and there may be a liberal Socialism, as there certainly is an illiberal.

There is a mechanical form of Socialism, with which Liberalism can have nothing to do. It attributes the phenomena of social life to the sole operation of economic factors, and in politics declares a class warfare based upon a rigid distinction between classes which is wholly non-existent. Modern Society, far from emphasizing and simplifying distinctions, is bringing about an increasingly complex interaction of class interests; a modern revolutionary cannot attack property in the interest of labour without finding that labour has an interest, direct or indirect, in property.

Against any authoritarian tendency in Socialism, against any scheme of life imposed from without, the liberal mind rises in revolt in the interest at once of the individual and of Society. It is determined to do justice to the individual and social factors in production, against the abstract individualism and the abstract Socialism which accentuate this or that element to the exclusion of the other. It conceives the rights of the individual as harmonious with those of the community, and defines the former in terms of a common good and the latter in terms of the well-being of individuals. Thus the growing co-operation between Liberalism and Labour, which has lately replaced the antagonism of the nineties, is not an accident or an expression of political opportunism, but is deeply rooted in the necessities of the new democracy.[1]

By 1906 English Liberalism had survived the crisis of Unionism; to-day it is in process of overcoming the graver crisis of war-time coalitionism, which beneath a mask of political neutrality concealed an actual prevalence of Conservative forces and authoritarian and Protectionist tendencies. The fact that in spite of its richly democratic and social content the party continues to use the name of Liberal shows that the emphasis in the English political point of view lies still upon liberty rather than upon equality. Thus all the changes brought about by a hundred years of history have not overthrown the traditional relation between the two terms by which the Englishmen of past generations distinguished themselves as lovers of liberty from the French as lovers of equality.[2]

[1] For a further account of the contemporary movement of English politics see my volume, *L'Impero britannico dopo la guerra* (Vallecchi, 1921).

[2] Hobhouse, *Liberalism*, in the Home University Library, N.D.

II

FRENCH LIBERALISM[1]

§ 1. CONSTITUTIONALISM

THE Bourbon restoration in France after the Empire of Napoleon did not imply a return to the régime of the years preceding 1789; politically it marked a progress not only upon the *ancien régime* but also upon the intervening Caesarism. Of all the restored monarchs, Louis XVIII was the one least influenced by the legitimistic and romantic outlook of the period, whose scepticism and common sense had most completely saved him from the dream of a revived medievalism.

The French preserved all the civil gains of the Revolution, sanctioned by the *Code Napoléon*. Individual and anti-feudal property continued to form the basis of economic society; the administrative centralization which, in spite of changes in political externals, had continued to develop ever since the time of Richelieu proceeded unchecked; and the Concordat of 1801 was preserved. In spite of the apparent restoration of the ancient noble dignities, the real governing class was the *bourgeoisie*, essentially a landed class but enriched from time to time with manufacturing and commercial elements as the industrial revolution, later and slower than the corresponding revolution in England, began to do its work.

Not only were civil liberties consolidated by the recognition given them by the new régime, renouncing as it did all attempt to reinstate the *émigrés* and the Church, at the expense of the landed proprietors created by the Revolution; but the political liberty which had been sought in vain during the Napoleonic period was granted by a constitutional charter guaranteeing the citizens their rights, and associating

[1] Belgian Liberalism will be discussed in the course of the present chapter, on account of its similarity of outlook and historical and political association with that of France.

them in a limited manner with the work of government. This charter satisfied the aspirations of the upper middle classes. It created two chambers, on which it bestowed the right to vote taxes and to collaborate in legislation, the initiative in the latter resting with the Crown. It made the vote a privilege of the propertied classes; the entire electoral body was composed of not more than a hundred thousand individuals, and the persons eligible for election did not reach one-fifth of that number, their property qualification being rated at a higher figure. Moderate opinion felt itself well protected by these restrictions against any attacks of a demagogic and revolutionary character. Indeed a Liberal, Benjamin Constant, was in favour of a stricter limitation, demanding as an essential condition of the suffrage not a property qualification, however large, but the payment of the tax on landed property, explicitly excluding the tax on personal property, as not providing the indispensable guarantee of stability and security required for the fulfilment of public functions.[1]

The charter of 1814 was sharply differentiated from the constitutions of the Revolutionary period by the fact that it was not based upon popular sovereignty, and was not a compact between equal and free individuals, but was an act of one-sided concession from a monarch to his subjects, implying that sovereignty belonged exclusively to the former. The charter of Louis XVIII begins with the express declaration that ' whereas all authority in France resides in the person of the king . . . we have of our own free will and in the free exercise of our royal power granted and do hereby grant the Charter of the Constitution'. Formally this was a reaction, even relatively to the medieval constitutions, which sanctioned a two-sided compact between the monarch and the people, thus recognizing on both sides an equally original right.

A second legal difference between the revolutionary constitutions and that of 1814 [2] consists in the fact that the latter

[1] Later Constant recanted, and advocated the concession of political rights to the industrial class.

[2] It was conceded after the first return of Louis XVIII to France.

speaks not of the rights of man in general but of the rights of Frenchmen in particular; this follows from the principle of the sovereignty of the monarch, for within the limits of his own realm any monarch may issue whatever ordinances he thinks best.

This identification of the monarch and the sovereign acted as a stimulant to Liberal political thought; for if the constitution, and with it all political guarantees, depended exclusively on the king, the king had the right of revoking it; or at any rate the possibility of its being revoked depended upon his conscience alone. The apprehensions of the Constitutionalists became graver as the abstract possibility threatened to become a reality under the increasing pressure of the reactionaries and with the succession to the throne of their leader, the former Comte d'Artois. On this point even the writers of moderate opinion, the so-called doctrinaires, Royer-Collard, De Broglie, and so forth, felt it necessary to dissent from the principles expressed in the charter. For Royer-Collard, a follower of Cousin, who had borrowed from his master's vague eclecticism the idea of a *raison universelle*, sovereignty belonged to this ' reason ', which resided in a sphere superior to the conflicting interests of individuals. This abstract reason of eclecticism took colour and shape in its political application from the fact that the *bourgeoisie*, which regarded itself as the depository of enlightenment, seemed destined to personify it. But if the sovereignty of reason was that which is manifested in the laws voted in parliament by the new privileged class, was it not the same thing as popular sovereignty, understanding by ' popular ' belonging to the ' legal people '?

This urgent question was put to Royer-Collard; but, as a later revolutionary pointed out, he omitted to answer it. Perhaps he thought that the logical interpretation of the sovereignty of reason would have led him to Rousseau's ' general will ', and that any democratic extension of the franchise might have been justified by the appeal to reason, however perilous it might be to right-thinking persons.

The reply was given by Constant, with great caution, in

his *Cours de politique constitutionnelle*, where he explains why in his earlier work *Principes de politique* he had shown himself hostile to the principle of popular sovereignty. It was at that time a dangerous weapon in the hands of Napoleon, who used it to justify his excessive power by the pretext that it had been delegated to him by the people. It was necessary therefore to attack popular sovereignty in order to combat a man who had abused it. At the Restoration the opposite motive came into play.

' None the less,' Constant remarked, ' one must not build upon an abstract idea, in the illusion that it can increase the sum of individual liberty; still less ascribe to it an unlimited applicability. The citizen body is sovereign in the sense that no individual, no faction, no association can arrogate to itself a sovereignty not delegated to it by the people. But there is a part of human life which necessarily remains individual and independent, and has the right to stand outside all social control. Where the independent life of the individual begins, the jurisdiction of the sovereign ends. Rousseau failed to see this elementary truth, and the result of his error is that the *Contrat social*, so often invoked in favour of liberty, is the most formidable ally of all despotisms.' [1]

The individual's true safeguard lies not in the recognition of popular sovereignty but rather in the limitation of its extent; and in the last resort on political guarantees against the sovereign, whether monarch or people. This is a return to the guarantism of the eighteenth century, the doctrine of Montesquieu brought up to date by the experience of 1789 and a deeper historical understanding of the English system.

Constant has the merit, as he himself complacently tells us, of discovering the key to the English parliamentary system, which consists in the separation of the royal power from the executive or ministerial power, the former irresponsible, the second charged with responsibility. Fifteen years later, in 1830, Thiers in a famous article was to express this

[1] D. Constant, *Cours de politique constitutionnelle*, Bruxelles, 1839, pp. 64 *seqq.*

principle in the formula : ' The king reigns but does not govern.' Its value lies in the fact that it leads to the separation of the various powers of the State in Montesquieu's sense of the phrase without impairing the unity of power. The monarchy forms precisely that neutral and superior unity (the expression is Constant's) from which proceed and into which return the various branches of public activity ; the system of checks and balances here finds its principle of harmony. Further, it offers a means of satisfying the demands of public opinion without overthrowing the government ; because the irresponsibility of the king, united with the responsibility of the ministry, permits any required change in public policy and indeed makes the king himself the author of such change.

The principle of ministerial responsibility destroyed the barrier which in the time of the Constituent Assembly had been erected against the entry of ministers into an elective assembly. They were now no longer mere functionaries of the Crown, and hence they did not represent an interest that might conflict with that of the people. The example of England demonstrated the point : here the opponents of the ministry saw in its power their own future position of authority.

As a further corollary of the same principle, the idea grew up that the ministry formed a single unity responsible as a whole for its corporate policy. This is the so-called Cabinet system, which is closely connected with a division of political parties, each putting forward its own distinct programme of government.

The most serious difficulties encountered by this complex system, so familiar to us to-day, were due to a continental people's lack of experience of the normal functioning of a party system. The French Revolution possessed in its clubs the embryo of political parties ; but their party conflict was carried on chiefly by means of the guillotine. Napoleon, whose Caesarism was based on the principle of the plebiscite, wanted no parties ; in his opinion, all Frenchmen ought to agree in loving their country and his government. The

memory of the Revolution and the levelling tendency of the
Empire tended to obscure the idea of party to such an extent
that many liberals of the Restoration declared themselves
hostile to parties as such. But new parties arose of their own
accord, through differences of outlook and interest that could
not be suppressed : reactionaries, moderates, and independents grouped themselves according to their similarities of
outlook and engaged in fierce mutual conflict. Thus the facts
proved that parties still existed, even though they might be
an evil; an avoidable evil according to the optimists, a
necessary evil according to the pessimists.

In order to understand the positive value of political
parties, the example of England is not enough ; there is also
required a religious experience which a Catholic people does
not possess, the experience of religious sects. If Constant
came nearer than any of his contemporaries to understanding
the party system, it was perhaps because he came of a Protestant family. That this was the source of his conception of
religious freedom is clear. The multiplication of sects he describes as a benefit which governments are wrong to ignore ;
their very number balances them and produces an equilibrium such that the sovereign need not treat with any.
Under a system of religious freedom, every new congregation
would attempt to prove the soundness of its doctrine by the
purity of its life and the skill of its propaganda ; the result
would be a beneficial conflict in which the victory would
belong to the most austere morality.

Now parties are nothing but religious sects, upon which
only religious experience can bestow that aspect of universality, that attachment to the common welfare, which com-
pensates and counteracts their original particularism. A
party is a particular way of looking at the whole, an individual conception of the common government : precisely as
a religious sect is a special way of worshipping the one God.
Now in Catholic countries there may be isolated and
emancipated individuals capable of understanding this
principle ; but the mass of the population will never be able
fully to grasp it ; and the parties will be forced to oscillate

between the two opposite poles of a narrow egotism and an undifferentiated universalism, unable to attain a point of stable equilibrium.

So closely are the various parts of the parliamentary system interrelated that if the function of party is ignored the political unity of the Cabinet and the right of parliament to demand its appointment must fall to the ground. For Royer Collard and the moderate doctrinaires, the ministry depends upon the king, and the right of appointing it is an exclusive prerogative of the Crown. Here we find in an embryonic form the two political systems known later as the parliamentary and the constitutional systems, the latter placing the centre of sovereignty in the king, the former in the parliament.

This first and most discussed type of political guarantee was followed by many others no less important, expounded in the period succeeding the Restoration by a throng of writers, Constant, Daunou, Tracy, Guizot, and Royer-Collard. At bottom they all say the same thing; and we shall state their views in a generalized and impersonal form.

There is another type of guarantee derived from the division of powers. The legislative alone has the right to legislate; citizens are not obliged to obey any laws but those constitutionally promulgated. This principle is in practice sanctioned by the independence of the judiciary, which is much easier to assert than to vindicate in a country like France with its tradition of centralization and bureaucracy, after a revolution which has fused all powers into one and left the individual defenceless against the public functionary. The Liberal writers of the Restoration go so far as to lament the abolition of the sale of offices, which had in addition to its many defects the great merit of rendering the magistrate as independent in relation to his office as a landed proprietor in relation to his estate, since no one could dismiss him. But since they could not put back the clock, they tried to gain their point by proposing that magistrates be not subject to dismissal, and that the magistracy should be distinguished in this way from the rest of the bureaucracy; and further, that the jury system be adopted not only in the case of serious offences, but in all cases closely concerned with the statutory liberties of the individual.

Another fundamental guarantee is the freedom of the press, not only as a corollary of the freedom of thought and speech, but also as a public or political liberty connected with the work of the press as mediator and interpreter between the public conscience and the established powers. Offences committed by the press can be dealt with by the common law, which is equally capable of protecting the individual and the government. Every restriction upon the freedom of the press injures those whom it is meant to help; the government becomes responsible in spite of itself for everything printed in the papers; every journalistic indiscretion may be attributed to the government and may compel it to excuse itself in terms which may appear a confession of the fault. Censorship of the press thus produces the serious result that it leads to the attachment of more importance to false statements contained in the newspapers than to truths. Besides, when there is no means of communicating with the public, every one is exposed defenceless to secret attacks prompted by hatred and envy. The statesman loses his honour, the merchant his credit, the private citizen his reputation, without being able to discover and unmask his enemies. Nor is it prudent to adopt the compromise—parallel to the religious toleration of a Catholic country—of having a government press and also tolerating an independent press; the result of this is the exact opposite of what is desired, for a government press commands as little credit as a censored press, while the independent newspapers probably command more credit than they deserve. It is better to trust in the example of England, where even ministers in office, when they communicate with the public or engage in controversy through the newspapers, write to the free press as private citizens and state their case. Liberty is thus an essential condition of veracity.

Another guarantee against despotism is provided by the independence of provincial and communal bodies. Local interests contain in themselves the seeds of resistance to authority, which can crush isolated individuals more easily than such groups. Patriotism, moreover, cannot exist without an active attachment to local interests, a fact disastrously forgotten by those patriots who have declared war on local interests and dried up the main source of patriotism by attempting to inculcate a fictitious passion for an abstract entity, a general idea robbed of everything that appeals to the imagination and speaks to the memory. Finally, it is in conformity with a rational division of labour that general affairs should be treated by the community, while that which concerns a part should be decided by that part.

Public administration, then, must be modified by introducing into it an element of federalism, understood not as a dismemberment of the State's sovereignty, nor yet as a mere administrative and bureaucratic decentralization, but as something between the two, something like the English local self-government, the delegation of certain governmental functions to local elective bodies.

But here too there were grave difficulties. What had become of the provinces? The departmental spirit had so far stifled them that only two or three still preserved their original individuality. What had become of the communes, and where were the ancient aristocratic bodies that might form the nucleus of local administration? The Liberal writers, in contrast with their revolutionary predecessors, began to recognize the immense gaps which impeded or delayed the application of the English constitutional system to the soil of France. They did not give up all hope that the new structure of property might gradually provide substitutes for the vanished aristocratic bodies; for this very reason they insist the more upon the importance of making electoral rights, not only political but administrative also, depend upon a property qualification. Only thus was it possible to create unpaid public offices whose holders should be economically independent in the face of government pressure and able to resist the expansion of bureaucracy.

One of the guarantees contemplated by the *Declaration* of 1791 was the right of resistance to oppression; a right much discussed from various angles, and expressing itself in the course of time by the organization of a National Guard to defend the rights of the individual and render unnecessary all isolated or violent forms of resistance. The Liberal writers of the Restoration see in this National Guard an important political guarantee, clearly distinguished from the army, the organ of external defence, and the gendarmerie, whose functions are merely those of a police force. The coexistence of the army and the National Guard may seem strange if we reflect that after the Napoleonic period the recruitment of the army was precisely national; but it must be remembered that after the fall of the Empire the spirit of the army excited a good deal of apprehension and distrust, and that, depending as it did on the king, it might be used by him to violate the Constitution. This justified the existence of a special National Guard recruited from the *bourgeoisie* and intended, in conformity with the *bourgeois* spirit which animated and controlled it, to resist every kind of absolutism, from above or from below, on the part of the Crown or on the part of the mob.

These political guarantees together served to safeguard the individual rights already enumerated : security of person and family, religious freedom, freedom of industry, security of property, and so forth. They go to make up that political freedom which was contrasted with the other kind of political freedom at whose establishment the Revolutionary democrats aimed : freedom in the ancient sense, the liberty of participation in the government. Constant gives us the formula of this opposition in his celebrated essay on *Ancient and Modern Liberty*.[1]

What is modern liberty?

' Liberty is every man's right to be subject to the law alone, the right of not being arrested, tried, put to death, or in any way molested, by the caprice of one or more individuals. It is every one's right to express his own opinion, to attend to his own art, to come and go, to associate with others. It is, lastly, every one's right to influence the administration of the State, either by

---

[1] Italian translation in volume v of Brunialti's *Biblioteca di scienze politiche*.

nominating all or some of its officers, or by his advice, demands, and petitions, which the authorities are in a greater or less degree obliged to take into account.

' Let us compare this liberty with that of the ancients. That consisted in the collective but direct exercise of many privileges of sovereignty, deliberating upon the public welfare, upon war and peace, voting upon laws, pronouncing judgement, examining accounts, and so forth; but while the ancients regarded this as constituting liberty, they held that all this was compatible with the subjection of the individual to the power of the community. . . . Among the ancients the individual, a sovereign in public affairs, is a slave in all private relations. Among the moderns, on the contrary, the individual, independent in his private life, is even in the freest states a sovereign only in appearance. His sovereignty is restricted, and almost always suspended; and if now and again he exercises it, he only does so in order to renounce it.'

Like all clear-cut historical oppositions, this may be shown to be fallacious.[1] The republics of antiquity, especially Athens and Rome, recognized many liberties of the so-called modern type; what they lacked, and in a limited sense this lack justifies Constant's assertion, was any idea of legal and political limitations of the individual's right. But, on the other hand, the moderns have begun to value liberty in the ancient sense of the word. What else is the primary democracy of Rousseau? and how else can be explained the claim of his disciple the Communist Mably, that the individual should be in complete subjection in order that the nation may be sovereign? And was not the Revolution based upon these writers' systems? Constant energetically opposes this so-called liberty, for him a dangerous reminiscence of that of the ancients; but in point of fact it is the logical development of the liberty of the moderns, because, granted the necessity of political liberty to guarantee the rights of individuals, this implies their participation in the government; and the progressive extension of this participation can only result from a complete development of political activities.

[1] Jellinek has shown this very clearly in his *Allgemeine Staatslehre*, Berlin, ed. 2, 1905, pp. 288 *seqq.*

But Constant shares with all the liberal writers of the Restoration an implacable hatred of democracy, whose recent excesses are fresh in his memory, and the illusion that the democratic heresy has been for ever crushed. Democracy, he says, reduces individuals to an atomic dust; as soon as the weather changes, they turn to mud. Guizot, with the prophetic dogmatism of even the greatest second-rate minds, asserts that the day of universal suffrage will never come.

These writers believed unswervingly in the goodness of the *bourgeois* régime, in which the private interests of a class assumed a vague air of universality. Was not the *bourgeoisie* the general class *par excellence*? Was it not the class of reason, as opposed to the class of dogma, or that of crude sensation? Reason here is no longer the headstrong Reason of the revolutionaries; it has become domesticated, legalized, eclectic, according to the spirit of the predominant philosophy, that of Cousin. No one denied that the property qualification constituted a privileged régime; but the word privilege, so lately detested, had gained a certain air of distinction and attractiveness. It had been worked upon by the romantic soul of the Restoration. The *bourgeoisie* was not and did not want to be a new class; it now wanted *s'ennoblir*. But this was a different nobility from that which it formerly sought; a *bourgeois* nobility with title of its own. Augustin Thierry writes the history of the Third Estate precisely with the object of discovering the truly noble, that is historical, titles of the glorious *roturiers* of France.[1] Madame de Staël had written the words which we have already quoted: in France, liberty is ancient; despotism is modern; and Guizot took this phrase as the text of his university lectures on the history of representative government, in which he set out to show not only the antiquity of the liberal tradition, already alive

[1] Recalling the past a few years later in the preface to *Dix ans d'études historiques*, he writes, 'Born a *roturier*, I demanded that the *roture* should be assigned its proper share of glory in history; that the memories of plebeian honour, of bourgeois energy and freedom, should be gleaned with reverent care; in a word, I demanded that science and patriotism should extract from our ancient chronicles a history capable of stirring the heart of the people' (*Œuvres*, Bruxelles, 1839, p. 566).

in the remotest feudal period, but also the evolutionary character of the history of freedom. Hence, he concluded, the error of those who sought it only in the infancy of Society; it did exist there, but as a seed which began to germinate only when individuals were strong enough to defend themselves and reach its full growth only when reason was fully developed.

' In this rational existence, capable as he is of discerning the truth, man is sublime; here resides the divinity of his nature; liberty is in him only the power of obeying the truth which he can discern and of shaping his actions in conformity with it. On this ground liberty is highly honourable, but on this ground alone; in the infancy of society, the liberty which all men desire and defend is only natural liberty, the liberty to do nothing except what one likes.' [1]

The liberal *bourgeoisie* could appeal to history with no fear of losing its self-respect; the recent gains of the Revolution, or at least those of them which were positive and permanent, were no novelty, no improvisation, but profoundly rooted in the past; and the most sentimental of the Restoration writers, Chateaubriand, can accept the constitution as a pledge of the continuity between the present and the past.

'We must preserve', he says, interpreting the aspirations of moderate opinion, ' the political work which is the fruit of the Revolution, and is consecrated by the charter; but we must eradicate the Revolution from this work, instead of perpetuating it, as we have hitherto done. We must so far as possible mingle the interests and memories of the old France with those of the new, instead of separating the latter and uniting them with revolutionary interests. We must construct representative government on the basis of religion, instead of leaving religion standing like an isolated column in the midst of the State. Hence I accept the whole of the charter, the whole of the liberties, the whole of the institutions which time has brought forth through the alterations of customs and the progress of enlightenment; but with all this I wish to unite whatever has not perished of the old monarchy, religion, the eternal principles of justice and morality,

---

[1] Guizot, *Histoire du gouvernement représentatif*, 2 vols., ed. 2, 1855 (ed. 1 consists of lectures delivered 1820–2), i. 214, 250.

and above all I wish to separate from all this the too notorious persons who have brought about our misadventures.' [1]

In this historical programme, accepted by most Liberals, may be seen an intimate and sincere attachment to English Liberalism, very different from the external imitation of representative institutions which satisfied the outlook of the eighteenth century. England was the country in which an uninterrupted continuity of representative institutions was combined with a system of sharply defined particular liberties. If Thierry, with a certain chauvinism and a reminiscence of Revolutionary Anglophobia, protests against the English yoke, and tries to turn the tables on Burke by condemning the Revolution of 1688 as a merely dynastic affair, transacted without the consent of the nation, the movement of sympathy towards England is widespread and constant in the other writers of the time. Continental thought was following the opposite path to that pursued by contemporary England : the former felt the need of tempering its abstract revolutionary attitude by the introduction of an historical point of view ; the latter, the need of infusing new life into its traditionalism by contact with a rationalistic point of view. Each bestowed upon the other the element most peculiar to its own historical and national genius.

As is clear from this short account, French Liberalism was definitely conservative in tendency. Fresh from the crisis of the Revolution, it felt the need of consolidating its gains instead of seeking new conquests. A secondary and collateral current of thought, led by the economists, showed itself more enterprising. In 1803 Jean-Baptiste Say wrote his *Treatise on Political Economy* ; but under the Empire he was officially forbidden to publish a second edition. Under the restored monarchy this work, composed with striking clarity in exposition and simplicity in design, but with little originality of thought, began to influence a wide circle of readers. It served to introduce the new English science to the continent, and to lead an assault upon the established principles of the physiocrats. The last of them, Dupont de

[1] Chateaubriand, *De la monarchie selon la Charte*, Paris, 1816, p. 147.

Nemours, took a tone of haughty superiority in controversy with Say.

The industrial system, he said, appeared to young students of economics, at a time when France was beginning to follow the lead of England towards industrialism, as a discovery no less important than that of Newton compared with the ancient Copernicanism. But if Say and his followers caused a considerable stir with their formulae of *laissez faire*, competition, and antagonism to the State, they were very far from convincing the economic and political forces of the country, as the English economists had done. In France, the traditions of industry were derived from Colbert ; and in the nineteenth century the development of manufacture was not only still receiving aid from the State, but it was not as yet giving rise to any serious conflict between the agricultural and industrial classes. Both classes, in spite of the economists, were always ready to join hands in a common protectionism and a common resistance to any proposals for free trade.

The manufacturers were most ready to be convinced when the economists spoke of the freedom of labour. Dunoyer wrote a large book on this subject, pointing out the advantages of setting labour free from the bonds of the medieval guilds, which condemned it to a stationary and unprogressive life. He uses hard language of workmen's associations : they were criminal when they used violence, but harmful even when innocent, because it was impossible for wages to rise above the natural limits laid down by competition.

' The condition of the working class depends not only upon wrongs inflicted by the upper classes of society, but also and especially upon its own faults : apathy, indolence, improvidence, lack of economic spirit, ignorance of the causes of the rise and fall of wages ; the abuse of matrimony, into which they are led by their grossness ; the ever-increasing number of competitors which they bring into existence, and thus diminish their wages, while an increasing demand for labour, following upon the development of industry, would tend to increase them.' [1]

[1] Ch. Dunoyer, *De la liberté du travail*, 3 vols., Paris, 1845, i. 390–404. The main nucleus of the work dates from twenty years earlier. Dunoyer

Very different language is used by Sismondi in his *New Principles of Political Economy*, published after his visit to England in 1819 and his observation of the first effects of the industrial revolution upon the working classes. He denounces the optimism of the Liberals, who wished the adaptation of labour to its new conditions to be automatically effected by the natural laws of competition, and did not realize what desolation these laws leave in their wake. The extension of national trade was bought too dear if it must result in the creation of a miserable and poverty-stricken class. Sismondi is opposed to State neutrality in economic struggles ; he demands intervention in favour of the working class : a proposal which to-day we can recognize as far from illiberal when we consider that at the time of which he writes the workmen were not free to form associations for their own defence. In political principles he is at bottom a Liberal, believing in the sovereignty of reason and hostile to universal suffrage, in which he sees a highly effectual and therefore dangerous reactionary force—an observation in which he shows himself more acute than the doctrinaires.

His work opens the flood-gates of the abundant social literature of the time of Louis-Philippe, and the vigorous party controversies of the period.

If the Liberals of the Restoration were in general of a moderate and conservative disposition, the old revolutionary spirit had not wholly vanished from French political life. It still existed and was especially represented by the reactionaries. These were the men who rejected all compromise between the new and the old, and while apparently desiring to restore the *ancien régime* were in fact only modifying the application and content of the revolutionary principles, leaving their form intact. De Maistre speaks of the constituent power of the Pope ; De Bonald devises a purely rational legislation ; Lamennais would overthrow all the traditional relations of Church and State. This revolutionary ferment

was the founder and editor with Charles Comte of the *Censeur européen*, the most active liberal paper of the Restoration period. Augustin Thierry wrote for it also, but made little success of journalism.

was not merely a matter of phraseology and literature; it had considerable effect on politics. The ' ultras ', or reactionary party, were the most active agitators; their attachment to absolute monarchy and divine right led them to oppose the constitutional monarch and become partisans of parliament : their quest for popular support led them to propose an extension of the suffrage far wider than that contemplated by the Liberal programme, because the love of throne and altar existed in greater purity and simplicity in the humblest people than in the higher *bourgeoisie*.

With the accession of Charles X in 1824, the reactionaries saw their wishes gratified. Their demeanour became more aggressive and their anti-constitutionalism, at first dissembled, was given free play. The ' ultras ' wished to re-establish the right of primogeniture, to repeal at least in part the confiscation of the property of the nobles and the Church, and to set up a personal government by the king; and thus subvert all the civil and political liberties which had been gained by the Revolution and the Restoration. This programme, as they began to carry it into effect, excited increasing alarm among the Liberal *bourgeoisie*; and finally extreme provocation, the edicts of July 1830, led them out into the streets once more in a second revolution for the protection of their rights.

It is not without historical interest to observe in the work of the reactionaries a curious element of Liberalism, a product of their very anti-Liberalism. We have already seen them posing on occasion as partisans of parliament and of a wider suffrage, out of hostility to the constitutional party. But of more permanent importance was the Liberal motive implicit in the religious policy of the section calling itself the Liberal Catholics.

This section was led by Lamennais, who in writings published as early as 1830 showed a strongly clerical and papist tendency of thought. He opposed the so-called Gallican liberties, in which he saw nothing but an odious and heretical means of enslaving the Church to the State. He also opposed the sovereignty of the people, as implying an assertion of atheism ; because, as Blackstone expressly recognized, it gave parliament the right to change or modify the religion of the country.[1]

But his own political ideal is incoherent, because the impossibility of establishing a rigid theocracy leaves him no alternative but to return to the old monarchy with its aristocratic and feudal bodies. But was not this the system that created Gallicanism? Lamennais would have a property-owning clergy, ' because it is in the nature of society that men consecrated to its service should have a secure and independent existence, and there is no independence except in property ; ' but a property-owning clergy is independent not only of the sovereign but of the Pope. As De Tocqueville was later to point out, it was the confiscation of ecclesiastical property by the Revolution that drove the clergy into the arms of Rome.[2]

Contradictory though it was, the desire to free the Church from its slavery to the State and to overthrow the Concordat had a strong hold on the mind of Lamennais, and from this time on formed the keystone of that wider Liberalism which took shape in his mind in the years following 1830 and was to be the inspiration of the journal *L'Avenir*, founded by him together with Lacordaire and Montalembert. The programme of this paper, represented by the motto *Dieu et liberté*, was to destroy the distrust of Catholics for Liberalism. 'We are afraid of Liberalism ; Catholicize it, and society will be born again.' It was also intended to demonstrate that freedom, not the freedom of privilege but the freedom of common rights, satisfied all the requirements of religion. The inevitable inference was the separation of Church from state, in the interest of the Church, which therefore must take the initiative in this step.

The movement represented by *L'Avenir*, opposing as it did the legitimistic and reactionary tendency of contemporary

---

[1] Lamennais, *De la religion considérée dans ses rapports avec l'ordre politique et civil*, Paris, ed. 3, N.D., pp. 39, 394.

[2] Lamennais, *Réflexions sur l'état de l'Église en France*, ed. 3, Paris, 1821, p. 65.

papal policy and religious circles, excited lively hostility. Lamennais appealed directly to the Pope; but the reply of Gregory XVI in the Encyclical *Mirari vos* was distinctly unfavourable. Unlike Montalembert and Lacordaire, he refused to submit, and, developing the logic of his thought relentlessly to its conclusion, wrote a few years later the famous *Paroles d'un croyant* which gave the renascent democracy a kind of mystical confession of faith.

Liberal Catholicism, arrested for a moment by the papal Encyclical, later reasserted itself somewhat timidly through the work of Montalembert and Lacordaire, now joined by Dupanloup and Ozanam. In this new orthodox form, no less than in the heretical and democratic form expressed by Lamennais, it served to detach a section of Catholics from the reactionary policy of the Restoration and bring them into touch with the mainstream of nineteenth-century Liberalism. We shall see these Catholics taking part in the revolution of 1848 and coming forward to oppose the Caesarism of the Second Empire. It was in large part owing to their work that the revolutionaries, who in 1830 were unanimous in hating the ' ultras ' and the priests, were in 1848 full of religious fervour, and asked the Church for its blessing upon the flag of liberty.

§ 2. THE BOURGEOIS MONARCHY

The Revolution of 1830, which drove the Bourbons from the throne and established the younger branch of the house of Orleans, was, as we have said, a conservative revolution, resembling in many ways the English Revolution of 1688. Symptoms of popular licence, a foretaste of struggles to come, were quickly repressed. The *bourgeoisie* obtained from Louis-Philippe a constitutional charter, differing from that of 1814 in omitting the invidious assertion of a one-sided concession on the part of the king, and substituting the idea of a mutual compact between king and people. The sovereignty of reason was preserved, and in its honour Louis-Philippe abandoned the traditional title of King of France and Navarre, and took that of King of the French, supplementing the phrase ' by the grace of God ' with the addition ' and by the will of the nation '.[1] All relations with the legitimism of the Restoration were broken off; at last the *bourgeoisie* had a government all its own.

But the reign of Louis-Philippe, whose establishment was regarded by the ' legal country ' as the final step in the realization of its social and political claims, was the reign which saw the most intense movements of reform in both fields. The *bourgeois* monarchy would make political rights the privilege of two hundred and fifty thousand individuals; but in a country like France, where landed property is divided among five or six millions of citizens, a dense stratum of small *bourgeoisie* forming a soil for the growth of all the scattered commercial, industrial, bureaucratic, and professional activities appropriate to such a class, the artificial barrier of a property qualification is powerless to divide the nation into two parts, and to disherit the larger part which feels itself politically no less capable than the other. This *petit-bourgeois* majority took an active share in the Revolution, and now felt itself defrauded by the constitution unexpectedly imposed upon it. The example of Belgium, which in 1831 obtained simultaneously its political freedom and a far more democratic charter, containing the express recognition of national sovereignty (the phrase ' by the grace of God ' being omitted) and a very low property qualification, reinforced the grievances of the disherited lesser *bourgeoisie* of France, and encouraged them to oppose the new régime. Their aspirations were mainly political; a democratic republic, universal suffrage, and the conservation of the existing social order; and when elements from the proletariate began to find an entry into their ranks and to raise the question of property, they hastened to ban the subject and emphasize its exclusion from their programme. *Moi aussi, je suis propriétaire* might have been their motto.

The proletariate, as a distinct class with a distinct out-

[1] According to Guizot's formula, which recognized the equally underivative character of the rights of the king and the people; hence the mutual character of the compact.

look of its own, was the most important historical product of this period, the period of the development of great industry in France. While the *bourgeoisie*, great and small alike, concerned itself with the question of monarchy and republic, the factory proletariate showed from the first a certain indifference to political claims, and demanded social reforms : the right to work and the duty of Society to provide means of subsistence. Its first manifesto was the constitution of Robespierre, which sanctioned this right and by a progressive property-tax tended to equalize the property of citizens.

Democracy and Socialism, which had already made a tumultuous appearance in the course of the great Revolution, and had betrayed their historical immaturity by the rapidity with which they vanished, now began to develop and organize themselves, because the extension and differentiation of the *petite bourgeoisie* on the one hand, and the growth of industry on the other, had prepared an environment upon which they could act more effectually and lastingly.

The most characteristic marks of these new or revived attitudes of mind may already be seen in the two schools of thought which, established at the period of the Restoration, enjoyed an ephemeral but brilliant success after 1830 : Saint-Simonism and Fourierism.

Saint-Simon was an eccentric and talented reformer, sharing with his eighteenth-century predecessors a belief in enlightened despotism, to which he assigned the new task of reconstructing society on industrial principles. The Middle Ages were organized for conquest and controlled by faith ; modern society must be organized for labour and directed by science. No more exploitation of man by man, but the exploitation of nature by the combination of human forces : that is the programme of the industrial system.

But between this and the old feudalism lies a third system, the Liberal system, able of itself, according to the politicians and economists who support it, to satisfy all the needs of modern industry.

For Saint-Simon this claim is groundless. Liberalism has

the merit of having destroyed feudalism, but this negative task of destruction has exhausted its strength ; adapted purely to criticism, it is incapable of construction and organization. Its error lies in being an invention of lawyers and meta-physicians, who do not ask themselves what is the purpose of social activity, or else replace the end by the means, namely legislation or abstract freedom, as if men joined together in order to legislate for each other or to be free from each other. Saint-Simon's *Parabole* is a witty satire on political formalism. If all the great dignitaries of the court and the State unexpectedly disappeared from the world, the world would go on without noticing their disappearance ; but what irreparable ruin would follow the disappearance of the great masters of industrial production !

The political ideal of Saint-Simon is collectivism ; the sub-stitution of the organic State for the Liberal or individualistic State. But this is not a socialistic ideal in the modern sense of the word, because it contains no conception of class distinc-tions, and productive forces are fused into a single mass, regardless of their *bourgeois* or proletarian structure. This distinction, and with it the emergence of a socialistic point of view, arises within the Saint-Simonian school, formed in 1829, four years after their master's death, by Bazard, En-fantin, and Rodriguez, whose organ was the *Globe*, a journal founded by Pierre Leroux. Here we find all the main points of the economic and political doctrine of the proletariate, forming a closely connected ' societary ' and ' organic ' system in opposition to the ' fragmentary ' and ' critical ' system of the *bourgeoisie*. Saint-Simon had divided society into the producers and the idle ; the only really idle people in his opinion were the landowners. His followers added to this category the capitalists, as exploiting the labour of the people no less than do the landowners. This is the beginning of the socialistic crusade against capital, against the ' lords of industry ', a privileged class no less than the feudal barons. Competition between manufacturers comes to be considered the source of all economic troubles, and is compared to the wars of medieval robbers ; freedom in the contract of labour is declared a fraud, because the workman is not free in his relation to the employer, but is forced to accept his terms for the sake of a livelihood.

The only escape from a ruinous individualism in production lies, for the Saint-Simonians, in the concentration of all production in the hands of the State, the organ of a higher distributive justice, which shall demand service from every one according to his capacity and reward every one according to the work he does. From this follows the abolition of all unearned gains, especially by way of inheritance; all profits won by labour must serve solely as credits for future labour; that is, they must be capitalized by the State as representing the society of producers. If it is objected that the abolition of inheritance will destroy the motive to accumulate wealth, the Saint-Simonians answer that this is untrue: in the army, the magistracy, or the universities, ambition is an effectual motive to exertion.

Once the imagination of the reformers was given free play, the Saint-Simonians overleapt all bounds. They transformed the family, property, the individual conscience and the religious consciousness, modelling all alike on the form of the State, making every activity a function and every man a functionary. Especially important is the religious aspect of their doctrine. For Saint-Simon, religion was a means of social progress; and in his last work, *Le nouveau Christianisme*, in which the socialistic tendency of his school is to some extent anticipated, he looks forward to a modernized form of Christianity, replacing its unworldly ideals with ideals of a more earthly and human character.

This immanentistic tendency to restrict the divine within man's earthly life was emphasized further by his school, indirectly influenced by German philosophy. Rodriguez [1] translated Lessing's *Education of the Human Race*, in which the German author, starting from the idea that revelation has passed through two stages, the Old and New Testaments, concludes that religion is progressive, and that a third phase

[1] Cf. P. Janet, *Saint-Simon et le Saint-Simonisme*, Paris, 1878, pp. 107 seqq.

is approaching. The Saint-Simonians proposed to bring it about. The fundamental error of old-fashioned Christianity was to transfer its ideals of liberty and fraternity to another world, and leave the earth a prey to evil; thus everything that appertained to the flesh was treated as evil, human labour became a curse and a punishment, and religion severed itself from all the living forces of society. The breach must now be healed. For the God of Christianity, pure spirit, must be substituted the spirit-matter God of the new religion of mankind : the God that is one and all, and includes all things. Enfantin, the chief inventor of this religion, defends himself, like his German authorities, against the accusation of pantheism ; he does not identify spirit with matter, he makes spirit the breath of life which vivifies matter and raises it to a moral and religious destiny.

It is characteristic that the new religion was not treated as an abstract theory, but was put into practice as far as possible within the circle of the Saint-Simonian school. Enfantin proclaimed himself its High Priest or Supreme Father; Bazard its head in matters of dogma, and Rodriguez in matters of worship. In conformity with the principle of rehabilitating the flesh, the priestly hierarchy was arranged not in individuals but in couples. This produced a certain atmosphere of scandal, and the last appearance of the mystical Saint-Simonian religion was in court, on a charge of outraging public morals.

But the exaggerations and eccentricities of this attempt at religious reform were based on a perfectly serious conviction that without a deep religious feeling there could be no transformation of the social structure, and that some attempt must be made to oppose the irreligion forced upon modern society by the intransigence of the Roman Church. The Utopian idea of a religion of humanity, ascribing an immanent divine value to human labour and satisfying man's thirst for justice through earthly rewards and punishments, was not an arbitrary invention of Saint-Simonism. It reappears in Leroux's book *De l'Humanité*, in Proudhon, and in general in all the democratic conceptions which aspire to

give a complete view of modern life.[1] Even the Positivist
Auguste Comte, who though a fervent follower of Saint-Simon
broke with his school on religious points, later in life returned
to the theological dreams of the companions of his youth.

Even Liberalism, though in a sense less Utopian, demanded
a religious reformation, necessitated by the hostility of the
Roman Church towards its social and political programme.
In Quinet and his successors the idea often appears that the
Catholic countries must have a Protestant Reformation of their
own, if they wished to raise themselves to the level of the
other nations. Catholicism was irremediably lost to the cause
of liberty; in its history and ideal structure freedom was
bound up with Protestantism, which had founded the whole
system of modern liberties upon the liberty of conscience.

Another social system which flourished in this period took
its name from Fourier, another original and gifted Utopian
who transferred into his dream a great part of the living reality
of his lifetime. Like Saint-Simon, he saw in the present a
period of transition towards a new and perfect society, which
he called Harmony. But unlike his predecessor, Fourier does
not entrust its realization to the State, which he ostentatiously
ignores. His conception is inspired by liberal motives, being
founded upon the free and spontaneous association of individuals without any coercion from outside. Such freedom from
coercion is impossible in the present state of affairs, which he
calls Civilization, because here labour is organized in the
most false and unnatural manner, out of all harmony with
the fundamental instincts of man, and is therefore devoid of
all cohesive force; but in Harmony labour is distributed
according to nature, that is, according to the free initiative
and spontaneous impulse of man. The principle of the
economic division of labour is that of attractiveness, which
makes it an enjoyment instead of a misery, and renders the
problem of remuneration unimportant or at any rate easy
of solution.

[1] As De Tocqueville says (*De la démocratie en Amérique*), the democratic
mind tends towards pantheism; the Germans introduced it into philosophy, the French into literature.

In the principle of attraction Fourier believed himself to have discovered a law more important than Newton's law of gravitation. He saw in it the means of redressing all the evils of industrial dispersion, competition, and property. Attraction organizes and connects the cells of the new society, which he calls phalanges (or phalansteries, from the point of view of their territorial distribution), which are small independent and self-sufficient communities harmoniously uniting agricultural labour (rendered attractive by the emphasis laid upon horticulture and fruit-growing) and industrial labour; which by living in common foster the social spirit of their members and reduce all the expenses of domestic life; which divide the produce of their labour by the system of the ' actionariate ', giving the individual an interest in the well-being of his society; which, lastly, stand in close relation to each other through those of their activities which relate to interests common to all.

How the freedom of association is to be reconciled with the rigid and uniform structure of the phalanstery, with the resulting monotony of life, which will resemble that of the factory, and with the fixed number of its members, Fourier does not tell us; here perhaps lies the inconsistency which will creep even into the most coherent dream. Yet Fourier's imagination is rich in suggestions and inspirations recalling, as a biographer remarks, those of Edgar Allan Poe.[1] His phalanstery is the ideal model of the modern factory; his principle that work in order to be productive must be pleasant is applied in many interesting ways to educational and social problems; his faith in the power of association is simply prophetic: he foresees taking shape by its means such masterpieces of modern industry as the Suez and Panama Canals. His school, founded in 1825 and surviving until 1850, was a training-ground for the best industrial, commercial, and financial brains of France.

Saint-Simonianism and Fourierism, the collectivist ideal and the associationist ideal, were the two poles between

---

[1] Charles Fourier, *Œuvres choisies*, ed. Ch. Gide, Paris, Guillaumin, N.D. Cf. Gide's introduction, p. iii.

which proletarian theory was to oscillate throughout the nineteenth century. The one expressed the tendency towards State concentration, the other towards decentralization and autonomy. The phalanstery is only a fantastic cross between a factory and a commune; it at once anticipates trade unionism and recalls the autonomous communes of the Revolution. There are two forms of decentralization : one economic, the other territorial, implying two different species of federalism ; but both alike are inspired by the anti-State outlook of extreme individualistic liberalism.

In the transition from a fantastic expression of desires to the practical organization of the working class, the centralizing or State tendency easily won the day. The tradition of an administrative and bureaucratic monarchy, which had already infected the *bourgeoisie*, infected the proletariate too as soon as it appeared under its own name upon the horizon of history. Saint-Simonism, stripped by Louis Blanc of its mystical trappings, offered the masses a simple and straightforward catechism. In Blanc's *Organisation du travail* we find the familiar criticisms of the liberal *bourgeoisie* ; we find the demonstration that the competition forced upon the working man is self-destructive because, by destroying the weaker businesses, it gives a monopoly to the strongest; we find the contrast between the abstract *bourgeois* idea of rights and liberties, and the concrete idea of liberty and right as real power. The organization of labour preached by the Saint-Simonians was to be brought about through *ateliers sociaux* financed by the State, which thus became not only the political but the economic centre of the nation. The people's right to work found a practical sanction in the providence of the State. The one practical departure from Saint-Simonism was the substitution for the formula ' from each according to his capacity, to each according to his *work* ', of the formula ' from each according to his capacity, to each according to his *needs* '; which is far less consistent than its predecessor. This catechism acquired great popularity in working-class circles during the last ten years of the reign of Louis-Philippe, and served as the manifesto of the working-class revolution of 1848.

The individualistic or libertarian current of thought met
with little support among the masses, and served only as an
antithesis, and therefore a critical stimulus, to the predominant Socialism. It was chiefly represented by Proudhon, who
opened his career as a brilliant and disconcerting publicist
in 1840 with his famous *mémoire*, *Qu'est-ce que la propriété?* ' Property is theft.' This reply has been compared to the pistol
shot which compels the traveller to halt. It caused an uneasy
excitement among the *bourgeoisie*, who felt in the increasing
flood of the proletariate a menace to their own possessions.
But Proudhon, though an enemy to *bourgeois* property, was
no less an enemy to Communism, in which he saw a new form
of the same tyranny. Property was the exploitation of the
weak by the strong, Communism the exploitation of the
strong by the weak. This is the first and fundamental antithesis which in his later work *Les Contradictions économiques* is
followed by many others, each polarizing in the form of an
antithesis some principle of economic and social life : labour,
value, competition, credit, or the like. All these antitheses
were based on the contradictory nature of modern life, which
attempted to affirm at once freedom and coercion, the individual and the State. As Proudhon later wrote in his *Idée
générale de la révolution au xixme siècle*, written after the revolutionary crisis of 1848, the contradiction goes back to Rousseau, who, starting from the demands of a reasonable individualism in the *Contrat social*, in fact overthrew them by
creating a compact of hate, a code of capitalistic and mercantile tyranny. The logical consequence of contractualism
is the destruction of the State ; the replacement of relations
based on a coercive authority by voluntary and spontaneous
relations. Individualism, pushed to its extreme consequences,
would lead to a mutualism, the rule of perfect social reciprocity, and would provide a fertile principle for the resolution
of all these antinomies.

Proudhon's so-called syntheses are the weakest and most
sophistical part of his work. He wished to introduce into
them the spirit of the Hegelian dialectic, but he was only
a dabbler in philosophy, and when he quotes Kant or Hegel

he commits the most elementary blunders.[1] These things are not his line; the real Proudhon appears in the brilliant art with which he develops his antinomies, where his caustic, eccentric, and penetrating wit is at its ease. In reality he is an anarchist, though he makes a show of rising above anarchy to autarchy; the political principles of Conservatives, Liberals, and Socialists are all equally distasteful to him, and he takes keen pleasure in riddling them and reducing them to shreds with a kind of malevolent fury. This explains the interest aroused by his work before 1848, when society was in a state of ferment. All parties could borrow from him with equal satisfaction; the Conservatives appropriating his anti-Socialistic themes, and vice versa; and both alike fulminating against that part of his work which contradicted their own views.

The *mémoire* on property was followed by an outbreak of French essays in defence of this ' palladium ' of modern liberty. Every writer in the country seems to have felt impelled to compose one of these on his own account; and during the Revolution of 1848 there were prize competitions for the most convincing and popular defence; but a contemporary reports that the result, at any rate as far as quality was concerned, amounted to very little.

The economists, on the other hand, feeling their prestige shaken by the contradictions discovered by Proudhon in their works, also felt bound to defend themselves and to engage in a counter-attack. Bastiat answered Proudhon's contradictions in his own *Harmonies économiques*, in which, by a curious phenomenon of mimicry, he comes much nearer to Proudhon, except as regards wit, than one might think at first sight. Bastiat, the last representative of the school of Say, was himself an individualist, and agreed with his adversary in desiring an almost complete suppression of the State. But this ideal was for him not a reconciliation of antinomies, but rather the natural expression of certain vague harmonies, slurring over the apparent discords of social life. It is diffi-

[1] See e.g. his interpretation of the Kantian doctrine of space and time in his *Système des contradictions économiques* (ed. Flammarion), ii. 398.

cult to see how an economist could have written so tedious
a work as *Les Harmonies économiques*, which very properly
became a butt for the satire of the Socialists. It is an echo of
eighteenth-century optimism with its identification of private
and public interests; and the hostility towards the State
which marks the earlier Liberalism finds in it a singularly
crude and grotesque expression.

In imitation of Cobden, Bastiat wished to found an anti-
protection league in France, and published a volume of the
chief speeches by members of the Anti-Corn-Law League,
translated into French; but he found himself confronted by
the invincible hostility of French landowners and manufacturers, and the book only served to introduce the continental
public to the English free-trade movement, and to prepare
the way for Cobden's enthusiastic reception on his continental travels following his victory in 1846.

The most important writer of this period, perhaps the
greatest French writer of the nineteenth century, is Alexis de
Tocqueville. His work on *Democracy in America*, published in
1835 and reprinted twelve times before the Revolution of
1848, marks a turning-point in the attitude of Liberalism
towards the changed historical environment which has seen
the revival of democracy and the rise of Socialism.

We left the doctrinaire Liberalism of the Restoration enclosed within the narrow confines of legal citizenship and
hostile to any extension of these limits: in the memory of
revolutionary excesses, combined with a stubborn class-
selfishness, it saw democracy in a sinister light. Nothing
could be better adapted to dispel this suspicion than a work
like De Tocqueville's, free from all apologetic intention,
composed with the cool lucidity of a man whose only care
was to analyse calmly and sincerely an historical phenomenon taking place on a stage far removed from the political
conflicts which were beginning to disturb France.

But while writing of America, De Tocqueville had his eye
on his own country; and even the somewhat abstract and
deductive character of his historical reflections facilitated
their application to an unnamed problem nearer home.

Not only the Americans, but the French too, had a love of equality leading them towards democracy; not based on an original equality of conditions and a widespread Puritan sentiment, but upon the assiduous work of a levelling monarchy and the completion of this work by the Revolution. Recently a new levelling factor had made itself felt, namely industry. As the principle of the division of labour was more and more completely applied, the workman became weaker, more limited, more dependent; as the art progressed, the artisan decayed.

Now the peril inherent in this democratic atomism was tyranny. As the resistance of individuals and groups decreased, the way was thrown open to those great administrative and political concentrations of which tyranny consists. Thus in the new industrial world the degradation of the proletariate was accompanied by an increase in the power of the masters. While the workman devoted himself more and more completely to the study of a single detail of production, the employer turned his attention towards an ever-increasing field, his outlook becoming broader as that of the workman became narrower. Before long the workman would need nothing but unintelligent physical strength; while the manufacturer, in order to succeed, must possess not only science, but almost genius. The latter was approximating to the ruler of a vast empire, the former to a brute. Thus, as the mass of the nation turned towards democracy, the manufacturers as a class became more aristocratic. The growing assimilation of the one was matched by the growing differentiation of the other. Industrial aristocracy was the harshest and most remorseless that the world had seen; first it impoverished and brutalized the men whom it employed for its own ends, and then it abandoned them in time of crisis and left them to be supported by public charity.[1]

But the danger due to industrial despotism does not only come from above. Perhaps this is the lesser danger, because it is on a smaller scale. There is also a danger from below.

[1] De Tocqueville, *De la démocratique en Amérique*, ed. 13, 1850, ii. 178 *seqq.*

In the end the workmen must prevail, because they have the force of numbers on their side, and the higher wages which they are extorting from their employers will make them day by day less dependent and more dissatisfied. The anonymous multitude carries in its heart a despotism less obvious than that of the privileged class, but more insidious and deep-seated, bent on destroying even the smallest inequality and on bestowing upon the mass all the power it can wrest from the individual.

As compared with old-fashioned personal despotism, this new despotism which is growing up in the democratic nations of our day is more sweeping and less painful; it degrades men without torturing them. It expresses itself through an absolute State power, detailed, uniform, provident, and mild, which would be paternal had it been designed to prepare men for a life of maturity; but its true intention is to arrest them permanently at the stage of infancy.[1]

What are the consequences of centralization? It succeeds in imposing upon the affairs of the nation a high degree of regularity, and reducing the social organism to a kind of administrative torpor. It excels in hindering, not in acting. When it is necessary to change society profoundly or to set it into rapid motion, its strength deserts it. Whenever its rules require the smallest co-operation on the part of individuals, one is surprised at the weakness of this great machine. Thus we find ourselves watching a twofold process of an increase of power on the one hand and its diminution on the other. In no previous period of history has the State appeared either so weak or so strong.

Our contemporaries often confuse despotism with autonomy. They console themselves for their condition of dependence by reflecting that they have themselves chosen those upon whom they depend. Many people to-day adapt themselves easily to this compromise between administrative despotism and the sovereignty of the people, by believing that they have sufficiently guaranteed the liberty of the individual when they have in fact surrendered him to the

[1] *Op. cit.*, ii. 356, 358.

central power. Yet this illusion is a symptom of a centrifugal force acting within democracy and tending to neutralize its effects : the force of liberty. In a highly centralized country, national representation certainly diminishes the evils of excessive centralization, but it does not destroy them.

The passion for liberty must not allow itself to be exhausted by a formal assertion of popular sovereignty, but must exert itself perpetually in every human activity. Since the advent of democracy is inevitable, and has indeed already taken place, we must neutralize its venom by means of all the antidotes which liberty can afford. Yet no task can be harder than that which democracy at once necessitates and impedes. It destroys all the barriers which ought to restrain it, and paralyses the individual energies which ought to resist it. In this state of things the school of liberty is a hard school, while despotism is rich in attractions, offering itself as the cure of all evils, the safeguard of rights, the champion of the oppressed, and the source of order. Nations sink into slumber amid the prosperity which it brings in its train ; when they awake, they recognize their wretchedness. Freedom, on the contrary, comes into being for the most part amid storms, is established painfully among civil discords, and yields its benefits only when it has grown old.

But how must we set it in motion? As democratic despotism attacks one by one the forms of individual and social activity, liberty must oppose it point by point : political guarantees, freedom of education, of religion, of opinion, of association, each has its place in the struggle. The whole field of history, levelled by despotism, must be broken up on every side, so as to create everywhere centres of resistance. The ' guarantism ' which the liberal thought of the Restoration elaborately worked out in opposition to the despotic claims of the Crown must be turned against this new monarchy, which differs from its predecessor only in being more widely and deeply rooted.

Thus the liberal thought which seemed to have grown old and stale in the selfish defence of class privileges found a new and wider field of action and an opportunity of drawing on new sources of strength. If doctrinaires like Guizot continued to show themselves impenetrable to these demands, more open minds threw themselves confidently and eagerly into the path pointed out by De Tocqueville. The programme of a liberal democracy attracted Lamartine, who devoted to it his *Politique rationnelle*; the philosopher Vacherot wrote a book *De la Démocratie*; the politicians who were to take the lead in the Revolution of 1848, Odilon Barrot and Ledru-Rollin, had democratic sympathies, and even Thiers included many elements of democratic origin in his programme of constitutional opposition to Guizot's ministry.

De Tocqueville dispelled a nightmare by showing that the democratic idea, far from being a revolutionary aberration, stood upon the highway of French history. To his penetrating mind, everything in the various periods of this history which appeared discordant with the preceding period reveals itself as exhibiting an uninterrupted and uniform continuity, which proves the French people, superficially regarded as fickle and inconstant, the most consistent and stable of all nations. The Revolution of 1848 was to provide only another proof of this consistency in the midst and in spite of change.

§ 3. 1848

On the 27th of January 1848, while Parliament was discussing its reply to the speech from the throne, De Tocqueville, in a famous speech, analysed the situation as follows:

' For the first time for fifteen years,' he said, ' I confess to the chamber that I feel a certain fear for the future. The feeling, the instinct of instability, the herald of revolution, exists in the country to a high degree. If I examine the governing class and the governed class, I find in both alike something which disturbs me and frightens me. What I see may be expressed in a few words : the customs of the people are changing day by day. Precisely because morality no longer reigns in the chief acts of life, it does not descend into acts of less importance ; and because in public life self-interest has taken the place of disinterested feelings, it controls private life also. Reflect,' he added, ' upon what is happening within the working classes, which to-day, we must recognize, are quiet. Do you not see that their passions, from being political, have become social? We discuss the justice of the distribution of property; but it is my profound conviction that we are sleeping upon a volcano. The régime of 1830 gave much less extension of freedom than might reasonably have been expected. Our rulers granted a kind of safe-conduct to vice and immorality. When I set myself to seek at different times and among different peoples the effectual cause that has brought about the ruin of a governing class, I see in such and such a man or event the accidental and superficial cause; but the real and effectual cause, believe me, why men lose power, is that they become unworthy to possess it. I believe in the value of electoral reform, and the urgency of parliamentary reform; but I am not so senseless as to be ignorant that laws, taken by themselves, do not make the destiny of peoples. No; it is not the machinery of laws that produces great events in this world : what brings events to pass is the spirit of the government.' [1]

This speech is an accurate judgement upon the régime of Louis-Philippe and a luminous anticipation of coming events. A *bourgeoisie* entrenched in the stronghold of its privileges, out of all relation with a renascent social world; a narrow government, anxious to keep the peace at any price, even at the price of its honour, which has nothing to say to its subjects but a crude *enrichissez-vous* : that is the political situation in France on the eve of the Revolution.

The occasion of the revolution was provided by that part of the liberal *bourgeoisie* which had lately come into contact with the democratic and social movements of the time ; these it hoped to check by means of political reforms, and set itself, led by Thiers, to oppose the government of Guizot and arouse public interest in its programme by means of political banquets. But these political reforms were soon swept away by the democratic revolution, and this in turn debouched into a yet wider movement of a socialistic character. As Laurent Stein, the most penetrating student of modern France, had already foretold in 1842, the new French Revolution would be not merely political, but social.

The year 1848 is a date not in the history of France alone,

[1] *Démocratie en Amérique*, appendix, ii. 455-68.

but in the history of Europe. In Germany, in Austria, in Hungary, in Italy, and to a limited degree even in England, the force set in motion by France produced a rapid effect, and its diffusion was complicated by the interference of a second motive : a claim on the part of peoples as yet deprived of national unity to freedom from foreign domination. The social character of these revolutions, even if attenuated, was everywhere perceptible. On every side it was the liberal and democratic *bourgeoisie* that excited the revolutionary movement and attempted to limit its operation, but was overwhelmed by the action of the masses which it had itself set in motion, and which were resolved to profit by it on their own account even at the expense of their allies. Confronted by this unforeseen outburst, the liberal *bourgeoisie*, terrified by the spectre of Communism, demanded a reaction. This it brought about at first by means of the National Guard, which took the field against the revolted masses in the towns and the country ; but, this weak barrier proving insufficient, it joined hands with the ancient forces of reaction, the lately detested tyrants where these still existed, or new tyrants where these could be improvised. Communism was checked, and the masses reduced to subjection ; but liberty was suppressed with them, and with liberty perished national independence where this had been gained.

It is in France that the revolutionary movement may be seen following this course in its strictest simplicity, because the case is uncomplicated by any factors other than the purely social question. In the first days of the Revolution the constitutional opposition vanished, and with it the government ; the Revolution created a democratic *petit-bourgeois* republic with socialistic trimmings designed to tickle the fancy of the mob. Blanc and Albert, representatives of the working class, were made members of the provisional government, but unlike their democratic colleagues they were ministers without portfolio ; as Proudhon sarcastically put it, they would have liked to figure as worker-bees of the Revolution, instead of which they were cast for the part of grasshoppers. The principle of the organization of labour, on which the eyes of the workers had been fixed for the last ten years, issued only in the creation of *ateliers nationaux* instead of *ateliers sociaux*; that is, in substance, the creation of legions of unemployed, paid by the State, whose number grew gigantically from day to day and whom the government was compelled to employ in the most futile manner. State industries cannot be organized by a simple word of command; a calm and methodical preparation is indispensable, and this the march of the Revolution did not permit. And the conviction that *ateliers nationaux* were a mere temporary expedient was so firmly rooted in the minds of the democratic rulers, that their organization was entrusted not to a Socialist, but to Thomas, a *bourgeois* strongly hostile to Blanc. The workmen soon felt that they had been deceived. Instead of gaining control of the State, they were offered a kind of degrading legal charity, imposing a heavy burden upon the taxpayers. The organization of labour was a farce, and an expensive farce; as was soon discovered by the peasants, whose taxes rose by 45 per cent.

The discontent of the small *bourgeoisie* began to affect the elections, now conducted by universal suffrage. The result was a majority in favour of a reactionary policy, ready to sacrifice all its liberties for the sake of exorcizing Communism. Such an environment favoured the fabrication and diffusion of skilful falsehoods, designed to throw a lurid light upon the proletariate and its leaders, by attributing to the latter a life of the most unbridled dissipation. Public morality was outraged and urgently demanded, what interest had already suggested, a military dictatorship to check the proletariate. The struggle between the *bourgeois* democracy and Socialism drew to a bloody end during the days of June, when General Cavaignac won the glorious title of saviour of his country and paved the way for the more lasting dictatorship of Louis Napoleon.

The most important political consequence of these events was the complete detachment of the *bourgeoisie* from the proletariate, democracy from Socialism, a detachment which had been gradually asserting itself in the course of industrial evolution and the development of party politics. For the moment, however, it seemed as though the conflict were to end very differently. The democracy found in Louis-Napoleon the dictator whom De Tocqueville had foretold: the *élu de sept millions*, the living expression of the will of the French people as expressed in a plebiscite. The working class seemed bent upon harnessing itself to the conqueror's chariot. Defeated and disorganized, it concentrated all its hatred upon its victor, General Cavaignac, and yielded to the blandishments of Napoleon, who nevertheless was raised to the throne by the very forces which had brought about a bloody reaction. But Napoleon had a socialistic record; he once belonged to the school of Fourier, and had been an ally of Blanc, with whom he had discussed the principles of the organization of labour; he was the avatar of the Napoleonic idea whose power was felt in the humblest cottage; and the proletariate put its faith in him, hoping that the pressure of reaction would at least lie upon it the more lightly. The partisans of law and order were quick to celebrate their victory; Reybaud, in a new edition of his *Étude sur les Réformateurs*, announced the death of Socialism. In point of fact this was perhaps the moment of its birth. What was dead was the illusion that the organization of labour could be improvised and bestowed as a gift from above, and that the right to work was a graceful concession on the part of the *bourgeoisie*. The death of these illusions was the condition of the birth of a Socialism that could educate the masses to organize themselves and to claim their own rights by means of class war. The *Communists' Manifesto* dates from the exoct time at which the death of Socialism was proclaimed.

The dictatorship of Napoleon was that mild and degrading power which De Tocqueville described as characteristic of modern democracy. The same policy of reconciliation which had succeeded with the working class was used by Napoleon in his dealings with the Catholics. If the groups of Liberal Catholics resisted his blandishments, and held firmly to their Liberalism, the main Catholic body, led by Falloux and Veuillot (editor of *L'Univers*), was ready enough to support a ruler who proposed to unite throne and altar : and the Vatican was the chief intermediary in the compact, and received in exchange a well-earned reward in the French *chassepöts* that destroyed the Roman republic. The dictator's attachment to the Pope, which began to show itself while the republican government was still technically in existence, naturally found a certain amount of support among democratic anticlericals. Odilon Barrot did not hesitate to approve the Roman expedition, for which he offered the truly Christian justification that spiritual power and temporal power must be united at Rome in order that they might be divided elsewhere. Napoleon accepted the premisses, which harmonized with his own views, and rejected the conclusion by reaffirming the Concordat. Thus the last hope of Liberalism, shared by Montalembert's Catholic group, was disappointed.

§ 4. LIBERALISM AND THE SECOND EMPIRE

The party which was really defeated by the Revolution was that of the Liberals, or those of them who felt the profound moral degradation of a dictatorship outraging their sense of their own human dignity. The professional Liberals were quite at their ease. Guizot, whose narrowness and political obtuseness was a chief cause of the Revolution, could still write an unctuous little work called *De la Démocratie en France*, with the complacency of one who could claim to have foretold the inevitable consequence of all democratic follies. Thiers, wiser and more subtle, held his tongue, and awaited another opportunity of seizing the power which had slipped between his fingers in 1848.

De Tocqueville, though he might more justifiably than any one else have claimed a foreknowledge of the course of events, looked at the situation with very different feelings. He saw in the loss of liberty a painful mutilation of his own human nature, independently of any social, legal, and political interest.

' I do not believe,' he said, ' that the real love of liberty ever arises from the consideration of material benefits, which often rather obscures it. That which has at all times won the hearts of a few for the cause of liberty is its own attractions, its own *charme*, apart from its benefits : the pleasure of being able to speak, to act, to breathe, without restriction, under the sole government of God and the laws. Any one who seeks in liberty something other than this is born for slavery.'

This is genuine Liberalism, not to be tamed by any dictatorship, against which it is the first and most direct centre of resistance. The Empire, based upon plebiscite and bureaucracy, and carrying the corrupting influences of a Caesarian democracy into the very cottages of the people, offered many opportunities for a revival of Liberalism by the mere fact that it revealed and brought to light the distinction between the servile mass and the man of will and character.

The Liberal theory of this period was inspired by Constant and De Tocqueville. The former put forward the political system of guarantism as against despotic government ; the latter, a programme of Liberal democracy, rendered the more urgent by the degeneration of democratic tyranny. The chief representatives of this tendency were Laboulaye, who constructed his theory of the State and its limits on the lines of *Ancient and Modern Liberty* ; Simon, the author of many works analysing in detail the various liberties of conscience, of work, civil and political ; and Prévost-Paradol, who set forth a plan of self-government in *La France nouvelle*. These writers show much the same tendencies of thought ; not only is their fundamental theory the same, but the situation upon which their criticism is brought to bear is not such as to permit any considerable differences of judgement. The Revolution of 1848, says Laboulaye, has shown how remote our generation is from Liberal ideas. After thirty-three years of constitutional government, it has been possible to revive the most disastrous errors of the first Revolution. Publicists who boast of being progressive have asserted that the individual is made for society and not vice versa, thus returning to the *Contrat social* and the tyranny of the Convention ; Utopians destroy the family and propose to turn France into a factory ; legislators imbued with the prejudices of 1789 can think of no better way of establishing the reign of democracy than by

weakening the executive power, as if energetic authority were
not the first guarantee of freedom.[1]

The one positive fruit of the Revolution, says Laboulaye,
was a fresh concentration of governmental power on the
ruins of the constitutional liberties of 1814 and 1830. To-day
the State is everything; the monarchy is unlimited; the
bureaucracy is omnipotent. The sovereignty of the people
has only succeeded in destroying itself and justifying Constant's profound distrust of this principle, a principle laid
down without guarantees and indeed with the intention of
rendering guarantees superfluous. The confusion of electoral
and parliamentary sovereignty with liberty has opened the
way to despotism, and has proved indirectly and negatively
that before citizens can exercise political rights they must be
carefully educated by a training in the affairs of their commune, department, church, institution, and school.

Local self-government is the true antidote to all despotism.
And the enemy to be resisted is not the form of government,
not political unity, which is the strength and greatness of
France, but administrative uniformity and bureaucratic encroachment. On this all Liberal writers now agree, and, like
their Restoration predecessors, take the old English system
as a model for their administrative reforms.

This recognition of local autonomy implies another autonomy, concerned not with local divisions but with a freer
and more mobile distribution of forces within an ideal and
spontaneously established organism : the right of association.
The recent Revolution has shown the importance of this right.
For Laboulaye the only remedy for political agitation is to
provide another channel for the outlet of these activities.[2]
Simon with profounder insight sees here a means of educating
the working classes, calculated at once to satisfy their demand
for equality and to create in them a loftier ideal of liberty.
But the idea of association must be completely separated from

[1] E. Laboulaye, L'État et ses limites (Ital. tr. in Bibl. sc. polit., ser. i,
vol. 7), p. 784.
[2] E. Laboulaye, Le Parti libéral, son programme et son avenir, Paris, 1863,
p. 43.

the dictatorship and from all supine dependence upon the providence of the State; its realization is the business not of the State, but of the workman himself, acting with perfect freedom.[1]

This is the new and peculiar feature of the Liberalism of the Second Empire, as compared with that of the Restoration. In other respects they are indistinguishable, at least in spirit; though the object of Liberal criticism is now no longer the old monarchy but the democratic Caesarism. The writers quoted have a tendency, favoured by the necessity of conducting their guerrilla warfare with circumspection, to ignore the form of government and to represent the conflict in a purely impersonal way, as a conflict between the individual and the State. They never regard this antithesis as ultimate, and therefore they never so far depart from the political tradition of their country as to display hostility towards the State as such. As Laboulaye says,

' the State, as representing nationality and justice, is the greatest and most august of human institutions; it is the country itself in visible form. But if it oversteps its own domain, it is a tyrant. Its limit is the freedom of the citizen, the principles of 1789. But to secure this freedom, constitutions are not enough. Constitutions are magnificent inscriptions cut on the front of the temple; but from the house that bears his name the god is absent, and in his place is worshipped a phantom which deserts and deceives its worshippers, Sovereignty.' [2]

While these writers are led by their individualistic temperament to emphasize the importance of the State's limits, without denying its positive function, others show an opposite preference, and point out that the rights of individuals acquire meaning and practical solidity only through the State. This argument is far from being anti-Liberal; but when it becomes the dominant motive of a political theory, it is in danger of creating a dangerous emphasis on authority to the exclusion of liberty. This is visible in one of the most vigorous political writers of the Second Empire, Dupont

---

[1] J. Simon, *Le Travail*, Paris, ed. 4, 1867, pp. 121-4.
[2] *L'État et ses limites*, p. 810.

White. The thesis of his chief work, *L'Individu et l'État*, is that freedom and the State, life and law, grow simultaneously on parallel lines. Freedom, legally speaking, means that no one is obliged to obey the mere will of his fellow man; obedience is due only to the law, the presumed expression of reason. Even the law can bind no one to do what is incompatible with the elements and ends of his nature: not only the rule of law, but the equity of law is implied by the spirit of freedom and human rights.

But this liberty and these rights appear simultaneously with the State. The reign of equity, of law, is full of complications; the procedure of force is simple and summary. A society in which a sense of equity is awakened exhibits increasing constitutional complexities; first it promulgates rights, then it particularizes them into regulations; then, in order to secure them, it creates guarantees, sanctions, compulsions, a whole hierarchy of authorities, a whole apparatus of procedures, limitations, and checks, rightly called an organization, because unless it is thus constituted a right is useless. Authority is created in order to make liberty possible.[1]

' Liberty, Equality, Fraternity: great words, if any words are great; but I know none less capable of realizing themselves unaided. Revolutions, to their eternal glory, utter these words; but it is the business of governments to perform what revolutions promise.' How can that average of rights which is called equality be established except by correcting here a deficiency of rights, there an excess or a privilege? This correction can only be effected by the State. What is liberty of worship but the supervision of worship by the State? Religious toleration is one of those advances which give one power the more to the State. That is the way in which freedom grows up: it only exists for all at the cost of a dependence and a discipline imposed upon all: that is the work of authority.[2]

The principle laid down by De Maistre, that the weaker an institution is the more people legislate and write about it,

---

[1] Dupont White, *L'Individu et l'État*, Paris, ed. 2, 1858, p. 37.
[2] *Op. cit.*, pp. 39 *seqq.*

is thus rejected by Dupont White. The progress of Society implies an ever-increasing legislative and regulative activity, an increasingly energetic expansion of authority from the centre to the circumference. Every growth of life is inevitably accompanied by an increase in the number of organs; thus the vast extension of the modern State, far from implying an intolerant oppression of the individual, represents the growth of his liberty.

This is true; but the path which it opens up is dangerous. It may encourage the illusion that freedom consists precisely in that complex of laws and regulations in which it clothes itself in order to survive in a social environment; and thus it may lead to the substitution of tailors' dummies for real people, unnoticed by an observer who only looks at the clothes. This is what happens to Dupont White in his volume *La Centralisation*, the sequel to *L'Individu et l'État*, in which the love of authority is pushed to the point of advocating a uniform centralization, and the self-government of the Liberals is condemned as a survival of feudalism.[1]

But the author is not unaware of the perils of centralization. The State becomes the butt for every criticism, and its very omnipotence thus renders its power precarious; in the last resort, centralization may lead to revolution. But no matter, he adds, if there must be criticism! A graver mistake leads him, in enumerating the means by which a centralized country may still be free, to mention, side by side with representative institutions, 'that outstanding force which is called the capital, which at once produces centralization and affords a ready-made counterpoise to the outstanding influence conferred by centralization upon the executive power '.[2] Unless we are mistaken, this means that the author appeals to the revolutionary Commune of Paris as a counterpoise to the Convention; in other words, finds a model for the Liberal State in the worst anarchy of the Revolution.

But in spite of his tendency towards authoritarian democracy, Dupont White preserves at least a touch of liberalism

---

[1] Dupont White, *La Centralisation*, Paris, 1860, p. 8.
[2] *Op. cit.*, pp. 117, 278.

which imparts a certain relief to the flat canvas of centralization. But this disappears altogether in the sociology of Comte,
who presents us with a pure and simple democracy, crude
and brutal beneath its scientific and ' positive ' vesture.
From the principle that Society is reality *par excellence* Comte
draws the conclusion that institutions made for the individual
must vanish. Freedom of criticism is the corner-stone of the
doctrine which, following the Saint-Simonians, he calls
' critical '; destroy that, and the rest will go. In a scientific
and ' organic ' Society, there is no more room for liberty of
conscience than there is in astronomy, chemistry, or physio-
logy. Popular sovereignty is a meaningless phrase; the word
right must be struck out of the political vocabulary as the
word *cause* is to be deleted from the philosophical; the individual man is an abstraction; the only thing which exists is
Society, and the only form of government is a dictatorship
exercised in its interests. The *coup d'état* of 1852 had in the
eyes of Comte the merit of initiating the dictatorial phase,
the only genuinely French phase, of the Second Republic.

John Stuart Mill described this conception as ' the most
complete system of spiritual and temporal despotism that
ever issued from the brain of any human being except perhaps Ignatius Loyola '. Even Comte's followers, the faithful
Littré and later the sociologist Durkheim, thought it monstrous, and repudiated its extreme consequences. Yet socio-
logical Positivism, even in a mild form, is for democracy a
swamp in which principles and programmes rot and fester,
and which as it encroaches upon modern political life has
degraded its intellectual character, deadened it and corrupted it. This disease has turned the finest and most aristocratic minds away from democracy in loathing, and has
converted the philosophical reaction against Positivism into
an anti-democratic crusade in the interests of exotic or out-
of-date political doctrines. This has been a serious loss to
European public life, because democracy, though still
remaining the predominant factor in politics, has become
an exclusive possession of ignorant and uneducated minds.

As compared with the theocratic despotism of a Comte,

a genuine old-fashioned theocracy like that of Montalembert appears not only dignified but even liberal. On the rise of Napoleon, Montalembert sadly remarked that silence had become the ideal of France, the country which had so long made an idol of free speech.

' But posterity will know,' he added, ' that there was one old soldier in the cause of Catholicism and liberty, who before 1830 already separated the Catholic cause from the royalist; who under the régime of July championed the independence of the Church upon the civil power; who in 1848 fought with all his might against the identification of Christianity with democracy; who in 1852 protests against the sacrifice of liberty to force under the pretext of religion.' [1]

The acquiescence of the Catholics is what most distresses Montalembert. Did they know that of all governments that which had always most endangered the Church was absolute government? did they know that the domination of a single man, claiming to act for all and think for all, was the ideal of paganism, as realized in the Roman Empire? Liberty and common rights were all that the Church and her believers demanded. A representative government, with a division of powers and a control over the work of government by the people, had been in all ages the condition of great and permanent influence upon the affairs of the world; the power of a single man had never produced anything except a brilliant but transient greatness and a brittle power like that of Louis XIV or Napoleon.

In practical politics, the various ideal motives of French Liberalism combined to form a single opposition to the Empire. But the exigences of the struggle brought them into alliance with very different elements, republican, legitimist, Orleanist. Every one who was discontented and restless united under the banner of Liberalism against the tranquillity of Napoleon's government. The result was a chaotic mixture, soon acted upon by the dictator's skill in those arts of corruption and blandishment which he had already put into prac-

[1] Montalembert, *Des intérêts catholiques au xixe siècle*, Bruxelles, 1852, p. 72.

tice in his dealings with the Socialists, the Democrats, and the Catholics.

The Liberal Empire was the second phase of Napoleon's kaleidoscopic policy, and began to appear about 1860. Liberty, in the Emperor's own words, cannot found a kingdom, but may in time consolidate it. In this remark, as in many others, he may have been sincere ; in a despotism there is generally one Liberal, the despot himself. But a Liberal of this type seldom displays a light or skilful touch. The conversion of Napoleon III to Liberalism turned his policy towards a path upon which the majority of the country were not disposed to follow him : the path of free trade. He became a convert to the doctrine of the economists on this subject, which we have already seen to be a superficial echo of the English system, and which had failed to win the support of a single nineteenth-century French writer or statesman outside the ' sect ' of the economists themselves. Having become a convert in theory, he hastened to become an exponent of free trade in practice, and negotiated with Cobden the commercial treaty of 1860.

But despotism is obliged to use coercion in order to create freedom ; that is, to destroy it by the very act intended to create it. The manufacturers and the agriculturists, the great majority of the economic forces of the nation, protested against Napoleon's move and formed a ' League for the protection of national labour '. The manufacturers might have gained by free trade : those of them at least who imported raw material from England, and perhaps even more definitely those producing objects of luxury, to which protectionism is wholly unsuited. This had been long ago observed by Cobden, when in the course of the Manchester School's campaign he called the attention of his countrymen to the complementary character of the textile industries in the two countries, and the consequent advantage of free trade, by which the English cotton and woollen manufactures would serve to clothe the French working man, while the fine French linens and the Parisian clothing industry would find a market in the upper classes of English society.

But the manufacturers were resolved, even if they lost by it, to maintain their old protectionist tradition, and refused to abandon it for a competition whose outcome was uncertain. They preferred to share the easy profits of State protection with the agriculturists. And after the brief interlude of free trade forced by Napoleon III upon the unwilling producers, the history of French finance presents a progressive increase of import duties on agricultural and industrial products, resulting from a compromise between the opposed interests of the two classes.

§ 5. THE LIBERALISM OF THE THIRD REPUBLIC

The fact that the Liberal opposition to the Empire did not prevent it from lasting eighteen years, and falling at last not through an internal crisis but because of a military disaster, shows how little a sense of freedom was diffused through the French public consciousness, or rather how completely it was dominated by the prevailing democratic and social tendencies. The Third Republic, born in defeat, and compelled from birth to struggle for existence against the Parisian revolutionaries' attempts to disrupt the State, has a strongly authoritarian character and a tendency towards the concentration of powers, resembling, except in externals, the attitude of the Empire. Against the Commune, which claimed for Paris the right to govern itself and form a federal alliance with other communities, the Republic took its stand on Napoleon's maxim that liberty is no foundation for a new State. Federalism has never brought success to its votaries in France, from the Girondins to the Communards ; and has only served to emphasize by their utter discomfiture the fundamentally centralized political and administrative structure of the French State.

This long-established historical tradition was in the present case reinforced by all those circumstances and impulses which emphasized and accentuated the activity of the State in contemporary Europe, and found in France an environment peculiarly favourable to their action.

Democracy provided a political platform for this encroachment of State activity, both because of its inherent tendency to centralization, and because of the expansive energy which propagates the idea of the State to the extreme limits of the circumference of society. But the triumph of democracy was bound up with other motives of a lower order : the selfishness, the parasitism, the corruption, which beneath the mantle of democracy pursued ends incapable of bearing open scrutiny. The sovereign people, as a writer has said, is like those fifteen-year-old kings who are officially declared to have attained their majority ; but, unlike theirs, we may add, the advisers of the sovereign people are chosen at haphazard and often with very poor results.

In this situation Liberalism, with its centrifugal tendency, its aristocratic outlook, and its predilection for the spontaneous and organic products of personal initiative, could only act, and can to-day only act, as a check and a corrective to French political life. If we look at the literature of modern France and modern Belgium, that which is inspired by Liberal ideas is at once the most copious and of the best quality. But this must not deceive us. In political society, writers are the exception ; and their Liberal sympathies emphasize the aristocratic character and critical function of liberalism.

The lead among these writers is taken by philosophers, Ravaisson, Fouillée, Janet; next to them may be named jurists and publicists like Anatole and Paul Leroy-Beaulieu, Molinari, Scherer, Laveleye, Prins (the last two Belgians), and finally Michel, who sums up and rounds off the movement. If we wish to discover the common characteristics of all these, we shall find that they are all alike derived from De Tocqueville, and that the programme of a Liberal democracy is their common ideal. But democracy is no longer the new and still indefinite historical phenomenon which presented itself to the eyes of their predecessor, and could mould itself to the shape of his lucid and comprehensive intellect ; it has a tradition, a complex and varied life, a structure, by now grown somewhat rigid, which obstruct the effort to shape it into the mould demanded by a Liberal outlook. Liberalism therefore must devote itself to preparing the way and clearing the path towards a distant goal at which the two ideals are to be united into one. Its critical attitude is often so prominent that disagreements are more visible than agreements, and even obscure the vision of the ultimate goal.

The greatest obstacle to this fusion lies in the profoundly divergent character of the authors' philosophical views of life. Democracy, trained in the school of scientific Positivism, shows itself utterly unable to grasp the idea of moral liberty, the value of personality, and the capacity of the individual to react upon his environment; it believes in necessity and historical determinism, it idolizes society and organization, and reduces individuality to a mere ingredient in a larger whole. Against this positivist outlook the philosophers of Liberalism rise in protest, convinced that unless liberty is recognized and asserted at the outset, any structure of civil, social, and political liberties is built upon sand. Certainly, neither the phenomenalism of Renouvier, nor the spiritualism of Janet, nor the attenuated idealism of Fouillée, can provide the foundation for a complete system of moral liberty; but they are well able to dispute the validity of deterministic arguments, and to transcend the theoretical agnosticism of the two opposed conceptions in the style of Kant by a practical postulate which is already an act of liberty. As Lequier says, even while denying that either liberty or necessity can be demonstrated or proved: ' We must choose between the two, either in one way or in the other.' [1]

Granted moral liberty, at least as a free right of choice, all other individual liberties acquire an enhanced and more intimate spiritual value. The liberty of thought, which democracy has petrified into a passive acceptance of positivistic and materialistic dogmas, is restored to the level of a right on the part of every man to search for the truth and the good in his own way, and to ask that others shall respect his work. Religious freedom, which under democracy has become a name for dogmatic irreligion, regains the consciousness of its own positive value: according to an often-repeated expres-

[1] Quoted by Michel in *L'idée de l'État*, Paris, ed. 3, 1898, p. 639.

sion of De Tocqueville's, man must believe if he does not wish to be a slave. The liberty of association, which likewise is in danger of degenerating into a brutal tyranny of the mass over the individual, is restated and justified in its original lofty sense as a means towards the formation and development of new individualities.

These, and the other personal liberties preserved by tradition, together form a system which demands that society and the State shall recognize it as an insuperable limit to their own activity. In this way modern Liberals are being led once more to the fundamental problem of the *Declaration of Rights*, and effectually deny that the problem is a thing of the past. In their eyes the demand on the part of the individual conscience to be released from the absorbing action of society and the State is ever living and present; because a rigid conformity, spiritual and moral, would be the worst form of slavery, and the surest way to dry up the sources of human progress, which flow from the rich variety of characters and temperaments.

But the justification of these immortal principles must not be that offered by the old jusnaturalism, when it asserted an imaginary and pseudo-historical priority of the individual to the State. A priority there is; but its character and significance are ideal; and thus, in place of a right of nature, Liberalism postulates a rational right, over and above all positive right, in which the individual and the State, which in the order of history arise simultaneously, find the definition of their limits and mutual relations.

In this way modern Liberalism is receiving a rationalistic *refonte*, linking it up more closely in fundamentals with its revolutionary predecessor. But the 'reason' of modern thinkers is not the mythical eighteenth-century *raison* which believed that it could invent history according to its own whims and caprices. It includes a critical consciousness which renders it cautious and respectful towards the historical order of human events; and therefore a tendency to act indirectly upon men's minds in order to bring about its ends, rather than directly upon institutions and constitutions.

No modern Liberalism has that naïve confidence in the omnipotence of legislation which the early Liberals had ; indeed,
it is when Liberals see that this confidence is to-day characteristic of democracy and Socialism, that they recognize the
political immaturity of these doctrines. This moderate scepticism shows itself in everything connected with the outward
forms of political machinery. The ideal of the perfect constitution is judged a chimera ; every constitution is good, if
a people will make use of it. Universal suffrage, the form of
modern democracy, is not accepted without reserve when
separated, as in fact it is, from a widely diffused culture and
a sense of political responsibility in individuals and classes.

The attention of Liberals is chiefly turned to the inner life
which animates political forms ; and this, once more, means
learning the lesson of English political experience. Representative and parliamentary government is only an illusory
appearance if it is set up by an isolated and transitory act of
popular sovereignty which has no roots in the public activities of the nation as a whole. It is only adequate to its highest
end of liberty and self-government when it forms the last link
in a chain of autonomous institutions, from the family to the
school, the union, the commune, the province, in which
power increases by exercise, and political ability is formed by
education.

The relation of Liberalism to democracy, and vice versa,
presents this difference in England and France respectively.
In England, Liberalism predominates, and gives its name and
its tone to a party, while democracy has no political organization of its own, and exercises only an indirect influence. In
France the opposite conditions prevail. Liberalism acts only
as a barrier or check, rendered necessary by the triumph of
democracy, because, as Leroy-Beaulieu says,

' were it not conquered in the name of liberty, democracy would
be the most ignorant despotism that the world has ever seen.
Apart from the liberal solution of the problem, democracy can
only offer a choice between two kinds of tyranny, both equally
crushing and humiliating : the tyranny of the masses, that is the
tyranny of the State and the commune, represented by omnipo-

tent assemblies, or the tyranny of a dictator, a civil or military master, embodying the forces of the people. Unless we can retain our hold upon the idea of liberty, unless we can set a limit to the continual encroachment of the State, if we sacrifice all the rights of the individual, the family, the living group, we shall never escape one or other of these tyrannies ; or rather, we shall endure them both successively, the one producing the other, as if by a kind of alternating generation.' [1]

[1] A. Leroy-Beaulieu, *La Révolution et le libéralisme*, Paris, 1890, p. 215.

III

GERMAN LIBERALISM

§ 1. ROMANTICISM

GERMAN Liberalism, in spite of appearances, presents a
spectacle of great historical interest, owing not only to
the unusual excellence of its theoretical statements, but also
to the peculiarities of its development, subjected as this has
been to a number of forces which have complicated its
character and turned it in unexpected directions.

In the eighteenth century, Germany presented a great
variety of territorial and political forms and mutually exclusive State traditions. Face to face with a feudal Empire, a
kingdom of Prussia was growing up, in which, although
feudalism had remained intact so far as civil society was concerned, a military and bureaucratic monarchy had established itself and taken in hand the political control of the
country in a manner wholly modern. Between the Empire
and Prussia lay a constellation of minor states of varying size,
some gravitating towards the two main centres of attraction,
others tending at least to remain outside this system and to
assimilate themselves to the political system of France, either
through geographical contiguity, as in the case of the
Rhenish states, or through a similarity of social structure, as
in the case of Bavaria.

The Revolution, beginning in France and propagating
itself in Germany, had the effect of accelerating these tendencies. In Western and Southern Germany it found a more
propitious field for its own diffusion : an agricultural society
already in great part liberated from feudalism, where small
and medium estates flourished, and where culture was prepared for that irruption of common rights which formed the
essence of the new Liberalism. But by destroying the Holy
Roman Empire, which during the medieval and modern
period had formed the ideal bond of the German people,

the Revolution made a new bond necessary. With its feeling for autonomy and independence, Liberalism aroused a powerful national consciousness, and directed it against the French conqueror. The idea of the Fatherland, of the German nation, was the new bond which replaced the broken fetters of the Empire. It had the same universalistic and mystical character. For the German of the beginning of the nineteenth century, to be *bloss deutsch* was to be *undeutsch*. His Fatherland was a cosmopolis, a *Weltbürgertum*, just as his Empire had been practically synonymous with Catholicism.

But side by side with this reminiscence of tradition, the spirit of modern Liberalism found a place in the new Fatherland. A nation cannot be constructed out of mere natural or historical facts; it must possess a consciousness able to transfigure and renew them. It is no mere historical accident that the national claims of the nineteenth century in Europe, especially those of Germany and Italy, had originally a Liberal character. To peoples possessing no tradition of political unity, only freedom could give the idea of a common citizenship capable of overcoming and dominating their political dismemberment. For the Germans, this citizenship was wholly ideal: their nation was a *Kulturnation*, in opposition to *Staatsnationen*; their freedom in fact consisted essentially in thought, and flourished in educated circles and in the schools, to a degree unparalleled in the most advanced *Staatsnationen* like France and England.

But if this ideal or literary unity satisfied men's minds in the first glow of romanticism, it became increasingly inadequate as the bitter experiences of the Napoleonic period revealed the weakness of the German nation relatively to its enormous potential strength, and the depressing effect of its political divisions upon all individual and public activities. The idea that the cultural nation must have its complement in the political nation gradually made headway in the German consciousness, and in the course of a single generation, that of Humboldt and Fichte, converted a naïve cosmopolitan patriotism into a national state.

The example which facilitated and directed this change

was that of Prussia, to which the attention of the whole nation was gradually drawn after the battle of Jena. Prussia united in her territory, as in a microcosm, the entire variety of historical and social conditions which characterized Germany as a whole. Her eastern provinces, enlarged by the partition of Poland, were still feudal. Here reigned the landed aristocracy, the *Junkertum*, rooted in the Middle Ages and ruling with almost sovereign power over its still servile agricultural dependents. The Prussian landed aristocracy, like the English, and unlike the French, discharged all the political duties attaching to the property which it owned. It lived in its castles, administered, governed, and preserved a prestige which the monarchy had never attempted to attack and had indeed skilfully fostered in its own interest. The alliance between the King of Prussia and the Junker caste was the distinctive feature of the German political system, which thus represented an intermediate term between the English system and the continental system of France. With the former it shared the aristocratic character of the governing classes with all the traditionalism and medievalism which that implies; with the second, a military and administrative monarchy. And while in England the aristocracy had succeeded in establishing its predominance only at the expense of the Crown, and in France the latter had risen to power over the ruins of the aristocracy, in Prussia the two political forces had come to an agreement whose roots are to be found in a vigorous blend of the individualistic Teutonic spirit and the historical needs of military defence due to the continental situation of the country.

A practical field for the agreement between the monarchy and the landed aristocracy was provided by the fact that the former had organized its army and bureaucracy by recruiting their higher ranks among the younger members of aristocratic families. It had thus been able to extend its own activities without creating friction, and had on the contrary won the loyalty of the nobles by attaching their sons to itself. By this means, while leaving almost intact the traditional privileges of the class, and turning its enormous conservative force to its own ends, the Crown had conceived and carried out a programme of State reconstruction held up by eighteenth-century illuminism as an unequalled model to every European sovereign.

The legal code drawn up by order of Frederick the Great and promulgated by his successor bears clear traces of this union. It proclaims that the good of the State and of its inhabitants is the end of Society and the limit of the law; and that the law cannot limit the freedom and rights of citizens except in the public interest. There is no mention of a hereditary patrimonial right on the part of the king and his family, nor of a private right distinct from that of the State. The name ' State ' is the only one used by the legislator to designate the royal power. It is, however, implied that the king personifies the State as its supreme functionary, and as the representative and agent of Society.

But beneath this very modern head, as De Tocqueville acutely remarked, one saw a Gothic body. The inhabitants of the country-side, with rare exceptions, remained in a state of hereditary serfdom; the greater part of the privileges of the landowners was explicitly sanctioned; the nobility was declared the chief body of the State: it alone could possess noble property and create trusts, enjoy the rights of chase and jurisdiction inherent in noble property, and so forth. And with a curious mingling of incompatible principles, it was proclaimed that all citizens must be equally subject to taxation, while provincial laws containing exceptions to this rule were left standing; the principle was laid down that the State has the duty of supervising the employment and wages of those who cannot maintain themselves, while the peasants were left at the mercy of their masters.[1]

But not the whole of Prussia was feudal. The *Junkertum* of eastern Prussia stood side by side with the *bourgeois* society of the west on the French frontier. Here lay the fertile and well-watered lands where small estates flourished,

---

[1] De Tocqueville, *L'ancien régime*, ed. Calmann-Lévy, appendix, pp. 336 *seqq.*

where the peasant was emancipated from serfdom, where property by common right was the vehicle of individualism and liberal rationalism. The *bourgeoisie* of the west was loyal to the Crown, whose breadth of outlook and assiduous care for the public good it valued ; but it detested the hybrid confusion of modern and medieval elements, and would have liked to shift the centre of gravity of the State in order to rid it of the relics of feudalism and permit the monarchy to pursue its task of reform to the end. The impulse of the French Revolution hastened the fulfilment of these wishes ; later, the defeat of Jena, unexpectedly revealing the weakness of the State, upon which the great name of Frederick still bestowed no small prestige, made it imperative to reform Society and the State and rid them of their antiquated elements. The country could never rise from its prostration and servitude without becoming the country of all ; only so could it unite in itself the energies of all its citizens. The rural population, therefore, weakened and degraded by serfdom, must be raised to the citizenship ; a public spirit must be created able by its unanimous action to carry the State with it, in place of the narrow particularistic outlook of a small caste ; freedom must become the source of new energies. The projects of Hardenberg were permeated by this spirit of freedom. He demanded so much liberty and equality as was compatible with monarchy and a free civil society : the abolition of the privileges of the nobility with regard to public office, possession of baronial lands, and exemption from taxes ; the abolition of the hereditary dependence of the peasants and the restrictions on the acquisition and use of land ; and the institution of national representation so far as this did not prejudice the principle of monarchy : not, that is to say, a true parliament, but a kind of elective and unpaid assessorate.

The proposed reforms of Baron von Stein, drawn up in 1807, were more organic in character. If their negative and critical part resembled that of Hardenberg's proposals and consisted in a programme of rural emancipation, the positive and constructive part attacked the political problem in all its complexity and attempted to unite the *bourgeoisie* and the rural aristocracy into a liberal system. This strictly realistic and historical attitude distinguishes them sharply from the generalized rationalism of the French system, and makes them a distinct type, and a model for all subsequent generations of politicians. For Stein, a Liberal government was not the same thing as a parliament; his dislike of the Cabinet system, as interposing between the king and his ministers a collective entity, capable of destroying the directness of their relations, rendered him reluctant to accept office under the King of Prussia. He would leave all political initiative to the Crown, limited only by the law, and controlled only by popular representation. But the most effectual liberal force, in Stein's opinion, was that of autonomous local administration. Here the participation of the people in government was actual and unimpaired by fictions. Hence Stein distinguished sharply between State administration and provincial administration : the former must be struck out of the duties of elective magistrates, on pain of falling into the dangerous anarchy of revolutionary France, which nothing but the despotism of Napoleon could bring to an end. The particular interests of the provinces, on the other hand, must be directly attended to by the persons interested, since this was the only way in which their public spirit and civic sense could be stimulated and the spirit of the nation reconciled with the authority of government. Provincial colleges composed of paid officials generated a mercenary spirit, a life enclosed within the forms and machinery of bureaucracy, ignorance of the region administered, indifference and distrust towards all innovation. To exclude the landowners from the care of the common interests meant refusing to profit by the bonds which unite them to the Fatherland ; a skilfully selected body of representatives from among their ranks was a powerful means towards strengthening the hands of the government.

This project of Stein, whose application begins with his rise to power in 1807, was the diagonal of the Prussian political parallelogram of forces. It strengthened the monarchy by broadening its basis ; it liberated the peasantry to the loss of the aristocratic class, but compensated this loss by offering the aristocracy an opportunity to renew its historic claims and prestige by an active participation in provincial government. It satisfied the more modest aspirations of *bourgeois* Liberalism; it introduced State reform under the guise of a corollary to the traditional self-government which the German communities had for centuries practised and which the encroachment of the monarchical bureaucracy had stifled without wholly destroying. In the sequel, Stein's Liberalism was regarded with great respect, even by the historians most hostile to ' radical ' Utopias, for the sake of its agreement with the German spirit; it provided a starting-point for the doctrines of constitutionalism and the ' State of rights ', the loftiest expressions of the political and legal consciousness of the German people.

The age of Stein was the golden age of Prussian Liberalism, inspired by patriotic sentiment, by the task of shaking off the yoke of Napoleon, and by the hope of restoring German unity under a single flag of liberty. But this success was transitory, because premature. The rural classes, emancipated by law, were unprepared to claim their rights, and preserved a feudal spirit which no care on the part of the government could dispel. The Junkers profited by their subjects' prostration to keep them in bondage despite the law, and attempted in their turn to draw the monarchy within their own orbit by availing themselves of the general movement of reaction which unexpectedly brought their antiquated feudal outlook up to date. The form of the patrimonial State, with its proprietary monarch and its medieval representation of privileged classes, came back into fashion, and was stated by Haller with an appearance of scientific cogency. In countries like France and England, the dream of an anachronistic revival of the Middle Ages would have remained confined to the heads of the dreamers; but not so in Prussia, where the monarchy found in the conflict between Liberals and reactionaries an opportunity to affirm its own supremacy unopposed and to govern the country according to its own views. The fact that the perplexed and vacillating Frederick III was succeeded by a king of the type of the Tsar Alexander, full of romantic medievalist fancies and wrapped up in a mystical mission whose fulfilment he regarded as a sacred duty, was enough, in all appearance, to ensure the realization of this anachronistic dream. But the German people was to find in its culture the antidote to an evil which culture itself had produced.

Before proceeding to narrate the events which took place in the reign of Frederick William IV, it will be useful to examine the genesis of German Liberalism from within, and to ask why Romanticism ended by rejecting it and promoting a reactionary type of thought inspired by the purest Junkerism.

The ideas of the French Revolution were at first enthusiastically welcomed by the ablest exponents of German culture. Goethe, Kant, Schiller, Fichte, Humboldt, recognized in these trenchant assertions a powerful historical reinforcement of the ideal of an autonomous spiritual life, as conceived by themselves in solitary meditation. Each transferred into his interpretation and commentary on the Revolation a part of himself. The Kantian conception of liberty as the capacity of the will to determine itself by itself according to its own rational law, the conversion of pure reason into practical reason, found practical expression in the work of the Revolution, which converted a philosophy into an act of human emancipation. It inaugurated the reign of personality, victorious over nature, narrow selfishness, and passive tradition. Schiller and Humboldt collaborated to write the text of this drama, whose hero had been depicted in sober and severe outline by Kant.

But to Kant belongs the merit not only of giving the highest expression to human freedom, but also of having modelled upon it an entire political organization, into which he transfused the more vital elements of the experience of revolutionary France. Kant based his theory of the State on the fundamental distinction of his practical philosophy, the distinction between legality and morality. Under the former head, an action is considered simply as conforming to the law, irrespective of its motives ; under the latter, as exhibiting a special kind of conformity in which the idea of duty, regarded as a law, constitutes the true motive of the action. The State controlled the sphere of legality, the sphere of actions in their outward conformity to law ; it had nothing to do with the sphere of morality, which lay wholly in the conscience of the individual ; for no authority except that of conscience could either create or judge the inner morality of human acts.

In these terms, with the utmost rationalistic clarity, Kant defined simultaneously the State and its limitations, discipline and spontaneity, law and liberty. The State is a strictly legal organization, whose chief care is to ensure the possibility of an ordered coexistence of individuals ; it personifies that universal law in which the free will of each may be reconciled with that of all others. But the single individuals enabled by the State to coexist are not its creation ; they have their own autonomous ground, and their claim to existence forms the primary right belonging to every man simply as man.

With Kant we are still within the circle of jusnaturalism. And in conformity with the individualistic outlook of that school, Kant explains the origin of the State by a social contract in virtue of which all, *omnes et singuli*, give up their outward liberty in favour of the community, to receive it again, converted into civil liberty, in their capacity as members of a political organization. In this exchange the individual does not sacrifice part of himself to a greater whole; by giving up a savage and lawless liberty, he finds the whole of his liberty in legal dependence, that is, in the legal state.

If the idea of the contract recalls not only Rousseau but the German tradition of the patrimonial and privatistic State, what emerges from it with a profoundly modern aspect is a juridical conception of the State destined to leave an indelible mark on nineteenth-century Liberalism. From this point of view the whole science of German public law has its origin in Kant, from whom it has learnt to regard the organization and defence of rights not only as an essential function of the State but also as the limit of the State's action. For the German people this has been a lesson of inestimable value, because their lively and constant preoccupation with this legal problem has made good the defects of their political evolution. The monarchical power has never pressed too heavily upon their shoulders, even in periods of the strictest absolutism, because it has always been tempered by a profound consciousness of this limit. Even when in the minds of the governing class the memory of the revolutionary declaration of individual rights has grown dim, its essence has been already transferred to the organism of the State; and even if claims on the part of individuals against the State could no longer be regarded as admissible, the principle expressed in such claims was alive and active in virtue of the juridical self-limitation of the State.

But in Kant's immediate followers this positive characterization of the Liberal State was submerged beneath a flood of anti-State individualism. Kant discovered in law not only the strength but also the antidote of revolution; he thus denied the right of resistance which the revolutionaries claimed in their *Declaration of the Rights of Man*.

A legal admission of revolt, he observed, meant a legal sanction for it; and that meant that the sovereign must have his hands tied by a provision in virtue of which he was no longer sovereign—an obvious contradiction. Less cautious than Kant, and less firmly sustained by a balanced legal sense, Fichte pushed the theory of contract to its most absurd consequences. Granted the social contract, that is, the right of self-constitution in the sense explained above, the possibility of constitutional changes, with the consent of all contracting parties, must follow. But the privatistic nature of the act implied that a person who did not wish for this change could not be forced to accept it. In that case he would withdraw from the State and re-enter the domain of the pure moral law, which for Fichte was the condition of the individual before the establishment of the State.

No less subversive of the autonomy of the State is the function, attributed to it by Fichte, of a mere guardian and custodian of property, an institution which he regards as foreign and prior to the State in origin, as an immediate and ultimate object of the individual will. Thus the legal provisions of Kant's conception degenerate into mere police provisions, and we meet with the figure of the ' policeman ' or ' night-watchman ' State, which was to be a butt for the derision of a riper German political consciousness.

The masterpiece of political individualism in the romantic period is Wilhelm Humboldt's little *Essay on the Limits of the Action of the State*, written in 1792 and posthumously published in 1851. Here the importance of liberty in the formation of human personality is shown in its most lively and attractive colours. Liberty is simply the possibility of a varied, because unlimited, activity ; it is thus the condition of all growth of individual powers. Even the most independent and unprejudiced man, placed in a uniform environment, progresses more slowly. The intervention of the State in regulating his private life paralyses the development of his faculties and talents ; and in the mutual relations of individuals it weakens the interest which each ought spontaneously to take in the others, and generates a mutual suspicion. Mutual aid is the more readily given as each citizen feels more vividly that all depend upon him ; and experience shows that in the oppressed classes, deserted by the government, the sentiment of solidarity redoubles its strength. Everything is better done when people do it for itself and not for an ulterior result. This is because action, provided it is free and spontaneous, is dearer than possession. The most active and vigorous man would rather do nothing than work at forced labour. And freedom not only increases men's strength, but through this increase it brings about a more generous disposition. Coercion, on the other hand, diminishes their energies, excites their selfish desires, and promotes the most abject and petty shifts. Coercion may perhaps impede certain errors ; but it also destroys the beauty of the most useful actions. Freedom may perhaps give rise to certain errors ; but even upon vice it bestows a less ignoble aspect.

Nothing so well teaches men how to deserve freedom as freedom itself. This will not be admitted by those who constantly appeal to an alleged immaturity as a pretext for oppression. The lack of a maturity sufficient for the enjoyment of freedom can only be due to a lack of intellectual and moral strength, and combated only by increasing this strength. To increase it, one must exercise it; and for its exercise the spirit of initiative which only freedom can confer is indispensable.

Faced with this exuberant assertion of individuality, the function of the State shrinks to mere security, to the removal of all disturbance or usurpations which may impede citizens in the free exercise of their rights. And if any one opposes this narrow police activity in the name of a more complex and organic function, capable of uniting into a unity the dispersed and fragmentary life of individuals, Humboldt, though attaching a high value to the organicism of the romantic conception, replies that only the free association of individuals can create anything really organic, while State intervention can realize nothing but an uncreative machine.

Humboldt's essay was written under the influence of Mirabeau's *Éducation politique*; in reading it, no less than in the contemporary works of Fichte and Friedrich Schlegel, we breathe the air of the French Revolution. But as these years of revolutionary excitement pass away, we see in the same men a profound change not only of tone but also of mental attitude. This is in part certainly due to the new turn taken by the history of the Revolution, with its creation of a new despotism more loathsome than the old within the very bosom of liberty, a military dictatorship, a lust for conquest, disappointing the generous hopes of German culture. But the conversion of the Romantics had causes more deeply seated than this, in comparison with which the changes of French policy were only accidental occasions and stimulants.

Liberal individualism is only one aspect or element in the romantic outlook; it is the first isolated and sporadic revelation of the German mind. The development of this revelation brings with it the consequence that this individual accent propagates and communicates itself to everything that the German mind has created in the course of its history. Above the single personalities stands the genius of the race, the German nation, with the unique individual features which make it a living and organic personality. This nation cannot be explained, like the State, as the creature of an arbitrary contract. It has its language, its traditions, its customs, whose origin lies in no artifice or convention, but in spontaneous and creative movements of the spirit of history. Towards this figure the romantic mind turns with the same love with which it had previously beheld itself, and there finds in a higher degree the same liberty which presides over the birth of individuals.

The historicism of the Romantics is only the self-recognition of the individual in an ever-widening sphere. In this vital contact the distant past is transfigured and reveals its hidden treasures. The nation is a living whole, including within itself many individual lives; and the German genius, even in its earliest medieval manifestations, is peculiarly endowed with that taste for ideal personifications which is so foreign to the dry and logical mind of the Latin nations. Thus to the eyes of seekers so ready to find them there appeared a whole world of ' personalities '—societies, corporations, communes, universities, classes, religious associations, and an entire network of legal and political relations binding this complex manifold together into the Gothic rigidity of national unity.

These historical experiences formed the best antidote to the abstract rationalism of the Revolution, which converts individuals into atoms, and having destroyed their organic bonds claims to replace them by means of artifice and convention, forgetful of those exigences of human freedom which it has itself discovered. And by way of the nation, German Romanticism learnt a deeper sense of the value of the State.

Already in the philosophy of Novalis, side by side with assertions of individualism, we find a demand that the idea of the State should penetrate more deeply into the lives of individuals, because the more living and spiritual are its members the more living and personal is the State. In

Friedrich Schlegel, who had at first been more infected by
republican radicalism than any other Romantic, the turn
towards conservatism is even more definite. In Schlegel the
love of the national spirit becomes a desire to restore all the
organization in which that spirit has historically expressed
itself. Hence the true national State of his dreams is that of
feudal monarchy, with the people arranged in classes and the
military aristocracy standing at the head. To the question,
What is a nation? Joseph de Maistre had answered : The
sovereign and the aristocracy. Schlegel's ideal is perfectly
consistent with this reply. And in the last phase of Fichte's
activity, beginning with the *Closed Commerical State* of 1800
and continuing through the *Addresses to the German Nation* in
1807 and 1808 to the political testament of 1813, there is seen
a growing attraction towards the Prussian State. Humboldt,
turned politician in middle life, finds in this new function the
natural corrective of his youthful antagonism to the State.

The conservative nationalism towards which German
Romanticism was tending resembled that of Burke, also
orientated towards history and respectful of traditional continuity. The writings of Burke were more eagerly read and
interpreted in Germany than in any other country. Friedrich
Gentz was the first of these interpreters ; his reactionary temperament emphasized and aggravated the anti-Liberal tendency of many of Burke's ideas. Adam Müller, who derived
from both these writers, expounded in his *Elements of the Art
of the State* a theory of the political organism from which all
trace of contractualism and jusnaturalism had vanished, and
the State appeared as a communion ' of the total inner and
outer life of a nation in a complete unity, great, energetic,
infinitely alive and active '.[1]

The idea of the nation was the link between romantic
individualism and this view of the State as an organism.
By its means, cultural and ethical ideals, which the German
thought of the Revolutionary period had set outside the
sphere of the State, and regarded as belonging exclusively
to the individual, were restored to the State. The legal

[1] A. Müller, *Elemente der Staatskunst*, i. 51.

attributes of the State, in their turn, undergo a profound change of spirit. The historical school of law, beginning with Hugo and Savigny, here attacked the revolutionary spirit in its last stronghold. To the rationalism which regarded rights as an innate principle applicable to all alike and subject to the laws of pure reason, the historical school opposed the idea of rights as a spontaneous and organic creation of the national spirit, like language, customs, and all other popular institutions. Savigny exaggerates and therefore falsifies the element of truth undoubtedly contained in this idea, to the point of denying that the spirit of his own times was ripe for the códification of law, and of disputing, with very feeble arguments, the value of the *Code Napoléon*. This was the subject of his famous controversy with Thibault. His dislike of codes extends not only to their formal and systematic character, but to their actual content; the abstract determination of juridical rules, he maintains, breaks the continuity of legal development, and turns a living organism into a lifeless *ens rationis*.

If this idea of development represents a real advance on the static hypostatizations of jusnaturalism, the conservative and reactionary interpretation put upon it by the historical spirit of the time turns the advance into a retrogression by opposing codification, not in the name of legal progress, but in the interest of a revival of ancient Teutonic law. *Historicism* did not conceal its sympathy for the quaint Gothic architecture of customary rights which the French Revolution set out to destroy, and which to early nineteenth-century students seemed the purest and most genuine expression of their national spirit.

The same tendency is to be seen in other fields of romantic activity: art, literature, religion, and politics. The love of everything strictly German, in the most medieval sense, led the Romantics even to repudiate the Protestant Reformation, which many of them regarded as a modern departure from the great Catholic tradition of ancient Teutonism. Friedrich Schlegel, Novalis, Adam Müller, Stolberg, and Haller joined the Church of Rome—a step which increased the difficulties already besetting the Lutheran churches. But even those whose conception of tradition was wide enough to embrace a religion three centuries old, and perfectly assimilated to the spirit of the people, turned Lutheranism into a principle no less conservative than that in whose interest the neo-Catholics had deserted that faith. Lutheranism has in fact a political character profoundly hostile to all revolutionary movements; it was therefore in complete harmony with the legitimistic tendencies current at the time of the Holy Alliance.

But the Romantics, with their dreams of medievalism and their national and political fervour, were torn by an inner conflict. In their hatred of the revolutionary lust for destruction which had laid their country low, they would rediscover the sources of national energy and create a strong State to express the organic unity of their nation. But their historical study of German national life directed them towards an age in which they found the soul of the people in all its purity, but did not find even the germ of the State which they desired. In the Middle Ages the German State was a mere shadow; and, what was worse, the only concrete realities to be found in medieval politics were far more like the contractualistic ideas of the detested jusnaturalism than their own ideal of a sovereign State. The source of the prince's power lay in property, in which the attributes of sovereignty inhered; the relations between prince and people were based on private contracts, analogous, at least in their privatistic character, to the social contract of democratic abstractions. A public law which, by clearly distinguishing sovereignty from the possession of property, could serve as foundation to a genuine State, was wholly lacking, and (by a profound irony) began to appear precisely through the operation of those democratic abstractions which, by suppressing feudalism, had pointed out the only way of distinguishing private life from public, property from sovereignty. The Romantics were compelled to hate what they ought to love, and to love what they ought to hate; hungry for concrete fact, they lived in a world of abstractions and dreams. A taste for the organic made them repudiate not only the Revolution, but also the machinery, as they called it, bureaucratic and military, of Frederick's monarchy; that is, all the more modern phases in the development of their national organism. Their love of history in the last resort turned into an anti-historical fetishism, which exalted one period to the detriment of all others and of the very laws of historical evolution.

This anachronistic spirit finds its most eccentric, precisely because its most complete and ' organic ', expression in Haller's work on the *Restoration of the Science of the State*. Here we find an encomium upon force as opposed to the abstraction of ' right '. It is a law of nature that the stronger should rule the weaker, and that instead of every one's being impossibly and uselessly free, some should be free and others in subjection. The source of independence is property, and here lies also the source of power. A realm is only a private estate, the property of a great lord ; hence the realm is made for the prince, not vice versa. The power and function of government are his right and not his duty, precisely because every man has the right to dispose of his own, and to enjoy a legitimate freedom in proportion to his means. Nothing, according to Haller, could be more rhetorical and false than the position, ascribed to the prince by Frederick the Great, of the first functionary in the State; he is its lord, in the strictest sense of that word, and depends on no one but God, whose viceregent he is upon earth.

But if sovereignty is a mere appanage of property, its limitations are determined by the limitations of property. The right of the prince is limited by the right of other lesser proprietors, in proportion to their autonomy as owners of property. This principle leads directly to feudal anarchy. According to the pseudo-philosophical system of the social contract, says Haller,[1] all men must be equally subject to the authority of the State which they have established in common, and must sacrifice all their liberty and so become slaves. But in States framed according to nature, liberty,

[1] Haller, *Ristaurazione della scienza politica*, Ital. tr., Naples, 1850, ch. 53, p. 518.

like dependence, has infinite gradations; the objects, the entity, the duration of services present great variety; each contracts at pleasure according to his means, his needs, and his ends; each is as free as he can be, each in proportion to his needs is dependent for the sake of the advantages which he himself seeks. As the son ceases to be subject to his father when he ceases to live in his father's house, so the duty of the subject disappears when he leaves the service of the prince.

It is easy here to see how Haller's hatred for the revolutionary contractualism which tries to bind all individuals in order to strengthen the State leads him to desire the restoration of a feudal contractualism destructive of the State. In no writer does the contradiction between the ideal of a strong and really monarchical State and the actual disintegration of the State's rights and functions appear so plainly as in Haller, upon whom the spirit of the times bestowed the unexpected honour of seeing his anachronistic dreams enter upon the stage of political realities and supply an inspiration to the reforms of Frederick William IV.

This conversion of Romanticism to a medieval Utopianism, while depriving the liberal and *bourgeois* spirit of some of its best forces, by its very exaggerations rehabilitated, at least in part, the thesis of Liberalism. If its medievalism expressed the spirit of the old aristocratic and feudal Germany, it was Liberalism that expressed the demands of modern Germany; the living nation had claims of its own, no less cogent than the claims of the nation that once lived. The problem presented by the coexistence of these opposed currents of thought was the discovery of a middle term to reconcile the demands of the present with those of the past, and permit a more genuinely historical expression of the continuity of the national life. Between the abstract rationalism of the revolutionaries, which would make a clean sweep of the past, and the no less abstract historicism of the reactionaries, which would make a clean sweep of the present, there was room for a synthetic conception, which, by interpreting reason itself historically, reduced the various phases of political evolution to a common denominator, fused individual and State into a single whole, united formal law and traditional custom, the patrimonial interests of classes and the sovereignty of public law. This synthetic conception, worked out in a brilliant and masterly manner, was achieved by Hegel.

§ 2. HEGEL

To a mind approaching it unencumbered by the prejudices of a philosophical school, Hegel's theory of the State reveals itself as something very different from a dry series of formulae. No political system, except perhaps that of Aristotle, is so rich in historical content as Hegel's *Philosophy of Right*. Even its systematic structure, far from being an arbitrary piece of mechanism, expresses the growing complexity of the problem of political organization in the ideal sequence of its factors: the individual, Society, the State. The mainspring of this development is freedom, which coincides with the idea of spirit, and therefore is not exhausted in the affirmation of isolated personalities, but gives rise to formations of a higher order which express the relations of individuals to one another.

Individuality is the factor which the philosophy of the Revolution asserted with all its energy. It is will in its immediacy, as subjective right, in which human freedom displays itself in the purest and most naïve particularism. But even in this first and narrowest sphere, liberty is no mere caprice, no abstract faculty of doing whatever one likes: that is the illusion of the doctrinaires, which lay at the root of all the wreckage and horror of the Revolution. Freedom, as right, has always a particular object, and tends to realize a personality, something limited and organic. Its first realization is already a determination of its abstract potentiality. This is precisely property, as based on an act of affirmation in which the will creates an external sphere for its own liberty, and completes the subjective energy of personality by supplying it with a proper object.

Thus it would appear that, since right is based on a pure act of will, to which Society and the State are altogether foreign, jusnaturalism is fundamentally right, and the idea of a declaration of the rights of man is sound. But in Hegel's view a right, as the expression of mere individuality, is not a concrete and independent existence, but a factor, a transcendental or abstract moment, in a process in which this primitive nucleus enriches itself by acquiring new and increasingly complex determinations. Thus property, which is at first asserted as the realization of the will in an object, can only develop the legal character, which distinguishes it from mere possession, in virtue of a recognition by other wills, other persons. Thus property ' passes over ', to use Hegel's phraseology, into contract; the immediate right *to* a thing is mediated by the right *towards* the persons.

The sphere of contract, implying the presence of various individuals and the combination of various rights, represents a higher form of liberty, but not so high that a theory of the State can be based upon it, as jusnaturalism tried to base it. The error of this school consists in transferring the characteristics of property and private rights into a sphere which is quite different and higher in its nature.

The idea of contract introduces us to a wider world of human relations, but leaves us standing on the threshold of this world. Even the family, the first organic nucleus above the level of the individual, transcends in its formation the sphere of contract. If we look at the family from the point of view of its relation to property, we see the individualistic and selfish aspect of property changing into something ethical, a function devoted to providing for the subsistence of a community. The right of inheritance cannot be justified by reference to the will of the individual; it requires a higher justification, which makes individuality itself an organ in a higher organism to which property attaches as the object of a more complex subject.

Family life, including marriage, the education of children, and inheritance, presents us with a system of relations which are incommensurable as a whole with the principle of abstract right. If in this narrower sphere I have a right, and another man has a duty, in relation to one and the same

thing, in the sphere of family life rights and duties are correlative; I have rights in so far as I have duties. The family
belongs to the world of *ethos*, where the subjective freedom
of the will objectifies itself and organizes itself into civil
Society.

Society is the intermediate factor between the individual
and the State. That is Hegel's great discovery, and the
turning-point of all German nineteenth-century political
science. The social organism, inserting itself between the
two extreme terms which revolutionary theory had brought
too perilously face to face, makes it possible not only to place
the idea of the State in a region secure against the assaults
of the individual, but also to canalize into that idea, in an
organic and disciplined form, all the claims and aspirations
that spring spontaneously out of the individual life. It parts
the two protagonists in the struggle, and at the same time
unites them by a firmer bond. It destroys the Revolutionary
fancy that the State is a product of convention and caprice,
but it equally rejects the reactionary fallacy that the State
is identical with the prince and stands over against the consciousness of the people as an external object.

The Hegelian theory of Society is only a formulation *sub
specie aeterni* of the historical content of the social life of his
time. It is easy to detect in it a rapidly changing world, in
which the relics of an ancient feudalism are mingled with
the seeds of a new *bourgeois* Society. The family, the guilds,
the classes, are displayed in an ordered hierarchy through
whose gradations the *ethos* of Society develops organically and
directs itself towards the *polis*.

Hegel shows us an essentially agricultural society, where
the class of cultivators, in the physiocratic sense of the word,
forms the broad base of the social pyramid. He has a keen
sense of the economic significance of class distinctions. The
effort to satisfy needs and acquire wealth, starting at the
level of purely individual selfishness, changes as it works
' into the contribution to the satisfaction of the needs of all
others, the mediation of the individual through the universal ;
thus each, because he acquires and produces and enjoys for

himself, produces and acquires for the enjoyment of others '. To this relation is due the division and solidarity of classes, each characterized by a close affinity of private interest, but containing at the same time a superior demand linking it up with the system as a whole.

Above the agricultural class comes that of the artisans, which Hegel conceives under the form of the medieval guild, with no presentiment of that industrial revolution which in the backward Germany of his day had not yet begun. To a higher stage in the social hierarchy belongs the middle class, the salaried class created by the monarchy of Frederick, in which political consciousness is more widely diffused; at the summit of the pyramid stands the general class, the class of independent proprietors. 'This class is adapted to a political function by the fact that its property is independent of the property of the State, the uncertainties of trade, and the desire for gain; it is set free from the dominion of its own caprice, because its members have not the right, which other citizens have, to dispose freely of the whole of their property, since this is entailed.' Thus Hegel's general class is simply the Prussian *Junkertum*.

But if the social hierarchy is in this respect still feudal, the end to which Hegel directs it is modern. The function of the classes is not exhausted by the care of their private interest, but has an increasingly general importance and serves to prepare the way by degrees for the function of the State. From civil Society emanate the representatives, deputies, and delegates, that watch over the work of government and enable the State to take account of the needs and interests of the people.

The principle that representatives are organs of Society, and not directly of the State, is an extremely important doctrine which Laurent Stein, under the influence of French Socialism and not without a reminiscence of Hegel, was later to introduce into political circles. But it is a principle peculiar to German public law, which rejects popular sovereignty and parliamentary government, and places the State in a sphere above that of civil Society, giving to the latter no direct part in the government, but only a critical function. In countries with parliamentary government, representation is strictly political, not social only; it thus forms an organ of the State. But the influence of Socialism, emphasizing the element of class as the foundation of the State, later gave this Hegelian view a more widely European importance, and aroused even in democratic countries a demand for the creation, side by side with purely political representation, of an organic system of class representation.

In Hegel the doctrine is to a great extent a reminiscence of the constitution of the ancient Teutonic state, subordinated as it was in his time to the monarchy of Frederick. It also contains an element, not easy to explain, of ideas drawn from French public law : for example, the statement that deputies are not mandatories or bearers of instructions, but are wholly free in their discussions and deliberations.

Another task which Hegel assigns to civil Society, in contrast with the prevailing theory, is the administration of justice. The protection of the property and life of individuals, the essential function of the State according to Kant's and Humboldt's Liberalism, belongs for Hegel to a sphere anterior to that of the State. ' People make a miscalculation ', he says, ' when they consider the State merely as a civil society, and assert that its proper end is merely to guarantee the life and property of individuals ; for such guarantee is not attained by the sacrifice of that which is guaranteed ; and this is precisely the sacrifice which the State demands in war.' The State thus expresses a claim higher than that attributed to it by the lawyers, which would be limited by the interests of individuals. All the errors of contractualism, which reduces the bond between the individual and the State to a contingent and arbitrary connexion, are derived from this failure to recognize the uniqueness and autonomy of the State organism and the true universality of its mission.

The State is to Society as the universal to the particular, as the ethical idea to the *ethos*. It is the expression of rationality, the world become spirit ; it is freedom in the fullness of its realization. These and similar statements of Hegel's are certainly emphatic; and since they have had the misfortune to be frequently quoted in isolation from their context in his system, and often by people otherwise wholly ignorant of his system, they have been regarded by incompetent and prejudiced judges as a shibboleth and a scandal. If we want to understand their historical significance, we must reflect that the idea of the State as something divine arose in Hegel's mind in opposition to the various political tendencies of his time which degraded it into a policeman, or a contingent product of tradition, or a special kind of private property. The contempt with which he speaks of Haller is a negative measure of the loftiness of his own political feeling. And the mere fact that the social materials at his disposal were insufficient, owing to their antiquated character, to form an adequate foundation for his highly modern idea of the State, forced him to make a sharp distinction between Society and the State, and to treat the latter as a kind of transcendent and superior entity.

It must also be remembered that when he speaks of the State as the incarnation of reason and liberty, he is not referring to any particular State, but to the genuinely modern State governed by a constitutional monarchy, impersonating the spirit of the people, and shaping the law which penetrates all their relations. This State is the living antithesis to that of the Middle Ages, in which the private interests of classes and corporations were the chief forces at work, and the whole was rather an aggregate than an organism. The attribute expressing the universal and public character of the modern State, as opposed to the particular and privatistic nature of the feudal State, is sovereignty, which belongs neither to the monarch, nor to the government, nor to the political bodies, taken singly, but to their unity in the State as a whole.

No less vivid is the contrast in Hegel's conception between the constitutional State and the despotic. In the latter, the monarch and the people stand face to face without those intermediate organizations whose function is to bestow a

legal and orderly form upon the interests of the multitude
Thus on the one hand the monarch acts arbitrarily; and on
the other, the people is a disorganized mass of atoms, which
does not know what it wants and whose strength is only
shown in acts of destruction.[1]

The constitution is essentially a system of mediation. Since
its nature is spiritual it is not something rigid and fixed, it is
a relation constantly coming into being and developing.
The constitution of a given people depends therefore upon
the character and completeness of its self-consciousness. The
attempt to give a people an *a priori* constitution, however
rational this constitution may be in itself, would imply a
denial of its truer rationality.

This is why, in determining the constitutional structure of
the State, even when he is generalizing most widely, Hegel
always keeps his eye on the German State. He accepts from
Montesquieu the idea of the division of powers, but tempers
and modifies it by his strong sense of political unity.

' The powers of the State ', he says, ' must certainly be distinct;
but each must form a totality in itself, and contain in itself other
moments. In speaking of the distinct activities of the powers, one
must not fall into the inexcusable error of implying that each
power must stand by itself in abstraction; the powers must be
distinct only as distinct moments in the concept. If the distinctions exist abstractly by themselves, it is obvious that two
autonomies cannot form a unity, but must produce a perpetual
conflict, resulting either in the destruction of the totality or in the
re-establishment of the unity by force. Thus, in the French
Revolution, the legislative now devoured the so-called executive
and was now devoured by it; the moral claim of harmony between them was reduced to absurdity.'

The unity of the State in the distinction of its powers is
visibly represented, according to Hegel, by the monarch.
But it is a mistake to require objective qualities in a monarch :

[1] Hegel makes the important observation, borrowed from Montesquieu and repeated by many subsequent writers, that in the despotic
State the people pays few taxes, while in the constitutional State taxes
rise because the people is conscious that it is paying taxes to itself. No
country is so heavily taxed as England.

he only has to say ' yes ' and to dot the ' i's '. In a well-ordered monarchy, the objective side, the *quid* to which the monarch has to add the *volo*, belongs wholly to the law.

In the legislative power the present and active elements are the Crown, to which belongs the supreme decision ; the government, as the consultative factor, with its concrete knowledge of Society as a whole ; and, lastly, the class element, the representatives of civil Society. These last are able to guarantee the interests of the general good and public liberty, not because of their individual intelligence, since the higher officials of the State have a deeper and wider comprehension of the requirements and institutions of the country, but partly because of the collective intelligence of the deputies, and more especially because of their stimulating effect upon functionaries relatively out of touch with the central government and capable of reacting to public censure or the fear of it. Considered as an organ of mediation, the classes stand between the government and the people regarded as a mass of isolated units. This position requires of them at once a feeling for the State and the government, and also a recognition of the interests of individuals. It is a mere prejudice to think of classes exclusively from the point of view of the conflict between them and the government, as if this were their essential situation. Absorbed into the organism, the class element reveals itself as a factor in a whole ; the conflict is reduced to a mere appearance. If it ever became a reality, the State would go to pieces.

Beside the legislative power, thus constituted, stands the executive or governmental power, which likewise has its head in the monarch. Its function consists in particularizing the universality of the law and applying it to individual cases. The judiciary power does not form a third element for Hegel, as it does in the traditional political trinity ; as we already know, the administration of justice is for him a function of civil Society.

Viewed as a whole, this system is as a summary or anticipation of modern German constitutionalism. The monarch, with the ministers emanating directly from him, at once reigns and governs; the representatives of the people collaborate and criticize in a subordinate sphere. The safeguards of liberty consist partly in this criticism, and still more in the sense of legality which binds at once the Crown and the classes. Kant's ' State of law' reappears in this emphatic assertion of the sovereignty of law. The antiquated and transient element in Hegel's constitutionalism is the hierarchical distribution of classes, which does not assign an adequate share to the *bourgeoisie*, already developing in Germany and soon to transcend in its industrial activities the stage of the artisans' guild, in its agricultural activity the feudal economy, and in its general professional activity the narrow bureaucratic sphere which Hegel ascribes to it. How could the development of this *bourgeoisie* be reconciled with a political organization of classes (*Stande*) giving to the aristocracy an overwhelming importance? This was one of the most serious problems for the German political consciousness during the reign of Frederick William IV.

The ethical conception of the State gives rise to an interference between the functions of Church and State, forming for Hegel a source of constant perplexity, from which he is unable to free himself by a solution that can satisfy him. On the one hand, the divine character and universal mission which he attributes to the State lead him to absorb the Church into it; on the other hand, his strong historical sense makes him realize the impossibility of asserting a theocratic idea in the presence of a religion like Christianity which refuses to be absorbed into the State, and he shrinks from the illiberality of coercing the conscience of the individual. Especially important in this respect is one of the ' additions ', No. 162, to the *Philosophy of Right*, where in order to save the distinction of Church and State Hegel runs the risk of compromising his conception of the ethical and divine state, and returning to the legalism of Kant.

' The State', says he, ' is essentially distinct from religion, because that which it claims has the form of a legal duty, and therefore it is indifferent in what state of mind the duty is performed. The field of religion, on the other hand, is the inward;

and as the State, if it makes religious claims, imperils the rights of inwardness, so the Church which acts as a State, and imposes penalties, degenerates into a tyrannical religion. If religion is to have the force of a political reality, all the laws are reduced to a farce, and subjective feeling dictates the law.'

But if the State is forbidden to trench upon that which is ' inward ', what becomes of its ethical mission? And even if the State is restricted to the sphere of legality, does not this sphere imply a doctrine, an inner spirit, which may interfere with the dogmatic spirit of the Church? And does not the doctrine of the Church transcend in its turn the inwardness of conscience, ' developing for itself a content intimately connected with ethical principles and the laws of the State? ' The difficulty of the problem lies in the fact that the rational content of the Church and that of the State are not separable, but are common to both : the difference between them is a formal difference, in the sense that the Church is truth in the form of feeling, the State is truth in the form of fully developed reason.

This leads Hegel to conclude, not without reluctance, that the relation of the two terms is a unity in distinction. The State is superior to the Church, in virtue of its more perfect form ; but it shows this superiority not by oppression but by freedom, because the State understands that the freedom of the Church is a means for bringing it to a fuller rationality. In other words, the doctrine expressed by the State is not a dogma to be supported by authority, but a consciousness of the autonomy of conscience, which therefore demands an infinite respect for the teaching of the Church, so far as that is freely accepted by believers. But if the Church claims to exercise unlimited and unconditional authority, which it may do owing to the very fact that its form is not fully rational, then the State must assert against it ' the right of conscience to its own point of view, its own convictions, and in general the thought of that which ought to prevail as objective truth '. Hence it is a mistake to affirm that separation from the Church is or has been a disgrace for the State; it is only through this separation that the State can become what it really is, self-conscious rational and ethical life.

The Hegelian conception of the relation between Church and State is in the last resort far nearer to the separatistic formula of modern Liberalism, 'a free Church in a free State', than to the disguised 'lay theocracy' which many interpreters have imagined themselves to find in Hegel. Its Liberalism lies essentially in the fact that the superiority of the State is manifested by permitting the maximum liberty to the Church, in the consciousness that since this freedom is the law of the spirit, it cannot prejudice the claims of spiritual rationality.

To conclude our rapid account of Hegel's political system it will suffice to note that, granted the full self-sufficiency of the State, there cannot according to Hegel be any higher entity to control the relation between State and State, and to resolve their conflicts. There is no praetor to judge between States; the only higher court is the universal spirit. The existence of a plurality of States is the condition of their growth to perfection. As the single individual becomes a genuine person only through his relations with other persons, so the State is only a real individual in relation to other States. But a conflict between States, when their several wills are irreconcilable, can only be decided by war. To this Hegel attributes a high moral value.

' Its highest significance consists in the fact that by its means ethical well-being is preserved against the encroachment of private interests, as the movement of the winds preserves the sea from the putrefaction to which it would be reduced by a permanent calm, like the condition in which peoples would be reduced by long and indeed an eternal peace.'

This ethical significance of war in the modern age reveals itself in the fact that the manifestations of military valour appear more mechanical and depersonalized, directed as they are not against single persons but against a hostile community; thus ' personal courage appears as impersonal '.

But the plurality of States and the multiplicity of their interrelations do not destroy, they rather postulate a higher unity, in virtue of which one nation may embody the universal spirit in a higher degree than others and may act as a guide to others. In all ages of history there has always been a constant succession of peoples thus taking the lead : in the nineteenth century, thinks Hegel, the leading people is the German. With this idea, the universalism of a *Menschheitsnation*, as conceived by the early Romantics, acquires a new meaning and a decisive tendency in the direction of the State.

§ 3. THE AGE OF FREDERICK WILLIAM IV

Hegel's doctrine is a theoretical synthesis of two opposed German tendencies struggling for predominance in the first half of the nineteenth century. In the field of militant politics their effective reconciliation, so far at least as concerns the fundamentals of public law, had to wait till a much later date.

Prussian Liberalism, which flourished after Jena, made its last appearance in the customs law of 1818, conceived according to the principle of free trade and containing only in a minor degree measures of retaliation against the protectionism of other nations; implicitly against that of England, which in 1815 had limited the importation of grain. In a country which was essentially an exporter of agricultural produce and devoid of industry, as Prussia was in 1815, this free trade was natural enough without appeal to the feeling for liberty, which at this time had almost vanished from the governing classes. But the Liberal consequences of the law were important, because it formed the centre round which all the other German States grouped themselves into the Zollverein of 1833. Thus the consequences of liberty survived the eclipse of the Liberal spirit in Prussia, and offer to political history a striking proof of the importance of liberty as a means towards national unification. Liberal opinion, widely diffused among the German States of the west and south, extracted from the Zollverein a powerful motive for a close union between the idea of freedom and that of the Fatherland, and for bringing pressure on Prussia to induce her to promote a general political movement towards liberty and to take the lead towards national unification.

But Prussia was now governed according to the ideals of the Holy Alliance, and disappointed all Liberal hopes. And the complications which Liberalism introduced into the national problem aggravated the Austrian government's inherent anti-Liberalism. Metternich realized that a Liberal Prussia would mean the end of the Austrian hegemony and of the Austro-Prussian equilibrium in the German federation; he therefore made every effort not only to arouse all Austrophil Germans against the Liberals, but also to encourage Frederick William III of Prussia in his policy of reaction. He regarded a monarchy tempered by representation of the feudal classes as the best government for Prussia; a view shared by the Prussian government, which in 1823 reorganized the provincial diets, redistributing them into three orders according to their territorial possessions, so as to give a safe majority to the landed aristocracy, the owners of the so-called *Rittergüter*, while the *bourgeois* not possessed of land, professional men, capitalists, and tradesmen, were entirely unrepresented.

The States of Southern Germany enjoyed a far more Liberal régime than that of Prussia. In most of them the constitutions of the period from 1814 to 1848 were modelled on the charter of Louis XVIII. The Liberal theories of these countries, too, much resembled the constitutionalism of Constant, Royer-Collard, and Daunou. They were represented in great part by university professors, the two Rottecks, Welcker, Friedrich Gagern, Jacob Grimm, Stockmar, Rümelin, Robert Mohl, Gervinus, and others. The programme of Carl Rotteck, the earliest of them, and therefore interesting as the original document of the school, is a defence of rational rights as against historic rights. By this Rotteck means a legal and political system directed to attaining the rational ends of man, and recognizing, in a Kantian spirit, the claim of every individual to a freedom compatible to that of the rest. In all these writers Liberal feeling is combined with national feeling, thus originating the movement of thought which was to have its epilogue in the parliament of Frankfurt.

But the first struggles of university Liberalism were con-

ducted within the schools and by academic weapons. Only
the extreme autonomy of the German universities could
permit professors living in the centre of Europe, between
a reactionary Prussia and a reactionary Austria, to expound
Liberal ideas to their students. Thus when, owing to government pressure, the freedom of teaching was here and there
violated, the universities became centres and hotbeds of
revolt. The most famous example is the protest of the historian Dahlmann of Göttingen, which bore the signatures of
the brothers Grimm, Gervinus, Eduard Albrecht, and others,
against the Hanoverian government in 1837 on its violating
the constitution it had sworn to respect. The protest was the
more significant in that not only the liberty of the university
but that of the country at large was at stake, and the professors felt the incompatibility of their function with the act
of a government that failed to abide by its solemn pledges.
' Must I ', said Dahlmann and the court-counsellor Albrecht,
' teach henceforward that the supreme principle of the State
is that whatever pleases those in power is law? As a man of
honour, I would cease to teach rather than sell to my audience for truth that which is a lie and a deceit.'

The seven professors who signed the protest were expelled
from their chairs; but the people of Göttingen, mindful of
the Liberalism which they had learnt to value under English
government, opened a public subscription on their behalf.
And the defences of their conduct written after their reap-
pointment by Dahlmann and Jacob Grimm are rightly
regarded by Germans as the loftiest examples of their own
Liberal literature. In them the peculiar *forma mentis* of
German Liberalism stands out, in contrast not only with
an arbitrary absolutism, but also with the anti-historical
rationalism dear to the Liberal extremists most influenced by
France. Thus Dahlmann denies the right of the people to
take the law into its own hands; and Grimm, answering
those Liberals who despised the barbarism of the Middle
Ages, does not conceal his deep sympathy for the ancient
medieval liberties of the people, and his delight in slaking his
thirst at the far-off springs of German life.

The greatest obstacle to the success of the national Liberal programme was the attitude of Prussia. Frederick William IV, coming to the throne in 1840, carried yet farther the reactionary tendencies of his predecessor. He was a belated Romantic, moved by the contradictory desires for a revived medievalism and a legitimatistic assertion of the divine right of kings. The great development of the *bourgeoisie* during the twenty years of his reign took place unobserved beneath his very eyes. Surrounded by a little clique of catholicizing Romantics, he devoted his political energies to a revival of the old feudal classes, and on the very eve of the Revolution of 1848 set about altering his predecessor's constitution by erecting a House of Lords above the representatives of the three classes, as if to accentuate a class distinction in order to impress the *bourgeoisie*. In convoking the new diet, he insisted on the special position of his State between the three Great Powers, by ordaining which ' it pleases God to make Prussia great by means of the sword, the sword of war without, the sword of the spirit within ; not the negative spirit of our age, but the spirit of discipline and order '. He added :

' No power on earth shall ever persuade me to exchange the natural relation between prince and people for a contractual and constitutional relation ; or to countenance the insertion, between our Lord in Heaven and this country, of a piece of written paper, like a second providence, to rule by its paragraphs and to take the place of ancient sacred loyalty.'

The increasing rigidity of Prussia in her traditional attitude formed a serious obstacle to the execution of the Liberal programme of a national unification by means of liberty, and split the party into two camps. The more moderate Liberals continued to hope for a change of heart on the part of Prussia, in the sense that if the king saw an opportunity to make a bid for the crown of all Germany, a feeling for his own dynastic interests might induce him to form a *mariage de convenance* with freedom ; the more radical Liberals began to look for a unification in spite of Prussia, at the price of the absorption of the Prussian kingdom in a Liberal Germany.

But in Prussia the same politicians who were farthest from the romantic spirit of the king, and shared with the Liberals a hope of national unification, recoiled from this extreme of radicalism. In their opinion the hegemony of an armed Prussia was the only guarantee for true unity, the only force capable of permanently uniting the numerous petty States of Germany, overcoming their anarchical particularism and arousing their dormant political feeling. Thus to the Liberal idea of a federation of autonomous sovereign States (*Staatenbund*) they opposed the idea of a federal State (*Bundesstaat*) with Prussia as its centre. The reactionary policy of Frederick William IV they regarded as an antiquated and out-of-date, but none the less providential, method of resisting the disintegrating forces of Liberalism, and saving the Prussian State in its existing form for its future task.

Thus the medievalism of the king became the vehicle of a highly modern imperialistic conception of the nation, in contrast with the Liberal conception. The realization of this change is the clearest proof of the profound historical sense of Ranke, Droysen, and Sybel, and of the political astuteness shown by Bismarck in his role of reactionary during the Revolution of 1848.

For these politicians the national idea was an inference from historical premises resembling those of Romanticism; but far from exhausting itself in a sterile reminiscence and passive admiration of the past, it brought its forces, drawn from the tradition of centuries, to bear upon the present and point towards the future, towards the expansion and domination of the German people. Not the nation as a vague sentimental entity, but the nation as an instrument of power, was the object of their love and, still more, of their political activity. They did not reject the nation of the Romantics; they wished to use its conservative energies, its archaic but solid structure, its narrow but powerful monarchy, as a platform on which to construct the new Germany. They took up the cause of Prussia not out of love of the old feudal Prussia, but because a strong Prussia could give to all Germany the form of a State, and enable it to take a place in the great international competition. Unlike their allies or tools, the pure reactionaries, they did not ignore the importance of the rapidly rising *bourgeoisie*, but wished to wean it from the philistinic ideals of a barren individualism, indoctrinate it with their own conceptions, and convert it into a progressive force to operate upon the sluggish landed aristocracy. While English and French Liberalism tended to shape the nation upon the mould of middle-class economic life, they proposed to mould this economic life to the needs of the nation, combining it with pre-existent and even outworn forces in such a way that each class should make its contribution to the common cause.

This was the motive of their protectionism, formulated for the first time, and with full consciousness of its national end, by Friedrich List in his *National System of Political Economy* in 1841. In this system the author's opposition to competition and *laissez-faire* is based not upon the social and humanitarian motives of the French and English Conservatives, nor upon the purely technical motives of Utopian Socialism, but on a totally different order of ideas. The aim of free competition, according to the classical school, was to increase the present wealth available for national consumption ; the predominant consideration was that of value in exchange. · List, on the other hand, introduced into the discussion two new ideas : the idea of nationality, as opposed to that of international free trade, and the idea of productive power, as opposed to that of exchange value. As against cosmopolitanism, he showed that individual prosperity closely depends upon the political power of the nation. As against the idea that productive activity ought to tend towards the creation of the maximum quantity of exchangeable values, he asserted the necessity of safeguarding the sources of labour and economic life, and ensuring the future development of these energies, on the ground that the power to create riches is infinitely more important than riches themselves.

Now according to the theory of free trade, it cannot pay a nation to create an industry when, as was the case with Germany about the year 1840, it can purchase the industrial products which it needs cheaper in foreign countries, in exchange for agricultural products which it can produce more cheaply. But this narrowly utilitarian calculation would, according to List, deprive the nation of its best energies. Industry best develops the moral energies of a people. The desire for a constant increase of intellectual and moral goods, the love of emulation and liberty, is characteristic of an industrial and commercial state; under the régime of a uniform agriculture, dullness of mind, sloth of body, and attachment to old ideas and habits are the rule. Even agriculture is powerfully stimulated by the presence of manufactures.[1] The State, therefore, by suitable legislation must encourage the birth and growth of industries.

Here economics are clearly subordinated to national organization. But not economics only; all the other energies of the people are to be treated in the same way. Freedom also, with its autonomous institutions, is a source of national energy; and the arguments which we have reproduced led List to distinguish clearly between the cause of protection and that of anti-Liberalism. Indeed, in the rise of industry, even under protection, he saw a means of a liberal education for the people. But freedom, like industry, like agriculture, like intellectual culture, has the value of a mere means to a higher national end. In a spirit not unlike that of List, Bismarck, the reactionary of 1848, later granted the nation universal suffrage when he came to see in this a useful means of consolidating the Empire; he was willing either to form an alliance with the Liberal Party or to set on foot the *Kulturkampf*, whose anti-Liberal character is obvious.

The danger of this tendency to subordinate and sacrifice every value to the idol of nationality is that the spirit of the people may lose its sense of direction, and that stability and firmness may disappear from the current of public opinion through the prevalence of the idea that these values are contingent and accidental; and in minds of a lower order, less strongly sustained by the consciousness of the higher end,

[1] Gide-Rist, *Histoire des doctrines économiques depuis les physiocrates jusqu'à nos jours*, Paris, ed. 4, 1922, pp. 310-24.

this means degeneration into a cynical opportunism. The nationalism of Bismarck, Droysen, and Treitschke failed to create a true governing class, because it was too much of an original work of art, requiring for its perfection a lofty intellect capable of mastering a recalcitrant and uninspiring matter. Now a political tradition cannot base its continuity upon a succession of great men. Bismarck could only create lieutenants; and when he vanished from the political stage, the technical and administrative subordinates who had worked under him in a complex and highly organized machine showed themselves unable to perform a task of synthesis for which they had not been trained.

Another danger of this form of nationalism is that by turning the nation into a weapon of aggression and conquest it threatens to destroy the basis on which the idea of the nation, and therefore the possibility of the coexistence of different nations, is built. The imperialism which inevitably proceeds from such a tendency not only claims the right of enslaving weaker nations, but runs the risk of corrupting the spirit of the conquering nation, by disintegrating its forces into a super-State composed of heterogeneous elements whose artificial cohesion demands a diversion of these forces from their normal function in the historical life of the nation. While the reactionary nationalism of the Romantics sacrificed the future of the national life to the love of the past, the new imperialism, which was not unconnected with its predecessor, sacrificed to ambitious hopes for the future the traditional historic character of the German people.

At this point the fundamental contrast between this conception and the political idea of the nation becomes clear. The one considers the nation only as an element in the power of the State; the other erects it into an independent value superior to the State, enclosing and entrenching the latter within the inviolable limits of the nation. Thus for Liberalism the peaceful coexistence of a number of nations, each organized as a State and conducting its relations with its neighbours on the same principles that govern the relations of free and self-conscious individuals, is a necessary condition of political stability and progress. From this point of view it is possible to appreciate the great difference between the national claims of most European peoples during the nineteenth century, directed to the achievement, through revolution and war, of a work of emancipation, and the projects of expansion and hegemony inspired by the spirit of an imperialistic nationalism.

The great campaign of German Liberalism for national unity was fought in 1848. The Liberals put forward three closely connected proposals : to liberate the German States from the paternalism of Austria; to obtain, especially in Prussia, genuinely modern constitutions in place of the old feudal diets; and to make these constitutions a bond of political union for the whole German people.

The first of these proposals could be carried out easily and almost instantaneously. Austria, weakened by a revolutionary crisis at home, a war against Italy, and a rebellion in Hungary, could offer little resistance to the German federation in its struggle for freedom. The weakness of Austria resulted in the paralysis of the pro-Austrian party, which called itself the Great German Party, and proposed to include the Austrian nation in a Greater Germany. This party, in a small minority at the parliament of Frankfurt, disappeared from the scene together with its patroness Austria, and the partisans of a smaller Germany remained masters of the field.

The second point in the Liberal programme was won at the first attack by the *bourgeois* revolution, which wrested from the terrified rulers the constitutional concessions that had long been demanded. This revolution was particularly violent in Prussia, where the monarchical reaction had been most energetic. Unlike the contemporary revolution in France, it had no marked social character, because industry had not yet developed in Prussia, and the agricultural masses were still in a backward state of feudal civilization which prevented their infection by the revolutionary feeling of the lesser *bourgeoisie*. The soul of the revolution was the city *bourgeoisie*, led by professors and students, the educated classes

among which the claims of Liberalism had been longer felt
and more vividly realized. But absolutism, defeated in the
towns, was uninjured and ready for the counter-attack in the
country, the stronghold of feudalism. Bismarck gives in his
Memoirs an interesting picture of this state of mind, which he
expounded to the king in order to engage him on the side of
reaction. But Frederick William no longer needed such aids.
In the army, a force of feudal origin so far as officers and
men were concerned, but educated in the school of monarchy,
he possessed the quintessence of the forces of ancient and
modern Prussia; and once the first period of dismay was over,
he employed this powerful weapon to put down the revolution.

The third task of the German Liberals was more complicated. It was taken in hand under the happy auspices of the
revolutionary victory in Prussia, which favoured the hope of
a unification of Germany with a Liberal Prussia at its head.
It expressed an ideal towards which no party, even the most
reactionary, could display a *fin de non-recevoir*. Yet this ideal
was opposed by the best representatives of culture and
politics, who, as we have seen, were partisans of a new
nationalism. These agreed in desiring unification, but not
by an act of popular sovereignty, which would create a weak
State, at the mercy of parties, and condemn Prussia to a
secondary position where she could make no use of her actual
military superiority. Hence we find an alliance in common
opposition to the Liberal programme taking shape, between
the old conservative classes, anxious for internal reaction,
and the most modern representatives of imperialism, ready
to use the former's power of resistance in order to oppose the
revolutionary project of a federation of German States. The
ancient alliance between the monarchy and the feudal
nobility was reasserted and confirmed.

And while the conservative classes seconded the efforts
of ' King Grapeshot' (as the King of Prussia was nicknamed)
to suppress the Liberal revolution, the nationalists criticized
and ridiculed the debates in the parliament of Frankfurt,
which, intended to settle the question of national unity, were
gradually degenerating into empty verbal disputes as the

people's representatives lost their prestige beneath the rising tide of reaction, and found themselves impotent to obtain any practical sanction for their resolutions. Nationalist historians have described the Frankfurt sessions as shining examples of doctrinaire abstraction and practical ineffectiveness. Partisan passions have prevented them from coolly realizing the exceptional conditions under which the representatives of the people were compelled to work, fettered by the heavy diplomatic yoke of two Great Powers, and, even more serious, hampered in carrying out their mandate by a permanent conflict between the sovereignty of parliament and that of the confederated States in whose hands any final decision must lie. But for the nationalists, the manifest impotence of the parliament was enough to discredit popular assemblies as such, and to create in the public mind a sense of distrust towards the futile and abstract sham-politics of professors and lawyers. The example of Frankfurt, aggravated by the historians' misrepresentations, was fatal to German political Liberalism. The people lost all interest in representative institutions, and made up its mind, to its own loss, that its political future depended wholly upon the Crown.

The closing scenes of the Frankfurt parliament, by a fiasco striking enough to impress itself permanently on the memory of the people, crowned the work of the doctrinaire impotence displayed by the representatives during the whole session. In the sitting of the 28th of March 1849, the assembly, after settling the internal crisis between the Prussian and Austrian parties in favour of the former, in spite of the Prussian reaction then in full swing, elected Frederick William IV Emperor of the Germans by 290 votes, 248 abstaining. But the King of Prussia refused the crown offered him by the representatives of the people, and explained in private why he had done so: the crown which a Hohenzollern could accept, he said, was not a crown created, even with the consent of princes, by a revolutionary assembly. If the ancient crown of the German nation, he added, which for forty-two years had lain idle, was to be conferred upon any one, it ought to have been conferred by himself and his equals, the other princes.

The king's haughty legitimism was a generation behind the times; but in its effects, if not in its motives, it harmonized admirably with the views of the most advanced politicians, who regarded unification as a problem of sheer force, to be solved by the sword. History has shown that both the king and politicians were right; for the Empire was created by the military strength of the Hohenzollerns, combined with the *Realpolitik* of the nationalists, to the complete exclusion of any expression of popular consent, or any aid from the spirit of an ' antiquated ' Liberalism. Yet the Liberal sense of nationality, outwardly ignored, never ceased to live and work silently in the depths of the popular mind; and in the darkest hour of the Empire, when the force which was to be its only effectual bond had failed, the nation was able to maintain its unity as a State in virtue of a right based on purely Liberal principles, and thus to feel itself still firmly united in spite of threats of internal disruption. The representatives united at Weimar at last did justice to the Utopian generosity of Frankfurt.

§ 4. THE JURIDICAL CONCEPTION OF THE STATE

Defeated in 1848 on the ground of politics, Liberalism as a party was unable to rally, and was only able to create unstable and ephemeral organizations, quickly dominated by stronger political forces. Yet the fundamental demands of the European consciousness have not been unfelt by the German people, but have found satisfaction in indirect ways. We can distinguish two groups of these, the first consisting of political claims, the second of juridical. The defective development of German Liberalism concerns the first group only, and is compensated by the rapid progress of the second.

The political institutions of modern Germany, down to the European war, remained in the stage of pure constitutionalism, consisting in the spontaneous gift of a charter by the Crown creating a system of popular representation with a merely critical function and no active part in the government. The act of governing belonged to the Crown, and was exercised through its ministers, who were directly responsible to the Crown and independent of the vote of the chamber. Later, the creation of the Empire as a federal State brought into being a collegiate political organism formed by representatives of the various States, with governmental functions belonging to it in virtue of this State representation.

This political system remained intact and uninfluenced by any parliamentary ideas of French origin, not only through the constant desire of the imperial government, but also by the consent of the educated classes, which regarded it as a genuinely German form of State, and the parliamentary system as a feeble and inefficient government with a sham popular sovereignty paving the way to the indirect influence of amateur politicians. The chapter on France, in Gneist's classical work *Der Rechtsstaat*, expresses this view with great clearness. For Gneist, the French system represents the triumph of politics over the legal sense of the nation. He finds the cause of this lack of legal feeling, quite rightly, in the political work of the monarchy, which succeeded in completing the unification of the State and in reducing the privileged classes to subjection by arbitrary and violent means. This was fatal to the development of public law. Later, the revolutions, for all the violence of their opposition to absolutism, carried on the same work in both its aspects, the positive or political and the negative or anti-legal. The incessant political transformation of the State destroyed all stability of government and involved public administration in the fluctuations of party politics and incessant ministerial crises. The idea of the sovereignty of the people, in the sense of a mere disorganized plurality of individuals, overthrew the legal basis of the constitution, enslaved the executive to the legislative assemblies, and made this slave a tyrant in its relations with the citizens. The functionary, himself at the mercy of the deputy, has the rights of the individual at his own mercy: his responsibility, civil and criminal, is practically non-existent. Hence arises the strange paradox that a sovereign people cannot safeguard the most elementary conditions of individual security from the caprice of the executive power.

The reason is that this sovereignty is a mere appearance,

and exhausts itself in the act of voting for the election of political representatives. From the complex organism of English law, France has gleaned only the idea of election. The vote has been regarded not as a right acquired by the exercise of an independent and energetic activity, but as an innate right: is it strange then that individuals cannot use it, and allow their abstract political power to be submerged by their actual political incapacity? The English parliament is a stable and organic force, because it is a combination of forces organized in varying degrees through every stage in the social hierarchy; the French parliament is an unstable, inconstant, disorganized force because it is an isolated apparition, arbitrary in its omnipotence, in a social world ruled by a uniform bureaucracy which by its operation prevents the citizen from habituating himself to those functions of self-government which ought to find their highest and completest expression in parliament.

This criticism of the French system shows that the Germans regard a political power, out of proportion to the legal capacity and social activity of individuals, as an evil. They are content with a very narrow constitutionalism, so long as it is effectual. The true basis of any constitution lies, they believe, in the widespread legal feeling of the people, which forms a limit to the caprices not only of the government but of political parties. Their Liberalism consists not in an empty show of political forms, but in a firm consciousness of rights, which without identifying government and governed, the State and the people, determines their relations in such a way that no political encroachment, whether from above or from below, can disturb them.

The conception of the *Rechtsstaat* (the State according to rights) in which the essence of German Liberalism finds expression is not the creation of a single jurist; it is the legal tradition of the whole people, from Thomasius to Kant and Hegel; and in the second half of the nineteenth century it inspired the great scientific constructions of Mohl, Gerber, Gneist, Laband, Meyer, and Jellinek. Even in the court of Frederick William IV a politician, Stahl, found in it an insurmountable limit to any reactionary programme.

The character of the *Rechtsstaat* is already familiar to us from our discussion of Kant and Hegel. The State is a civil juridical association. This does not mean that its only end is the declaration or sanction of rights, but only that the achievement of its ends, whatever they may be, must take place within the forms and limits of law. The merit of later writers, especially Gneist, is to have shown that this legal function of the State can only be effectively discharged when ' through the intermediate organizations between the State and the social body there is promoted and maintained in society that sense of right and understanding of the law in which, under a constitutional government, all parties ought, in their political activity, to be indistinguishable '.

From this point of view the English parliamentary system, understood and imitated in France only in its outward political manifestations, assumed a new and deeper significance. Before ever she affirmed the omnipotence of parliament, England had established juridical government and secured it against the abuses of political parties. Definite limits to the interference of parties in the work of government were laid down. The approval of the budget was required by law, the control of parliament over administration was limited by the courts. It made no difference to the administration whether a Whig or a Tory ministry were in power. But the foundation-stone of the *Rechtsstaat* consisted in self-government, understood not as the participation of the people in a legislative and governing parliament, but as the possession by local bodies of governmental functions conferred upon them by the general judiciary, administrative, and financial laws of the State. ' The complex organism of the English State is based not on a conventional division of powers, but on the unity of political power, which calls the social classes to take part no less in the autonomous execution of the laws than in their formation.' Blackstone in his *Commentaries* confined himself to the external elements of the parliamentary constitution, ignoring the intermediate organism, the local judiciary and administrative power, which stands between parliament and the central government : thus the continent received a mutilated view of the system, giving the false impression that nothing was required except to represent the will of the nation through a political assembly. And England has in her turn been exposed to the effects of the continental democratic reaction.

This being so, the German rejection of parliamentary government did not mean a rejection of modern constitutionalism, but prepared the way for a deeper understanding of its real importance. Like England, Germany has an ancient tradition of self-government, marked by the autonomy of the three orders, the flourishing *Genossenschaften*, the independence of the courts, and a constant exercise of administrative functions by the aristocracy. The downfall of the feudal State with its three orders and the self-government that it implied began with the Reformation. The legal equalization of religions by the Peace of Westphalia was the greatest step which mankind had taken since the Middle Ages; but it was purchased by Germany at the price of the dismemberment of the Empire. It destroyed the bond which the rich and privileged classes had found in the unity of the Church; the divisions between nobility, *bourgeoisie*, and peasantry became deeper.

In these conditions the monarchy embarked on the difficult task of reuniting a society divided in faith and social interests. The chief organ of this task was the bureaucracy, which gradually took upon itself certain public functions hitherto exercised by the feeble and quarrelsome provincial diets of Germany, created a unitary jurisdiction in the place of class-tribunals, became the legislative adviser of the king, and subordinated patrimonial authorities to itself.

The faults of administrative and bureaucratic monarchy were the lack of a clear distinction between laws and edicts, and the danger of an insecure and over-detailed legislation. Thus, while absolutism was uniting the people, it was destroying their legal sense by destroying those traditional institutions which had served as a school for legal capacity. Later, the revolutionary influence of France, by subordinat-

ing all other public interests to the problem of formal
politics, helped to accelerate this process.

The political degeneration due to the Revolutionary spirit
was to some extent repaired by the Restoration, with its lively
feeling for historical tradition. But the error of the Restoration monarchies, like that of Frederick William IV, was to
confine themselves within the limits of antiquated and narrow
feudal system; the idea of self-government, which the French
Revolution had sacrificed to the mob, was sacrificed by the
Prussian monarchy to the ancient feudal orders.

It was natural that the German Empire, on emerging
victorious from two wars, should reassert the *Rechtsstaat* in
a form adapted to modern conditions. Bismarck brought
about a great administrative reform based on self-government. Between the feudal party which wanted autonomous
administration, but of a patrimonial type and in its own
interest, and the Liberal *bourgeois* party, which meant by
self-government a communal elective administration on the
French model with a wide suffrage, Bismarck succeeded in
finding a middle path, reconciling the old territorial interests with the new industrial and commercial interests of
the *bourgeoisie*. His reform was based on the principle that the
classes, in the modern sense of the term, must accept the
task of personally discharging those public duties for which
our times provide far more opportunity than any previous
age. In modern conditions, it is impossible to get rid of the
salaried State employee; but it is possible to supplement the
rigid bureaucratic system at certain decisive points by calling
in the help of the classes. Side by side with salaried officials,
a system of unpaid officials can provide a juridical check on
the administration, and at the same time train the educated
classes in the practical exercise of political functions and so
restore to them their lost legal consciousness. In this way
Prussia effected a reconstruction of the political basis of the
State which Gneist describes as unparalleled in Europe. On
this foundation was rebuilt the whole structure of German
juridical government, which, while recognizing the necessary rights of the State, draws an inviolable legal circle, un-

known to antiquity, around the subject, with his family, his association, his commune, and his church.

The mere extension of the suffrage to the whole adult male population seems to Gneist, on the other hand, a danger to social order, and in no way essential to public law ; to take part in the government is not an innate right, but must be acquired, like any other, by the personal discharge of duties. In this spontaneous participation of the citizen in public business, Gneist finds the true spirit of German Liberalism as opposed to French.

A simple objection may be brought against Gneist's theory. Granted that the political forms of parliamentary government are a mere façade, the constitution of the *Rechtsstaat* is a building without a façade. Gneist has learnt from England everything except the art of finishing off his work.

But the relations between the legal and political elements in the State are in reality very different from those between the structure and façade of a building. In order to realize this, it is enough to reflect that the drawing of this legal circle round individuals and social groups, in which the *Rechtsstaat* consists, depends essentially upon a political view of the State. A State may be a legalized system of oppression ; a governing class like the German landed aristocracy may practise self-government to the detriment of the other classes ; and then what becomes of guaranteed rights? They are inseparably connected, though not identical, with the political ideas inspiring the Revolutionary declarations of the rights of man, and may be systematized by a complex legal organism, but cannot be created out of nothing. The mistake of German legal science is that, wishing to make rights an autonomous reality, it makes them an abstraction, something unreal : the true reality of right lies in its connexion with all the activities of a nation's historical life. Hence the ' State of rights ' acquires solidity when Gneist treats it as an aspect of the development of the English ' political State ' ; taken by itself, it is only an empty form, equally capable of justifying feudal claims like those of the Restoration, if these should again be made.

Happily, in spite of the attempt to eradicate from the
Rechtsstaat every element not strictly legal, German thought,
by a process of unconscious mimicry, ends by adapting its
constructions to the political requirements of nineteenth-
century Europe, thus expressing in narrow juridical terms
an historical fact of far wider scope. This is how it brings
itself into line with the general European consciousness.

From Gerber to Jellinek, this gradual process of assimilation makes great advances. The character of the present
work forbids our examining it in full; we will confine ourselves to the consideration of a single element, closely relevant
to the political problems hitherto discussed, namely the
relation between the rights of the individual and the State.

If we look at the underlying motive of political science as
a whole, it seems impossible to justify the idea of an original
and inviolable right on the part of the individual. This
science generally regards the State as an organic unity, which
therefore cannot permit the existence side by side with itself
of separate and unassimilated elements, and tends to reduce
individuals and groups to cells and organs of the State.
Even when rejecting an exaggerated organicism, it aims at
conferring all sovereignty upon the State, according to the
German tradition, and in opposition to the two antithetical
conceptions of absolutism and French Liberalism, which
ascribe sovereignty to the prince and the people respectively.
For the German jurists, the idea of the State represents a
higher synthesis of two conflicting elements, and reconciles
them in a reason more truly universal than that upon which
the abstract thought of the French doctrinaires would
bestow the attribute of sovereignty.

But if the State is sovereign, the individual is a mere
subject; and any claim to a right of his own as against the
State is inadmissible, because it would destroy this sovereignty. And in fact the most rigorous scientific deduction
leads Gerber and Laband to deny any such thing as subjective public rights, at least in the expression which these
rights received from the French Revolution.

But the evolution of political consciousness makes its in-

fluence indirectly felt, even by the rigid deduction of the
jurists, and restores in another way what they have rejected.
Thus Gerber, in his work on *Public Rights* published in 1852,
makes subjective right a reflex of objective right. The right to
vote, for example, is not in his opinion a right of the individual, but rather a function imposed upon him by the organization of the State; that is, a duty.

Passing over the intermediate links in the legal tradition
beginning with this doctrine, we find in Jellinek the fullest
development of the tendency, implicit in it, to restore subjective public rights in an indirect manner. The work of
Jellinek marks an epoch in the history of German legal
science, and is of the utmost interest from our point of view,
that of political history. In his treatise on *Subjective Public
Rights*, a fundamental distinction is drawn between two
kinds of subjective rights as a whole, public and private.
Some consist in a *licere*, others in a *posse*. The former are
private rights, separable at will from the personality of their
possessor; the latter are public rights, inseparable from the
personality unless this is diminished; hence they form the
inalienable status of the individual.

As opposed to *licere*, which represents a mere faculty left
at the discretion of the interested party, *posse* expresses a
function, that is, at once a right and a duty. The public
character of this right consists in the fact that it forms part
of the State organism, and is at once the means by which
the activity of the State shows itself, and a limit which
that activity cannot overstep. This does not contradict
the principle of the sovereignty of the State, for reasons
of two kinds: first and foremost, because the subjective
public right is a part or moment of sovereignty; secondly
(so far as concerns its significance as a limit), because sovereignty does not mean unlimited power, but capacity for
self-limitation.

The sovereignty of the State is sovereignty over free men,
that is, over persons. By recognizing the personality of the
individual, the State limits itself, by drawing a legal line
between itself and the personality of its subjects, and recog-

nizing a sphere of individual freedom withdrawn on principle from the State's authority. The notion of this sphere and its express recognition are essentially a product of modern civilization. In antiquity it was ignored, though in fact it existed even in ancient States. From this point of view Jellinek accepts in a limited sense, in his *General Theory of the State*, Constant's distinction between ancient and modern liberty. It is not true that the ancients ignored individual liberty and regarded freedom solely as participation in government; the truth is that individual liberty existed *de facto*, but had no legal sanction.

But the assertion of an individual sphere independent of the State does not imply the ascription to the individual of an absolute personality in no way subordinate to the will of the State. This would be incompatible with the nature of the State, and would apply only to the mystical pre-political personality of speculations concerning the state of nature. All personality is relative and limited, including the personality of the State, which is legally bound by its own juridical organization and morally bound to recognize the personality of its subjects.[1]

From this conclusion important inferences can be drawn. According to jusnaturalism the individual's original rights, existing as they do before the State, are purely privatistic in nature; and therefore the public rights based upon them are rooted in private rights. It is enough to recall the doctrine of the social contract. This whole system of ideas is reversed by modern juridical thought. Not only are subjective rights consisting in a *posse* strictly public; but even those consisting in a *licere*, that is to say private rights, are based in the last resort upon public right. Jellinek actually restricts this principle to the limitation of rights of *licere* (for example, the limitation of the right of property on grounds of public interest); but his doctrine is capable of extension and development in proportion as the prevalence of democratic and

---

[1] Cf. Jellinek, *Sistema dei diritti pubblici subiettivi*, Ital. tr., Milan, 1912, p. 97. The word *morally*, in the passage quoted, would be better replaced by *politically*.

socialistic tendencies in politics implies an increasing subordination of the individual to the State.

Down to the present day, the theory diametrically opposed
to jusnaturalism has only been asserted in the legal conceptions of Socialism. Thus Anton Menger, in his work on *The
Socialist State*, makes the social reformation of the legal system
consist in the conversion of modern private rights into public
rights, not only as regards property, but in all other cases :
for example, in cases of contract, where the Socialist State
denies the employer's right to engage men at will ; in cases of
succession, where it claims the right to dictate the future
structure of society by dictating the future disposal of property ; and so forth.[1]

This digression has served to show that legal formulae, for
all their apparent impassivity, are in reality modified and
influenced by the development of political ideas, and that
German thought has followed, from its own special point of
view, the general evolution of the European public consciousness. The demands which we have seen put forward in
France and England, on purely political grounds, for an
introduction of the principles of the *Declaration of the Rights
of Man* into a more modern conception of the State, for the
addition of a system of self-government to a parliamentary
régime, and so forth, appear no less in Germany, but
formulated in the language of legal science. And from the
point of view of European Liberalism, Jellinek's great work
on *The General Theory of the State* is an important witness to
the close bond between Germany and Western Europe, in
spite of a difference of constitutional form. It contains an
exposition of the concepts of sovereignty, representation, constitution, distinction of powers, and so forth, in a form
entirely acceptable to Western and English Liberalism ; indeed, in his lucid and penetrating historical introductions to
his analyses of the various institutions of public law, the
author abandons a strict legal formalism, and proceeds to
sketch suggestive pictures of European political evolution in
order to illustrate the relations and differences of the various

[1] A. Menger, *Lo Stato socialista*, Ital. tr., 1915, pp. 99 *seqq.*

nations. And it must not be forgotten that the *Declaration of the Rights of Man* has found its best interpreter in Jellinek, a student belonging to the nation which, according to a widespread but superficial view, has stood aloof from the Liberal movement of the nineteenth century.

It might, however, be suspected that in Germany the jurists have enjoyed a monopoly of this enlightening grace, and that their work has met with no echo in the spirit of the nation and the minds of politicians. To convince oneself that this suspicion is unjust, it is enough to examine the work of one of the political writers commonly regarded as most hostile to Liberalism, Treitschke. We shall there find, no doubt, many ironical or contemptuous references to Jacobinism, Liberal rhetoric, and the spirit of hostility to the State; but we shall also find, transformed into a new shape, the entire legal organization of the Liberal theory of the State. No one has criticized more keenly than Treitschke the monomania, ascribed to Hegel but in reality characteristic of the Hegelians, for making the State absorb into itself the entire life of the individual. Let the State content itself, says Treitschke, with external order, and not force its way into the intimacy of conscience. No Christian can live solely for the State, for he cannot renounce his eternal destiny. But if pan-Statism is false, no less false is the excessive individualism which would reduce the State to a night-watchman. There is a cultural end which the modern State must not neglect; but its activity in this expansion is ' beneficent and wise when it promotes and strengthens the autonomy of the free and wise man; but it is an evil if it restricts and sterilizes the autonomy of the free man. People use mere words, when they speak of educational discipline as restriction of freedom; they ought to call it restriction *to* freedom.' [1]

On the other hand, to give the name of liberty to a denial of all authority, as the Poles did, is to ensure the complete dissolution of the State. An excess of liberty becomes slavery, because when all authority is suppressed the strong are un-

[1] Treitschke, *La Politica*, Ital. tr., Ruta, 4 vols., Bari, 1918, i. 80 [Engl. tr., 2 vols., Constable, 1916, i. 76].

restrained and the weak are exposed to the right of might. A fanatical attachment to liberty not only leads to slavery, but is itself slavery. It is a false conception of freedom which asks for freedom not *in* the State but *from* the State : the power of the State and the freedom of the people are inseparably connected. It is not always that the true partisans of freedom are the so-called Liberals : it is undeniable that at the time of the Great Elector the real champion of liberty was absolutism ; Leibniz, Pufendorf, and Thomasius, to whom we owe the reawakening of Germany, were all rigid absolutists. Who were the reactionaries of that time? The friends of so-called liberty, Conrad von Burgsdorff and General Kalkstein, the leaders of the noble party who wished to enslave the common man in the interests of a caste.[1]

This is not an isolated case. To-day, asks Treitschke, who are the true Liberals? Are they the partisans of universal suffrage? It is quite untrue that the effect of universal suffrage is radical ; the truth is that its effect is incalculable. The man who thinks that the external mechanism of the vote can create a true liberty is a mere radical doctrinaire. It leads visibly to a weakening of parliament. It is impossible out of this welter of clerical, political, and economic groups to form a majority capable of exercising a decisive influence upon the government. And that, quite apart from the true observation of a French historian that nothing can be less Liberal than the people.

Those who affirm that Germany is illiberal because she cannot establish party government overlook the peculiar character of the Imperial constitution. The Chancellor, the only responsible functionary, has the exclusive duty of obeying the orders of the Federal Council, whose members represent twenty-five governments. It is therefore his duty to represent opinions which in certain circumstances are not his own. Moreover, the constitution of the Empire lays down that a member of the Federal Council cannot be at the same time a member of the Reichstag, while the heads of the main branches of the Imperial administration must be *ipso facto*

[1] *Ibid.* i. 150 *seqq.* [Engl. tr., *cit.*, i. 154].

members of the Federal Council. Thus a parliamentary government is impossible by the terms of the constitution.

None the less, Treitschke adds, there is no State in Europe in which the parliamentary criticism of administration is so strict or so honest as in Germany; and this is because in Germany the government stands face to face with parliament as a real and genuine power. In England it is only the opposition that can criticize the acts of the administration. And the criticism is always moderate in tone, because it is a case of one hand washing the other : the opposition knows that it may very soon be itself in power and the butt of criticism. In Germany, on the other hand, the opposition can push its criticism to extremes because it knows that it will never be in power.

But liberty does not consist only in a central constitution. The constitutional life of the State, if it is to be healthy and active, presupposes a vigorous local self-government. It is of the essence of political freedom that the will of the State should be carried into effect not only by means of permanent officials, but by means of the administrative autonomy of communes and groups of communes. From this point of view the north of Germany is more free than the south, despite appearances to the contrary. There is no administrative autonomy in Bavaria ; there is a system of prefectures, though in a tempered form, a thing absolutely foreign to the Prussian organization. In general, Northern Germany is far more careful than Southern to preserve the free movement of personality, habituated as the latter is to a Napoleonic régime.[1]

As the reader can see, Treitschke's political conception harmonizes exactly with that of the jurists, and represents a form of Liberalism doubtless in many respects at variance with Western Liberalism, but at bottom inspired by the same motives, and equally tending to find in the autonomous personality the source of a rich and varied political life.

[1] Treitschke, iv. 84, 136, &c.

§ 5. SOCIAL LIBERALISM

Legal science is not the only field in which the Liberal consciousness of modern Germany has found room to display itself; economic science is another. In saying this we are not thinking of the doctrines of the classical and Manchester schools, which through the work of Schulze-Delitzsch have come to form part of the progressive Liberals' programme. Lassalle's criticisms of these anachronistic revivals, though in their tone perhaps unjustly contemptuous, are decisive. To tell the workman, in the middle of a factory system in full swing, that his salvation lies not in the trade union but in freedom of contract, and to enlarge upon the sense of dignity and responsibility resulting from that freedom, is unconsciously to make a mock of him. And to repeat the old phrases about profits on capital being the rewards of abstinence, is to invite the ridicule of all who know that capital does not nowadays originate in the same way in which it did in the early days of capitalism. The source of the capitalist's accumulations is not his own labour but the labour of others, and his handsome rewards are the fruit not of his own abstinence but of other people's. In these terms Lassalle replied to Schulze-Delitzsch, whose *Working Men's Catechism* betrays an outlook at least a generation out of date.

The social Liberalism of which we are now speaking is based upon the great development of German industry, which began in the second half of the nineteenth century as a result of the nationalistic economic programme laid down by List; it is also based upon the formation of trade unions, whose legitimacy and value it does not dispute. The problem which it raises is whether the only function of these unions is that ascribed to them by the Socialist ideology, and whether the so-called *bourgeois* economic system is inseparably bound up with the theories of the classical and Manchester schools.

The problem thus assumes a double aspect, historical and theoretical; and the school which makes the most important contribution towards its solution is in fact the historical school of economists, founded by Roscher, which in opposition to the abstract and doctrinaire methods of classical economics attempts to prove that economic forms and institutions, and therefore the scientific laws which regulate them, are historical in character. This point of view already constitutes a presumption in favour of the thesis that the classical theories of the relations between capital, profits, and wages, adequate to a certain stage in the development of industry, are inappropriate to a more advanced and complex stage; and that the Socialists' apocalypse, based as it is by a kind of dialectical opposition on the immobility and eternity of these laws, is a fallacy, and may safely be ignored in the attempt to give a theoretical and historical account of the latest phase in the development of industrialism.

This is the position taken up by Brentano in his works on trade unionism; and the impulse which he gave to a liberal outlook upon social questions gave rise to a flourishing school of economists, whose chief representatives are Herkner and Schulze Gaevernitz.

Brentano criticizes the socialistic idea of the workman-employer. This union of functions which industry in its development has separated is a departure from the line of historical progress: it is possible only in small industry, not in large or even moderate undertakings. He would prefer a reform of a quite different character, based on a wages policy not only fair but even in the long run favourable to the masters. In fixing wages, this policy would aim at the application of the principle that low wages do not necessarily imply cheap labour or vice versa, and that the highest wages are paid for the best and most important work.

Now there are only two means of preventing the employer from dictating the terms of the labour contract, with consequences fatal to the workman and indirectly to himself also: the united strength of the workmen, and the State. But State interference in the determination of wages is an infraction of the freedom of person and property; and what is even worse, it hinders instead of helping the solution of the social problem, because the workman, instead of relying freely on his own strength, finds himself in a position of complete dependence on the State. The result would be that the working classes would attempt to seize, or at least to influence, the government, and the employers would do the same; so that both classes would be exploiting the public power in their private interests. The resulting situation would resemble that of society in the ancient world; every political conflict would turn into an economic conflict, and in this conflict class hatred would be the predominant motive.

More conducive to the end is the other means, the spontaneous and free organization of workmen and employees, and an agreement between the two competing groups brought about by a court of arbitration. Thanks to the influence of trade unions, the ruinous consequences of identifying labour as a commodity with the labourer who sells it disappear, and it may be said that labour truly becomes a commodity and the labourer becomes a free vendor, no longer selling himself as a commodity. He puts his will into effect by means of a skilful control of the sale of his labour. The opposition of the classical economists to trade unions, as an artificial means of raising wages beyond the point permitted by the needs of production, falls to the ground when it is shown that the wage-fund theory, according to which the capital used by the employer for wages is a sum fixed in advance, is erroneous.

Experience has proved that this fixed limit does not exist, and that the progressive improvement of the conditions of the workman, far from being detrimental to industry, is a condition of its development.[1] From this point of view Herkner was able to regard social reform as a means of industrial and capitalistic progress.

This conception, framed in a full-length historical setting, appears in Schulze Gaevernitz's work on *Great Industry*, which from a close inquiry into the growth of the English cotton industry, as a type of modern industrial development, rises to a comprehensive view of the social problem in its successive historical phases.

The first generation of great manufacturers drew its

[1] Brentano, *La Question ouvrière*, Fr. tr., Paris, 1885, pp. 167 *seqq.*

strength from the consistent and ruthless application of economic principles. The rule, buy in the cheapest market and reduce the cost of production to a minimum, was to them so important that the chorus of economists which accompanied the drama of the Industrial Revolution pronounced it an eternal law of human life.

When it is said that the factory system has created a class of wage slaves, something more is intended than a mere figure of speech. In spite of certain external differences, the condition of the labouring proletariate created by great industry truly resembles that of slaves. From this fact the economists inferred the brazen law of wages, a scientific formula adequate to the industrial period marking the transition from small industry to great, and to that period alone. But great industry in its turn, finding itself in possession of a monopoly, in order to lower the cost of production requires a gradual improvement in the conditions of labour, not unlike that which formerly led from slavery to freedom. This industrial proletariate, whose condition recalls that of a slave population, disappears by degrees as great industry grows. This has actually occurred in the cotton industry, where, in order to increase the rapidity of the shuttles and the number of shuttles controlled by a single workman, it has been necessary to raise the workman's standard of living. Thus from indeterminate claims upon a vassal class, determinate claims arose, and from these, liberty; from the slave bound to industry arose the slave bound to tribute, and from him the free artisan: the workman has risen in the scale, but always to the master's advantage.

This being so, what is the relation between wages and profits, which the classical school regarded as standing in irreconcilable opposition? In the first phase of industrial development the cost of production rose, either because capital was scarce and dear, or because manual labour, however low its wages, was expensive on account of the quantities of it which were necessarily employed. Profits were high because the growing businesses enjoyed a monopoly. From the social point of view the opposition described by the economists was perfectly real: bare subsistence on the one hand ; on the other, the concentration of immense fortunes.

But internal and international competition produces fresh progress. The continual lowering of the cost of production becomes the dominant motive of development. Raw materials become of less importance ; and the greater part of the produce is distributed between labour and capital in such a way that the so-called profits of the employer, being of a two-fold character, may be considered as comprised partly under the one head and partly under the other. Machinery lowers the cost of labour, the latter being progressively displaced by mechanical methods ; capital charges are diminished because technical progress renders capital more productive and economic progress renders it cheaper. The workman gains, because this diminution in prices has the effect of an increase in wages. An equal capital to-day produces more than fifty years ago ; but interest and profits have remained the same, or have decreased; the balance has gone into the pocket of the labourer.

Competition from above is reinforced by pressure from beneath, exercised by trade unions ; and the two together have reversed the old relation between profits and wages. Formerly the employer received everything left over after paying the interest on borrowed capital and the wages of his men ; now labour receives the balance, after the payment of interest and profits. Profits, like interest, tend to become a fixed quantity, while wages absorb the variable margin produced by industrial progress.

The facts of economic evolution thus disprove both opposite doctrines, the conservative and the socialist, both of which are based upon a false assumption. Great industry, it is said, proletarianizes society and destroys the middle class; the poor become poorer, the rich richer. The tension between the two parties increases, and a violent conflict will at last become inevitable. Hence the *bourgeois* classes often look upon social progress with an anxious eye. The labouring classes, on the other hand, regard it with satisfaction, as leading to the time when the expropriators, reduced in numbers, will be in their turn expropriated.

These fears and hopes are groundless. The social results of economic growth may be summed up as a beneficent tendency towards equalizing the extremes of wealth. So far from its being the case that the rich always become richer and the poor poorer, statistical inquiry shows that the opposite is taking place.[1] The Liberal significance of these consequences of industrialism is undeniable. Great industry tends to form a new middle class to replace the lower middle-class artisans whom it has destroyed. It is creating an aristocracy of labour with an ever-increasing sum of physical and intellectual demands, which, rescued from the brutalizing and servile poverty of the past, is beginning to develop a political outlook of its own : the clear mark of a power of independent reflection upon the problems of its own future. Slaves have no political programme ; they create nothing but violent and destructive insurrections.

From this point of view, the contribution of the working classes to the political life of modern nations is a fresher and keener feeling for liberty and self-government. The trade unions, and still more the co-operative societies, are new forms of social self-government which, as compared with those forms which yet survive from the old landed aristocracies, have the merit of being the fruits of labour alone and of implying no privilege. The creatures of freedom, these institutions have moreover an organic character which shows the measure and the tendency of modern Liberalism, as opposed to the atomistic individualism of the early nineteenth century. The co-operative movement, as opposed to the political movement known as social democracy, has the advantage of a great historical capacity of adaptation to the political institutions of the day, a practical demonstration that over and above the class conflict which alone social democracy recognizes, there are elements of solidarity and peaceful evolution.[2]

[1] Schulze Gaevernitz, *La Grande Intrapresa* (tr. Jannacone in *Biblioteca degli economisti*, ser. iv, part i), pp. 42 *seqq.*

[2] Cf. the interesting remarks on the co-operative movement and its Liberal character in Herkner, *Die Arbeiterfrage*, Berlin, ed. 5, 1908, pp. 185 *seqq.*

§ 6. POLITICAL LIBERALISM

The great development of legal and social theories in Germany, though indirectly influenced by the general evolution of European politics, has not succeeded in overcoming the lack of a political point of view in the proper sense of the word : of a widespread training, on the part of the government, parliament, and parties, in strictly political problems as distinct from the technical problems of law and social science. The Germans have not lived in the political atmosphere in which their great State organization ought to have been steeped ; this organization has remained isolated, in a rarefied atmosphere, in comparison with States like England and France which have behind them a great political tradition. From this point of view the disastrous tendency of the Germans to state every controversial question in terms of military force may be explained as a symptom of their political weakness.

Even before the Great War, signs of discontent with the rigid constitutionalism which condemned the people to a perpetual political minority had begun to appear. The best elements in the country were withdrawing from public life to devote themselves to industry and trade, despairing of playing any part in the government through the adoption of a parliamentary career. Government had sunk into a technical and bureaucratic function, wholly dependent upon the Crown, to whose capricious and often arbitrary initiative it was compelled to submit. The absence of any real political responsibility necessarily paralysed that particular form of sensitiveness which has enabled governments in countries far weaker than Germany to manipulate and overcome far more difficult and delicate situations. The political parties in their turn suffered from this bureaucratization of the government, which sterilized their work by denying effective co-operation to the great currents of public opinion, or by subjecting these currents to an underground influence designed to play off one against another in order to leave the will of the monarch and his military and bureaucratic satellites in undisputed control of the situation.

The faults and defects of this system of government were displayed in all their irremediable gravity by the Great War. An acute German writer, Max Weber, has the merit of explicitly recognizing this fact in a work on *Parliament and Government under the New Régime in Germany*,[1] whose publication coincided with the profound transformation of the German political system.

For Weber, the world-wide coalition against Germany was due to the German people's lack of political training, due in its turn to the passivity which that people had learnt from Bismarck. Under Bismarck's rule, ' the nation lost the habit of that positive and decisive co-operation in its own political destiny by means of elected representatives, which alone can educate political judgement '. His intolerance of all disagreement towards ' every independent brain and every consistent character ', his constant practice of surrounding himself with non-political collaborators who merely obeyed his orders, left the country utterly deprived of political education and political will.

Such a régime favoured the immense development of the bureaucracy, by enclosing within its rigid boundaries that which should have remained outside them. Weber does not deny the positive value of the bureaucracy within the limits of its technical and administrative function ; but he strongly opposes its extension to political life, which is regulated by wholly different principles. Political activity shrinks from the hierarchical arrangement of ranks, which conceals the personality of the agent beneath an impersonal system of ranks and offices ; it is essentially a free activity, individual and responsible. For this reason political ability cannot be recruited by tests of technical competence, but by means of a political selection exercised by parties, organizations formed by a free enrolment which is necessarily renewed at every moment of their history, and thus contrasting with any kind of close corporation circumscribed by law or contract. In-

[1] Italian translation by Ruta, Bari (Laterza), 1921.

wardly and outwardly, their life is a struggle, an unceasing selection of political talent, as war is a selection of military talent. For this free and mobile school of politics substitute bureaucracy, and you have lost all free initiative, all rapidity of movement, all skill in discerning the political value of something technically defective, or the political ineptitude of something which from a technical point of view is perfect. A Parliament of experts and civil servants, the ideal of modern State Socialism, would be merely 'an organ for effecting purely material compromises, devoid of political orientation as a State'. It would increase the temptation for the bureaucracy to preserve its own power by playing off one material interest against another and by a thinly veiled system for the distribution of offices and emoluments. The true function of a parliament is the exact opposite : to set up a body with strictly political interests to counterbalance the particularism of the expert and the routine of the State servant.

Reflecting on the history of Germany in the light of these ideas, Weber finds it easy to show how the bureaucratic structure of the German Empire made it impossible for the Government to restrain the political vagaries of the Kaiser or nullify their disastrous international consequences, which any kind of parliamentary government could have done with ease ; and thus exposed the monarchy to grave risks and colossal responsibilities, to the danger and detriment of the entire nation. Moreover, it deprived the State of the aid of the most intelligent men in its hour of need ; it reduced the activity of the political parties to a war of words, destitute of practical sanction ; even when it placed party men in power, it severed them from their party by turning them into bureaucrats, and thus surrendered the prestige which it might have drawn from their contact with the currents of public opinion that they represented. A further consequence was that France, with a technical and administrative organization far inferior to that of Germany, and a democracy torn and rent by internal crises, was able to triumph over her enemy in the field of politics by effecting against her a coalition of the whole world.

The work of Weber coincides, as we have said, with the new political and parliamentary orientation of Germany which is the greatest triumph of post-war Liberalism.[1] The actual political fruits of this régime cannot as yet be precisely estimated. But if one thinks of the internal and external difficulties under which Germany is labouring, and of the severe trials which the constitution of Weimar has already undergone, one may conclude that the omens are favourable towards the capacity of the German people to win for itself that liberal education in politics which the old régime denied it.

[1] It is interesting to note that the end of German authoritarian constitutionalism coincided with a profound change in the agrarian system of the country, which, by breaking up the large estates, tends to decrease the political power of the *Junkertum*. On the other hand, the simultaneous appearance of parliamentary government and of small and middle-sized estates forms an important subject worthy of separate study.

ITALIAN LIBERALISM

§ 1. THE PERIOD OF PREPARATION

IN the general economy of European political evolution Italian Liberalism plays a modest part. It is a mere reflection of foreign doctrines and tendencies; yet noteworthy by its effort to adapt them to the special conditions of Italy, and by its close connexion with the process of national unification. In the latter aspect, it represents the most significant example of the efficacy of Liberal ideas in cementing the union of a people; for if in Germany also it was in the name of freedom that national feeling first asserted itself, political unification came about in another manner and by other means; in Italy we find a loyalty to the first ideal which is highly instructive to the historian of Liberalism.

The lack of originality and inherent vigour in the Italian Liberal movement was partly due to the causes which, after the luxuriant growth of the Renaissance, produced in Italy a general lowering of vitality in comparison with the other European nations. Political divisions impeded the formation of great movements of public opinion and limited the activity of parties to the narrow sphere of communal and regional rivalry. The subjection of certain provinces to foreign rule was detrimental to the liberal education of the people, because it concentrated their best energies upon an attempt at emancipation which led to a confusion between independence and freedom, and thus reduced the latter to something contingent and in a sense external. The spirit of the Counter-Reformation crushed the individualistic feeling which is the life-blood of modern Liberalism; not so much stifling it by force, as drying up its sources by a Jesuitical education designed to sap the freedom of the will and employ its energies in a passive acceptance of authority. Culture, surviving only in the persons of professional writers and antiquaries, withdrew from the sphere of the present, with its vital interests, to an imaginary other world, the last relic of the squandered inheritance of humanism. And even when, at the beginning of the nineteenth century, it tried to draw inspiration from contemporary history, it betrayed its origin in a literary and bookish tradition.

Another cause is to be found in the backward economic state of Italy, which retarded the social differentiation of classes and in especial the formation of a large middle class. Foreign trade had shrunk owing to the displacement of the great trade routes ; internal trade was impeded by the customs barriers resulting from the political divisions of the country. The transformation of the artisan system into a modern industrial system was delayed, partly by lack of raw materials, partly by the smallness of the markets ; hence no Italian district, except to some extent Lombardy, had passed through its industrial revolution till after the middle of the nineteenth century.

Taking as our starting-point the state of Italy in the eighteenth century, we find that the economic forces of the country were wholly agricultural. Here reigned a great variety of crops and methods, connected with differences in the distribution of landed property. Richer in the valley of the Po and in Tuscany, poorer in the south, impoverished by ecclesiastical misgovernment in the territories of the Church, Upper Italy is the first region in which a widespread landed *bourgeoisie* arose ; and, since technical and economic necessities favoured large-scale farming and led to very little subdivision of land, this *bourgeoisie* essentially consisted of substantial and enterprising tenant farmers, manifesting already the industrial spirit of the new age.

In the other regions, less favoured by nature, the large estate was for technical reasons not susceptible of this transformation ; and hence feudalism lay heavier upon economic and social life, and delayed the formation of middle classes. From a political point of view, on the other hand, the weight of feudalism was in general less perceptible : in Italy the aristocracy did not form a political body worthy of the name. From the time of the *Comuni* and the *Signorie*, the first and heaviest blows had always fallen upon the aristocracy ; later, foreign rule and the small size of the autonomous principalities had constantly lowered its prestige and diminished or destroyed its activity and ability to govern. Thus the rise of the Third Estate in the Revolutionary period caused no internal struggles comparable to those of France or even of England ; indeed, the most progressive and enlightened elements in the aristocracy, as individuals and not as representatives of a distinct political body, welcomed and championed the new Liberal doctrines.

The feudal texture of society was further much weakened by the fact that from the earliest medieval times, the tradition of Roman law never lost all its hold upon Italy, and its persistence effectively opposed the exclusive dominion of feudal law. The results of this fact are somewhat complicated. Roman private law, with its institution of quiritary property and its general tendency to make all juridical institutions a common possession of citizens, prevented the rise of exclusive privileged rights, and thus maintained the civil liberties of individuals. But at the same time, being a law of subjects, of men equal in subjection, its influence prevented the growth of the idea of inherent and original rights independent of the State and opposed to the rights of the prince. The vital experience of the antithesis between prince and people, which elsewhere created a feeling and love for political liberties, was thus lacking to the Italians. Estates General, Diets, Parliaments, which in France, Germany, and England arose out of this antithesis and formed, from the Middle Ages onwards, the first school of political Liberalism, are almost entirely unknown to Italian tradition. Here from its origin the State is strictly monistic : such is already the character of the *Comuni*, whose liberties are wholly different from those of feudal states, and may be called not so much Liberal as democratic institutions, in the ancient sense of that word. It is at any rate true that the sequel to their development is afforded by the *Signoria*, the monistic state *par excellence*, which denies all autonomous right on the part of the people and fuses people and prince into a single State organism.

Thus on the whole an age-long juridical tradition brought about in Italy a livelier sense of civil liberty, which prepared people's minds, by the beginning of the nineteenth century, to welcome legislation destroying feudalism and instituting *bourgeois* property; but at the same time it brought about a lack of training in political liberty, further aggravated by the vagaries of the municipal spirit and the other causes already described.

To the rise of an Italian Liberal movement in the eighteenth century, while Upper Italy contributed a substantial and industrious *bourgeoisie*, Southern Italy made a very different but not less important contribution. It was her privilege to consist of a kingdom of some size, with a long tradition behind it, and a political class trained to think and act from the point of view of the State. This kingdom had long been engaged in a controversy with the Holy See, which claimed over it an ancient title of feudal superiority; and this struggle served to bring into relief the principle of State sovereignty, which was vigorously championed by eminent jurists, protected and honoured by the monarchy, in whose service they did their work. But the value of this work went beyond any merely dynastic interests, and laid the foundations of modern legislative theory. Such at least is the importance of the *Storia Civile* of Giannone, the culmination of this study of public law and the inspiration of the reforming programme of the eighteenth-century Bourbon monarchy. No one who remembers that throughout its development Italian Liberalism shows itself most alive and most original when dealing with the problems of religious politics, owing to the peculiar relations between Church and State in Italy, can forget the great value of the southern tradition which developed the Liberal principles of separatism and of the secular character of the State.[1]

An interest no less autonomous inspired the economic

[1] For a fuller treatment of these problems, and in general for an analytical investigation of the contribution made by southern writers to the formation of national political thought, see my volume *Il pensiero politico meridionale nei secoli XVIII e XIX*, Bari, Laterza, 1923.

studies which flourished in Naples in the second half of the eighteenth century, and were, no less than the legal, penetrated by an intimate sense of the State as an end immanent in all the problems of economics and finance. Whereas in France the physiocrats preached a rationalistic liberalism, abstracting from the conditions of liberty in time, space, and manner, the two greatest Neapolitan economists, Genovesi and Galiani, made no secret of their inclination towards protectionism. This was due to the fact that they were studying a kingdom like Naples, whose resources were small, and which required to preserve its autonomy against the aggressive efforts of the great Mediterranean Powers, France and England, which might have made it the tool or the theatre of their rivalry, had it not resisted the bait of so-called Liberal commercial treaties. For the southern economists, especially Genovesi, economic liberty ought to begin at home, by breaking down the barriers which feudalism had opposed to trade in the national produce and to the development of agriculture.

Thus, through the converging efforts of lawyers and economists, arose the first manifestations of a Liberal idea, consisting essentially of a programme of reforms, involving the removal of all political, legal, and economic relics of feudalism, to be put into effect by an enlightened and educated government, a description certainly applicable to the Bourbon monarchy. The subsequent influence of French illuminism added nothing really new, but reinforced and broadened these original motives through the rationalistic spirit which now inspired and propagated them. All the efforts of a mind trained in simplification and clarification were required to disentangle the intricacies of feudalism and to grasp the fundamental principles of law and of the State with sufficient clarity to demonstrate their ability to safeguard civil liberties.

In reading any of the more important works of the period which drew its inspiration from illuminism, such as Filangieri's *Scienza della Legislazione* or Pagano's *Saggi politici*, one soon observes that, if the ultimate nature of the problems is the same, the intellectual atmosphere has undergone a

change. The love of the particular, the historical jurisprudence of a Giannone or the strictly national economics of
a Genovesi, has given place to a love of broad generalizations which renders the principles clearer and their application less certain. Thus in the works of Filangieri and Pagano
we find a clear statement of the conception of civil liberty,
as a liberty developing within the inviolable barrier of the
law; but at the same time we find an exaggerated belief in
the power of law itself to transform and renew society. It
was not for nothing that Rousseau depicted the legislator
as a god, and gave him the function of converting a chaos into
an ordered and harmonious cosmos. And the old feudal
world in which they still lived, and from which the quasi-
magical power of a new legislation was to rescue them,
seemed to the illuminists nothing else than a chaos.

The true meaning of liberty had been far better grasped
by a philosopher whom these men admired much but understood little, Vico; who, far from restricting the significance
of freedom to an abstract policy of legislative reform, made it
consist in having one's own laws, one's own institutions, one's
own government, free because one's own. Thus freedom was
an historical category, a counsel of prudence, a check on
revolutionary violence; but the age was not yet ripe for the
acceptance of this untimely lesson.

Civil liberty was the limit common to the new illuminist
generation and that which preceded it. Politically, Filangieri openly professes himself a partisan of enlightened
despotism, after the fashion of Voltaire and the physiocrats.
In Pagano the influence of Montesquieu and, through him,
of English Liberalism is visible; thus we find in his *Essays* the
antithesis between absolute government and free government, and the expression of a wholly new feeling of distrust
towards the enlightened activity of a single individual. The
opinion that the happiness of all citizens should be entrusted
to a will other than their own he explains as the effect of
habitual passivity; behind his cautious expressions we already
see a growing disappointment of the hopes of monarchy. The
revolutionary changes that were soon to come about set

the seal on this disappointment, and confirmed these earliest demands for political liberty, by elevating it into the true safeguard of a civil liberty which cannot safely be entrusted to the will of a benevolent despot.

While the political thought of the south was chiefly concerned with the State, that of Upper and Central Italy, where the municipal traditions of the past were still alive, was more open to the influence of the new individualism. The hardworking *bourgeoisie* of the north were far more conscious of the value of their own activity, as the private activity of individuals, than they were of the value of the State, which was an idea wholly foreign to the Lombards, real but feeble in Venice, crude and merely military in Piedmont. It was precisely in Piedmont that the age of enlightened despotism, then at its height, heard the first summons to the war on tyrants : Vittorio Alfieri's *Della Tirannide*, written in 1777, in which the figure which was to be the protagonist of future tragedies already appears. In its inspiration this book betrays a literary origin, because the picture which it gives of tyranny is abstract, conventionalized, abstracted from time and space ; but it is a literature very unlike an empty academic exercise, a literature into which there breaks a spontaneous and intimate feeling, and which is turned to the interests and ideals of contemporary historical life. In this aspect, it heralds the national and liberal tendencies later exemplified in the culture of the Risorgimento.

Tyranny for Alfieri means any government in which the person charged with administering the laws may make them, destroy them, break them, obstruct them, suspend them, and even evade them, with assured impunity. Hence one kind of tyranny is monarchy : ' the soft name which ignorance, flattery, and fear have given and still give to such governments.' It is said that a distinction can be made, depending on the difference between use and abuse : but if the laws in themselves, independently of the prince, have no force and authority, who can prevent abuse? And the laws which distinguish a free government from a tyranny are understood as mutual and solemn social pacts, necessarily a product of the will of the majority, as determined through legally elected representatives of the people. But even elected legislators become tyrants in their turn, if they have the power to take upon themselves the administration of the laws.[1] This is the keynote of a democratic conception in which democracy is tempered by the Liberal doctrine of the division of powers. And Alfieri did not contradict himself when, more than twenty years later, in his *Misogallo*, he scourged the tyranny of the Jacobins, to which he had by anticipation assigned its place in his treatise of 1777.

Granted the intellectual education of its author, the reader does not expect in this work any great breadth of political outlook; yet there is a vivid psychological picture of the environment which the tyrant creates for himself. A soulless life is the likeliest to prove a long and secure life under a tyranny, which surrounds itself with small-minded and commonplace men, flatterers and self-seekers; always inferior to those elected by a free people, however corrupt, because the people's favour is proof of a certain capacity or virtue.

The safeguards of tyranny are the army, which annihilates even the appearance of civil life, and the Church. 'The Christian religion is not in itself favourable to the free life, but the Catholic religion is practically incompatible with the free life.' Thus, the people being oppressed by every sort of vexation, 'the land in which a man is born is under a tyranny called in mockery by the name of fatherland; for people do not reflect that the only true fatherland is the land in which man enjoys freely, and under the security of invariable laws, those most precious rights which nature has given him '.[2]

Happily, tyranny brings with itself its own cure: in the cruelty, the constant injustice, the rapacity and the outrageous dishonesty of the tyrant lies the quickest and surest remedy, because the greater the development of the abuse, the greater the hope that the multitude will rise against it.

The opposite idea, of a free government, is less clearly

[1] Alfieri, *Della Tirannide*, Book I, ch. 2.   [2] *Op. cit.* i. 5, 6, 8, 10.

defined. Alfieri is thinking of the English government as interpreted by Montesquieu, but the aristocratic spirit which pervades this government renders its transplantation difficult. The creation of new titles, which in England is habitual and unattended with detrimental consequences, would in other countries be a weapon of oligarchical tyranny. This is because the English nobles by themselves are less powerful than the people; united with the people, they are more powerful than the king; united with the king, they are never more powerful than the people. Hence in England there exists that equilibrium between the one, the few, and the many, which is the political ideal, expressed later in various comedies, that Alfieri borrowed from the common literary tradition of political science.

More important than these attempts at a mechanical equilibrium or chemical combination of elements are the realistic observations added by Alfieri to explain the actual strength of English Liberalism.

'If in some things', he says, ' the English republic seems more firmly based than the Roman, this is because there is in England a permanent and vitalizing disagreement, not, as in Rome, between the nobles and the people, but between the people and the people : that is, between the ministry and the opposition. Thus, because this disagreement is generated not by disparity of hereditary interests, but by disparity of changing opinion, it does perhaps more good than harm ; for no one so completely belongs to one party that he might not often pass over to the opposite ; neither of the two parties having interests permanently opposed to and incompatible with the good of the whole.' [1]

This sentence expresses a very profound insight into the essence of political Liberalism, which consists in an opposition of parties transcending the opposition of classes. The conflict of social classes compromised the power of Rome ; the conflict of parties nourishes the strength of England.

[1] *Op. cit.* i. 11. I have not come across this thought anywhere in eighteenth-century literature ; yet I cannot make up my mind to give Alfieri the credit for inventing it, so incompatible does it appear, in inspiration and political penetration, with the literary orientation of his treatise.

Side by side with these notions of Alfieri's, important because they mark the beginning of a new point of view, civil and political, in the world of culture, arise Liberal notions of a very different kind, practical and economic, originating in the more advanced representatives of agriculture and trade. Their centre was naturally in Lombardy, the richest and busiest part of Italy, which, just because more deeply inspired with an expansive economic energy, was less tolerant of the obstacles and impediments which the survivals of feudalism in agriculture and industry opposed to its progress, and the customs barriers by which Austria deprived it of contact with Italy. It is in Lombardy that we find for the first time united, as at their source, the principal streams which will later meet in the unification of Italy: independence, unity, and freedom. Independence of Austria is the necessary starting-point from which the productive powers of Lombardy may find their natural outlet in the other parts of Italy; unity of market, of civil regulations, of political control, is the complement of this effort after emancipation: freedom forms its effective means, because, removing the arbitrary coercion of the subject and the habits of an inveterate tradition, it enables the people to translate their most vital aspirations into action.

These different but converging demands begin to appear of their own accord in the second half of the eighteenth century; but only at the time of the French Revolution and conquest do they acquire a definite and organic character and a wide diffusion among the *bourgeoisie*. Till then they were the privilege of an intellectual aristocracy, a few choice spirits forming the contributors and readers of *Caffè*, a journal which enjoyed a bare two years of life, from 1764 to 1766, but succeeded in revealing a few really modern personalities and uniting their views into a common programme. To this group belonged Pietro and Alessandro Verri, Beccaria, Carli, and Frisi; but other kindred minds were already in process of formation, whose leaders were afterwards Gioia and Romagnosi.

The idea of a common Italian fatherland took shape in

the minds of these writers in its most realistic aspects; they were endowed with a culture mainly economic and legal, and thus saw in the unity of the nation at once the cause and the effect of commercial and industrial development and of uniform and rational civil government. The subdivision and dispersion of all values, the melancholy heritage of feudalism, were the chief objects of their aversion and their criticism. Pietro Verri, intellectually the strongest of them, rises to a wider conception of Liberalism. He demands freedom not only in trade, but in all human actions: all limitation of activity is detrimental to social life, because every unnecessary exercise of governmental power weakens the moral ideas of the people, and renders them at first timid, then deceitful, and finally passive.

Verri is therefore an enemy of enlightened despotism. In a dialogue between Joseph II and a philosopher, he makes the philosopher criticize the work of the Emperor as follows: 'When you have deprived the clergy of authority, the ministers of "condecoration", the nobility of power, and the people of laws, how do you imagine that the public spirit can rule itself, by means of such a clergy, by means of degraded ministers and an army without officers?'[1] A constitution must be sought; an inviolable law, ensuring to the monarch's successors the devotion of good and loyal subjects, and to the citizens that security of property which is the sole end of government. This constitution must be guaranteed and defended by a permanent body interested in preserving it, whose voice may at all times freely warn the monarch of any encroachments on its integrity made by his ministers.

To this argument in favour of constitutionalism Verri adds another, more strictly logical in character. Great enterprises demand energy in execution, but must be preceded by doubt and quiet examination, without which the people is in danger of knowing nothing of its sovereign except his force.[2] Therefore if action belongs to the government, deliberation demands the aid of those who represent the interests of the people.

[1] P. Verri, *Scritti inediti*, in appendix to Ottolini, *P. Verri e i suoi tempi*, Palermo, 1921, p. 253.   [2] *Op. cit.*, p. 257.

With the outbreak of the French Revolution, thoughts of civil and political liberty spread rapidly through the districts of Upper Italy, which were better prepared to receive them than the rest, and had greater opportunities of contact with the revolutionaries. Here conditions existed analogous to those which accounted for the success of the Revolution in France : feudalism was already shaken to its foundations, social well-being was widespread, and the sense of liberty and civil equality was already to some extent inspiring the ordinances of the government ; the last relics of feudalism thus appeared all the more oppressive and intolerable.

From 1790 onwards essays and tracts began to appear in shoals, canvassing before an ever-increasing audience the political, economic, and national questions raised directly or indirectly by the French Revolutionaries. Later, at the period of the conquest, the freedom of the press gave rise to a yet livelier discussion, now carried on through political journals. Writers now discuss economic freedom, the abolition of feudalism, the introduction of a more uniform and rational legislation, the creation of a customs union ; and point the contrast between monarchy and republic, aristocracy and *bourgeoisie*, liberty and equality. Those who during the preceding period had already provided themselves with a solid background of ideas brought to the discussion a note of balance and moderation, to temper the zeal of the hotter revolutionaries. Verri, in his *Thoughts on the Political State of the Milanese*, in 1790, unites all the most essential elements in the claims of the new age. The headlong current which seemed to be overwhelming everything tended in fact to create a more stable and permanent order of things, by setting law in the place of human caprice. Now the security of property, the real foundation of civil and political order, depends solely upon the security of the laws ; and this in its turn would be altogether ephemeral, if the power of the ministers were by itself sufficient, as it hitherto has been, for the creation of new laws. Thus the security of property depends upon the constitution, and finds its ultimate safeguard in the representation of the people, because every written constitution must be an empty illusion in the absence of a body destined to maintain it and interested in doing so.[1]

The same legalitarian interpretation of liberty and equality is given by Romagnosi in his two essays, *What is Equality?* (1792) and *What is Liberty?* (1793), where he shows in a popular manner and by way of instances that equality of property is a chimera and an injustice; and that the real equality, that of rights, justly involves inequality in fact. Hence, ' nowhere is equality so well promoted, protected, and defended as in a good civil society, that is, a people ruled by a strong and well-ordered government in which all serve the law and no one serves a private person '.[2] Similar considerations apply to liberty.

These ideas of a moderate Liberalism were interwoven with the theme of national unity, to which the French occupation gave a powerful impulse. In 1796 the general administration of Lombardy announced a competition on the question ' which of the free governments best conduces to the happiness of Italy? ' A northern writer, Gioia, to whom the prize was awarded, and a southern, Galdi, were in substantial agreement: each maintained that only a united and indivisible republic answered the needs of a free government for Italy. But the term republic was taken, with a reminiscence of classical usage, as a synonym for a State ordered according to law; and the feeling against monarchy is explained by Gioia as meaning that ' the passions of a single man change in time and cease to exist with himself; those of a body that exists for ever, animated by the same spirit, urged by the same interests, are in their nature immutable and immortal '. Thus the republic at which Gioia aims is not the concentrated and tyrannical republic of the Convention, but that in which the power of making laws is, in the interests of liberty, separated and independent of the executive power.

---

[1] Verri, *Pensieri sullo stato politico del Milanese* (London, 1825), pp. 42, 64, 65.

[2] G. D. Romagnosi, *Che cosa e l'eguaglianza?* in *Opere*, Milan, 1843, vol. iii, part i, pp. 792, 795-6. *Che cosa è la libertà?* is contained in the same volume.

If it is objected that the establishment of such a republic would necessarily be followed by the rise of a thousand different parties in mutual conflict, till one or more tyrants arose once more to dictate laws over their heads, he answers that he does not fear this; that ' a certain ferment of spirits, an oscillation so to speak in the mass of the people, instead of being a seed of destruction, is a preservative against the death of liberty and the extinction of energies '.[1]

The largely reflected character of Italian Liberalism in the revolutionary period is betrayed by the constant changes in Italian public opinion resulting from the events in which France took the leading place. At first, feelings of naïve confidence and fervent hope were uppermost: the success of the French Revolution, first internal and then external through its victorious armies, seemed a providential means of universal salvation. But later, news of the horrors of civil war, and, later again, first-hand experience of the oppression and spoliation which accompanied and followed the French occupation, destroyed the first confidence in the Liberal watchwords of the invaders, and turned the nascent energies of the Italian nation into a stubborn hostility towards France. Of this new attitude the most finished expression is Vittorio Alfieri's *Misogallo*, the forerunner of an abundant anti-French literature.[2]

Nevertheless the French occupation throve and was consolidated by Napoleon's campaigns of 1795 and 1796 and still more that of 1800. It brought with it, together with the evils of foreign rule, the benefits of a civil and enlightened government, which satisfied many popular hopes entrusted in vain to the old governments. The *Code civile*, the Magna Charta of modern property, was introduced; administrative unity was achieved, an effective means of blotting out the last relics of feudalism, which, driven from the field of law, had taken refuge in local traditions and customs; and the heaviest of the fetters that hampered the movements of

[1] M. Gioia, *Dissertazione sul problema: quale dei governi liberi meglio convenga alla felicità d'Italia*, ed. 3, Lugano, 1833, pp. 21, 27, 107.

[2] Collection in Hazard, *La Révolution française et les lettres italiennes*, Paris, 1910.

agriculture, industry, and trade, were removed. The formation of a kingdom of Italy, though limited to a part only of Upper Italy, Piedmont being annexed to France, gave opportunity for a practical test of the value of the new reforms as a whole. They realized the aspiration formulated in the following words by the author of an anonymous pamphlet of 1801 :

' We invoke the formation of these two codes, civil and penal, as the palladium of our public liberties. Only after their adoption can it be hoped that the partial rivalries which now visibly mark the divisions of the ancient state may be overcome : and as in the tenacity with which they maintain their own laws Rousseau has seen the only reason why the Jews have preserved their national spirit, in spite of so many centuries of dispersion, so, by the adoption of a code of their own, so many and such diverse peoples, recently united, will succeed in forming a single harmonious Cisalpine mind.' [1]

Piedmont and Central Italy, in large part annexed to France, and the Napoletano, formed into an independent kingdom but with a French king and a French government, were less completely severed from the kingdom of Italy than the various Italian states had been from one another before the conquest. If certain political accidents still severed them, the spirit of the new régime, circulating through all alike, was identical ; and no less identical were the legal system, the recruitment of the army, the system of finance and customs, and the organization of public magistracies, whose members were selected in great part from among the Italian *bourgeoisie*. Thus intellectual and economic relations grew up between the various parts of Italy, creating at once the need and the opportunity for a permanent understanding. Especially after the victory of Marengo, many southern exiles, survivors of the unhappy Neapolitan republic, found refuge in Milan, which at this period of preparation performed a function of national concentration like that which Turin was to play on a larger scale during the Risorgimento.

From the point of view of Liberalism, these first attempts

[1] Del Giudice ascribes the work to Bonaventura Spannocchi. Cf. Ciasca, *L'origine del programma per l'opinione nazionale italiana*, Milan, 1916, pp. 182-3.

at national cohesion are important not only because they show the unifying value of free civil government, but also because they mark the beginning of a new orientation in Italian public opinion, very like that which was taking place at the same time in France. No sooner had it emerged from the anarchy of the Revolution, than the people, or rather the *bourgeois* class which represented the people, welcomed with relief the peace created by Napoleon, as the herald of tranquillity and order and of a life ruled by stable laws. Civil liberty appeared as the most solid gain achieved by the Revolution, under the auspices of Bonaparte, who by his work had brought to an end the chaotic and convulsive movements of a mob unconscious of the goal in which its revolutionary impulses were to find rest and satisfaction. And in comparison with the benefits of civil freedom, bestowed by an act of imperial command, political freedom, associated as it was with the detested memory of past convulsions, necessarily appeared as a delusive benefit, or as a first crude and chaotic incarnation of a truer freedom. This explains why the Italians, whom their own historical experience had taught to value civil liberty higher than political, were satisfied with the Napoleonic régime and set themselves to profess a Liberalism resting ultimately upon a dictatorship.

This is the spirit which dominates the numerous petitions presented to the French government by Italian patriots, demanding the completion of the unification of Italy which the French had already begun. It is also the ideal of Foscolo, who in his *Address to Bonaparte*, in 1802, exclaims : ' If then thou canst not live as one of ourselves, may it be the seal of our liberty that thou thyself hast left it inviolate. And, with the whole people, I mean by liberty the having no magistrate (except Bonaparte) who is not an Italian, no captain who is not a citizen.'[1] But the most vital and organic expression of Bonapartist Liberalism is furnished by a great southern writer, Vincenzo Cuoco.

The focus of Cuoco's political thought is popular monarchy. The consciousness of the people can only express

[1] Foscolo, *Prose politiche*, Florence, 1850, p. 63.

itself in its synthetic unity in monarchy; its historical continuity has its tangible symbol in hereditary monarchy. But what he demands is not any kind of monarchy; he is too hostile to the lately vanquished despotism; he demands a popular monarchy, the immediate expression of the people, the supreme magistracy of the State, and therefore a responsible power. ' With heredity and responsibility ', he says, ' are united two things which in their nature appear irreconcilable, freedom and power.' Only in this monarchy can the legislative and executive powers be fused into one, whose dissociation produces inertia and caprice; it possesses the power to vivify institutions, and the capacity to adapt every action of the government to the needs of the people.

In this conception Cuoco is of course thinking of Napoleon, in whom he sees the fruit and positive result of the entire Revolution. ' If the Revolution has produced anything good, it is owing to Bonaparte; for a revolution, which by nature is an evil, becomes good only when it is over; and Bonaparte is the man who by his powerful grasp has arrested it in mid-career without retarding human progress through a counter-revolution.' At first this positive significance of the Revolution escaped him; his hatred of Jacobinism, for the spirit of turbulence and disorder, hid it from him, and he came to see it only when the Revolution itself was over, but its spirit was still active and beneficent, through Napoleon's wise control of it, and his skill in keeping it within the limits of law and institutions.

The conception of representative government, an expression of political liberty, is foreign and hostile to Cuoco's mind. Representation is a mediation which destroys the strict immediacy of the people's life; it interferes with the direct and intimate communion of ruler and ruled; it duplicates the single and compact life of the people, by attempting to extract from a diffused sensibility, in which the popular mind expresses itself, a concentrated reflection intended to represent it.

A certain interest in constitutional government appears only at the beginning of his career as a writer, when as yet the Napoleonic idea had not taken shape in his mind; namely in 1799, when a Constitution was being elaborated for the new Neapolitan republic. But even then he did not understand the spirit of political Liberalism. In a letter to Vincenzo Russo on Pagano's project of a Constitution, he criticized the principle that each representative was to represent not his constituency but the entire nation, because he saw no connexion between this universal, abstract, indirect representation and the immediate needs of the various groups of the people. This representation was neither a people nor a government; it contained neither the manifold interests of the one nor the active unity of the other. Cuoco suggested for his own part a political system based on municipalities, within which parliaments should be formed suited to the particular needs of the various communities. In this way the idea of representation was in substance denied : from the assumption that the particular could not be reproduced or replaced, it followed that in the last resort nothing except itself could represent it. Representative forms were thus contaminated with those of an immediate and direct government, or rather, not so much the forms of a government as those of a narrow and as it were domestic administration, as soon as municipalities were made the basis of the political system.

Where then shall we find the unity of these particular forces? It was only some years later that Cuoco was able to understand the formation of this unity, when it appeared incarnate in Napoleon. Not an abstract unity, the residuum of a process of reduction through a series of representations becoming emptier as they became more general; but a concrete and living unity, possessing at once the life and activity of the particulars, and the weight and energy of their synthesis.[1]

This political view, which found many adherents in Italy during the French occupation, was closely bound up with

[1] I have transcribed the above remarks in great part from the chapter on Vincenzo Cuoco in my volume quoted above (p. 278) on the political thought of the South.

the Napoleonic Empire: it arose and declined with it. But even before the Empire passed away, there were signs of growing hesitation and doubt. The idea that all the gains of the Revolution were bound up with the fortunes of a single man, even if that man were Napoleon, began to make people uneasy. What became of the safety of property by common right, if the laws which sanctioned it had no guarantee but the will of the monarch, and might be revoked by a stroke of the pen, leaving the people powerless to safeguard their rights?

Moreover, Napoleon's government oscillated between legality and caprice. The betrayal of Venice at Campo Formio created an insuperable difficulty for many Italians; and later, the annexation of Piedmont and Central Italy to France, and the contemptuous silence which alone replied to all requests and petitions for the unification of the peninsula, increasingly emphasized the discord between the people and the monarchy which was to have been its direct and pure expression. Not only were actions and deliberations of political import effected without the consent of the people, but even those of civil import in the widest sense of the word were effected, in spite of the citizens' desires, by this very political action which was withdrawn from their control. It is enough to refer here to the imposition of the continental blockade, as an interference with the economic freedom which forms an integral part of civil liberty. This meant that civil liberty itself was illusory unless provided with an effective guarantee against the caprice of the monarch. And what guarantee could it have, except a liberal compact between the king and the people, that is, a Constitution together with a political organ consisting of popular representatives and designed to protect it?

Thus in Italy, as in France, the demand for political liberty as a guarantee of civil liberty reappears, and becomes a part of the tradition which we have seen growing up in the period preceding the Revolution and including its earliest years. Not only Napoleon but the princes whom he set up in Italy were increasingly petitioned in the last years of the Empire for a constitutional charter in order to consolidate their thrones by the express consent of the people. But they grasped the importance of these demands too late, when the European coalition was on the point of overthrowing them.

With the triumph of the legitimist restoration, the demands of constitutionalism became more vigorous. What had been a remote danger or a partial limitation of rights was now an actual programme, the declared intention of recapturing all the positions that the Revolution had won. The Treaty of Vienna created a host of little Italian states; in each one the old customs barriers and the old government by police reappeared; and if the old feudal régime could no longer be reinstated, the survivals of its spirit were treated with all respect. From the summit of the social hierarchy, the spirit of legitimism spread to the intermediate strata; if sovereigns could demand reinstatement, could not the ecclesiastical orders and the other privileged classes, which anti-feudal legislation had stripped of part of their property, make the same demand? Thus the reality of present evils foreshadowed graver dangers to come, threatening the new *bourgeoisie* of the Revolution, already deprived of the military glory which it had won in Napoleon's armies, and the civil dignity which it had acquired under the government of the Empire, with the loss of its economic freedom.

The *bourgeoisie* threw itself into the constitutional movement in order to preserve the possessions which it still held against the assaults of despotism, and to regain what it had lost. In Italy this constitutional movement presents no originality of thought; it is modelled upon the French political ideas of the Restoration, and is thus indirectly connected with the English eighteenth-century tradition. The only difference, accidental in itself but highly important in its consequences, was that in France a constitution actually existed, and therefore the constitutional movement developed within the parliament and by the activity of political parties; whereas in Italy, where governments were absolute and administered by the police, the movement found its channel in secret societies and ' sects ', which to some extent distorted its natural character. A struggle soon began between moderate public opinion and the spirit of the sects, which was regarded as a corruption of the spirit of the people. As early as 1815, Foscolo headed his four *Discorsi della Servitù d'Italia* with the motto ' If Italy is to be remade, the sects must be unmade ', which was to be the watchword of the Moderates at the Risorgimento.

What does Foscolo understand by a sect? ' A sect ', says he, ' means a perpetual state of schism created and maintained by a number of men who, separating themselves from a civil community, profess either publicly or among themselves religious or political opinions designed to justify secret interests, and subserve them by actions contrary to the common weal.' Thus the idea of a sect is opposed to that of a political party. ' The parties in a state are, in my opinion, two or some small number of associations of free men, having different opinions or interests as regards the particular manner of governing public opinion ; but, in matters touching the common safety or honour, always agreeing with their adversaries.' [1]

The distinction is just, and the view of the function of parties is lofty ; but in the political circumstances of Italy after 1815 was it possible for parties to exist, and was not the evil of sects inevitable? Driven out of public life, were not the citizens compelled by their own governments to turn their activities to factious and selfish ends? Foscolo himself shows that he recognized this melancholy necessity by the contrast which he draws between the state of England and that of Italy. ' Individual passions and self-love exist in England as elsewhere ; but since man cannot find his own advantage except in the public advantage, in England men become citizens. In Italy, on the other hand, every citizen is forced to become an animal, because his inability to benefit his country deprives him of duty towards it.' [2]

The first phase of Italian constitutionalism, culminating and collapsing in the revolutionary movements of 1820 and 1821, arose in a sectarian atmosphere, and its spirit betrays

[1] Foscolo, *Della servitù d'Italia, Discorso I* (*op. cit.*, p. 196).
[2] *Op. cit.*, p. 247.

its origin. Its centre of gravity was the Carboneria, an essentially *bourgeois* society, recruiting its most active and resolute supporters from the surviving elements of Napoleon's armies, discontented with their unfavourable situation under the Restoration governments. But these soldiers had a higher motive for taking part in the conspiracies of the Carboneria. The *cadres* of the Napoleonic armies were the first organized expression of the new *bourgeois* class, and therefore the first to be equipped for action; the other elements of the *bourgeoisie* were not ready to act till a generation later.

It is characteristic that the highest expression of this Liberal and revolutionary spirit among army men was given to it by a nobleman and an anti-Bonapartist, the Piedmontese Count Santorre di Santarosa. So strong was the spirit of the age and of the historical environment, that this aristocrat conceived the function of the army in a strictly *bourgeois* manner; and his anti-Bonapartism did not prevent him from recognizing that ' Bonaparte by the scourge of military conscription was in spite of himself preparing the day of the Italian war '.

Santarosa was a Liberal in the sense which that word bore in the years 1816–20, that is, a supporter of constitutional monarchy. ' Absolute power, even when wisely and humanely wielded, necessarily deprives mankind of many precious and useful possessions, and renders insecure and transitory those that they enjoy.' The absolute king, wishing to be above the law, places himself outside Society, because Society only exists as between persons subject to a common law. ' Between an absolute prince and his people there is therefore a state of nature: or, to use a more correct but terrible word, a state of war. A calamitous state of things, which men may tolerate if they will, but which they cannot by any reason human or divine be obliged to tolerate.'

Granted the imprescriptible right of demanding an express and stipulated pact between monarch and people, the particular question which concerns the army is, why cannot this right be equally exercised by the armed portion of the people, that is, by the soldiers? Because they are armed, because they can will more efficaciously, ought they to abstain from willing a thing so just as the legal existence of their country, the constitution of the national family, without which private families can have no secure protection? It is objected that their arms were given them by the prince. ' But to whom did he give them? To men who, before they received them, before they were soldiers, were members of civil society, children of their country, towards which they had obligations and duties contracted by birth and education, strengthened by the sacred bonds of the family; duties that can never be destroyed or repudiated.' Nor could the soldier's oath be legitimate and binding except with this necessary qualification, that service to the prince should be compatible with the necessities of the country.

This right to put their arms at the service of national freedom was not claimed by the soldiers in virtue of privilege or hope of personal gain; they knew that in a free state the military class, though its intrinsic dignity may be greater, is less rich, less 'cherished', less feared than under an omnipotent prince, and even tends to lose its identity among the other classes of Society; when they desired and sought a Constitution, their thoughts and their actions were those of generous citizens who put civil moderation before soldierly pride.[1]

Such was the spirit of the military risings of 1820, as indicated by the fact that these movements led not to a military oligarchy but to a constitutional régime in which certain ' civilian' elements of the *bourgeoisie* took an active part. The final collapse of this régime was due not so much to its incompetence—the Neapolitan parliament of 1820 and 1821 showed remarkable political capacity—as to international action expressing itself through Austrian bayonets. The lack of co-ordination between the constitutional spheres of Naples and Piedmont made a speedy repression possible; but it also lent the weight of practical experience to the demand for a closer connexion between the claims for liberty, unity, and

[1] S. di Santarosa, *Delle speranze degl' Italiani*, reprinted by Colombo, Milan, 1920, pp. 17, 59, 64 *seqq.*

independence, which, separate, had proved themselves weak and ineffective. At first indeed, under the fresh impression of Austrian tyranny, the problem of independence was not only given the first place, but allowed to eclipse the others. This explains why the earliest thought of the Risorgimento treats the question of the salvation of Italy in a manner which is in some ways anti-liberal.

§ 2. THE LIBERALISM OF THE RISORGIMENTO

The intellectual movement of the Risorgimento is certainly of extreme importance for the history of Italy, whose political unification it prepared; but some of its chief protagonists, followers, and commentators claimed for it an altogether exaggerated European significance, and thus gave rise to hopes and disappointments, the one as mistaken as the other. The reason for this exaggeration is to be sought in literary tradition, the only or chief element of continuity throughout the centuries of Italian life. Italy had produced humanism and the Renaissance, intellectual phenomena of European and world-wide significance, and had lived on this inheritance of culture long after she had lost every trace of originality, converting her original supremacy in civilization and science into a supremacy in memories. A narrow feeling of self-sufficiency, characteristic of the Italian literary world, made men less able and less ready to thrive in the climate of general European culture; and even when foreign influence prevailed, as in the eighteenth and nineteenth centuries, an inveterate national pride attempted to belittle its importance or to deny its value by means of the comparisons, antitheses, and parallels which form the least pleasing part of Italian patriotic literature.

A book like Gioberti's *Primato* [1] becomes perfectly intelligible and satisfactory when framed in this traditional style, but seems clumsy and out of key as soon as it is regarded from a more broadly European point of view. And Gioberti in his long years of exile was better qualified than most Italians to acclimatize himself to an international atmo-

---

[1] [' On the Moral and Civil Primacy of the Italians ', 1843.]

sphere. Now when one looks dispassionately at the Italian Risorgimento as a whole, one cannot help seeing that it creates in the main the same impression. In its most serious significance, its most permanent value, it represents the attempt of a few men, but a chosen few, to raise Italy to the level of the other European nations by a rapid assimilation of the most vital elements in their culture and political institutions; yet the goal appears distorted and disfigured by a literary fiction which treats a reproduction as if it were an original creation, and fills the gaps in the present with rhetorical references to the past.

The whole of Italian culture in the nineteenth century has an air of narrow provincialism, reminiscent of decayed gentlefolk whose isolation has deadened their consciousness of their actual condition, while their pride leads them to despise the benefits of the civilization in which they nevertheless share. This false patriotic shame, which deprives a nation of the courage to look within itself and recognize its defects and limitations, not only vitiated certain manifestations of the national consciousness at the time of the Risorgimento, but falsified the judgement of that period formed by later generations. It has been surrounded with a halo of rhetoric; even when made the object of learned curiosity and study, it has been withdrawn from the sphere of genuinely critical examination; and its intellectual expressions have been admired and praised the more, the less their real nature has been understood. Few people have ever seriously asked themselves why in the nineteenth century, the century most active in the international exchange of ideas, hardly one of the writers of our Risorgimento achieved anything like a European reputation, or why, which is far worse, none became familiar to the Italians themselves. To answer this question one need only open the works of Rosmini, Gioberti, Mazzini, Balbo, D'Azeglio, or Tommaseo to be conscious of a certain stuffiness, a smell of literary mould, which betrays the narrowness of the national outlook.

But the reader who can overcome this first impression ends by seeing through the books to the men who wrote them, and finding that the men are far better than the books they wrote. The Italian Risorgimento is essentially a matter of moral values; honour, justice, devotion, disinterestedness, loyalty. The very indifference of the populace towards the problems of unity, liberty, and independence gave rise to a silent selection from all parts of Italy, unaided by any party activity, of a little band of men, who, through having been in touch with their various governments, had already some experience of public life, and brought to their common enterprise a narrow but austere sense of honour, the fruit of their provincial education. This was the real ruling class at the period of unification : and if any one in Italy wishes seriously to appeal to the tradition of the Risorgimento, he ought to appeal to the moral ideals of this class, which discharged its function of government apparelled in an almost domestic virtue. But this authentic tradition of the Risorgimento has vanished from Italy, replaced by fabrications like that expressed in Ferrari's *Filosofia della Rivoluzione*, which opened the floodgates of false history and literary and rhetorical exercises.

In proceeding briefly to examine the political thought of this period, so far as it concerns our subject, we must not forget that its centre of gravity is strictly ethical and expresses the outlook of the small governing class described above.

The most important phenomenon is the doctrine and programme of the so-called Moderate party : a party without organization, without rules, a party which refused to recognize itself as a party, because it cherished the higher ambition of representing the hopes of the citizens at large ; but which spontaneously gathered round itself the widespread support of a class already largely homogeneous in economic structure and rendered even more so by its close cultural affinities.

This party began by adopting the motto that if Italy was to be remade the sects must be unmade. It rejected all sectarian spirit, partly by moral and religious conviction, partly because it saw in it a dangerous incentive to the violence and revolution which it profoundly abhorred. As D'Azeglio said in his Programme of 1847, two periods are to be distinguished in recent Italian history; one from 1783 to 1815, the other from 1815 to the present time: the first was dominated by the idea of rights maintained by force, the second entrusted the vindication of rights to reason. The revolutions of 1820 and 1830, brought about by the secret societies, belonged to the spirit of the first period; the new faith in moral force implied a search for means calculated to work on public opinion, and the renunciation of all secret and violent methods.[1]

Was it necessary then, instead of secret societies, to organize associations and parties for the work of public propaganda? In the opinion of some highly influential interpreters of Moderate opinion, parties and secret societies were indistinguishable. The gentle Rosmini used language of unaccustomed bitterness when, in his *Philosophy of Politics*, he spoke of parties as the ' worms which devour the fabric of society, because they consist of men who are not resolved to do that which is morally right and virtuous '. Their origins were various: interest, opinion, popular passion; ' but their source is equally ignoble and dark. Justice and morality do not enter into the minds of party men . . .; the society which conserves itself by an incessant party conflict is a society within whose bosom an implacable war is being waged.' [2]

As an example of political obtuseness, this is hard to beat; but it is redeemed by a rectitude so exquisite as to convert a defect into a merit. At bottom, the Moderates' hatred of parties was due to the fact that they had no desire to win recruits for their policy among the masses. Rosmini reminds us that Christianity saved Society by appealing to the individual and not to the mass; similarly he and his friends would save the national Society by appealing only to those able and willing to think for the common good. The people, which for Hegel was that part of the nation which did not know what it wanted, was for Gioberti a simple nonentity, an indifferent

---

[1] D'Azeglio, *Proposta di un programma, &c.; Scritti politici e litterari,* Florence, 1872, i. 261.

[2] Rosmini, *Filosofia della Politica, Opere Ed. ed Ined.,* xx. 207 *seqq.*

and inert matter upon which any form might be impressed. Nothing could be more foreign to these Moderates than the democratic idea of popular sovereignty and self-government : the two functions of governing and being governed are for them sharply distinguished, and subordinated to the rule *Tout pour le peuple, rien par le peuple.*

The Moderates' attempts at persuasion were therefore directed towards members of their own class and the princes of the Italian States, to whom they wished to entrust the initiative in the work of national federation. Works like Balbo's *Treatise on the Hopes of Italy* are justified only when placed in the environment in which and for which they were created ; the attempt to make them documents of a true Italian Risorgimento reveals them in all their poverty. Seen from this wider point of view, ' The hopes of Italy ' was not unjustly rechristened 'The despair of Italy', and became a butt for popular satire, because, as is well known, Balbo places the chief hope of independence for Italy in the destruction of the Turkish Empire, which would permit Austria to expand in the Balkans and relieve her pressure on Italy. This theory had a certain vogue in the small circle of students of political problems to whom this most moderate of the Moderates addressed his work. In the year 1843, in which the *Hopes of Italy* was published, Balbo was as yet unconnected with political Liberalism. His capital problem (*Il porro unum necessarium*) is independence : he asks himself whether liberty can make any contribution to this end, and answers that it cannot. Great changes in the State were effected with difficulty and danger if entrusted to the many ; it was therefore necessary to entrust them to the few. The modern invention of constituent assemblies and conventions had been a retrograde step which experience had proved the cause of ceaseless disturbance, especially in countries where the effort after liberty was complicated by an effort after independence. But if constitutional initiative was in the hands not of the people but of the prince, did these dangers still exist ? ' Let us speak accurately : even when taken by princes, such a decision may be full of dangers, fertile in controversy, distracting men from the pursuit of independence. Deliberative or parliamentary assemblies live on divergences and divisions of opinion.' Finally, however, Balbo grants that if a prince succeeds in effecting the constitutional change with great courage and skill, 'It is not doubtful that this prince would have acquired a very powerful weapon of popularity and of Italian unity '.[1]

Happily, not all members of the Moderate party were so perplexed and inconsistent as Balbo ; and even he, returning to the problem of constitutionalism after the experience of 1848, was to achieve a more mature view of it. Even before this crisis, however, men were not wanting who, attaching themselves to the Liberal tradition whose origin we have already described, stoutly asserted the necessity of representative government in the national interest. A somewhat remarkable indication of the degree to which scientific study of this subject had led to an understanding of it is provided by Romagnosi's *Scienza delle Costituzioni*, in which the system of ' guarantism ', borrowed from the French, is developed in great wealth of detail.

With the majority of the Moderates, constitutionalism was a useful starting-point for the federalistic proposals with which their programme opened. Shrinking as they did from all revolutionary tendencies, and anxious to lead the people towards national federation while leaving intact the existing forms of political organization, they proposed a compact between the populations and their respective princes, expressing this harmonious will and binding the contracting parties to execute it. Hence constitutions should tend to bring into being two kinds of guarantee : one directed against the prince, to check any secessionistic tendency on his part, or other divergence from the national ends ; the other directed against the people, to restrain their political aspirations within the bounds of law and order. The principal organ of the constitution, parliament, had therefore the function of forming an intermediate political body between the prince and the people, partaking of the nature of both.

[1] C. Balbo, *Delle speranze d'Italia*, ch. ix.

But in order that parliaments should be able to discharge this function, they must be wholly free from the faults inherent in constitutions of French origin, which Rosmini attempts to enumerate in full. They fostered excessive ambition for promotion to ever higher offices, they generated extremes of party feeling, they gave excessive proponderance to popular changes, they did not sufficiently guarantee the freedom of citizens, they abandoned religion to the mercy of political interests, they did not give a proportionate representation to landed property, equalizing as they did the rights of large and small landowners ; Rosmini, an extremist of moderation, would actually like to see the electoral vote commensurate with the direct taxation paid to the State by the voter; so that the tax should be paid not by the person but by his property.[1]

But short of these radical remedies, the more reasonable Moderates were content with a raising of the electoral property qualification, to ensure that the political body should be preserved from democratic contamination and form a tolerably faithful expression of large and medium agricultural property. The political ideal of the Moderates was the semi-feudal liberalism of eighteenth-century England, tempered by a livelier feeling of social justice, the fruit of the new age. But the psychology of the two historical forms was profoundly different. The eighteenth-century Englishman was proudly conscious of his privileged and traditional freedom, never as yet challenged by any claim for the universal rights of man as man ; his modern imitator had a fresh memory of the rationalistic and Revolutionary freedom whose subversive consequences he remembered with fear and wished to forestall by safeguards which would render it harmless. The spirit of modern Liberalism is as remote from this outlook as

[1] Rosmini, *La Costituzione secondo la Giustizia sociale*, Milan, 1840, pp. 6, 8, and 47. ' The universal vote is in its consequences identical with an equalization of all properties : it is the agrarian law which in our days leads to communism. . . . What is the proximate and efficient cause of the Revolution of 1789? The granting of the vote to *persons* and not to *things*.' And the man who speaks thus is a spiritualistic philosopher !

anything can be. The idea of progress as due to great conflicts, the idea of a rich multiplicity of forces finding their
political focus through freedom and arduous labour, and
conferring upon this focus, when found, all the wealth of the
historical life of a nation, can never be grasped by such a
mind. Its conception of national politics is homely and sedentary; democratic agitation disturbs and annoys it; it regards
homogeneous mediocrity in the political class as a necessary
qualification for the ordered conduct of public business.
Hence the Moderate party was to provide competent administrators, upright judges, clean-handed ministers, ingredients
of priceless worth to the whole, but at the same time politicians of less than mediocre ability, submitting grudgingly,
under the influence of Cavour, to the forces of Jacobin democracy, and losing all sense of direction when deprived of their
indispensable guide. Out of touch with the people, they saw
a threat of revolution in every sign of popular awakening,
and could only stiffen themselves in an attitude of defence
which was a far more real danger, leaving those forces to
develop outside and against the State, which they ought to
have been able to include within it.

The philosophy of the Moderates was in perfect harmony
with this arrested Liberalism. The fear of liberty in the political sphere exactly corresponds with a fear of reason in the
theoretical sphere. The two have in history been found together. In the name of rationalism individual and political
rights were pronounced inviolable, the tradition and authority of the *ancien régime* were spurned, and all the excesses
of an unbridled liberty saw the light. Faced by the subversive consequences of such principles, Italian thought, like that
of Europe at large, seemed inspired by an impulse towards a
restoration. It had felt the crisis of anarchical rationalism in
all its gravity, and wished to erect a barrier against new outbreaks of individual force.

Two paths offered themselves, each the opposite of the
other. The first was to improve upon the rationality of the
Revolutionary mind, and complete the criticism of life which
it left half-finished, at a superficial level where destruction

was more prominent than reconstruction; to reflect, to mediate that which was still unreflective and immediate. What was the cause of the destructive excesses of reason? The fact that it appeared as a quasi-physical principle, all extension and expansion, never returning upon itself, but moving from one thing to another, levelling instead of differentiating, atomizing under colour of individualizing. The new reflection must give to reason its *ubi consistam* : must involve a critical and historical outlook; must give back to the spirit, transfigured and renewed, all that it had taken away in the first phase of its criticism. It was necessary, in a word, to press home the revolution of Cartesian rationalism, and find a new foundation on which a stable society could be built; whereas this revolution, arrested half-way on its course by Descartes and his eighteenth-century followers, lost itself in extension, and destroyed without reconstructing. That is precisely the meaning of the great work achieved by German philosophy.

But another path was open to thought : to deny and renounce this destructive rationalism; to seek an external, transcendent principle of stability, exempt from all arbitrary encroachment. This principle was provided by religion, with its dogmas, its faith, its authoritarian structure, and its age-old institutions resisting the assaults of modern times. Was not this a safe and certain foundation? So it appeared to the first generation of counter-revolutionaries, De Maistre, De Bonald, Ballanche, and Schlegel. To the Italian mind this possibility seemed even more attractive and promising, for no sooner did it awake to a sense of its own nationality, than it saw in the Catholic Church the most strictly national of its institutions, the one survival of its work in past centuries.

Now the characteristic feature of the philosophy of the Moderates, represented at its highest in Rosmini and Gioberti, but implicit in all the others, is that it proceeds simultaneously along both these paths, and applies itself at once to criticism and dogmatism, reflection and tradition, free examination and authority. But this proceeding soon causes it discomfort, which later becomes torment. Stated as they are, the two terms are irreconcilable; and thought, in the vain attempt to grasp them together, wavers eternally from one to the other and never finds a position of equilibrium.

The reason for this inner inconsistency is that the Italian mind had never deeply experienced the crisis of revolution, but had felt it only at second hand; and had similarly never had a Romantic counter-revolution of its own, but only a reflection of one. The terms of the antithesis therefore presented themselves to it in an attenuated and impoverished form, susceptible of an eclectic compromise. It seemed easy to divest Catholicism of its reactionary clothing, and Liberal rationalism of its revolutionary ferment, and make them friends. Thus arose the idea, which took the field in the unsuccessful Revolution of 1848, of a liberal Risorgimento with the Pope as its centre of gravity.

This is the entire argument of Gioberti's *Primato*; but an inconsistent and fallacious argument. From a philosophical point of view, once embarked upon the way of rationalism, it is impossible to stop, because whatever limit is set to reason will always be a self-limitation, and therefore virtually capable of being transgressed, never a dogma in the Catholic sense. From a political point of view, the attempt to make the Pope the centre of an Italian tradition, not as head of the Catholic Church but as a temporal prince, is an illusion whose existence in the country of Machiavelli is inexplicable.

The enormous popularity of Gioberti's argument with the Moderates only proves their political inexperience, and also, to some extent, the lack of harmony between the interna-structure of the party and its historical task. At bottom it was a conservative party, placed in spite of itself in a revolutionary situation: and the inconsistent eclecticism of its theories merely betrayed the abstractness of its desire to save both the old and the new, the princes and the national unity, Catholicism and rationalism, enlightened despotism and freedom. To put it brutally, the Moderates wanted to make an omelette without breaking eggs.

Beside and opposed to this great mass of Moderate opinion,

the Risorgimento presents us with more individual figures and more modern views.

The first close criticism of the programme of Gioberti, Balbo, and D'Azeglio appeared very early in 1846, in the shape of the Piedmontese general Giacomo Durando's work *On the Italian Nationality*. Durando came forward as an opponent of Guelphism, an ancient tradition in which he saw not so much a national force as a perpetual cause of Italian disunion. He also opposed the Ghibelline tradition, whose monarchical principle is ' the only unifying and organizing power for our nationality '. What then is to be the ' regenerative ' principle? Freedom.

On this second capital point too, Durando is in open contradiction with Balbo, who regards the sacrifice of political liberties as indispensable to the great end of the redemption of Italy. What liberties had Balbo in mind when he expressed this hard judgement? Merely the old medieval liberties; ' liberties ignorant, fanatical, ill-defined and worse understood, corrupted by feudalism, irreconcilable with the dignity of man': which for that very reason ' were a safe weapon by which Roman Guelphism could hinder our national unification '.

But there is a modern liberty very different from the medieval, which, by means of representative government, liberty of thought, publicity of governmental acts, and a wise co-operation of the nation in public administration, might be ' the one point of moral concentration and the one banner of our redemption '. Modern representative institutions alone are capable of fusing into a common nationality the scattered, reluctant, and even hostile fragments of the Italian nation. Moreover, they render the great tasks of the modern State in many ways easier of fulfilment. With regard to taxation,

' in the mutual pact established by representative institutions between sovereigns and nations, taxpayers find a guarantee of the right employment of the new taxes, and creditors a moral security for their loans. Whereas, if the cause of dynasties is separate from that of peoples, the force of public credit is diminished by half, for it rests chiefly upon the inalienability of the political capital which serves to guarantee it, and on the certainty that the dynastic sovereignty which represents it will not perish.'

In the military sphere, in which Durando is especially interested, as that which in the last resort is to solve the national problem, it is impossible to provide a strong reserve of fighting men except by a citizen army : ' nor can these armies exist without the energy and devotion which the public spirit of the country finds in the political guarantees it has obtained.'

' If a civil people,' Durando adds, in a fine page which we may quote entire, ' at the first beginning of its political regeneration, is surprised and threatened by an external or internal enemy, it will not undertake the defence of the State with the necessary resolution, unless it is fully assured that the new order of things will be safeguarded in exchange for its sacrifices. It will not hasten to the frontiers, or it will do so only with reluctance, if it leaves behind it silenced speakers and a silent press, the sure mark of tyranny renewed or imminent. In the terrible moments in which a nation is fighting with the enemy in the gate, factions, movements, tumults do indeed arise, but are only the abnormal products of abnormal circumstances. Absolutely to reject the application of a great regenerative principle, merely because the first steps are difficult, would be like rejecting a medicine on which life depends, merely because the first dose displeases the palate. Do we wish (and if we wish it we can do it) to lead a degenerate people against the mouths of cannon, to suffering and death ? Let us inspire them with confidence, passion, enthu-siasm ; let us endeavour to rouse them with all the activities and attractions of public life. They may frown, murmur, and show their teeth, but they will fight ; they may fall into excesses, but they will fight, and they will save their country. Such fears of internal discord at the time of danger are the common pretext and the eternal bugbear of traitors and cowards.' [1]

This is true modern Liberalism. It is the spirit of Santa-rosa reincarnate, more experienced, in a soldier of the new generation ; but it is an isolated apparition. More fertile is

[1] Giacomo Durando, *Della Nazionalità italiana, saggio politico-militare*, Paris, 1846. Cf. esp. ch. xii, xiii, on *Il principio rigeneratore*, sub-titled : ' Modern political liberties considered as elements of moral force.'

the economic branch of Liberal thought, which borrows its
theoretical programme from the classical economists and the
Manchester School, and at the same time finds in the
economic development of Northern Italy conditions favourable to effective action. The economic freedom advocated
by the economists, whose leader was the fervent propagandist
Ferrara, signified in practice a spontaneous direction of the
productive energies of Upper Italy, which despotic governments were directing away from their goal and allowing to
languish in a narrow local market, towards the greater
market of Italy. Here the value of liberty as an element in
the national unification appears in a more persuasive light,
and forms a second and decisive argument against the
attempt of the Moderates to separate the two problems.

In any attempt to estimate the contribution of economic
studies to the modernization of the agricultural and industrial *bourgeoisie*, it must always be remembered that these
studies shaped the personality of Cavour, the only truly
European figure of the Risorgimento. Cavour shows no
trace of the congenital narrowness which delayed the intellectual emancipation of the agricultural classes. Sprung
though he was from the small landed nobility, he succeeded
in ridding himself completely of the intellectual attitude of
his class, and attaining a wholly modern conception of the
economic functions of Society. His scientific education was
in the school of Manchester Liberalism. The studies which he
published before 1848 on the Anti-Corn-Law League and the
Irish question are as good as anything in the literature of the
day ; unlike the rhetorical exercises of a Bastiat, they reveal
a sense of reality and a preference for facts over doctrinal
formulae. To the Manchester School Cavour owed not only
a general view of the laws governing exchange, but also
something deeper and more intimate, not to be expressed in
abstract scientific terms : a consciousness of the expansive
power of modern industrial Society, and a confidence in
individual initiative and enterprise, destroying old habits in
order to launch out on a new path fraught with hopes and
dangers. This is the true value of the Liberal ferment com-

municated by the English middle class of the nineteenth century to sluggish agricultural societies. In Italy the demon of industrialism came later, and was less vigorous; but its absence at the culminating period of the Risorgimento increases one's admiration for men like Cavour, who had enough spiritual energy to anticipate within themselves its appearance, and to infect with its energy, so far as that was possible, the torpor of contemporary Moderate opinion.

The genius of modern business is present in Cavour's programme of railway construction,[1] out of all proportion with the modest interests of the little Piedmontese kingdom of the time, but commensurate with the needs of the future. The same outlook, the same vital lack of equilibrium between the present and the future, is revealed by his participation in the Crimean War. And Cavour's internal policy, which won the co-operation of conservatives and revolutionaries, Moderates and democrats, however hostile to each other, in a single national scheme, and fitted admirably in its turn into a complicated international policy, gives the full measure of the powers of this genius. In the work of Cavour we feel for the first time in Italian history the living spirit of the modern Liberal State; the State which feeds upon mighty conflicts, which reconciles violent passions any one of which in isolation would be destructive and disastrous, while each, in its union with the others, is an element of life and progress. Take the single Italian parties of the Risorgimento: their outlook is so narrow that each believes not only that it alone can save Italy, but also that the opposite party is working for certain destruction. Yet above this conflict there is a co-operation in which all are equally, though in different ways, serving the common cause. Now it is clear that this higher resultant or synthesis can only be elicited by means of a State, and by an art of government which gives to each party its fair opportunity, trusting in the rationality which presides over the competitive and selective evolution of

---

[1] It began to develop in his mind during the years preceding his rise to power; cf. the important essay *Des chemins de fer*, published in the *Revue nouvelle* and reprinted in Zanichelli's ed. of *Gli scritti*, 2 vols., 1892.

human liberty. It was Cavour who in his own person represented this State and this Liberal art of government through which the conflicting variety of Italian forces at the Risorgimento were concentrated into a single political focus.

The spiritual outlook of Cavour as an economist, to which we have referred above, recalls another figure, modern too, but more limited in interests and in sphere of action : the Lombard Carlo Cattaneo. Like Cavour, Cattaneo was an expression of the new industrial and Liberal spirit which was already pervading the agricultural Lombard *bourgeoisie*. There are, he says, two very different agricultures. The one is primitive, barbarous, abject, without buildings, without machines, without roads, without irrigation, without trade; much of its produce, unable to be exported, is wasted as useless lumber. The other agriculture is the late-born daughter of an old-established trade, provided with all the aids of economic power and all the guidance of science. This is the difference between the numerous and splendid municipalities of Upper Italy and the wretched cities of Lower Italy and the islands. Agrarian industry is a part of the mercantile life of a people : it does not spring from natural genius, from bucolic inspiration, but issues in its own time from institutions and laws which give capital and industry access to the soil. Agriculture is the act of civilization, not of barbarism ; it springs from the city.[1]

As such, its progress demands the same development of the human factor which in industry strictly so called made possible the transition from the medieval artisan system to the great modern business. Industrialized agriculture, too, requires intelligent labour, reflective, living at a high standard, and enjoying all the rights of modern citizenship. The Liberal demand inherent in the new agriculture must therefore be extended so far as possible to all cultivators of the soil, arousing in them the sense of human personality, initiative, and responsibility. Cattaneo's Liberalism therefore leads to democracy, that is, the extension of liberty to

[1] Cf. Salvemini's excellent anthology *Le più belle pagine del Cattaneo*, with a highly instructive introduction by the editor, Milan, 1922.

the rural masses, instead of its restriction to the privileged landowners.

Here the agricultural Liberalism of the north differs profoundly from that of the south, personified by Poerio and Spaventa. The latter rises, it might be said, above agriculture rather than from agriculture; it is the expression of a narrow class of *bourgeois* landlords which has inherited almost unchanged certain rights of the old feudal lords, living on rents or at any rate on the margin of agricultural production, and devoted to the liberal professions or to public life. The Liberalism of this class is the fruit of culture, of political and legal education, and its connexion with the soil is only indirect and does not tend towards the emancipation of the agricultural producer. No southern Italian, either before or after 1848, realized that the elevation of the agricultural masses might be a factor in the reconstruction of the State. The most intelligent of the southern Liberals, Silvio Spaventa, was alone in recognizing, late in life, the existence of a democratic problem within Liberalism.

Here lies the explanation of the superiority in this respect of northern Liberalism to southern. The latter, recruited from too narrow a field, left outside itself a degraded rural and urban population, extraneous and hostile to all the demands of modern life, held in a state of servile subjection by those who ought to have been moved by duty and interest to raise it to a more worthy condition. By compensation, this very narrowness permitted southern Liberalism to select its statesmen more rigorously, trained as these were in the older and more important of the Italian monarchical traditions. Even after the end of the Neapolitan kingdom, these men were able to maintain intact the State organization of the South, so that this region, in spite of its social backwardness, played an important political part in the establishment of a unified monarchy.

To complete our review of the political tendencies of the Risorgimento, it remains to notice democracy, towards which we have already been led by our observations on the thought of Cattaneo.

Giuseppe Mazzini is rightly considered the founder of Italian democracy. But in this estimation of his work it is commonly forgotten that long years of exile made it hard for him to acquire a thorough concrete knowledge of that ' people ' to which he addressed such fervent but such abstract words from afar. The social, political, and religious problems in which Mazzini was generally interested, really concerned England and France more than Italy. His political and religious mysticism belongs to the tradition of Lamennais, the Saint-Simonians, Leroux, and Vinet, which forms as it were a secondary branch of the Reformation and is as foreign as anything can be to Italy, the country in which the outlook of the Catholic Counter-Reformation finds almost its only complement in a religious scepticism of humanistic origin. The formula ' God and the People ' was destined to add one more to Italy's collection of formulae, but not to awake an echo in the heart of the nation.

Nor is this an element of Mazzini's thought that can be detached from the remainder ; it is the centre of gravity of a system which, without it, loses much of its historical and ideal character. It was in the name of his own religious view of Society that Mazzini criticized the anarchical and materialistic individualism of the Liberals, competition, freedom of contract, and subjective rights, which degrade the labourer to the status of a commodity and break up the divine unity of the popular spirit. These criticisms, which we do not repeat because they are familiar both to Mazzini and to ourselves in the works of Sismondi, the Saint-Simonians, the Fourierists, Owen, Kingsley, and many others, are perfectly justified in the social environment in which they arose. Like those who inspired him, Mazzini was thinking of the industrial Society of early nineteenth-century England, with its ruthless individualism, which spread such misery among the working classes, and, by contrast, excited such humanitarian fervour in the Conservatives, the Methodists, and the Romantics. What Mazzini was not thinking of was Italian Society, as yet unfertilized by the industrial revolution and entangled in a net of feudalism which, largely banished from the sphere of law, survived in tradition and custom. An attack on Liberal individualism was in Italy, to say the least, premature : it would have been more to the point to wish Italy a little individualistic energy capable of dispelling the dead weight of custom ; and this would in its own time have created spontaneously, by antithesis and for purposes of defence, a democratic organization based upon free association or State support. But what, in Italy, could be the meaning of the associationism which Mazzini saw arising upon the ruins of an anarchical and merciless liberty that Italians had never known? Who was to form such associations, in an agricultural country whose agriculture was in a backward and semi-feudal condition?

Mazzini's democracy was utterly foreign to Italian realities, and it was in vain that he attempted to force it upon Italy as a duty, since, arising as it did from no spontaneous need, it could only remain a dead letter. Hence arises the preaching tone which makes Mazzini's works tiresome to read. For it is of the nature of preaching that it sets before its hearers a duty not, in general, directly arising out of the facts of their life.

The chief ambition of Mazzini's democracy was to give a full and all-embracing content to the forms of politics. It was the time, between 1830 and 1848, when the announcement was made in France that the age of merely political revolutions, changes in the external forms of government, was over, and that the next revolution would be strictly social : that is, would have as its protagonist not a clique of politicians but the people, and as its end a redistribution of social values. Mazzini dreamed of something like this for Italy, a revolution by the people, inaugurating a kingdom of justice and labour, and at the same time realizing the political unity of the nation. It was a fine idea ; but all Utopian ideas are fine. The actual work which fate had in store for Mazzini was to be the chief actor in that political revolution which he fancied, following his French and English teachers, a thing of the past. The ineffective preacher of social religion and the ethical State became in practice the highly efficient organizer of secret societies, the supporter of republican ideals, the champion of unity against Guelphian federalism. He took his stand on the ground of purely formal politics, thinking that he could meet there the people of his Utopia, but met in reality only small but active bands of conspirators, republicans, and anti-clericals.

Thus Mazzini produced his chief effect upon the Risorgimento not in the role of an unheard prophet but in the role attributed to him by tradition in its least sophisticated form, the role of a ' Jacobin ' agitator, overthrowing and falsifying the calculations of the most practised political wisdom and throwing himself into the adventure of unification, which the common sense of the moderate majority judged chimerical or absurd; but achieving definite political success, while the skill of his ablest opponents only entangled them in a fruitless federalism. This is why the action of Mazzini could enter into close relation with that of Garibaldi, and in this union could destroy the barriers which those in charge of the government opposed to the realization of the warmest national hopes.

What then is the sum of Mazzini's democracy? Something very different from what is meant by democracy in other European countries. In England and Germany it is a vast organization of industrial labour; in France, a widespread *petit-bourgeois* point of view, conscious of the value of equality and jealously safeguarding its immortal principles. In both cases it is a great social movement, organic and permanent in character. Nothing of the kind exists in Italy. Here democracy is the party of action. It is the *piazza*, dominated for the moment by a few political agitators, which reduces cabinets to futility and creates the new and unforeseen fact. This action was providential: without it, the Moderate mentality being what it was, the unity of Italy could never have been achieved. But at the same time a democracy like this contains nothing lasting and organic which can survive the momentary explosion of a revolution; it has no capacity for government or for enjoying the permanent fruits of its conquest. Hence the success of democratic action depended upon the political wisdom of the Moderates, which converted the victories of the *piazza* into a stable political fabric. This is the explanation of the apparent paradox by which Italy was brought into being by the so-called democrats, but organized and governed in their despite by the regular political parties.

This result, however intelligible to us, must have been a profound disappointment to a man like Mazzini, who fancied that he had created a genuine democracy, able not only to destroy but also to govern. His judgement was warped by an abstract ideology which prevented him from recognizing in the new Italy that Italy which he believed himself to have willed but which in reality he had only dreamed. In point of fact, the new Italy was just what he himself had helped to make her by his work as a political agitator.

A democracy, as an independent and lasting popular organization, was to arise in Italy only with the rise of Socialism, the first political movement to have a strictly social content and to come into permanent touch with the masses so as to rouse them from their apathy. The most obvious proof that Mazzini's democracy lacked this genuinely popular character was his own profound dislike of Socialism, whose first efforts he had observed, and had realized the distance which separated it from the lofty moralism of his own social conceptions. But the people to whose welfare Socialism truly dedicated itself was after all the actual people; the wretched non-political masses, in whom the gospel of crude self-interest aroused a first glimmering of humanity and a demand for association, leading in its turn to the most precious gifts of human freedom and personality. These were the very things whose value Mazzini had assiduously preached ; but he had conceived them in the hands of an abstractly rational being, and when they actually appeared disfigured by the base uses of a mob he could not bear to look at them.

The year of crisis in Italy was 1848 : a beneficent crisis, even though politically not final, because it revealed the contradictions and illusions of the Moderates and democrats,

showed the disastrous consequences of their failure to understand one another, and indicated the points in which they
might be able to co-operate. The best results of this crisis
were to be found in the busy and active years from 1849 to
1859, which, in spite of appearances, were the golden age of
the Risorgimento.

The Moderate programme, which gave the political campaign of 1848 its keynote, was soon exploded. The Guelphian
Utopia fell to the ground, as did federalism and all timid
compromises between political unity and the *status quo*. At
the same time something unexpected happened, which revealed the latent conservatism of the Moderate party : the
agrarian revolution, which, under the banner first of liberty
and then of Socialism, aimed, especially in the south, at the
seizure of the land by the peasants.

Was this the revolution which the democrats had dreamed
and preached? Far from it. It was a blind instinctive movement of revolt on the part of the non-political rural masses,
men without a country and without land ; it was the curse
which hangs over every nation where politics are an affair
of a few privileged persons, while the majority are left in a
servile condition, seemingly favourable in normal times to
the rule of their betters, but broken at times by movements
the more savage and uncontrollable, the more the social
passion underlying them is politically virgin and unformed.

The democrats of 1848 did not attempt to profit by the
social diversion in order to prolong their strictly political
agitation, once the moderate programme was proved bank-
rupt ; their last hopes disappointed, they left the revolt to its
fate, to the mercy of the restored absolute governments. The
latter, in the role of champions of the threatened rights of
property, were able to recover the allegiance of many of the
Moderates and even of the democrats.

This social episode in the Revolution of 1848 is a proof of
the strictly political and national character of Italian democracy, whose programme, as we observed, extended over the
same field as that of the Moderate party, in the sense that
it concerned only the external forms of government, republic

as opposed to monarchy, unity as opposed to federation, leaving the social content common to the two parties untouched. This observation is of great importance, because it is due not to our subsequent experience but to the experience of the leaders of the Risorgimento themselves, and therefore gives a new direction to their political activity. One chief cause of the failure of the political revolution was the opposition and lack of understanding between democrats and Moderates. This was partly due to the ambiguity of the social programme, and the fear that Italian democracy might prove to be like that which had so gravely shaken France. The equivocation was cleared up and the fear exorcised by the discovery that the claims of Italian democracy were strictly national and political; and this provided an opportunity for understanding and compromise. Had not the democrats and Moderates taken their differences too seriously? Did they not belong to the same political class, divided for the moment by accidental contingencies, only to be reunited on a calmer and wiser view of the facts? The Moderates had been deluded by excessive trust in their own principles into a belief in federation; could they not embrace the democratic programme of unification, without ceasing to be Moderates? And was the form of a republic, which at Rome and Venice had never been given a genuine national welcome, really essential to the democrats? Was the republican tradition in Italy favourable to unity, and not rather a municipal tradition, destructive of nationality? The democrats in their turn thus offered to bridge the gap that divided them from the monarchical programme of the Moderates.

This compromise, however, after the fierce struggles of 1848 and the mutual recriminations of the following year, was not entirely easy. It was necessary to find a basis of agreement to soothe wounded feelings, to pave the way to a better mutual understanding. This was the great work of the years 1849 to 1859. The kingdom of Savoy, with its loyalty to the *Statuto* and to the national cause, provided the basis of agreement. Cavour, with singular skill, succeeded in bringing the conflict of the parties into a single political focus, using towards the realization of the national programme not only their points of agreement but also their points of difference. The Moderates and democrats, on their side, made Cavour's work easier by a serious revision and criticism of their previous political programmes and attitudes.

It would be interesting to follow the chief figures of the Risorgimento through the labours of these ten years, following the dreams and illusions of the forties. It would completely dispel the legend that 1848 was the year of the great national movement, and that the ten following years were those in which revolutionary energy decayed and gave place to second-best solutions and a submission to monarchy, and similar fables. The truth is that during these years the boys of 1848 grew into men, learnt to distinguish between chimeras and possibilities, and acquired a truer knowledge of the Italy which at the Revolution they had rather fancied than known.

We shall confine ourselves to a few remarks upon two of the leaders of 1848 in whom the spiritual crisis went deepest and produced most results : Balbo and Gioberti. Balbo, who had felt obliged to sacrifice freedom to independence, saw that he had been wrong. The Revolution taught him that where there is not a political freedom well controlled by law, there is a false and licentious freedom, giving rise to factions which in their turn reduce the political conflict into a war to the knife, a war ruinous to all the combatants and to the cause for which they are fighting. As D'Azeglio saw even more clearly, the Moderate party, by its refusal to recognize the fact of party division and party conflict, converted those who ought to have been in their own way collaborators in a common work into implacable enemies, and thus created an internal crisis which paralysed the energies of the Risorgimento.

' Free governments in general have the virtue of converting factions into parties, representative governments the virtue of leading these parties from the market-place to the chamber. Another virtue of these same governments, but especially of monarchies, is to reduce the complex series of parties to the smallest possible number, or even to two, the ministry and the opposition.' [1]

Once on the path of constitutionalism, Balbo devoted the last years of his intellectual activity to the study of representative forms, basing his studies on the experience of Piedmont, where during these ten years political contact was re-established between the democrats and the Moderates by means of parliamentary institutions, and the conflict between these parties brought within measurable distance of termination.

More profound and complex was the spiritual crisis which took place after the catastrophe of Novara within the mind of Gioberti, because the personality of the man was incomparably richer and the passion with which he had taken part in the national rising more violent. Eloquent witness to this struggle is borne by his work on *The Civil Renewal of Italy*, which involves not only a recantation of the chief arguments of the *Primato*, but also a general revision and much deeper understanding of all the problems of the Risorgimento. Before the fall of his government, Gioberti, with the quick perception of his versatile mind, saw the necessity of an alliance with the democrats, because the Moderate element, too slow and cautious, would never be able to bring the national enterprise to an end. Later, embittered by the Moderate opposition which had prevented him from pursuing his new policy, he had time, during his last residence at Paris, to go over the recent events in Italy and compare them with those of the French Revolution; and this comparison deepened his alienation from the Moderate party and increased his inclination towards democracy.

In the *Renewal* he connects the Italian Moderates with Guizot's Liberals (a connexion too flattering to the Italians), and turns against the former the same criticisms which the French democrats, beginning with the Saint-Simonians, had directed against the latter. For the natural representation of the people, based upon intellect, they substituted an

[1] Balbo, *Della monarchia rappresentativa in Italia*, unfinished posthumous work, Florence, 1857, p. 289.

artificial representation, based upon property, and thus revived and accentuated the privileges of feudalism under a new name : ' The bank and the rich factory replace the landed estate by the work of these very *bourgeois* who, with the help of the people, had abolished it.' Thus arose ' a new aristocracy, hardly less unjust and more contemptible than the old, whereby the war waged against it has rightly acquired the principles and spirit of democracy '.[1]

The chief end of this democracy was the salvation of those masses to which Gioberti himself had recently denied all political existence, but in which he now saw the very pulse and soul of the civil world, ' which possesses a real primacy that no one can take from it, because it is the nursery of the other classes and the matrix in which the perennial life of the community resides '.[2] The salvation of the masses ' resolves itself into a gradual modification of property, without attacking it, proceeding not by way of arbitrary dictation by the government, but by way of public opinion and good laws propounded by the nation, rendering the transmission and successive distribution of this property conformable to the good of the greatest number '. Property is capital; capital is accumulated labour, exploited by means of new labour.

' The right to live by labour is thus in substance the universal and common economic right both of landowners and of the proletariate, with this sole difference, that the labour of the latter is fresh and in small quantities, that of the former ancient and concentrated. Hence it is seen that labour is the principal agent in creating and ennobling property and not vice versa, since man is born a landowner only so far as he receives his property from the precedent labour of others.' [3]

Owing to the rise of the working classes, revolutions to-day are no longer merely political, but have an economic and social purpose. ' While political revolutions were governed by abstractions or strictly rational concepts, those of the other kind are rooted in a living, sensible, palpable fact, the unhappiness of the masses and their need of redemption.' But

[1] Gioberti, *Del rinnovamento civile d'Italia*, reprinted by Laterza, i. 52.
[2] *Op. cit.* iii. 8.　　　　　　　　　　　　[3] *Op. cit.* iii. 185, 187.

the goal of the democratic revolution ought not to be the monopoly of power on the part of the masses, as is suggested by the idea of popular sovereignty. The masses are not the whole, but only a part : the other part consists of intellect, which creates an aristocracy of reason. Sovereignty is a synthetic principle uniting in itself both elements : by its essence it belongs to reason, but it manifests itself through the contingent expression of will, by popular suffrage. 'Let us modify the democratic formula by saying that the will of the people *conformable to reason* is the supreme law.'

Now the division of society into two parts, the masses and the aristocracy of intellect, gives rise to two political parties, the democratic and the conservative, each destined to supply what the other lacks by their mutual opposition.

' When the conservative element separates itself from the progressive, it loses all its credit with the multitude and deprives them of all trust in those who support its policy, who, deprived of this aid, reach a goal the opposite of that which they set before themselves. This is not surprising, when it is seen that in political affairs, as in cosmic, conservation is a perpetual creation.'

Similarly democracy, deprived of a strong conservative check, ' becomes a despotic rule, the more intolerant because for the firm mastery of one or a few is often substituted the cruel and inconstant tyranny of violent and unscrupulous factions '. Democrats and conservatives have therefore a dialectical function, as elements in a higher synthesis ; apart from this synthesis they degenerate into ' sophistics ', as are in effect the narrow Piedmontese conservatives, whom Gioberti calls ' municipals ', and the fanatical Mazzinians, whom he calls ' puritans '.

The point at which the two parties must converge in order to fulfil their dialectical function is provided by the nation. In the political order this concept stands at the head of all others and comprises all others : ' Nation implies stability and movement, maintenance and progress, unity and variety, authority and liberties, capital and labour, masses and educated people, &c.' [1] Thus in the national individuality

---

[1] *Op. cit.* ii. 3.

are reconciled the two opposite but equally essential demands of the modern age: the supremacy of thought and the salvation of the masses. The new historical age which is called to realize this programme takes the name of Rinnovamento. It differs from the Risorgimento in that it concerns not exclusively Italy but Europe in general, and therefore does not imply any supremacy of one nation over the others.

Here Gioberti's thought is very close to that of Mazzini, in spite of the constant care taken by these two haughty opponents to make a recognition of their substantial agreement impossible. Gioberti, like Mazzini, formulated his doctrine more with a view to conditions in France than in Italy, which at the time offered little hope for success to a programme of social democracy. And in fact the idea of a Rinnovamento was almost unobserved by his contemporaries, and even for Gioberti himself it was no more than the ultimate justification for his gradual conversion to the strictly political and national programme of Italian democracy. By way of the doctrine of popular government he was led to assert the necessity of political centralization, without which ' federal forms, far from being the best type of State, are actually the worst '.[1] This implied bringing the problem of federation within the limit of the State, whereas previously it had been treated as a problem of relations between one State and another. The doctrine of unity once accepted, the point of union must be not the Pope but the Piedmontese monarchy; the very existence of a temporal papal sovereignty finally proved a dead weight which had to be removed.

Thus the most practical and immediately valuable part of Gioberti's new programme coincided with the new orientation of national opinion, and to some extent preceded it and gave it a lead.

§ 3. THE RIGHT

From the strictly political point of view from which we are narrating this history, the unification of Italy is the result of a happy compromise between democratic initiative, in the

---

[1] *Op. cit.* ii. 202.

sense above defined, and the stable political attitude of the Moderates; a compromise effected under the auspices of Cavour. The Right, the party which gathered this fruit and controlled the destinies of Italy for the first sixteen years of the new reign, consisted of men who in the past had fought in the ranks of the two opposed parties, and had made peace over the strictly political programme of national unity. It would be not only a misstatement of fact but a serious falsification of the whole ideal significance of the Risorgimento to see in the Right the successor of the Moderates and in the Left the successor of the democracy of 1848. The Right by itself is the synthesis of the previous antithesis, as is clear if we consider the principle which in reality lay at the root of the conflict, and not the ideological or abstract expression of the antagonism. On the other hand, the Left, which defined and developed itself in opposition to the government of the Right, and was ultimately to inherit its position, was really in great part a new formation, bringing for the first time into the field of actual politics that complex of democratic and social demands which in 1848 had appeared on the Italian horizon as a reflex of the European Revolution, but only as a passing episode.

That this was the character of the Right is proved by its position with regard to the chief political problems with which it has to deal during its tenure of office : the problem of centralization, and the problem of the relations between the State and the Catholic Church.

As for the first, we find in the programme of government worked out by the Right, a restatement of the conflict between the old federalist tendency and the unitary tendency, represented respectively by Minghetti and Ricasoli. But during the period which paved the way for unification the problem came to be stated in a new and improved way, in that, whereas at first two opposed political views stood over against one another in mutual exclusion, so as to cancel out and produce no political result, the later conflict was between two tendencies within the sphere of a single political view, and therefore took the form of a less radical and more soluble question concerning political and administrative centralization or devolution. The tendency represented by Ricasoli ultimately prevailed, and the new kingdom received a centralized organization.

This solution was already to some extent anticipated by the triumph of unitarism over federalism, after the collapse of neo-Guelphism. All things considered, it was a benefit to Italy, if one reflects on the conditions in which political unity was achieved. Those who lament the suppression of regional autonomy forget that this autonomy consisted in the existence of regional States, and that these States must be at all costs suppressed in order to convert a country in which unitary feeling was very scanty into a single kingdom. Even political centralization, in view of the extreme narrowness of the country's political divisions, would have been insufficient to promote the circulation of the idea of the State throughout the national organism, unless assisted by administrative centralization, supplementing and increasing its effect by an action capable of affecting the entire nation.

But granted this necessity, it cannot be denied, from the point of view of Liberalism, that it favoured the tendency, already inherent in the mentality of the Right, towards an authoritarian or even despotic form of government. Raised to power not through a spontaneous development of Liberal ideas in the minds of individuals, but by a virtual act of conquest sanctioned by a merely nominal plebiscite, this party confined liberty to the narrow political caste which took actual part in public life, and even, in its highest theoretical expressions, came to identify liberty with the State itself. Now it is certainly true that the State is the highest and most complex creation of human freedom ; but only if the State is the term or culminating point of an ideal process connecting it with the individual, nourishing it and nourished by it in a constant interchange of influences. In other words, it is not *any* State, but the State as the organization of liberty, that forms the goal of Liberalism. But was this the State which was brought into existence by the Right? In theory it was.

One of the best theorists of the party, Silvio Spaventa, was thinking of this when he said :

'What is most truly novel in the consciousness of Europe is that the State is not something divine or inevitable, casual or conventional, outside ourselves; it is as intrinsic to ourselves as our own natural organism; because law, right, authority, which are its essential functions, are pure human will; a will of which we feel ourselves capable, and which has as its immediate end not our individual good but the common good, in which our own, as contained in it, is purified and idealized. This will, organized outside us under the name of the State, like a great individual distinct from the little individuals, commanding, binding, and compelling them to act for the common good, is our own will. Such is the principle and such is the supreme liberty of the modern spirit, filling every sphere of its activity with their echoes and constituting its greatness and its pride.' [1]

And Silvio Spaventa's brother, the philosopher Bertrando Spaventa, explained in his *Principles of Ethics* how by means of constitutions the State personified the ethical substance of the individual, realizing the universal form of the human spirit, purged of that particular and selfish content which flourishes in the inferior sphere of civil Society.[2]

But in fact the government of the Right was widely separated from this lofty ideal, and tended not so much to vitalize the State within the consciousness of the individual, as to erect it into an independent principle, isolated from all that spiritual process which justifies it and unifies it with the will of the citizens. Thus, by a slow and imperceptible degradation, two things were in practice dissociated, which in the idea of the Liberal State should have been, and theoretically were, conjoined : authority and liberty, law and autonomy, active citizenship and passive citizenship. No one who remembers how far the men of the Right and their successors were prepared to go in justifying reactionary excesses by appeals to the principle of the State can fail to recognize what degradation the original idea had in practice undergone.

[1] S. Spaventa, *La politica della Destra* in *Scritti* collected by Croce, Bari, 1910, p. 198.

[2] B. Spaventa, *Principii di Etica*, ed. Gentile, Naples, 1904, pp. 158 *seqq.*

This solidification of the State into an illiberal entity was favoured by the fact that a narrow distribution of political rights restricted the circulation of political life within excessively narrow limits. Hostile as they were to all extension of the rights of citizenship, the men of the Right endeavoured to correct or temper the stifling narrowness of their political conception by means of a wide and impartial legal discipline, capable of offering the citizens an effective guarantee of their civil rights. Thus freedom, strictly limited in the political sphere, was formally unlimited in the legal sphere, every individual having the power to move within the circle of the laws without arbitrary impediment.

This conception of the ' State according to rights ', borrowed in its theoretical basis from the *Rechtsstaat* of German jurisprudence, upon which the legal training of the chief statesmen of the Right had been based, doubtless represented a great advance on the arbitrary police government of the older régime; and the Right cannot be denied the merit of having partly at least realized, by immense legislative labours, by impartial administration of justice, and by a constant diffusion of legalitarian sentiments, its ideal of a ' State of rights '.

But the formula of ' liberty within the law ', a formula of which extraordinary abuse was to be made in the future, was inadequate, and vitiated by an equivocal formalism. If law is unjust, or oppressive of the individual's rights, what is the value of the liberty to move freely within its circle? A valid guarantee of freedom is provided not by *any* law, but by a Liberal law, a law inspired by the same spirit from which all modern liberties proceed. This means that it is not law as such, which may sanction any content, but law framed in a political atmosphere consonant with liberty, that gives its true significance to the Liberal formula. The 'State according to rights' has its source and justification in the ' State according to politics ', which is the State *par excellence*. Now it is clear that the narrow conservatism of the political State created by the Right necessarily infected the juridical State, and reduced to very slender proportions, or even degraded into instruments of oppression and reaction, those legal means towards which it displayed such ostentatious respect.

Other causes helped to render the Italian imitation of the 'State according to rights' greatly inferior to its original, as created by Anglo-Saxon practice and German theory. As we have already seen in our study of English and German Liberalism, the juridical conception of the State had its necessary complement in self-government, regarded as a means of promoting, strengthening, and rendering effective the legal sense of individuals and organic bodies within the State, and erecting them into an insuperable legal barrier against attempts by the political and administrative organs of the State to enlarge the limits assigned to them by law and encroach upon a sphere of action not their own. Now the government of the Right was centralized and bureaucratic, that is, it was in conflict with this fundamental requirement of the juridical State, and was therefore driven, even against its will, to neutralize its own legalitarian tendency. Concentrating all powers into the hands of the State, it not only in fact deprived individuals and particular bodies of the effective means of legal resistance, but it opened the door to all manner of illegitimate interference, by the narrow dominant political caste, with the organs of administration, and by these in their turn with the rights of citizens; so that the principle of liberty within the law was in effect reduced to an illusory appearance.

The evils of such a system became far more perceptible with the rise of the Left to power. This party, leaving intact the principle of State concentration, and even finding itself compelled to extend it, added on its own account a certain laxity of political conduct, which emphasized the faults which the probity and scrupulosity of the men of the Right had to some extent kept within bounds. This explains why the most intelligent statesmen of the old Right felt obliged to undergo a severe examination of conscience after the fall of their party from power, when, on going into opposition, they were free to carry out a thorough revision of their programme, on the strength of experience gained at their own expense.

After 1876, in fact, we find the outlook of the Right undergoing a fruitful change. About 1880 Minghetti began his famous campaign against the interference of political parties in the sphere of administration, which, with the questions raised by Spaventa concerning ' administrative justice ', forms one of the most genuinely Liberal episodes in the history of the Right.

In an essay published in 1869, Count Iacini had already shown that administrative concentration had resulted in the concentration of every kind of influence in the person of the deputy, and had concluded that parliamentary government was detrimental to administration. The same argument was restated by Minghetti, supported by a wider range of facts and accompanied by indignant protests in political circles ; he was even asked to refer the question to the High Court of Justice. From observation of abuses, Minghetti proceeded to the statement of the positive political problem, how to secure impartial justice and administration under a party government. Faithful to his old contention, he advocated decentralization : a solution which in 1880 began to assume a new political interest, now that the obstacles which stood in its way at the time of the unification no longer existed.

Now according to Minghetti there are three channels by which authority may flow from the centre of the State to its circumference : delegation, by which the central government confers authority on its agents ; the conferring of wider powers upon local elective bodies ; and the institution of independent juridical units. The central government would still retain national defence, the safeguarding of rights, and the general control of internal and external policy. Even so, however, the problem of decentralization would not yet be solved : local bodies might reproduce all the evils attributed to the central government. This, Minghetti adds, is a question seldom considered : most people think that freedom consists solely in the choice of a government, whereas in fact it consists in a general maintenance of rights. With local elective bodies, political interference with the administration does not cease; it is merely transferred to these bodies. The most radical remedy would be what Spaventa also is inclined to adopt : self-government after the English pattern, according to the juridical interpretation given to it by the school of Gneist in Germany. But for Italy this presents an insuperable social difficulty.

' The facility with which real property may be conveyed and divided among heirs prevents the formation of a stable class of rich landowners trained to undertake and carry out the tasks of public life. And to-day not landed property, but personal property, is the centre of gravity of social relations, and its owners are less disposed than any one to take up work outside their habitual occupations.' [1]

This is the heart of the difficulty. There remain only subsidiary, yet not wholly valueless, means for checking the interference of political parties in administration; for instance, the determination of the legal status of government servants, the principle of the responsibility of State officials, the institution of mixed administrative tribunals, and so forth.

Silvio Spaventa takes the same general line. He too is convinced that the problem of effective legality in the State is for Liberalism an essential condition of life : the State has lost its *raison d'être* if it merely subserves the interests of the stronger party and ignores or tramples upon the rights of the weaker. Impartiality, necessary to all forms of civil government, is indispensable to a party government; but is rendered more difficult by the fact that this government is exposed to all the dangers of party control. If nevertheless it overcomes the temptation to infringe the rights of the citizens, it will find it still harder to avoid the danger of taking under its patronage the interests of its own partisans.

The remedy for these evils cannot be the diminution of the powers of the State, which is irreconcilable with the ever-increasing demands made upon it by modern Society; nor yet in a wide and unconditioned delegation of these

[1] M. Minghetti, *I Partiti politici e la ingerenza loro nella Giustizia e nell' Amministrazione*, Bologna, 1881, p. 255.

powers to local bodies, which is irreconcilable with the industrial tendencies and habits of the classes now predominant in Italy; but in good actual administrative legislation, a well-organized jurisdiction of public law, and a strict responsibility of administrators. One part of this programme is the institution of a fourth jurisdictional section of the Council of State, which counted Spaventa among its most authoritative supporters.[1]

Thus, beneath the banner of administrative justice, in a campaign against the government of the Left, but in the last resort against the faults of a system created by itself, the Right brought its labours to an honourable close.

Another problem with whose solution the name of the Right is permanently connected is that of the relations between the Italian State and the Catholic Church: a problem rich in theoretical and political difficulties,[2] chiefly due to profound differences of opinion with regard to the precise nature of the function of the modern State as compared with that of the Church, the collision between the rights of the Italian State and those of the Holy See on the Roman question, and the international complication proceeding from this collision.

The political preparation of this problem, in the period preceding the unification, was very slight. The Moderate party, which comprised the great majority of the Italian political class, had never studied it closely, because, regarding the unification of Italy as a chimera, it had not contemplated the possibility that the Holy See might be dispossessed of its territories. And on the other hand, the federation of Italian States, which formed the highest goal of its hopes, was not a true and proper State in the modern sense, capable of a well-defined religious policy and able to give rise to a conflict of sovereignties. A federation presupposes the sovereignty of the States composing it; and having no true consciousness of its own sovereignty, it cannot feel

---

[1] S. Spaventa, *La politica della Destra, cit.*, p. 63 *seqq.*

[2] For a more general treatment of this problem, see Part II of the present work, Chapter V, State and Church.

very keenly the conflict between its own principles and those of a Church.

Moderate opinion, moreover, was in general Guelph, and, as such, inclined to belittle all the religious dissensions arising from modern Liberalism. Its Guelphism stopped short, indeed, of demanding the complete subordination of State to Church required by the rigid principles of Roman theocracy : according to Catholic custom, it was ready to compromise, and if it attributed a pre-eminent position in the federation to the Pope, it felt the need of disguising and attenuating this ' primacy ', and justifying it as an act of deference towards the most august of Italian potentates. In practice, the Guelphism of the Moderates confined itself to asserting the need for the full liberty of the Church in its own sphere, in agreement with the main lines of French Liberal Catholicism, and to opposing the Revolutionary rationalism which claimed, in the name of the sovereignty of reason, to oppress and enslave religious authority.

With the elevation of Pius IX to the Papacy, and in the first political and religious fervour which accompanied and followed this event, down to the Revolution of 1848, Guelphism seemed on the high road to success ; but before long the Pope's desertion of the national cause, and later the reactionary policy pursued by the Church, hand in hand with the restored governments, necessitated a complete revision of the Guelph programme. The fact that in the new phase of the Risorgimento a unitary conception was taking the place of a federalist implied of itself the necessity of taking up a definite line towards the Church, and probing to the bottom the antithesis between Church and State. Now Mazzini's idea of unity already contained a solution of the religious problem in outline, a solution consistent with the monism of modern democracy. In the formula ' God and the People ' a lay theocracy was implied, which, locating the divine revelation directly in the people, without requiring a mediation through the Church, made the popular State the centre of the religious spirit, and conferred upon the State the tasks which every Church claims as exclusively its own. At bottom

it was the programme of the Convention, modernized by
a more consistent philosophical view, through which the
rigid principle of State consciousness acquired an apparent
justification based on reason and consent. But in practice
what could this political theology mean, when confronted
with the Catholic Church, an institution with an age-long
history, deeply rooted in the consciousness of the people?
It meant that the State, conscious of its own religious mission, must not only subject the organization of the Church
to its own legal principles, but must also affirm its own competence in the field of dogmatic instruction, and require the
Church to revise its doctrines and bring them into line with
the religious motives of the State.

These demands, however restricted in interpretation and
application, imply a despotism incomparably more onerous
than any that had been exercised by absolute monarchy.
The latter had confined itself to affirming its jurisdiction over
the Church, without attempting to claim dogmatic authority
as well as legal supremacy; the new democracy aggravated
this subjection by bringing it within the Church and the
consciousness of the believer. The logical development of
Mazzini's principles could only mean an extension of the
Reformation to Catholic countries: an idea actually can-
vassed in Italy, in imitation of France, after 1848, that is,
after the monistic tendencies of democracy began to prevail.

But further, Mazzini's religious programme was based on
a complete failure to understand the political and historical
terms of his problem. Even in Protestant countries, where
the Reformation had united the two heads of the imperial
eagle, the influence of Liberalism had brought about a new
movement for the separation of Church and State; thus the
example on which the would-be reformers rested their case
was of little value. But what shall we say of the proposal
to introduce the Reformation into Catholic countries, three
hundred years after its time, when its most vital elements
had already been absorbed in other ways by the educated
classes, while the masses, for whom alone the change could be
intended, rejected it in their unsophisticated but stubborn

attachment to the Catholic Church? Moreover, the change
would have to be carried out by means of the State, an
entity towards which these masses were as yet hostile and
diffident; in the teeth of a Church which, conscious of its
strength, would have fought tooth and nail for its spiritual
integrity; and in contempt for the most elementary principles of the freedom of individuals and associations. Yet
such is the force exercised by absurd suggestions, that the
idea of a reformation of the Catholic Church, to be effected
from without, has never been wholly abandoned down to
the present day.

Thus the religious policy of unitary democracy came into
conflict with popular religious feeling and the political views
of the Moderates, who, asserting the liberty of the Church
and the necessity of setting a limit to State interference in
matters of dogma and cult, were far nearer to the spirit of
modern Liberalism. Here as elsewhere, the great merit of
Cavour was to find a political mediation for the two opposite
positions. From the unitarists he accepted the idea of State
sovereignty; but instead of understanding by that an absorption of the religious content of the Church into the State, he
confined it within its own juridical limits, and interpreted it
as the right of the State to insist that all who lived within its
boundaries should respect its laws. The right, therefore, to
demand that the Church, as an association for purposes of
worship, should enter into the sphere of common rights.
But within these juridical limits, he left to the Church full
doctrinal and practical freedom, simply because the State,
granted its liberal character, not only had no right to invade
the conscience of the individual and to encroach upon the
autonomy of associations, but actually rested upon this conscience and this autonomy. Thus arose the famous formula,
' A free Church in a free State '.

The policy of the Right followed the principles thus laid
down by Cavour. It was fortunate for Italy that these were
firmly planted in the minds of the most responsible statemen,
and gave them strength to resist the conflicting pressures
brought to bear, within the Right itself, by the supporters

of the two conflicting theocracies, that of the Church and that of the State. Both were agreed in criticizing Cavour's solution as a worthless compromise or a temporary makeshift ; in asserting the practical impossibility of separatism ; and in denouncing the ' agnostic ' or even ' atheistic ' state. They merely showed themselves bad philosophers and worse politicians. Cavour's solution was certainly a compromise, but only in the sense in which all political acts are compromises. At bottom, and this was the gross error of these pseudo-philosophers, it was not a question of a speculative discussion of the relations between religion and philosophy, or of ' transcending ' or ' validating ' the one by the other, but only of finding a political solution for an historical problem, whose terms were institutions, not pure conceptions capable of dialectical treatment. And on the other hand, separatism was so far from being impracticable that it has inspired the ecclesiastical legislation of many European States. But here, too, there was a philosophical confusion. A juridical separation between two institutions, whose effect was limited and contingent, was confused with an impossible division within the consciousness of the citizen ; the Liberal solution had the merit that, limiting the competence of the State within definite juridical bounds, it left the individual free to harmonize the spiritual discord between religion and philosophy, or faith and reason. But did not the State thus become agnostic or atheistic? If words are ever nonsense, these words are nonsense. The State has no cure of souls in the confessional sense ; it is agnostic in relation to everything which it need not and cannot know. This does not mean that it has no doctrines : but, since we are speaking of the Liberal State, its doctrine is liberty, that is, a conception according to which the conscience of the individual is inviolable, every religious or moral doctrine not freely accepted is harmful, and the energy of the nation shows itself not in acts of barren coercion, but in the free competition between opinions and beliefs.

Cavour's religious policy found its clearest interpreter in Minghetti, whose work *State and Church* expresses the central and ultimately dominant tendency of the Right in relation to this problem.

' Cavour's thought,' says Minghetti, ' was that the situation of the Church was such that it ought to be held superior to the possession of a slice of territory or a handful of subjects to govern ; and he thought that he was adopting a policy calculated to reassure all good Catholics, when he proclaimed the separation of the two powers and the principle of freedom, broadly and loyally applied to the relations between civil and religious society.' [1]

It was a legal separation which did not exclude a moral union. Piola, Mariano, and Bertini, in opposing this view, made the mistake of extending the sphere of the State so as to make it identical with that of Society ; now, replied Minghetti, it was true that

' the State is the organ of Society in the noble and important function of safeguarding rights; not only does it remove many obstacles to private activity, but it also supplies and makes good the defects of private activity where general interests are at stake. But this does not mean that the State can take the place of the individual and the association, or that its own proper end embraces and comprises every other social end.' [2]

The separatist Radicals, on the other hand, denied that the law guaranteeing the status of the Church was conformable to the ideal of a complete separation between the two powers. It was impossible, they said, to speak of a separation of State from Church, of freedom and of common rights, when the ecclesiastical hierarchy was privileged with special rights and extraordinary immunities.

' This objection', Minghetti replied, ' contains some truth; the contradiction between the separation and the law of guarantees lies principally in according to the Pope the quality of sovereign, and therefore inviolable, granting to him certain specified personal and local immunities, and so forth. But it must be remembered that the said law was politic and opportune; its aim was to convince Catholic governments and peoples that the end

[1] Minghetti, *Stato e Chiesa*, Milan, 1878, pp. 66–7.
[2] *Op. cit.*, p. 184.

of the Pope's temporal power did not imply the spiritual servitude of the Church.'

This political aspect of the question was just what his opponents overlooked, or allowed to be overshadowed by philosophical considerations which would have led them into the most mistaken policy, ' that of discussing the religious question without a definite end in view, and giving the Church a pretext for raising the cry of persecution and posing as a victim, without making any advance towards the solution of the religious problems of our times '.[1]

The best judgement on the political value of Cavour's policy is that recorded in the form of an anecdote by Silvio Spaventa, which I will here repeat, because its force as an argument is far superior to that of any formal discussions I have read. ' A foreign diplomat ', says Spaventa, ' resident at the Court of Italy in 1872 and 1873, who in his own country belonged to a party very jealous of the temporal power, said to me one day, speaking of the (wild) discourses of Pius IX :

' How fortunate you are ! this old man who throws in your teeth every day the most outrageous insults, which are repeated all over Europe, does Italy more good in Europe's opinion than all the ability and the moderation of your papal policy. His discourses prove that the Pope is still the most free and independent man in the world ; if Europe doubted it before you took away the temporal power, she cannot doubt it now.'

Spaventa adds on his own account this valuable reflection : ' The acquiescence of the Catholic people in a *fait accompli* settled the question ; because nowadays it is discussed by nobody except the Roman Curia, which is only a single party : it is therefore no longer a question. . . . It is now clear that the question has lapsed precisely because conciliation has failed.' [2]

One point alone of Cavour's programme may be called

---

[1] The one mistake in Minghetti's extremely sensible book is his attempt at a superfluous justification of separatism by a very unsuccessful sketch of a dualistic philosophy. There was no need for it ; his political argument stands on its own legs without any such support.

[2] S. Spaventa, *La politica della Destra, cit.*, pp. 195–7.

a failure. 'Perhaps,' he said at the end of his life, 'I shall
be able to sign in the Capitol another religious peace, a
treaty whose consequences for the future of human societies
will far outweigh those of the Peace of Westphalia.'[1] Instead
of that, Italy had to conquer her own capital by force, and
the hoped-for peace never came : yet a careful observer will
conclude that the disappointment of this hope promoted the
success of the more substantial elements in Cavour's policy.

§ 4. TOWARDS THE PRESENT DAY

With the rise of the Left to power, Italian Liberalism entered upon a period of crisis. The political and legal structure
of the State remained formally intact ; but the extension of
the vote, and the consequent claim on the part of the ruling
class to a patronage of the non-political and unorganized
masses, which could only understand their new rights as
a means of obtaining corresponding benefits, led to a visible
deterioration in the content of that form.

The Right had been founded upon a limited but homogeneous electoral body, composed of small and medium
landed proprietors, in perfect sympathy with its conservative
spirit and not disposed to hinder its legal and administrative
organization of the State. The introduction of new and untrained elements, devoid of any definite social and political
individuality, was bound to complicate the simple patri-
archical relations between representatives and their constituents. And since the new recruits made no contribution to
the State, or practically none, the State itself had to equip
them ; in other words, the governing classes had to buy the
support of their constituents with favours bestowed at the
expense of the State.

The government of the Left appears from this point of
view as a slow consumption of the State capital accumulated
by the Right. The highly centralized structure of the State
created by the Right facilitated the wide extension of political
patronage ; and new forces arose to increase this concentration : the rise of industrialism, the development of social needs

[1] Quoted by Minghetti, *op. cit.*, p 67.

and of means for satisfying them, the diffusion of democratic doctrines, and the pressure of the political *clientèle*, itself the effect of concentration, and now reacting upon its own cause.

But this system, while it found material to its hand in a certain economic awakening of the country, was bound to weaken the political organism of the lately created State, either by training the masses in the wrong direction, or by impairing the legal and administrative framework constructed by the Right. The government of the Left was in fact marked by a serious weakening of the legal sense and of integrity and administrative probity in the governing class. Thus the State grew in bulk and became more interfering, and simultaneously relaxed the cohesive force of its own inner structure : power became at once broader in extent and less firmly rooted.

Elements of new life were certainly not absent from this changed political atmosphere. Some influence from the great European democracies made itself felt in the Italian democracy, as had previously been the case with Liberalism. It was the first awakening of that popular spirit which had been symbolized in literature and invoked by political rhetoric at the time of the Risorgimento, but had not in fact played any part in the struggle for unity. Hence, as with other awakenings, it revealed a reality less attractive than the dream. The governing class could not help recognizing this, finding as they did that their representation of this people gave them no new strength, but only a more exacting political *clientèle*. The extension of the suffrage therefore immediately resulted in a policy of practical compromise at the cost of party principle, democratic only in the sense that it used democratic pleas to disguise the continued patronage of a narrow governing class over a fluid and unstable populace.

Thus with the rise of the Left began the period of breaking up political parties into groups, the period of transformation and coalition. Political divisions sprang up all over the field of parliamentary activity, no longer corresponding with principles deeply and intimately rooted in consciousness.

In spite of appearances, the political life of the country was not really diversifying itself into new and individual forms, but was undergoing a process of reduction to the colourless uniformity of dust.

Unfortunately, the Right did not succeed in arresting this process of disintegration, but assisted it by offering new materials to the process of transformation and coalition. Some of its more intelligent members, like Spaventa and Minghetti, attempted at first, it is true, to form a conservative opposition designed to safeguard at least the legal and administrative framework of the new State. But the Right was prevented from taking up a firmly conservative attitude by the fact of its own revolutionary origins, by its religious policy, and by the Liberal sentiments of its leading members, which forbade them to oppose any extension of political citizenship. And in fact Minghetti and Spaventa, whom we have seen as partisans of an opposition at once Liberal and conservative, based on the programme of administrative justice and the limitation of interference on the part of political parties, were in reality themselves progressives, and followed the growth of democracy with anxious sympathy.

In this way the non-existence of a conservative opposition to check its activity impaired the political education of the Left, and rendered universal the disintegration and confusion of the parties, thus creating an amorphous mass, substantially devoid of political views, and for this very reason providing excellent materials to the alchemy of the few skilful holders of power. This mass retained the name of Liberal much as a noble title is retained by a decayed family; it was in fact only a governing majority, capable of supporting indifferently the policy of Depretis, Crispi, or Zanardelli. No consciousness of any distinction between one party and another could survive the transformation and coalition which made party programme a question of bargain and compromise. The only real relic of Liberalism was a skilful art of governing, which succeeded in uniting the disconnected groups and tempering a substantially oligarchical government with outward respect for civil liberty and constitutional forms. Here lay the singular skill of Giolitti, who succeeded not only in governing the country with a minimum of coercion, but also in preserving without serious interruption the continuity of the life of the State and the political organization of social forces, in the early days of Socialist agitation.

The fault of this art of government was that behind an impressive façade of Liberalism and democracy it concealed a decadent governing class and a non-political populace. The social convulsions that followed the War revealed the illusion, stripping off the pretence and laying bare the facts. It then appeared how far the Italian people were from having assimilated modern Liberalism, with its opposed but complementary elements, individual liberty and State organization. From Bolshevism to Fascism, the annals of Italy have been strewn with morsels of undigested history : the factions of the Communi, the Condottieri and the princes, the grovelling servility of the viceregal period, the narrow views of absolutism, clerical hypocrisy, mob violence, the easy acquiescence of the Moderates, and many other things. After more than sixty years of existence as a single State, the Italian people is not yet an organic unity.

This fact, realized to-day by an increasing number of Italians looking with pain on their country's situation, is grave enough. But the very consciousness of its gravity may mark the beginning of a reaction and a renewal. It has been observed before now that the revival of the old police despotism, modernized and degraded by co-operation with the demagogic despotism of the *piazza*, is stimulating Liberal feeling to a lively re-awakening after a period of quiescence. It is a ferment that is spreading through all classes, and this is a new fact in Italian history ; this is the first time that the people as a whole, not merely a small intellectual minority, has shown any tendency to assert its solidarity in the name of freedom. Liberalism is being reconstructed from the foundations : its foundation is the personality of man, which has been more oppressed and flouted than any other social and political value. The energy which the Italians will in the future bring to their reaffirmation of human personality will be the measure of their ability to share in the entire life of modern Liberalism.[1]

[1] I should like to support my confidence in a revival of Italian Liberalism by appeal to the judgement of Benedetto Croce. In a ' postil ' on Liberalism, published in *La Critica* in March 1925, while this book was in the press, Croce rightly places on one and the same plane the two authoritarian conceptions of Socialism and reaction, and contrasts them both with the Liberal conception. ' The efforts of Socialism, like those of every democratic movement, have not been and never will be barren ; the ideals which it pursues have been realized and are being realized, even though not precisely according to the schemes devised by its theorists and constructors of Utopias. Nor is the force of authoritarianism and reaction either vain or evil, intervening as it does from time to time to save society by creating a dictatorship and restricting liberty. But far wider and more constant is the value of the work of Liberalism, which does not concentrate on any single part of social life, but looks at the whole, and is not only of use in times of disorder and unrest, but has to do with what is called normal life, whose conflicts it so rules as to render them fertile, and whose perils it diminishes by reducing to a minimum the loss which they involve.'

History, adds Croce, shows ' that authoritarian governments endure only among decadent peoples, and are never permanent among those which are developing and progressing ; and that repression only prepares the way for more terrible explosions of these forces, which ought not to be repressed but to be allowed to develop among the oppositions which they excite or contain within them.' The two forms, then, cannot be placed on the same historical plane : but ' while Liberalism goes out to meet the future, authoritarianism bears upon its every act the stamp of its transitory and provisional character. And whereas a truly intelligent Liberal can never be converted to the authoritarian or reactionary ideal, or to the communistic ideal, because he already contains these ideals within himself, within those limits where alone they are acceptable, and is equally hostile to the ideal of the abolition of the State involved in the first tendency, and the State-worship of the second tendency, it is quite natural that Socialists and authoritarians should be converted to Liberalism, according as experience and reflection progress in their minds or claim control over them.'

PART II

LIBERALISM
IN ITS
EUROPEAN SIGNIFICANCE

I

WHAT LIBERALISM IS

§ 1. LIBERTY AND LIBERTIES

THE study of the historical forms of European Liberalism has shown us, through all the differences of the various national minds, a process of mutual assimilation, gradually building up a European Liberal consciousness pervading its particular manifestations without destroying their differences.

If we take the two typical forms of Liberalism, the French and the English, which at the end of the eighteenth century seem irreconcilable in their mutual contradiction and exclusion, we find that their differences tend to disappear in the course of the nineteenth century, as a result of two converging movements; the one leading English Liberalism towards a more democratic rationalistic form, the other leading French Liberalism, and continental Liberalism in general, towards a more historical outlook and a more individualized application of its rational content. The hostility and mutual incomprehension of the two political worlds culminates in Burke; yet it was Burke who introduced continental Liberals to the spirit of English Liberalism; and this English spirit in turn, by means of a Radical rationalism adapted to the outlook of the new governing class, accustomed itself to the 'general principles' of the continent, which to Burke had appeared a tissue of empty metaphysical fantasies.

The antithesis forming the primary source of the conflict, and creating the primary demand for a reconciliation, is that between liberty in the singular and liberties in the plural. These expressions symbolize two different political systems: the one treating liberty as an abstraction, a concept intended to express the essence of human personality, exalted above all historical and empirical contingency; the other treating liberties as a complex of particular rights and immunities, acquired one by one as circumstances dictate, independently of any conceptual formulation which might unite them and deduce one from another.

For the Frenchmen of the Revolutionary period, the liberties on which Englishmen prided themselves were mere privileges enjoyed by a minority to the detriment of the community as a whole; they implied as their complement the enslavement of the majority, and were therefore a contradiction of true liberty, which formed the very essence of human personality. For the English of the same period, the liberty of the *Declaration of Rights* was an abstract right devoid of practical sanction and guarantee, which, by destroying as irrational and unjust privileges all historical guarantees and sanctions, tended to reduce individuals to a congeries of indistinguishable atoms, the easy prey of a despotic government.

The historical experience of succeeding generations developed the two terms of the antithesis separately, till at last each revealed itself as totally denuded of that Liberal spirit of which it had claimed the monopoly. The exponents of English eighteenth-century Liberalism, Whigs and Tories alike, stiffened in their privileges and attempting to exclude the new social classes from any share in them, lost their original political character and appeared as conservatives and reactionaries. The Liberals of the Revolution, in their turn, labouring to devise constitutional formulae capable of expressing the pure essence of rational liberty, allowed government to go on breaking down the last remaining traditional immunities and liberties, and in reality reducing the whole of the individual's life to subjection, while leaving him the empty show of a formal liberty and an ineffectual sovereignty.

The positive and fruitful result of these historical experiences was a deep-seated demand, dominating the whole political consciousness of the nineteenth century, for a synthesis of these two opposite conceptions, by which liberty and liberties, inconsistent in their mutual exclusion, might reciprocally complete and safeguard each other. Liberty in the singular, as a formal concept, is necessary to liberties, to

prevent their degeneration into privileges and monopolies.
It connects them once more with their fountain-head, perpetually renewing both them and itself, in human personality; it reveals their solidarity and their expansive and
diffusive force, it redeems their title from the passive status
of hereditary transmission, and reveals the original and permanent origin of every historical title in human consciousness.

But liberties, in their empirical particularism, are in their
turn necessary to liberty, if it is not to evaporate into an
abstract formula. They provide the content without which
the form is empty; they give a tone of interest to the general
expressions of reason; they render the vindication of rights
more easy, presupposing as they do the possession of objects.
The experience of liberties, even in the form of mere privileges,
prepares an articulated historical environment capable of
resistance to the levelling action of despotism; it creates, not
only in the ruled, but also in the rulers, a feeling of the inviolability of certain rights, and opposes organized defensive
points to the threat of encroachment.

The fact that England and the continent approach this
common task of synthesis from opposite sides, gives rise, as
we have seen, to opposite historical tasks, each impeded and
disturbed in its execution by a peculiar difficulty. For the
English, the chief obstacle to the universal extension of a
Liberal consciousness lay in the nature of their liberties, and
was aggravated by all the survivals of feudalism and the
stubborn resistance of the old privileged classes. The
obstacle was sufficiently powerful to distort, as we have seen
in our discussion of Bentham's Radicalism, or to weaken, as
appears in general from the feeble constructive energies of
English political thought, the formulations of Liberalism.
For the continentals, who at the first onset of revolution
destroyed their traditional liberties in the name of liberty,
the problem was the far more difficult one of reconstructing
what had been destroyed. Now the reconstruction of particular liberties in the face of a predominant democracy is like
digging a trench in the presence of the enemy: it is an
exceedingly difficult task, to which the political energies of

the Latin races are as yet unequal; the German peoples have shown themselves more equal to it, partly because for them the Revolution implied a less radical levelling than for the former, and left intact many of the defences of feudalism, upon which Romanticism early began to concentrate its resistance.

These respective deficiencies reveal the limitations of the assimilative process in the two historical forms of European Liberalism, and the tenacity with which certain peculiarities of the two original points of view have survived. This limitation and this survival must be borne in mind, now that we are entering upon a consideration of the problems of Liberalism in their synthetic and broadly European aspect.

§ 2. NEGATIVE FREEDOM AND POSITIVE FREEDOM

We have spoken of individual and social freedom, civil and political freedom, freedom *from* the State and freedom *through* the State; but in all these inquiries we have in some sense presupposed a freedom unqualified by any adjectives, lying at the root of these various specific forms. We must now undertake a more fundamental inquiry, which alone can justify these others, into the essence of human freedom itself.

History presents us with two conceptions, one inspiring the political systems of the eighteenth century, the other those of the nineteenth and twentieth. According to the first, freedom is the ability to do what one likes, a liberty of choice implying the individual's right not to be hampered by others in the development of his own activity. Considered in itself, in its strict essence, this liberty is all but a nonentity, precisely because it is devoid of content, and exhausts itself in the formal assertion of an abstract capacity, wholly arbitrary in its indifference to any particular determination. It therefore acquires coherence and character only in its historical or polemical expression, which reveals it as liberty *from* something, as the rejection of some external impediment which hampers the free expansion of the individual will. The extreme vitality of eighteenth-century Liberalism is due entirely to its polemical tone, to the critical energy with which it attacks and dissolves the rigid world of custom and authority, and liberates in this dissolution a myriad of new-born individuals living for the first time a life of their own.

In this way abstract liberty begins to acquire a content, produced by its conflict with the historical environment forming the object of its criticism. It is no longer the indifferent caprice which it appears to be in its inadequate theoretical formulae, but the affirmation of a definite *something*, namely the modern individual with his beliefs, opinions, needs, and activities; no mere ultimate natural fact, purged of all the accretions of historical life, but the product of modern history, the outcome of education, culture, and work. If resistance to oppression asserts itself in the name of an abstract universal faculty, that is only because concrete particular faculties are already at work, capable of generalizing from their own experience.

Thus the negative or polemical notion of liberty leads to a positive or constructive notion, systematically developed during the nineteenth century. According to this, freedom is not indeterminate caprice, but man's ability to determine himself, and thus by the spontaneous act of his own consciousness to rise above the necessities and the bonds in which practical life imprisons him. Thus it is not a natural fact, but the result of an unremitting education of character, and the mark of civil maturity. The really free man is not the man who can choose any line of conduct indifferently—this being rather a frivolous and weak-willed man—but the man who has the energy to choose that which is most conformable to his moral destiny; to realize, in his own act, his universally human nature. The absence of external compulsion is the merely outward aspect of this freedom; its inner value lies in the concentrated strength of the personality which dominates and controls all the factors and elements of its spiritual life. To be free is to be *sui iuris*, independent of others in the sense that all natural and coercive dependence is abolished and replaced by a dependence spontaneously affirmed in the consciousness of duty towards oneself and others. This notion develops by opposing, point by point, the notion that preceded it. Negative freedom consisted in denying all authority and all law; the new positive freedom consists in transferring the source of authority and law to the intimacy of one's own mind. To be a law to one's self, or in other words autonomous; to obey an authority recognized by conscience, because springing from its own law, is to be truly free. The eternal glory of Kant is to have demonstrated that obedience to the moral law is freedom.

Freedom thus coincides with the reality of the mind. It is not a faculty, an adventitious mode of being which might be withdrawn, leaving the substantial structure of mind unmodified and unimpaired. It is the spiritual energy which presides over, nourishes, and regulates all the activities of man. To act and to act freely are the same; without freedom there is not action, but passion, mechanism, habit. This is why ability in any art, creative vigour in any science, initiative in any enterprise, progress in any branch of human activity, are rooted in freedom, because freedom is nothing but the creative spontaneity of the mind and at the same time the law which controls its development.

As such, it is not restricted or atomically isolated within the narrow sphere of the individual life. This would be the result of a merely negative freedom, tending to exclude all interferences from without, and to justify caprice. In the higher conception of which we are speaking, the individual is more than a mere individual, because his conscience represents for him a law, an authority, in which are already expressed the universal elements of his nature, and from which arises the demand for an organization of human life transcending the demands of mere selfishness. The man who acts according to duty is no longer alone in the world; he stands face to face with an *other*, in whom his original *self* is duplicated; and this fundamental relation is the source of all human relations.

It was the great merit of Hegel to have extracted from the Kantian identification of freedom with mind the idea of an organic development of freedom, coinciding with the organization of human society in its progressively higher and more spiritual forms. The historical experience of the nineteenth century had vindicated Hegel's view, by showing that freedom has the force of a bond capable of holding men together in associations the more lasting and fertile according as they are more spontaneous in their origin and autonomous in their choice of ends. The destruction of outward bonds, which the timid conservatives of the early nineteenth century believed would bring about a ruinous anarchy, proved on the contrary the best means of effecting, without undue violence, a redistribution of social forces and of facilitating their expansion. The generations that followed the Revolution, still trained in the sensationalism and naturalism of illuminist philosophy, were unable to recognize that ideal bonds are far more effective than material facts in uniting men, and that consent is the real force of modern Society.

Thus freedom not only created a rich variety of subordinate associations, replacing by degrees the historical organizations which the Revolution in its first onset destroyed, but found a further expression in the highest and most complex human association, the State; and here provided the most irrefragable proof of its own constructive power. We are to-day so much accustomed to the idea of the Liberal State that we do not notice its paradoxical character, which was plain enough to its first inexperienced observers. The State, the organ of coercion *par excellence*, has become the highest expression of liberty; the traditional enemy of the individual has reconstructed itself after the pattern of the individual consciousness.

These experiences have emphatically disproved the opinion of despots and their partisans, that liberty can destroy but cannot construct, and can at most add ornamental features to a fabric constructed by servile labour. Of these two opinions the first applies only to the freedom of revolted slaves, the second to that of slaves liberated by grace of their masters; in both cases the freedom in question is a servile freedom, the creature of despotism. True freedom, the freedom of a man *sui iuris*, can both destroy and reconstruct; it only adorns the fabric which itself has built. To a free man nothing can be more repulsive than the opinion entertained by courtiers, that freedom is an ornament and a luxury : he knows that it is something far more serious than that, a discipline, a responsibility, a sacrifice. A free action is by no means synonymous with an easy action : freedom deprives a man of the comfortable support of ready-made decisions imposed from without, which save him the pains of an inner struggle ; it leaves him naked in the sight of his conscience, burdened with the unshared responsibility for the consequences of his own actions, which no kindly authority can conceal or disguise. The joy of being the sole author of his actions is inseparable from the torment which preceded it : both alike are equally elements in his spiritual progress.

This explains the great difference between the eighteenth-century notion of liberty as a natural fact and what we may now call our own notion, which treats it as a development, a becoming. To say that man is born free involves admitting that he becomes a slave ; because every bond that connects him with his fellows, every relation in the life of the family, Society, and the State, implies a surrender of this original and fundamental freedom. A strange freedom this, which man possesses only when he is not human, and which begins to vanish as soon as he is born ! Everything which we regard as a spiritual development, an enlargement of our sphere of action, the acquisition of a wider experience, is on such a view a diminution of the freedom of the will, a restriction of human personality.

We, on the contrary, are profoundly convinced that men are not born free but become free. This applies both to the life of the individual and to the historical life of humanity. The child is not free, dominated as he is by impulses, by transitory and changing passions ; we place him on the contrary under watchful control. Childish peoples like those which are not controlled by stable laws and organic government are not free, though they may seem to be ; among them we find only caprice above, among the dominant strong, and servitude beneath, in the dominated weak.

Liberty does not exist at the origin of human development, but comes into being as it proceeds. As the action of man widens its field, it becomes more free, because focused in a more complex personality. As children we are dominated by the senses and the passions; in our youth we begin to dominate them; adult, we possess them more completely in the calm of our reflection. The isolated individual is less free than the man who lives in the family, in Society, and in the State; because family, Society, and the State offer him an increasingly wide sphere of activity in which to strengthen and enrich his personality. If freedom were an abstract individual faculty, the faculty to do whatever one pleases, it would disappear as the individual began to live more genuinely in the world; but that faculty is what we call caprice, the opposite of the freedom which men feel to be their social and moral mission.

Freedom exists so far as it is exercised, so far as it faces the increasingly complex demands of life. What is the freedom of an outlaw, a savage, or an exile? Slavery to his own passions or caprices, slavery to nature and necessity; in either case the motive of a brutal and deadening existence. The true freedom is that of the man who lives in civil Society, with all its bonds and all its burdens, from whose servitude he is continually liberating himself by the very fact of finding in it the necessary means to the development of his own moral personality.[1]

Are the two notions of freedom, here sketched in outline, merely two historical systems of thought, one of which follows the other in an irreversible order, the first wholly vanishing when superseded by the second? Or are they also two ideal elements in our present life, the one subordinated to the other, yet incapable of being entirely suppressed, and reappearing with an insistent claim to survival whenever we think we have destroyed it? To deny the second alternative would be to discredit the direct experience of our psychological and social life, and—more serious—to deny the genetic

[1] See the author's *Problemi della conoscenza e della moralità*, Messina, 1924, pp. 120-1.

character of freedom. However we try to confine the freedom of caprice and selfishness to the lowest stage of social evolution, we can never deny that it contains a spark of spiritual and spontaneous life, that is, of true freedom. The negation of custom and social mechanism, however lawless and arbitrary, marks the first liberation of the mind from that which burdened and paralysed it; the first act of faith in itself, the first movement of its creative energy. The experience of error and evil, necessarily acquired in its long pilgrimage, is a vital element in its growth, without which truth and goodness could not be its achievement, its joy, and its pride. And even in its highest stages of spiritual progress, when freedom is a sure possession that has already borne fruit, the work of negation and criticism must still be renewed if the mind is not to lose itself in a passive stagnation.

The simultaneous presence in the same social world and the same individual life of different stages in the development of freedom creates the first political problem of Liberalism. Ought we to recognize freedom only in its most mature and highly developed form? Ought we, for example, to make the State an assembly of free men, separated from the servile mass which must be governed by authority? This would amount to recognizing as the only form of freedom the freedom to do right, a doctrine consistently taught by the Catholic Church and all but embraced by some professedly Liberal politicians. But clearly such a policy destroys even that freedom which it would preserve, whose existence is inseparable from the entire spiritual process that has produced it. Without an inferior freedom, an elementary school of character, no truly free personality can ever emerge into the light. And if these experiments demand a great expenditure of energy, it is not wasted, for all the energy that is used returns multiplied to its source.

Yet this solution, however straightforward in outline, becomes more difficult and complicated in the rich variety of circumstances perpetually presented by historical reality. There is a freedom which, in the shape of caprice or licence, while promoting the activity of one person, impairs that of others; to permit this would be to destroy civil life, and with it the very root of human freedom. Here then is the first Liberal limitation of freedom, which consists in guaranteeing the coexistence of different free wills in the same society. Together with liberty comes into existence law, equality of rights. Again, individual caprice may injure not the rights of others, but the growth of new beings emerging into a free spiritual life; and here again public interest demands another and an even stricter limitation. For example, a person who employs a child in work that is too severe for it is smothering a nascent personality: the veto of Society on such employment is therefore just and liberal. Further, there are cases in which the caprice of individuals hurts nobody but themselves, squandering their chances of a higher and worthier freedom; so that here again Society is right to intervene. For example, Society may prescribe compulsory elementary education, may limit the purchase of unwholesome beverages, and so forth.

The innumerable cases presented by everyday experience cannot be dealt with by deduction from a general notion of liberty. The main thing is a liberal spirit, able to pierce the often deceptive appearances of formal liberty, and to grasp its more substantial and genuine content.

§ 3. LIBERALISM

Various definitions of Liberalism have been given. It has been called a method, a party, an art of government, a form of State organization. These descriptions are complementary rather than exclusive, since each expresses a particular aspect of the Liberal spirit. One might endeavour to arrange them in a progressive order of complexity.

(a) First and foremost, Liberalism appears as the recognition of a fact, the fact of liberty. Every mental habit, every method, every art, presupposes this single act, which is the first organic element of Liberal experience. Now, only one who is himself free can recognize the freedom of others. Only the man who has experienced in himself the value of intelligent and autonomous personality is in a position to understand another's right to assert himself as a person. This understanding or recognition does not imply a merely theoretical observation; it also signifies a respect for that which it observes, a personal moral adhesion. *Homo homini res sacra*, said the ancient writer, and this mutual reverence can be established only through a profound sense of human identity, originating within us before it can arise between us.

(*b*) But the individual act, the isolated recognition, is not sufficient; as we have already seen, it may be deluded, it may let itself be deceived by appearances and attribute freedom to that which does not possess it, or deny it to that which does. Such acts must occur habitually, and thus form a watchful and discriminating experience. Liberalism has rightly been called a method, that is, a capacity to reconstruct within oneself the spiritual processes of others, and to estimate their purposes and results. Not all the manifestations of freedom have the same value and deserve the same respect : these values belong only to the moral and genuinely free personality, and can only be indirectly ascribed to the personality as yet in process of formation, as the capacity and ability to pursue a moral end, the hope of future goodness. The Liberal method begins with the presupposition that this capacity belongs to every man as man, and is not the privilege of a few. Every man must therefore have his opportunities, through the removal, so far as possible, of obstacles to his development, yet without the substitution of another's work for his own. The Liberal method is equally hostile to the solicitude of an impatient moralism claiming to shape everything after its own image, and the arrogance of an enlightened despotism which would create human progress by its own *fiat*.

Liberalism is conscious that the formation of human individualities is the work of freedom. No demand of the higher life can be effectually made, unless it is made spontaneously by the spirit; no progress will be enduringly achieved, unless it is a conscious development from within. To raise to our own level those who are living a lower life, we cannot either by grace or by force excuse them from the labour and pains that are the price of human progress, or from the necessity of traversing step by step the distance which divides them from us. This freedom is therefore no privilege, but rather a task which the spirit imposes as the price of the benefits it confers : no one can obtain them freely; any one can obtain them by application, toil, and sacrifice. Hence the error of the authoritarians and the moralists, who arrogate to themselves the functions of a providence.

More modest, but far more difficult, is the task which a man may reasonably take upon himself in relation to other men. It begins with a conviction of the autonomy of every spiritual process, and proceeds by the rare art of arousing within himself, as a demand of his own, that which he would impart to others, and thus in causing these others to impose upon themselves those principles which he wishes to impose upon them.

(c) In the world of politics, this method has for partisans the so-called Liberal parties, social groups peculiarly interested in the free play of individual forces because, from their own experience, they understand their vital importance and energizing power. The function of these parties is especially critical and polemical : it consists in removing all artificial and harmful impediments to the expansion of individual energies, in refuting the sophisms of a degrading authoritarianism, and in leaving men so far as possible to act for themselves. But the end to which these Liberal means are directed is nothing but freedom ; if freedom is the means, freedom in a higher and more organic form is the end. The conviction that liberty arouses energy, trust, and consent, and creates a spontaneous spirit of association and co-operation, is characteristic of all Liberal parties worthy of the name.

Those tasks proper to the State which authoritarianism discharges with immense toil and waste of energy, through ignoring or repressing the voluntary consent and co-operation of individuals, are therefore discharged by Liberalism more speedily and efficaciously. For the older Liberals, this self-government of freedom was to serve the purpose of reducing legislative and governmental functions to a minimum; but since their time experience has shown that to extend the benefits and responsibilities of freedom to all citizens and to interest them effectually in a great common task, it is necessary to embark upon new and more complex legislation and a watchful governmental activity, in order to guarantee the free development of all energies and to support them without replacing them. Thus has come about not only an enlargement of the State's action, but also its intellectual and moral advancement, since these new functions demand a power of psychological penetration and moral judgement concerning the needs of citizens, which despotic governments were not called upon to possess.

But Liberalism is only in part identical with a Liberal party; to a great extent the two may be divergent and even opposed. The critical and polemical zeal which inspires a party on the eve of its rise to power is commonly destined to languish and decay when power has been attained. It is easier to criticize others than to criticize oneself; the habit of government becomes inveterate, leads to action where none is required; administrative routine blunts quickness of perception; and the tendency to erect freedom into a monopoly for oneself, a privilege of some at the expense of others, after having demanded it for everybody, is inevitable. Thus by degrees the Liberal spirit deserts the Liberal party; and at times it appears equally in opposing or competing parties which affirm their own right to exist and to destroy the privileges of those in power.

There is also a danger, inherent in every Liberal party, of creating a fanaticism of liberty, an intolerance in the name of respect for the autonomy of the human conscience. The sectarian bigotry of the partisans of free thought is notorious; but it is not an isolated case; it often happens that the very energy with which Liberals defend their own cause destroys their calm estimation of difficulties and makes them unjust towards their adversaries and therefore, in the last resort, dogmatic and illiberal.

These limitations and distortions are accidental; but there

are more essential reasons why Liberal parties cannot enclose within themselves the whole of the Liberal spirit. They start with the presupposition that the life of individuals, whether men or peoples, develops through competition; that it constantly renews itself by overcoming the inertia and passivity of habit, tradition, and servile obedience. There is here the implicit assumption of a hostile resistance, something immovable which opposes motion, but nevertheless is its necessary condition. Now a Liberal party, as a part or division of a whole, cannot contain within itself, in its limited programme of action, the ideal motives of its opponent: if it recognized the necessity of the thing against which it was fighting, this recognition would end by paralysing its activity. Its strength, but also its weakness, lies in being partial. A more comprehensive Liberalism would recognize the dialectical ground of the antithesis and would see resistance and movement, conservation and progress, justified and validated in a higher synthesis which is political life in its concreteness. And from this point of view, the development of the struggle between Conservatives and Liberals, and their alternation in power, represent not an alternation of freedom and unfreedom, light and darkness, but the rhythm of an uninterrupted movement. But no Liberal, in his capacity as a party man, could ever consider the defeat of his party a triumph of Liberalism.

There is another aspect of this party conflict, which has been acutely analysed by Silvio Spaventa. The spirit of modern progress and of the political renewal of the European peoples, he says,[1] is rooted in the principle that the world is reconstructed by thought and through thought. But this principle, the instrument by which the face of Europe has been changed, is essentially Radical, and stronger in criticism and demolition than in reconstruction. This is because reconstruction is the work not of the thought of one man or of one generation, but of every one's thought, present and past generations alike. Now a respect for this work and the moral

[1] S. Spaventa, letter to Camozzi (1882), in *La politica della Destra, cit.*, 1910, pp. 470 *seqq.*

interests enshrined in it is a spirit not of innovation but of conservation, not a Radical spirit but an historical spirit.

This consideration helps us to grasp the ideal value of the principle which lies at the root of Conservatism and nourishes the dialectical antithesis of the Liberal thesis. It confirms our view that Liberalism, as a synthetic reality, rises above the terms of the conflict, and justifies them both. In this wider form, it embodies itself in the activity forming the focus upon which the action of all parties converges, and the resultant of all their conflicting energies: the activity of government.

(d) Liberalism has been defined, with profound insight, as an art of government. To govern, said Bismarck, is to find the diagonal of the parallelogram of forces. A Liberal government, in this task, always depends upon the spontaneous and sometimes involuntary co-operation of the public. It allows the conflicting opinions and interests to check and balance each other, the forces of Society to reach a state of equilibrium; and thus, working with a material already of itself reduced to equilibrium, without the intervention of the government, it imparts movement to the whole with a minimum expenditure of energy on the part of the State. And when we think of the immense complexity of modern societies as compared with ancient, we can easily understand why modern societies have given rise to Liberal governments. To rule them by force, to control and direct them from outside, would be an impossibility, an absurdity.

The function of government has a synthetic character. A government, even if derived from one party, governs for all and has in view the interests of all. It is obliged, as a party is not obliged, to consider fairly the motives of its late opponents and to reconcile these with its own. Care for the interests of the minority is the most strictly liberal of its tasks.

As an art of government, Liberalism consists of a capacity to unite the principle of conservation with that of progress, Radical initiative with historical tradition. To distinguish what is feasible from what is chimerical, that for which the mind of the people is ripe from that which must be postponed; but at the same time to permit the discussion of all opinions, and indeed to keep alive in the social organism the active spirit of inquiry, the love of the new, the trust in initiative, upon which the spiritual wealth of the government of to-morrow will be based ; all this goes to make proficiency in this art. ' Trust the people ' has been the motto of the most sincerely Liberal governments, the governments which have set before themselves, as the ideal goal of their action, the self-government of the people.

This Liberalism cannot be the exclusive property of this or that type of government. It comes into being in the continual exercise and impartial discipline of governing, in the alternate rule of parties each of which learns that in this activity there is something that a mere party can never know : the mutual criticism of parties and of the currents of public opinion ; the legal, administrative, and financial skill which the act of governing calls into existence. Thus it comes about that governments pass away ; widely differing political views follow one another on the stage of public life ; but through all these fluctuations something remains unchanged, and asserts itself by degrees with a prestige and an authority which nothing contingent and transitory can impair. This is the Liberal State, a being which in its inmost essence is sanctioned by no law, no statute, but is an historical growth to which all generations of politicians have contributed, on which all governments have left the traces of their activity, and which is different from every one of these because it is the work of them all.

§ 4. THE LIBERAL STATE

These characteristics, stability, permanence, impartiality, are intimately bound up with the idea of the Liberal State. A free play of all social forces, opinions, and initiatives could not give rise to an organized civil society without a common channel uniting in itself the fluctuating elements of historical life and ensuring the continuity of their movements. This function, by which the Liberal State makes for peace and normality, proceeds through various great convergent aspects: political, legal, economic, and social.

(1) The political aspect is fundamental, and constitutes the specific differentiation of the Liberal State as compared with all other historical types of state. It is based on the notion that the synthesis of the interests, economic, administrative, cultural, military, and so forth, which go to form the unity of the State, has a character of its own distinct from that of its various elements. These have a limited and partial character, since each, being unable to contain within itself the grounds of the others' claims, tends to assert itself at the expense of these others, or at least without consideration for them. The synthesis, on the contrary, is characterized by unity and generality : it unites and fuses not only the interests belonging to a single group, but also those which belong to different groups ; and this combination is not abstract and indeterminate—a mere receptacle into which everything can be put—but is sharply individualized in time, in place, in cause, in manner, so as to represent the historical, circumstantial, and indivisible action of an entire people. Suppose, for example, it is proposed to issue an edict regulative of industry : the State cannot content itself with tracing the diagonal of the industrial forces of the country, but must consider these forces in connexion with all the others, must examine the consequences which its action may have on the present interests of production and distribution, on finance, on military defence, and so forth. All the problems of social organization are thus profoundly modified when brought to the focus of this synthetic activity : they become political problems, in which the original technical element does not disappear, but is subordinated to the demands of a higher perception, more comprehensive and all-embracing, more formal in the best sense of the word. The chief organs adapted to this function are parliaments ; which, in the course of constant experience and by means of constant modifications and adaptations, have so developed and organized themselves as to sharpen and heighten their political sensitiveness. They are composed of representatives of the people, and thus by their very composition constitute a first selection and purification of social energies, a higher struc-

ture which moderates the violence of the interests that under-
lie it, expresses them in a form which already to some extent
anticipates the final political antithesis, and softens the contrasts between them. The representatives, chosen from the
people, bring with them the outlook and interests of the
various classes; and their number, which is generally large,
combined with a carefully arranged electoral system,
guarantees a fair degree of conformity between parliamentary
geography and the social structure of the country. But the
particularity of interests and classes is subordinated to the
general principle that the deputy represents the entire
nation; a legal formula which has its deepest significance in
the universal and synthetic character of the function which
he is called upon to perform.

The historical evolution of parliaments has successively
emphasized two functions of popular representation: to act
as a check on the government, which is regarded as opposed
to the people in accordance with the dualistic medieval
tradition, and, later, to govern on its own account, in conformity with the democratic monism of the modern age.
Liberalism has accepted both these views, without however
regarding them as fully expressing the inmost essence of parliamentary institutions, which it regards as consisting in their
function as organs of the political sensitiveness of the State.

Parliaments are accused of talking too much and doing
too little, as if their proper work was not precisely to talk;
and of having insufficient technical knowledge of the questions which they discuss, as if their knowledge was not
required to be simply political knowledge. The hostility to
parliaments that is visible in our days is only the mark of
a political obtuseness due to excessive love of technique:
generations educated by industrialism, positivistic philosophy, and historical materialism were naturally unable to
grasp the ideal and spiritual character of a synthesis like that
of politics, and could not help disintegrating it into the
materiality of its various elements.

(2) The second function of the Liberal State is legal. It is
less fundamental than the foregoing, not in the sense that

political interests may disturb or influence the legal order, whose validity is a necessary condition of the strong and well-organized life of the State, but in the sense that, while the political activity expresses the positive result of a combination of social forces, the legal organization constitutes its negative defence against external interference.

' The State of rights ', with which we have already become acquainted in our historical inquiry, is the organic complex presiding over this function. It has its ultimate origin in feudal Liberalism, which by definite rules guaranteed the privileged rights of individuals and associations against the encroaching power of lords and princes; but its further development presupposes the equalizing and levelling work of modern administrative monarchy, diffusing a sense of the equality of men, at least in their condition as subjects; it also presupposes the individualistic reaction which elevated and ennobled this equality, making it depend not on the will of a ruler but on the stable and impartial rule of law.

In the rise of modern Liberalism, the legal guarantee of individual rights first came about by the prevalence of private rights over public : that is, by withdrawing from the sphere of State interference everything exclusively belonging to the individual, until the whole organization of public rights was resolved into an organization of private rights, by a constant encroachment upon the traditional rights of the State. At the Revolution, the triumph of the contractual theory, as held by the school of natural rights, marks the culminating point of this absorption and the simultaneous commencement of a counter-movement; because, as the individual inserted his personality into the State, he by degrees created new public rights, and felt the need of reasserting the distinction between these and merely private rights. Indeed, the more deeply he committed himself to this development, the more completely the original relation between the two categories of rights was reversed : feeling himself engaged in building up a higher individuality, he came to value all his own subjective faculties not as ends in themselves but as means to this higher end ; his rights thus became duties and functions, and the whole system of these rights began to appear as subordinate to the public interest. The modern 'State of rights' tends progressively, though no doubt only within limits, to acquire this publicistic character. For us, individual rights are guaranteed not, as for the authors of the *Declaration of the Rights of Man*, by the alleged recognition of an entity prior to the State, but by a sanction due to the fact that the modern individual is essentially a political being; a sanction, therefore, belonging to the sphere of public rights.

Similarly, the rights of association and of local self-government are no longer justified on the merely privatistic ground that the interested parties are the only judges of their own interests. These rights show no trace to-day of their origin in the patrimonial state; they are based on the necessity of exercising and training the political consciousness of individuals. Gneist's conception of self-government as an organ of sovereignty, a channel of public rights uniting the individuals to the State, has opened up to legal theory a path rich in promise.

But the most important mark of the reciprocity between the individual and the State recognized by modern public law is the fact that both are bound by the same legal system, which neither has the power to contravene. The State, unlike the princes of a former age, is not *legibus solutus*; its sovereignty is not an unlimited power, but, as jurists put it, a power of limiting itself. This limit consists not only in the rights of individuals, but also in the internal structure of institutions and constitution. The most concrete embodiment of this principle is that which sanctions the responsibility of public functionaries, not only for the violation of the citizens' rights, but also for the violation of their interests, and permits them to be judged by the ordinary courts or by courts independent of the executive powers. The effective legal protection of individuals against the power and caprice of the organs of government is the mark of a people's civil maturity.

Taken as a whole, the Liberal conception of the 'State according to right' forms the precise opposite of the conception of the State as force, force being understood in its most

direct and brutal sense as (to use the expressive phrase of
the Germans) Fist-right (*Faustrecht*). This pseudo-theory of
the State was definitively criticized by Rousseau. Force, he
says, is a physical power; it is incomprehensible that it should
produce moral effects. To yield to force is an act of necessity,
not of will. If force creates right, the effect changes with
the cause: every force which overcomes another inherits its
rights; the instant disobedience goes unpunished it becomes
legitimate; and since the stronger is always right, the only
question is how to become and remain the stronger. To
speak of the rights of force means no more than to speak of
force alone. If it means ' yield to force ', the advice is good
but unnecessary; no one will ever disregard it.[1] This criticism
does not intend to deny that the State must always possess
force, but only to assert that, so far as it is a State, its force must
be simply that which imposes and sanctions the legal order.

But the doctrine of the State as brute force has no supporters, except possibly a few weak or morbid minds. The
writers to whom so insane a doctrine is commonly attributed
as a rule understand by force something very different. One
example may stand for all. The unjustly abused Treitschke
defines the State as force; ' but a force which tramples upon
all rights is doomed to final overthrow, because in the moral
world nothing can stand which has not sufficient virtue to
survive. An honourable and guileless policy wins for itself
a credit which is a very real force.' Thus in the last resort
the force of the State belongs to the moral order.

(3) A third class of functions belonging to the Liberal State
concerns the more mobile sphere of administrative, economic,
and in general social interests. Early Liberalism was opposed
to the recognition of these functions, and regarded the
State as unable, or less able than individuals, to deal with
matters concerning essentially private interests. The Manchester School held that any one who has a personal interest
in a problem is in a better position to solve it than any one
to whose interests it is indifferent. This opinion was especially directed against bureaucracy, through which the

[1] Rousseau, *Du contrat social*, i. 3.

activity of the State is displayed. The political programme of the Liberals who held it therefore consisted in ' minimizing ' the functions of the State, restricting them so far as possible to the maintenance of law and order by the courts and the police. One of their favourite maxims was ' Beware of too much government '.

In time this hostility to the State diminished, partly through the Liberals' rise to power, which forced them to take up the work of government and administration ; partly through the transformation of the State into a synthetic expression of individual forces, which could no longer be an object of hostility ; and partly through the great intensification of social life, perpetually creating new problems which individual activity was incapable of solving. It began to be recognized that the non-intervention of the State in the economic struggle implied, not, as the Radicals imagined, that the State was passively uninterested in it ; but that it was interested in the higher sense of securing fair play for the contending parties, and preventing the use of weapons detrimental to the principles of civil Society. Later, the Liberal principle that all the energies of Society must be able to compete effectively among themselves, and that none must be deprived, by the strength of caprice of another, of its fair opportunity, led to the multiplication of interventions apparently limiting the freedom of individuals, but really facilitating the free movement of the whole. The freedom of the entire people, instead of a few privileged persons—freedom as the positive capacity of developing one's own personality, not an abstract faculty which the less fortunate could never possess—that is the ideal goal towards which genuinely Liberal governments have learnt by degrees to direct their action.

Thus their social and generally cultural functions have acquired an increasing importance. By the mere fact that the State has become a creation of the individual, it has become conscious of its duty to contribute positively to the individual's education, and to broaden and strengthen the energies of individuals and of their free and voluntary associations. By nourishing the cells of its body it nourishes itself.

II

LIBERALISM AND DEMOCRACY

§ 1. UNITY AND OPPOSITION

THE relation between Liberalism and democracy, as it has appeared in the course of our inquiry, is a relation at once of continuity and of antithesis. No one can deny that the principles lying at the root of the democratic idea are a logical development of the ideal premises of modern Liberalism. They may be summarized in two formulae: the extension of individual rights to all members of the community, and the right of the people as an organic whole to govern itself. Now these two formulae are only the two aspects, or rather the two poles, of Liberalism. The one is the negative liberty of guarantism, the formal guarantee that the individual's activity shall not be interfered with in its proper development; the other is positive liberty, the expression of the free individual's effective power to create his own State.

As soon as Liberalism passes out of its feudal phase, and exchanges the idea of freedom as the traditional privilege or monopoly of the few, for the idea of freedom as a right common, potentially at least, to all, it has already set its feet on the path of democracy. No doubt the transition from the first phase to the second has often been stubbornly resisted by more moderate Liberal opinion; for instance, by the French constitutionalists of the early nineteenth century, and, far more strongly, by the German and Italian Liberals. In the first part of this book we referred to the contrast between ancient and modern freedom, as stated by Constant: the one corresponding to the modern idea of democracy, in its positive sense, as government of the people by itself, the other to the doctrine of guarantism. This is a simple and clear statement of the distinction between Liberalism and democracy, which would avoid the perplexing questions arising from their confusion. But only a barren Liberalism could be content to assert the rights of the individual as if they were a kind of private property, only to ignore the question of their use and their effective validity, and deny the higher significance of freedom, its power to create men capable of governing themselves.

The anti-democratic prejudice of the constitutionalists, justifiable in its own historical period as marking the transition from the old administrative monarchy to the Liberal State, is now everywhere out of date. The provinces of Liberalism and democracy can no longer be separated; they occupy common ground. Nor can they be distinguished by their manner of governing this territory. Here, too, time has gradually obliterated their original differences. Democracy, in its first appearance in the stormy sky of the French Revolution, was something hybrid and confused: it contained in itself both what is now strictly called democracy and what is now distinguished by the name of Socialism. These distinct elements implied two distinct views of government, confusedly united. The first proposed to limit the principle of equality to a merely legal expression, and therefore tended to advance social progress by organized and legal methods, respecting rights and recognizing the ' individual ' fruits of liberty. The other aimed at a violent redistribution of social values and property, and at divesting the individual of all rights to confer them upon the community. To this expropriation, not only of goods but of individual rights and values, Liberalism is profoundly hostile; whereas it has no objection to the strictly democratic programme, which harmonizes with its own. As the nineteenth century proceeded, the two tendencies of this early democracy were separated and distinguished, and the second acquired a new name; as a result of this process, Liberalism and the new form of democracy have come to coincide in their formal conception of the State, a conception based on the recognition of individual rights and the people's capacity for self-government.

The democratic extension of Liberal principles has its practical complement in the extension of political rights to all citizens, and the admission of the lower social orders into the

State; and this assimilation has come about with no essential change in the political and legal structure of Liberal institutions, a fact which proves the unity in principle of Liberalism and democracy.

But it would be wrong to infer that the identification is so complete as to leave no residue. To disprove such a suggestion it would suffice to recall the constant and bitter struggles, mentioned in the course of our history, between Liberals and democrats. No doubt these struggles are in one way accidental and transitory, representing the disinclination of privileged classes to share their privileges with others; but in another way they have a permanent character, based upon a profound divergence of political outlook which causes serious and lasting conflicts in the field of practice. First and foremost, democracy implies a strong emphasis on the collective or social elements in political life at the expense of the individual element. Culminating as it did in the second half of the nineteenth century, it was influenced by the intense 'organicism'[1] of its historical environment; by the industrial expansion which was leading to a twofold concentration of capital and labour into trusts on the one hand and trade unions on the other, associations in which isolated initiative was swallowed up; and by materialistic and positivist philosophies, which likewise tended to merge the individual in his environment and deny him any genuine individuality and uniqueness. These converging causes gradually reversed the original relation asserted by Liberalism between the individual and Society. It was not the spontaneous co-operation of individual energies that created the character and value of the whole, but the latter which determined and created its constituent parts. The individual was the creature of Society: by himself he was almost a nonentity; his particular physiognomy was a stamp set upon him by his environment. Hence political action in the widest sense must begin not from the individual but from Society, and must be brought to bear on the former by means of the latter.

[1] [The tendency to see Society as a 'social organism', in which the human individual has no independent existence of his own.]

This is the ground of the impatience characteristic of the democratic mind towards all gradual development of individual activities, and the formation of human personalities from within ; and this is why it tends to anticipate the results of these processes by determining the direction of social development from without. The logical result of this tendency is not only to deny the creative efficacy of freedom, but to repress and destroy freedom altogether. Under such a régime, freedom may belong potentially to all members of society, but it produces actual results only in a few, thus creating a kind of aristocracy, which, however mobile and fluid, inevitably appears as a privileged body. Now the democratic dislike of everything inconsistent, with its feeling for equality and social uniformity, leads it to reject the consequences of this spontaneous social differentiation, either by an arbitrary degradation of those members that have risen, or by an artificial elevation of those that have remained beneath. The art of arousing an inner demand for elevation, which alone can give it significance and value when gained, is utterly foreign to democracy, which contents itself with scattering broadcast rights and benefits whose gratuitous character destroys their value in advance, and whose dissipation is promoted by the fact that their value is neither felt nor understood. Such a policy is calculated to hinder the education of the people, to make them pay for material wealth by spiritual poverty, and to teach them the demoralizing habit of trust in a social providence that spares them the trouble of looking after themselves.

The practical consequence of all this is the virtual negation of that self-government which ostensibly stands at the head of the democratic programme. Or rather, self-government is permitted only to the highest rank of the social hierarchy, as the total and indivisible power of Society over its own members, but is denied to the other ranks, namely subordinate associations and individuals. No doubt these associations exercise a power of resistance which impairs the supremacy of the whole, and is therefore intolerable to democracy, as an impediment to the free and rapid circulation of governmental activity from the centre of Society to its circumference. But they also possess a power of educating people to self-government, which ought to assist Society as a whole to govern itself, but is lost through the fault of democracy, which, from denying the autonomy of the parts, is led to deny the autonomy of the whole, and to leave it, in spite of an ostentation of popular sovereignty, a prey to bureaucracy and the arts of demagogues. From a formal point of view, democracy does not deny the rights of private associations and local bodies; but in substance it corrupts them by its failure to understand the constructive value of the liberty which should govern their creation and operation. It is notorious that the democratic administration of communes and provinces, instead of something genuinely autonomous, becomes a mere link in the bureaucratic chain, hierarchically subordinated to a central policy and acting as a long arm to the levelling work of the government.

Granted these tendencies to concentration, democratic politics naturally emphasize the economic, social, and cultural functions which Liberalism regards as playing the minor part of supplying deficiencies in the activity of individuals. For democracy it is a question not of supplying deficiencies, which would involve the explicit recognition that individuals are the true motive forces of Society, but of replacing, of imposing, and of effecting a positive redistribution of values. The initiative in progress belongs to Society; the individual is only a means or an ingredient in a work whose end transcends him. State interference is the 'open sesame' of the democratic mind, destined to make good every lack of experience and of energy.

§ 2. THE DEMOCRATIC WORSHIP OF THE STATE

The growth in the bulk of the State, due to a conscious political tendency, brings with it a change in the character of the Liberal State. Signs of this change are already present in Rousseau, who formulated the ideal archetype of the democratic State. As we saw in the Introduction, the social contract is the means by which the natural rights of the individual are transformed into civil rights. This transformation appears at first sight to leave the subject of the rights unchanged; but in reality the individual which acquires these new rights is no longer the free man, but a collective entity, Society itself; and the original subject enjoys them only indirectly, as an organ of Society, that is, in the discharge of his function.

Thus the democratic State is the result of depriving the citizens of their rights and conferring them upon a general will, a single and indivisible sovereign people. Formally, the individual loses nothing; as member of the sovereign, he recovers all that he loses as an isolated person. But in practice this equation is illusory. If it is to be a genuine fact, the general will and the will of all must exactly coincide; that is, the collective interest must be the arithmetical sum of the individual interests. But in point of fact, to continue our metaphor, it is their algebraic sum; in other words, it involves the neutralization of all individual differences. The general will, as democracy demonstrates in practice, is only the will of the numerical majority. The omnipotence of the majority is the practical corollary of democracy; and the formal respect for the rights of minorities loses all effectual sanction just because the individuals have forfeited all power to insist upon their rights, by conferring them bodily upon the State.

The concentration of an immense power in the hands of an often fictitious majority is genuinely tyrannical; and it is therefore no error to place democracy and despotism on the same plane. Indeed, the gravest and most dangerous form of despotism is that which arises from democracy, precisely because it begins from the lowest strata of Society and proceeds by levelling, by destroying the forces which might limit and temper it. The victims of this tyranny include not only the minority, but the majority itself, whose actual social composition is very different from that of the representatives appearing under its name on the political stage. This difference is generally ascribed to the crudely numerical and non-qualitative manner in which political representatives are elected. But this is in part an illusion. When people speak of democracy as the triumph of numbers, they forget that they are speaking of numbers of men, not numbers of sheep or of cattle, and that therefore this quantity is the symbolic expression of something qualitative. The extension of the franchise is in reality an extension of consent, of adhesion to an ideal, a programme, or a personality; it is therefore the first stage in a synthesis. And if we look around us, we shall soon see that none of these protests against election has led to the discovery of a superior method of choice.

The evil of democracy is not the triumph of *quantity*, but the triumph of *bad quality*, which is revealed by numbers no less clearly than by every other manifestation of the democratic spirit. Lack of education on the part of the masses whom a *fiat* has raised to the position of sovereignty; the necessity of making oneself acceptable to a body of electors untrained in politics, which leads to the display of the least creditable abilities calculated to subserve the lower interests and confused passions of the mob; the omnipotence of the State, which makes it an attractive prey to those who intend to turn it to their private ends;—all these circumstances widen the gulf between the actual majority and the majority of representatives, and threaten to make of democracy a tyranny over the many in the interests of the few.

In the course of history the more watchful interpreters of Liberalism have frequently pointed out another reason why this new form of tyranny is more oppressive than the old, namely, because it does not confine itself to bodily or material domination but tends towards a slavery of the spirit also. The traditional figure of the tyrant, as drawn by writers of the past, and as manifested in history down to recent times, is that of an overbearing but external and transient force, demanding an outward conformity of act and word, but caring nothing for the mind within, which its weapons cannot reach, and which it leaves master of itself, as if to compensate for the tension produced by the rigour of its laws.

But the democratic tyranny is aimed directly at the spirit. It exacts that consent without which its own action would be unavailing; its work of levelling and equalizing would be impossible without a widespread sense of equality, degraded into the meanest envy. That Society is all in all, and contains everything in itself, is a principle which cannot be applied merely from above, by the action of government, but demands a universal collaboration of the public, by means of mutual hatred, envy, and delation. Democratic tyranny finds a spy in every citizen, and therefore knows no limit to its extension. As Mill has vividly shown, it influences not only actions, but also and especially opinions, precisely because the prestige of democracy rests upon opinions, and any difference, any singularity, is easily represented as an attempt to subvert the State.

This tyranny, thus brought home to the human spirit, has a quasi-religious sanction in the worship of the State. The idea that the State is a kind of earthly providence, that everything which belongs to individuals is its creation, that it has the right to control all thought and all belief, and therefore possesses the principles of truth, justice, and goodness, brings with it that adoration of the State which is the most degrading form of modern idolatry. For what is idolatry but the worship of the creature instead of the creator, the adoration of the works of men's hands?

The new form of idolatry stands in the sharpest opposition to the Liberal feeling for the State. The history of Liberalism, it is true, contains certain records of this superstition; but they are inconsistent with the general attitude of the Liberal mind, and are justified in part as a too emphatic expression of a legitimate pride in the imposing structure of the modern State on its foundation of freedom. In general, Liberalism has always been keenly conscious of the opposition between the State as the creature of liberty, and the State as creator of liberty and of the personality of its citizens. No Liberal worthy of the name has ever thought that his consciousness might be totally absorbed in the consciousness of the State; he knows that the autonomy of his own consciousness possesses an absolute spiritual value which is the very source of political progress. All the fruits of the Liberal conception of the State as a human reality in perpetual process of growth, and susceptible of endless modification and transformation, would be lost by its erection into a deity, the transcendent object of passive reverence and worship. That idolatry can be accepted only by one who fancies the individual a mere product of Society : and this is why it is characteristic of modern democracy.

§ 3. LIBERAL DEMOCRACY

Are these the inevitable consequences of democratic theory and practice? Do this theory and this practice necessarily turn against the freedom which at first they began by asserting? From our historical point of view, these consequences can only be contingent; they depend not on an abstract deduction of concepts, but on the historical outlook of modern democracies, the deterministic and illiberal views of the positivist philosophy underlying them, and the encroaching 'organicism' attending the upward path of industrial evolution, which by degrees has reduced the margin of individual independence. It is an undeniable fact that the rigid and unintelligent application of the principle of equality tends to mutilate the necessarily unequal and differentiated products of liberty, and to diffuse not only mediocrity itself, but a love of mediocrity. The democratic envy of personal wealth reduces the practical opportunities for individual independence, self-government, and resistance to oppression by the central power ; it concentrates all property and all values upon increasingly abstract anonymous and impersonal entities ; it makes every individual a civil servant or an official, and thus bureaucratizes the life of Society, with a depressing effect upon its rhythm and tone. Thus is created a slavery without masters, milder and more degrading than the old slavery, as De Tocqueville said, robbed of the vital incentive to revolt in the hostile presence of a master. But often the master is merely in concealment, biding his time to gather for his own advantage the harvest of servility which he sees ripening for his benefit. It only needs a dot on the i to turn a democratic tyranny into the dictatorship of a single man.

But the consciousness of this danger, inherent in a strict democracy devoid of Liberal spirit, soon excited in the best minds both of Liberalism and of democracy a sense of the desirability of liberalizing the structure of democratic Society in order to break up the stagnant uniformity of its elements, to vitalize them from within, and to make them into centres of spontaneous co-operation and of resistance to the oppressive action of the whole. This demand resembles, while exceeding in complexity, that which we have seen discussed within Liberalism itself between the partisans of liberty in the singular and liberties in the plural; its tendency being to effect a higher synthesis of identity and difference, unity and multiplicity. The feasibility of such a task depends on the original unity of Liberalism and democracy, and the dialectical character of the opposition between them, which is of such a kind that each requires and depends upon the other for all their mutual polemics.

Granted the preponderating importance acquired in modern Society by democracy, this synthesis takes the name of *Liberal democracy*, where the adjective Liberal has the force of a qualification, and serves to emphasize the demand for specification and differentiation which makes itself felt within the oppressive and deadening uniformity of democratic society. The partisans of this tendency are aiming at a democracy of free men : at instilling a sense of autonomy into the masses, fostering a spirit of spontaneous association and co-operation to break up their shapeless bulk, and at paving the way for the self-government of the State by means of varied and independent forms of particular and local self-government. It is a difficult task, because its execution cannot be entrusted to a State providence, operating from above, but must assume that the passive reliance upon external aids is already dispelled from men's minds ; it can only be effected by patient and assiduous education, and practical training of individual talents and abilities.

In the field of party politics, this Liberal democracy cannot hope for rapid triumphs. In the present state of general political education, the great masses from which parties are recruited have not the capacity to understand the synthetic task that is required of them, far less to execute it. Nevertheless, there is an indirect means at hand to remedy this deficiency. The great expansion of democratic parties has everywhere reduced the old Liberal parties to the position of a slender minority. This Liberal defeat may have, and is already having, great results in a selection and reorganization by which the reviving Liberal parties, reduced in numbers and freed from the dross that encumbered them, will be better able to fulfil a function of critical examination, or opposition in the best sense of the word, within democratic society. Unable to compete with democracy in the work of electoral campaigns among the masses, they may carve from the great common territory a small district to be cultivated in their own way, as a nursery garden of freedom. A permanent influence of Liberalism upon democracy is possible only if its action begins from below, from the humble experiences of association and organization, rising by degrees to the wider manifestations of social life. A practical demonstration must be given of the origin and development of aristocracies of freedom, or as they are sometimes called social *élites*, drawn from the shapeless block of the masses, so that in various ways, by efforts distinct in kind but converging in their purpose, the entire block may by degrees shape itself into a multiplicity of definite forms and figures.

The distinction between Liberalism and democracy in the field of practical party organization seems therefore, at least in view of this preliminary educational work, providential. A sense of the difference between their respective points of view, as developed in the course of recent history, is an essential condition of their synthesis; without it, this would degenerate into an empty and barren confusion, doomed to lose the fruits of both tendencies.

III

LIBERALISM AND SOCIALISM

§ 1. CLASS AND PARTY

THE appearance of Socialism on the political stage in the second half of the nineteenth century, and the rapid progress which it made, created a profound perturbation in the Liberal mind, but at the same time introduced elements tending to clarification and a new orientation. Distinguishing itself from democracy in general, the democracy of numbers, with which it was originally confused, Socialism constructed a theory of its own and a method of action calculated to emphasize that social content which democracy had hoped to model on the already existing structure of the Liberal State. It formed the ideal of building up a new State, and, not content with Utopian predictions of its appearance, like the earlier and cruder Socialism of the early nineteenth century, set to work to bring it about by actively organizing and educating the democratic masses.

This action was facilitated by the development of industrialism, which, by generalizing and concentrating the factory system, afforded it an ever-increasing number of recruits, already gathered together and united by strong affinity of interests. It was thus enabled to extract from the total mass of democracy a section already to some extent displaying the structure of a new social form, namely the industrial proletariate, and to a more limited extent the agricultural proletariate, where this, owing to the industrial development of agriculture, had acquired a social character resembling that of the former.

Socialism is thus a specific form of democracy, and in its specific way it expresses a demand resembling that which we have seen expressed by Liberalism. But this differentiation produces something distinct and even antagonistic both in

form and in content; hence there is an open and definite conflict between Liberalism and Socialism.

First and foremost, the organization of Socialism is inspired
by the principle of class war, in its modern historical form,
as a war of the proletariate against capitalism. It is not our
task to go deeply into this principle; we are only concerned
to observe the peculiar way in which it comes into conflict
with the notion of political parties, owing to the fact that
Socialism, pending the appearance of its new State, develops
its action within the Liberal State and bestows upon a social
class, organized for an economic struggle, the further character of a political party competing with other parties.

Now a class is a particular group of homogeneous individuals, and is so far the same thing as a party; but differs in
that, whereas a party is a particular group directed towards
a universal end, a class is a pure and simple particular, containing within itself no wider *raison d'être*. As we have already
seen, the idea of party is only an element in the idea of the
State, and therefore the partial interest which serves to differentiate it is embraced and transfigured in a common and
higher consciousness, in the idea of a task of national import, to be performed on behalf of the whole community.
Once in power, a party governs not for itself but for all; and
this universality is, as we have remarked, the political transformation of the social and economic particularity by which
parties are differentiated. In a class, on the contrary, there
is nothing but the direct expression of interest, without this
transformation and this demand for synthesis; thus the conversion of Socialism into a party causes a profound disturbance in the organization and functioning of the Liberal State,
owing to the fact that its structure is strictly that of a class.

This disturbance was hardly perceptible while Socialist
parties formed an inconsiderable minority; but with their
growth and rise to power, they disturb the entire orientation
of the State by bringing to the work of government a partisan
outlook and a programme of class dictatorship which is the
crude negation of any genuinely political consciousness. They
assert, indeed, that the class element in their conception is

provisional and transitory, and that, capitalism once destroyed, the class war will cease and it will be possible to govern in the interests of all. But it is extremely curious that Socialism, which has so dramatically emphasized the class war, and has devoted its historical researches to pointing out its leaders and following its fortunes in all periods of history, should be able to cherish so cheaply quietistic an illusion, and should fail to see that the causes of the struggle do not depend on external contingencies, but lie at the roots of human activity, and that class divisions are as eternal as the specific forms of that activity. Men like Lassalle, Marx, and Engels, in the very act of creating a new and profound historical cleavage, dreamed of a moribund and stagnant uniformity as the goal of their labours.

But ever apart from these considerations, the idea of a single and all-embracing class, as the outcome of the class war, is very far from representing the transformation of particular interests into the universality of politics, as it tries to do. The mimetic tendency here displayed recalls the attempt of the Benthamites to create moral values by a combination of interests; for politics, like morality, is not a receptacle, but an original *forma mentis*. Just as, in order to discover the moral value of an act, it is not enough to consider its consequences in connexion with all the other acts of Society, so the universality of politics cannot be reached by adding up the various interests of humanity, but may be discerned in any one of them by itself. The Socialist theory seems doomed to waver eternally between a narrow particularism and a vague and ineffectual universality, a sectarian present and an apocalyptic future, without ever uniting into an articulate unity the sundered elements of the social synthesis.

By becoming a political party, Socialism alters not only its own character but that of the other parties. By degrading the political conflict into an economic conflict, by insisting upon its own class consciousness, it compels its opponents to organize themselves into class parties, and teaches them to suppress that sense of the universality of their political function which the presence of Socialism makes it all the more necessary for them to cherish. The Liberal parties of the past have doubtless erred through selfishness, class prejudice, and excessive narrowness ; yet they have never raised selfishness to the rank of a fundamental principle of government, and have always tried to rise superior to a narrowly *bourgeois* point of view. The conviction which to-day is growing up under the influence of Socialism, that they represent the exclusive political expression of the *bourgeoisie*, and therefore ought to undertake the defence of the interests of one class as against another, threatens to frustrate every effort to express economic conflicts in the higher terms of politics and to discover an ordered and civilized *modus vivendi* for the classes.

Once the political struggle degenerates into an economic struggle, its end, the achievement of power, instead of being the triumph of a policy for the State as a whole, valid for all members of the community, becomes the triumph of one group at the expense of another, subserving the interests of one faction as against those of another, and in the last resort against those of the whole. The tyranny of the majority, which we have examined in the case of democracy, is now aggravated by a new perversion : for democratic majorities at least have a political character, and a consciousness, even if not a very strong consciousness, of their duty to the State as a whole ; whereas in the case of Socialism the particularity of interests is asserted in the most direct and brutal manner without even an appearance of political mediation.

When the struggle is thus distorted and degraded, it threatens to compromise the permanence of the State and the continuity of its historical life ; the triumph of a party class is in danger of becoming the triumph of a party State, and the alternation of parties in power, instead of presenting a regular development safeguarded by the identity of the State, is perverted into a series of revolutionary convulsions.

Of this peril Liberalism is not sufficiently aware. It has lost touch with its own tradition. It has allowed its outlook to be narrowed into a few out-of-date formulae, in which no sane man would expect to find the ready-made solutions of the new problems offered by the real world. Hence it has been easily swayed by the economic and social storms which have driven it from its historical path. Its first and worst error was to accept the restatement of the political struggle in terms of an economic and social struggle, and to give its parties the character of *bourgeois* parties. But even if it ought not to recruit, and does not recruit its followers solely from the *bourgeoisie*, it ought incessantly to repudiate all class qualifications by vigorously asserting that in the field of political conflict there are no classes, but only parties, particular points of view within a whole which because they are particular do not cease to have a necessary universal validity.

This does not imply that a class struggle does not exist. It does exist; but only in the subordinate sphere of economic and social life. To confuse Society with the State, and to make the latter a mere agent and administrator of social interests, is one of the deepest and most disastrous errors of modern political science, especially that form of it which inspires Socialism. The State is not Society, but its political organization; it is therefore a higher form in which the heterogeneous and conflicting elements of social life are united into an organic whole.

The political character of this form is, as we have observed, a transformation of the narrow content of economic and social relations : class selfishness, which in itself can find nothing to limit its expansion, finds in the sovereignty of this political form the checking and tempering power necessary to civilized life, and also finds a purified and universalized expression in the programmes of political parties, because each party is bound to consider this selfish interest as an element in the synthesis of government; and the conflict and mutual criticism of parties further develop this synthetic motive and prepare it for receiving the final seal of State authority. Thus the superior form of State sovereignty is not forced upon the content of social life from without, but emerges gradually from within itself, through a spontaneous selection of its elements. That is the inner structure of the Liberal idea. Take away the idea of the State as something superior to Society, take away the mediating work of political parties, and there is nothing to check the savage fury of social strife; all appeal to a higher court is precluded.

But the political parties which have arisen from Liberalism (and this does not mean only the Liberal parties strictly so called), losing sight of their original political function and degenerating into *bourgeois* parties, that is, economic class organizations, have often attempted to transfer to the sphere of Society that synthetic task, proper to the State, which they have deprived of its appropriate theatre of action. Not to mention those who have attempted simply to deny the class struggle, and have put out their own eyes to avoid seeing it, there are others who have tried to degrade the State into an 'economic' arbitrator in this struggle. The attempt has been unsuccessful, because the State is not a technical expert: the arbitration which it effects is simply that of politics; and its intervention in the capacity of an expert only means arbitrarily conferring that name upon a prefect or civil servant who has no title to it.

But the most serious political error of this type is that which has appeared in Italy from 1923 to the present time, through a hybrid union between ill-digested reminiscences of trade unionism and ill-managed Liberal institutions. It began in an attempt to bring about by coercion a collaboration of classes which, in the present stage of social evolution, is impossible; it went on to the worse error of transferring the whole apparatus of trade unionism, thus manipulated, into the sphere of strictly political institutions, which implies degrading the latter to the level of the former. After all that has been said, the error is clear. The political disguise of the trade unions could only infect the State with the immediate particularism of social interests, annihilate the genuine political functions of the State, sanction the social conflict in all its brutality, and render its effects irreparable. But the most grotesque aspect of these endeavours lies in the fact that they were intended to bring peace to Society by means of the State, at the very moment when, politics being degraded into the expression of a class and the State into the expression of a party, discord was being sown broadcast in the very

State which was to play the part of peacemaker. The failure to recognize the proper sphere of politics, in which the divisions and conflicts of Society are healed and pacified, has led clumsy reformers to begin their work from the wrong end, trying to unite that which is necessarily divided, and dividing that which is the sole instrument of union. This grotesque picture will perhaps have the merit of affording a text for future manuals of politics, to prove by *reductio ad absurdum* the autonomy of their object of study.

§ 2. HISTORICAL MATERIALISM

The neglect of political values by Socialism is due to the conception of historical materialism which underlies its whole system. According to this notion, the economic factor in Society is fundamental, and all others, including the political, are not only secondary but mere reflections of the economic. The structure of the building is economics; religion, politics, and morality are a superstructure. Hence, in its programme of action, Socialism concerns itself essentially with the economic factors of production and distribution, in the belief that everything else will follow automatically. It has refused to undergo a genuine political education, being convinced that in the technicalities of economics it already possesses the secret of politics. In the constant attempt to translate all political problems into economic terms, it has brought to their solution a narrowly technical outlook and an administrative and bureaucratic spirit.

The conversion of politics into bureaucracy, begun by democracy, is completed by Socialism through its blind worship of the technical expert. How, indeed, could the representatives of trade unions possibly form the political organ of the State, except as an administrative and bureaucratic board? The State character, the universal character *par excellence* of the political synthesis, degraded into a universal expression of economic interests in their own sphere, is confused with the character of the bureaucracy, which is the impartial organ administering the general interests of the country. The great Socialistic invention of making politics a matter for technical experts is merely a revival of the principle of administrative monarchy, which Liberalism succeeded, not without difficulty, in destroying by the creation of a political State rising above the sphere of ordinary administration.

The bureaucratic idea of Socialism pervades all grades of the social hierarchy and tends to convert every individual into a State employee. And one of the most deplorable principles of historical materialism is that the individual is a mere impersonal product of his social environment, with the practical corollary that, since he owes everything to Society, his rights must all belong to Society, making him the mere agent or administrator of interests that are not his own but those of the community.

Here the antithesis between Liberal individualism and Socialism, concealed to some extent in democracy, emerges into full daylight. For Liberalism, every dispossession of the individual is not only an injustice but an error, or whole series of errors, because it ignores the spiritual and autonomous character of the individual's growth ; destroys the value of the voluntary associations which Socialism itself has so impressively built up, and which so clearly demonstrate the individual's ability to react on his environment ; and threatens to lower the tone of social life, by deadening the consciousness, and thus indirectly impairing the activity, of its chief motive force. Without for a moment doubting that the civil servant is a useful person in his right place, it may be admitted that the extension of his characteristic mental qualities and modes of action to spheres which are less suited to them and require initiative, personal responsibility, energy, quickness of eye, and in general the qualities that may be called political, is bound to impair all the constructive forces of Society.

As against this absorption of the individual by the environment, Liberalism champions the opposite policy, the liberation of the individual by means of Society. It recognizes that the social environment often has a limiting and repressive action upon human personality ; but instead of treating this fact as a law of nature, and trying to atone for the repression of one by the repression of all, it regards it as due to an immature condition of social consciousness, and makes it a motive for turning the already free forces of Society towards the work of liberating the rest. A truer estimation of the negative side of the action of Society upon the individual facilitates a truer estimation of its positive side, the importance of social co-operation, in the widest sense of the words, for the expansion and multiplication of the individual's powers. This is the genuinely Liberal function of society, brilliantly exemplified in practice by Socialism itself, whereas a deluded ideology can see in it only a function of brutal enslavement whose direction may be altered but whose substance must remain the same.

The attitude of Liberalism towards this problem might be expressed in the formula, ' through Socialism to a higher individualism'. This implies making Society into a means of individual development and salvation; making the individual, like a living organism, absorb all he can of the world in which and on which he lives, using his own powers to render it free and spiritual.

Lastly, to confine ourselves to the essential points in the Liberal criticism of historical materialism, our repudiation of the idea that politics is a mere reflection of economics must not be regarded as substituting one particularism for another, the triumph of the political expert over the economic. The mistake of historical materialism was to forget not only the value of politics as an autonomous reality, but the value of all the other factors of social life, which, no less powerfully than the economic factor, go to make up the political synthesis. This synthesis is the expression of an historical activity in which all the determinations of the mind are present: interests, opinions, convictions, beliefs, and moral judgements. Materialism proposed to reduce all these elements to one; and the reduction necessarily implied mutilating many values, perverting others, and misunderstanding their complex play in the life of Society.

To believe that economic interests are the master-key to all human relations is to expose oneself to serious disappointments. To deny the importance of the moral convictions of individuals is a sign not only of moral degradation, but of political incapacity, not because politics and morals are the same, but because the object and the agent in politics is the whole man, in whom the voice of the moral consciousness is a genuine force. Even prejudices, errors, and illusions have their own effect on the total result, and politics must not forget them; otherwise its finest architectonic plans become impracticable.

In its view of the class struggle, historical materialism fails by harping on a single string. The resulting theory is a simplification useful in the scientific laboratory, like its predecessor the ' economic man'; but the struggle as so described is not a struggle between living men, not an adequate statement of the infinite complexity of human relations. In real life, the rectilinear development of the conflict is interfered with by numberless circumstances transforming its original economic motive; even the structure of its protagonists, the classes, is not fixed and rigid, but, under the operation of the most various causes, shows a continual formation and disintegration of social groupings, an alternate drawing and obliterating of class divisions, which no merely economic schematism is adequate to describe.

Liberalism, based as it is not on schematism, but on the consideration of human personality in the fullness of its spiritual determinations, is better able to understand the complex play of psychological factors which go to make up the synthesis of politics. It possesses that kind of tact or flair, sometimes degenerating into an unscrupulous opportunism, which in its highest manifestations is true political sensitiveness, and serves to recognize everything that is human—human strength and human weakness, human reason and human passion, human interest and human morality—in the relations between rulers and ruled; and is able to turn this experience to the ends of the elevation of human society.

§ 3. THE LIBERALISM OF PRACTICAL SOCIALISM

While recognizing the political faults of historical materialism, we must also recognize that Socialism, as an actual force
organizing the working classes, does not stand wholly condemned by this condemnation of its doctrines. Its work has
a significance transcending that of its narrow ideology.

In uniting working men for the purposes of class warfare,
Socialism has achieved something of permanent spiritual
value. It has raised a mass of men, whom it found in a state
of brutalizing servitude, to the human level of antagonists in
a battle; has aroused in them a sense of their dignity and
autonomy; and has advanced their differentiation as a class
from within. The present position of the working man, as a
man and not a mere machine or commodity, is largely due
to Socialism, which thus appears as the greatest movement
of human emancipation since the French Revolution. If we
remember the mean and inhuman harshness displayed by
early nineteenth-century Liberals towards the urgent social
problems of their times, we cannot deny that socialism, for
all the defects of its ideology, has been an immense advance
on the earlier individualism, and, from the point of view of
history, has been justified in attempting to submerge it beneath its own social flood.

The intellectual narrowness of its programme has even
helped to promote an action whose limitations lent it vigour.
Upon men rendered insensible by servile labour and extreme
poverty, it worked through the conviction, learnt by experience, that a certain minimum of economic welfare is necessary for the rise of any higher impulse of humanity. The
economic gospel of Socialism acted like the first message of
mind to a materialized world. The rise of wages, the reduction of hours of work, and the improvement of factory conditions, which were its immediate effect, were not only an
economic advance, but a step towards civilization, culture,
and moral life. The workman, at first undistinguished from
the labour which he sold, and sold himself with it, learnt to
distinguish himself from his labour and to sell it freely; and

this distinction was the first step in forming his personality, as an autonomous reality, withdrawn from the sphere of the market, and capable of understanding its own moral destiny. Thus labour itself, the tangible sign of his slavery, was redeemed and converted into a means of salvation.

Through association, the workman not only gained these individual advantages, but learnt to cultivate a social spirit destined to increase his first gains. If at first these associations were violently and forcibly dragooned by a dominant few who could see farther than the majority, and could overcome their inertia, this was a typical example of men being forced to be free, of an imperious summons to all those who as yet could feel nothing but force, to the duty of making men of themselves. And the first blow did the work; afterwards the direct experience of the benefits to be won by association gave the force of persuasion and consent to the common bond, and lent a higher tone to the work of propaganda and proselytism. Trade unions became more and more free: not only the development of their organizing powers, but also the increase of their internal freedom became the mark of their progress and attested a real emancipation of conscience.

The value of these associations, apart from their relation to external forces and their opposition to organizations of masters, which they have succeeded in so far balancing as to equalize the two parties to the contract of labour, appears also in the internal relations of their members. The men who had known nothing of social life except the heavy chains of dependence, learnt to deal like men with other men on a footing of equality; to discuss, to argue, to persuade, to criticize. They found currents of thought taking shape and struggling for mastery within these bodies, with the consequent emergence of synthetic talent, the political temperament of the statesman. Seen from outside, as a weapon of economic warfare, the trade union appears as something narrow and incomplete; but seen from within, it reveals the ferment of a whole human world, a complete miniature political organism, in which economic factors are intertwined with all the other elements of psychological life; in which the controlling minds find at their disposal a rich variety of human points of view.

Socialism in action thus contains Liberal and democratic motives of great importance. How could it be otherwise, when Socialism was born with freedom, drew its strength from the crisis of Liberalism, and has adapted itself to the forms of the Liberal State and Liberal politics? The necessity of living together has an educational force capable of overcoming the bigotry and rigidity of any theory. By the mere fact that Socialism demanded freedom for its organizations, it was compelled to submit in some degree to the laws of freedom; by the mere fact that it entered into relations with other political and social currents within one and the same State, it was bound to submit to the play of political competition, in which it found its abstract theoretical schematism of less practical value than the mature experience already won by Liberalism. This was an invaluable training for the young Socialist party; a school of life, in the highest sense of the word, teaching it to distinguish the feasible and the chimerical, the partial and the universal, administration and government. Socialism began to learn the barrenness of force and the value of consent, and moral factors generally, in government, and the profound transformation which strictly economic interests undergo when brought into the focus of political activity. It increased its power of penetration and psychological synthesis, to make up for its loss in formal theoretical consistency.

On the other hand, the rise of Socialism has been of great value to Liberalism. It has shown that the problem of freedom cannot be disposed of by an abstract declaration of rights, leaving the stronger in a position to vindicate their own rights to the detriment of the weaker; but that this declaration must be supplemented by practical sanctions and means towards vindicating these rights for all. Such a task implies that formal respect for the freedom of individuals must sometimes be subordinated to emphasis on the effective content of this freedom, and wholly surrendered when it is found tantamount to an instrument of oppression. This is *par excellence* the case with the freedom of the contract of labour, which has permitted unscrupulous employers to conceal a policy of slavery beneath a cloak of Liberalism.

By following the action of Socialism for the improvement of wages and the general condition of the working classes, Liberalism has had occasion to see how groundless were the arguments by which employers justified their stubborn resistance. So far from destroying profits and capital, these improvements, by raising the productive powers of labour, became a means of industrial progress and of consequent welfare for all classes. This discovery brought about a profound change in the attitude of Liberal policy towards the social problem. Whereas at first it regarded this as a strictly economic problem, and interpreted non-intervention on the part of the State as due to a mere lack of interest in economic problems as such, it now began to understand that there is such a thing as a wages policy, or, in other words, that here too the economic element is fused in a wider synthesis in which the moral factors of production are the main point at issue. The elevation of the labourer into a man is a gain not only for Society at large, as an association of men, but also for economic society in particular, as an organization of forces for the production of wealth.

Finally, Liberalism came to see in the self-governing associations of workmen, due to the spontaneous activity of the men themselves, an example of those autonomous bodies which it regards as expressing the creative energy of free individuals and providing the best safeguard of collective freedom against all forms of government tyranny. This recognition is certainly not free from serious reservations, which we shall not here repeat, because they have their ground in the historical materialism which inspires such associations; but together with these reservations, there is also the hope that their immanent spirit of liberty may vanquish everything in them that still impedes its development.

IV

CHURCH AND STATE

§ 1. LIBERALISM AND ORGANIZED RELIGION

A STUDY of the Liberal view of the relations between Church and State must begin by distinguishing protestant from Catholic countries.

For the Germanic peoples, the great consequence of the Reformation was the break-up of the spiritual and political unity of the Empire and the creation of a plurality of particular and autonomous States. At first this break-up favoured the cessation of the long-standing conflict between Church and State. The Empire was Catholic indeed, but in this very catholicity it had an invincible rival in the Roman Church, itself organized in the form of a State; by the Treaty of Augsburg the new Germanic States acquired the right of sovereign control over the religious bodies of their respective territories. The tendency to unite the Church and the State made headway in all reformed countries, not only where the spirit of the Reformation was slender, as in Tudor England, but also where it was most robust, as in Calvin's Geneva.

But if in this respect the Reformation was one of the most potent factors in the monarchical absolutism of the modern age, in another way it contained in itself the antidote to the enslavement of the religious consciousness by the State. Illiberal and theocratic in its manifestations, it was nevertheless based upon an act of freedom and an invincible love of free thought. Hence, wherever it established itself, it gave rise by a kind of spontaneous generation to innumerable sects, whose simultaneous existence within a single State counterbalanced the tendency to political and religious unification, and implied a dissociation of Church from State in fact, whatever might be the case in theory.

Moreover the Reformation, arising as it did from a profound religious feeling, was bound at heart to recoil from the

paralysing servility of a State religion. A parliament or a
monarch, imposing doctrine and cult by force, destroyed its
significance and its spiritual energies by degrading a mystical
love of the divine into an instrument of worldly policy. Faith
and feeling obey no command. What the State can win from
the individual is only an outward conformity of acts and a
hypocritical consent, not only destitute of all religious value,
but actually deleterious to the character of the citizen. This
explains why their conscience drove Protestants to rebel
against the State religion which Protestantism had itself
created, and to claim freedom of worship. The struggles of
the English puritans against the pharisaical legalism of the
Thirty-nine Articles had their origin in a deep-seated religious fervour.

The old conflict thus began again by the consent of both
conflicting parties, agreeing to redistinguish what had lately
been confounded. The State, confronted by different sects,
was compelled by degrees to distinguish its own interests from
those of any one sect as distinct from others, in order to avoid
incurring the hostility of the sects and permitting a religious
crisis to degenerate into a political crisis. The sects, on the
other hand, rejected the protection of the State, as depriving
their propagandists and proselytes of spontaneity and fervour.

The principle of religious freedom, an indirect but lasting
result of the Reformation, thus finds practical expression in
the policy tending to separate Church from State, which finds
adherents among both clergy and laity in Protestant countries. The meaning and limitations of this separatism will be
explained in the sequel ; here we must only point out that,
granted its origin, it is wholly free from the spirit of irreligion
and scepticism often marking a separatistic policy in Catholic
countries. In Protestant countries, both Church and State
have organized themselves progressively on the principle of
the emancipation of conscience, and the distinction which at
a certain point divides this historical process into two parts,
or is beginning to divide it, for the end is not yet, does not
imply that the two branches of the stream do not meet again
in the unity of the individual ; on the contrary, it implies that

they do so meet. Only the spontaneity of the individual consciousness can resolve the discord within the spiritual life
between earthly reality and heavenly hopes. Apart from this
free solution, there can only be either a State oppressing a
Church, or a Church oppressing a State, neither able to throw
off the other, since each is equally and eternally rooted in the
human spirit. Alternatively, Church and State may conspire
to oppress the individual, when their common triumph only
serves to dry up the springs which feed them both. The
periods of theocratic rule are those at which all civilization
is stagnant, and the State is itself paralysed in its attempt to
oppress the individual.

In Catholic countries, during the formation of modern
monarchies, we can observe an effort towards the unification
of politics and religion analogous to that in the reformed
monarchies. The Articles of the Gallican Church, and, later,
Febronianism or Josephism in Austria, assert the sovereignty
of the State in matters of cult, and attempt to detach the
national Church, so far as possible, from Rome. In these
cases, unlike Protestant governments, monarchical absolutism encountered no serious resistance on the part of popular
religious feeling, because the authoritarian spirit of the
Counter-Reformation had dried up its sources, and the
educated classes, imbued with deistical or atheistical rationalism, supported ecclesiastical reform more out of hatred to
clericalism than out of love for religion.

The vital task of defending the individual conscience against
State oppression, which religious feeling could not discharge
in Catholic countries, was undertaken by the Roman Church ;
which thus, in spite of its theocratic principles, performed a
great Liberal function in modern Society. By a providential
law of compensation, where the individual was less able to
resist the State, he was given as guardian of his faith a Church,
unlike the reformed Churches, claiming complete independence of the State and having an organization of its own
capable of resisting the claims of monarchical absolutism.

The struggle between Church and State during the modern
period thus forms one of the most striking episodes of Liberal-

ism. Its deepest Liberal significance lies, not in the attempt of the State to assert its independence, and even control, of the Church; nor in the attempt of the Church to resist interference on the part of the State; for, as we know, each of these liberties conceals an aspect of servility; but in their conflict itself, as cancelling out many of their several claims, and thus facilitating the free development of the individual conscience.

But the fact that support against the excessive claims of the State came to the individual from without, and that the Church which provided it was a political organization complete in itself, gave to the providential conflict of the two powers the character and significance of a struggle between external forces, in which the individual figured rather as a spectator than as a participant. This necessarily led to the illusion that his fate was not in his own hands; that his salvation was to come by taking the side of one or other combatant, and looking upon it as the victor in a gladiatorial contest. At the same time a true solution of the conflict, which could only come about within the sphere of consciousness itself, was deferred by treating it as something external to consciousness. The partisans of the State declared war on the Church in the name of the rights of reason and liberty; whereas it was the Church that was organizing the forces of defence against the concentration of State power which threatened to suppress liberty and reason. The triumph of State idolatry would have meant the unopposed reign of that monstrous force terribly, but transiently, exemplified by the Convention, through which the rational State devoured its own offspring. On the other hand, the partisans of the Church, in the name of the freedom of Rome, would have rekindled by their victory the fires of the Inquisition. Happily, the economy of historical reason effected a just distribution of illusions between these Ghibellines and Guelphs, so that each cancelled the other and the fatal consequences of a union of powers were averted.

§ 2. THE CATHOLIC CHURCH AND LIBERTY

A just view of the conflict between Church and State as materially promoting liberty was made more difficult to Liberalism both by an exaggerated confidence in the State, with which, as its own offspring, Liberalism was more familiar, and also by an exaggerated distrust of the Church, whose activity was inspired by manifestly illiberal principles. Few could understand that the presence of the rational and Liberal State did not relieve reason of the task of criticism and limitation, but made this task even more urgent. The first lesson of modern rationalism is that reason must begin by distrusting itself and subjecting its own work to critical examination. In the sphere of politics, this means that the rationality of the Liberal State lies not in the unlimited extent of its powers, but in its ability to impose limits on itself, to prevent the rule of reason from degenerating into the rule of dogma, and to ensure that the triumph of truth shall not close the road to the laborious process by which truth itself is reached.

Liberals, and democrats still more, have sometimes forgotten this warning in their relations with the Church, which they have sometimes wished to deprive of the rights of free citizenship in the State, without realizing that by so doing they were degrading their Liberalism into a form of dogmatic absolutism.

The Church, by its reactionary attitude, certainly gave occasion for this recrudescence of anti-clerical spirit, which has deformed Liberal policy in many Catholic countries. The peculiar situation of the Holy See, during the period of Italian unification, aggravated the Catholic Church's opposition to Liberalism by the expressions of a merely transitory hostility and bitterness. But at bottom there is a permanent reason for this opposition, independent of all transitory facts, in the authoritarian structure of the Church, as claiming to be invested with power from above ; in its doctrine of sin, redemption, and grace, implying the fallen character of human liberty and reason, and the need of external aid ; and in the function which it claims, of a supernatural mediator between man and God : whereas Liberalism assumes that, without any intermediary and by his own unaided efforts, man is fully able to realize all the values of the spiritual life.

If we wish to realize the distance which separates the Catholic Church from modern Liberalism, we may take as our standard, not the *Syllabus,* in which the distance is over-emphasized by certain accidental historical facts, but a far more moderate document, representing the limit of the concessions which the nineteenth-century Church thought itself able to make towards the Liberalism of its time: the Encyclical *Libertas* of Leo XIII.

Here liberty is described as a supremely noble gift, proper only to reasonable beings, and conferring on man the dignity of completely controlling his own actions. His rationality consists in the fact that human reason discovers the contingent character of each and all of the goods which surround it, and therefore, excluding the necessity of embracing them in its own despite, leaves the will free to choose that which is pleasing to it.

Reason thus comes into play, not (in spite of first appearances) to sanction freedom as a spiritual value, and to assert its own essential connexion with it, but to declare its contingent character. The Encyclical itself takes care to emphasize this fundamental opposition to modern Liberalism, by developing a whole series of contradictions on points of detail. The Liberal theory, it says, claims that in the practical life there is no divine power to be obeyed, but that every one is a law to himself, and makes himself the supreme principle, source, and criterion of truth. Hence arises that moral philosophy which is described as ' independent '; which, by releasing the human will from observance of divine precepts, under colour of liberty, bestows on man an unbridled licence. Once granted that man has no ' superior ', it follows that natural and civil Society depends not on a principle external and superior to man, but on the free will of each. Hence public power emanates from the people as its original source; and just as for each individual the only guide and rule of life is his individual reason, so, for the public life of all, the only guide and rule is the reason of all.

In order to show by comparison the opposite consequences to which the two conceptions lead, the Encyclical enumerates the so-called modern liberties, pronouncing its own judgement and interpretation of each.

In the first place, there is the liberty of worship, which means that every one is free to profess what religion he pleases, or none at all. Thus, ' leaving to man the power of professing any religion, it gives him the power of forgetting or distorting at his pleasure the most sacred of all duties, and thus turning his back upon the highest and immutable good and his face towards evil : which is not liberty, but the licence and servitude of a mind hardened in sin '. Reason and justice condemn the atheistical State, or, which is the same thing, the State indifferent to forms of worship and extending the same rights to all : 'granted then that a religion must be professed by the State, that must be professed which is alone true ; and this is not difficult to recognize by the marks of truth which visibly distinguish it, especially in Catholic countries.' Here, passing over the weaknesses and ambiguities in the argument, the practical conclusion is that freedom of worship is restricted to Catholic worship.

As for the liberty of speech and the press, the Encyclical recognizes that unless this is properly tempered, unless limit and measure are observed, this cannot be a right. True and honourable things, except as the rules of prudence may demand, have a right to be propagated freely and to become so far as possible matter of common knowledge ; but errors, diseases of the mind, vices, corruption of heart or manners, ought to be diligently repressed by public authority, to prevent their being disseminated to the common detriment.

But who can distinguish the true and honourable from the false and vicious? Obviously, the Church ; hence liberty of speech and press, like liberty of worship, holds good only within the circle of the Church.

A similar judgement must be passed, continues the Encyclical, on what is called liberty of instruction. Jesus said that only the truth makes us free ; and since the Church is the depositary of truth, that instruction alone is free which agrees with the precepts of the Church; consequently, every other form must be forbidden.

We need not pursue this summary farther, in order to show that the freedom which the Church claims for itself is, from the individual's point of view, sheer slavery; and that if the doctrine here expounded could be sanctioned by the State, which it would if the union or agreement between State and Church, demanded by the Encyclical, were effected, it would imply the most paralysing oppression of human conscience.

But the Liberals, who in the name of a higher conception of liberty would prevent the Church from professing this doctrine, and would subject it to State control, as is demanded by those who favour a new reform of Catholicism, degrade themselves by this very act to the level of the view they are opposing, and convert their own Liberalism into an equally oppressive and intolerable dogma.

The real superiority of the Liberal theory is revealed by its gift of free citizenship even to the most illiberal opposition, owing to its profound conviction that such an opposition is not only impotent to prevail over the rational and free activities of the mind, but is bound to develop and improve by contact with them.

The freedom of the Church, in its instruction and ministry, redeems the servitude of the believer towards dogma, which in a theocratic or other compulsive system would be intolerable and degrading, and gives it its proper place in the life of the mind, by the fact that it is freely chosen and an act of spontaneous submission. Thus referred back to the intimacy of conscience, religious doctrines and practices acquire a nobility and purity of which compulsion in any form would deprive them. In a free State, as the most intelligent Liberals have clearly recognized, the positive values of Christianity emerge of themselves; political society in its own interest makes manners become more humane, fosters benevolent and sociable feelings, and lightens the task of law and authority.

One of the most undeniable duties, as the Encyclical *Libertas* warns its readers, is to respect authority and obey just laws, in order that in the strength and vigilance of the law the citizen may find protection and remedy against the violence of the wicked. Legitimate power is of God, and he who resists power resists the ordinance of God; by which principles obedience is greatly ennobled, becoming submission to a righteous and august authority. Thus, adds the Encyclical, where the right to command is absent, it becomes a duty to disobey men in order to obey God : in this way, the road being blocked to tyrannical governments, the State cannot concentrate everything in itself; the citizen, the family, every member of Society, will be able to live in security, and true freedom, which consists in every one's ability to live according to law and right reason, will be the possession of all. Here the possibility of a conflict between the Church and the powers of the State is clearly contemplated ; but this conflict is no obstacle to liberty, but actually promotes it, by facilitating the destruction of an authority which may oppress the conscience of the individual. And no one who reflects upon the harshly authoritarian character of modern democratic civilization can deny that the resistance of the Church to the ' tyranny ' of the State, though far from Liberal in its inmost motive, may represent in point of fact a protection and defence of liberty.

§ 3. SEPARATISM: ITS NATURE AND MEANING

These and similar Liberal values attaching to religion depend upon the political idea which by separating the Church from the State preserves the autonomy of the Church in its own proper vocation, and prevents it from becoming an instrument of tyranny. Separatism is thus a strictly Liberal doctrine, which in the course of history has been accepted by those Catholics who have been most convinced that the prestige and efficacy of religion depend upon conscience in all its intimacy, and by those politicians who have been most aware that the freedom of the Church is better adapted than any legal authority, or any expedient in the nature of a *concordat*, to strengthen the spiritual sources of the life of the State.

We have already laid down the main lines of separatism, in examining the programme of the Italian Right; we will now complete and generalize our discussion. Separation is a legal and political term, not, as some have misunderstood it, a philosophical. It does not imply a dualism between soul and body, the spiritual and the temporal, the divine and the earthly; it implies a separation between two historical institutions, not between two moments in a spiritual dialectic. Thus separation has a contingent character and a merely approximative significance; because two institutions, which in the course of their development have come into contact and conflict in a thousand ways, cannot in practice be distinguished from one another with formal preciseness.

Separatism, in its limited legal and political sense, is a limiting conception, tending to prevent the State, so far as possible, from interfering in ecclesiastical worship and doctrine, and conversely to prevent the Church from competing with the State in those tasks which the internal structure of the State marks out as its own. The sovereignty of the State is in no way compromised, because the liberty enjoyed by the Church is simply the liberty of common rights, within the limits of the laws of the State, which all individuals and all associations equally enjoy.

Nor is the State reduced to agnosticism, as if its refusal to intervene in the establishment of dogma and worship deprived it of a doctrine of its own. It is certainly true that the conception of separatism, which in the course of its historical development has worked in an intellectual atmosphere of positivism and agnosticism, has often been influenced by this atmosphere; [1] but these influences are in substance accidental, and can be easily dissociated from it. In declining to intervene in doctrinal matters belonging to the sphere of organized religion, the State is asserting a doctrine of its own. It is taking its stand on the assertion that the individual conscience is able by itself to achieve a religious view of life, and can manifest its sense of the

[1] See, for example, the theory of Minghetti quoted above (p. 338, note).

divine in all its purity only in a spontaneous and autonomous manner. It is too often forgotten, when the doctrine of the Liberal State is crystallized into a dogma, that it really consists in freedom, and that its source lies therefore in the individual. In the same sense the Liberal State may be called agnostic in economic questions, because it leaves the care of economic interests to the initiative of private persons ; whereas here, too, the apparent absence of State activity is really the presence of a higher activity, namely the State's confidence in the powers of the individual. Thus in both cases the limit to the action of the State is imposed not by a principle outside or higher than the State, which would be a proof of agnosticism, but by a principle internal to the State, and recognized by it, so far as it is a Liberal State, as its own generating principle.

Nor can the State be called atheistic, if, by extending identical rights to all forms of worship, it shows a recognition of their higher divine kinship in spite of their differences of name and form. This recognition is due not to a new religious formula, wider than the others, invented by the State, but simply to the respect which it has for the conscience of individuals. Granted that the spontaneous manifestations of conscience may have a religious significance, it follows that the differentiation which necessarily springs from this free activity also has its significance.

A reconciliation, like that desired by the partisans of union, between reason and faith, between the duties of the citizen and the believer, will never be reached through the relation between two positive institutions like the Church and the State ; it can only be the personal act of the individual. Only in the intimacy of consciousness can there arise that vital dialectic between opposed values, divine and earthly, mystical and rational, which some would in vain endeavour to transfer to historical institutions of fixed and largely unchangeable character. All that the State and the Church can do is to remove every obstacle and to facilitate the work of the individual, leaving him master of his own fate. If they attempt to impose upon him a ready-made solution, a theoretical view of the problem of his own inner life, they at once degrade it and pervert its proper function.

So interpreted, the historical rivalry between Church and State is, as we have already said, a precious guarantee of freedom, sheltering the conscience of the individual against the dangers of a too great concentration of power. Separatism, as a new phrase in the age-long struggle, preserves the essential historical motive, but at the same time rises above the terms of the conflict, by subordinating both combatants equally to the profounder demands of the life and development of the human spirit.

V

FREEDOM AND NATIONALITY

§ 1. NATIONALITIES

DURING the nineteenth century Liberalism and national feeling[1] arose and developed together. Freedom inspired not only a struggle for the assertion of nationality on the part of peoples not yet politically united, but also an international policy, among nations already formed, favourable to such claims.

What is the cause of this relation? It may at first sight seem strange that freedom, in the individualistic sense in which it was understood at the beginning of the nineteenth century, should have served as the foundation for a group of claims concerned with an organic reality formed in the cause of an age-long tradition. How could that same Liberalism which, in the name of the rights of man, had claimed to annul the traditions of the past, set itself up, immediately after the French Revolution, as the interpreter and champion of these same traditions? Such a task might seem more suited to the reactionary spirit of the Restoration, the declared partisan of a return to the past.

And in fact, as we have already seen, a reactionary view of the importance of the nation was actually put forward by De Maistre, who considered it as composed entirely of the king and the aristocracy, the institutions rooted in a distant past and threatened with destruction by the Liberal revolution. Wider and more comprehensive, but equally traditional in character, is the national conception of German Romanticism, which tends to emphasize all the historical elements

---

[1] I do not say nationalism, because in the sequel this word has acquired a different and in some respects opposite significance. Johannet, in order to indicate this difference, thinks it desirable to coin a new term, and to distinguish *Nationalitaires* from *Nationalistes*: cf. *Le Principe des Nationalités*, Paris, 1918.

that go to make up the spirit of a people : race, language, religion, customs, institutions ; and opposes this living and organic complex to the abstract conventions by which Liberal contractualism attempts to unite a congeries of atoms into a State.

But these historical elements, which Romanticism with the passion of the scholar sets itself to study and bring to life, though necessary to every nation, cannot by themselves make a nationality. How could a distant past exist by itself, unless something in the present brought it back to life? Flourishing nations have been seen to decay and fall, even while all the elementary conditions of their rise persisted. If the force of tradition is reduced to a passive habit or mechanism, it is subjected to that perpetual loss of energy which every mechanical system undergoes through friction and the resistance of its environment. And even if an ancient nation might succeed in surviving through strength drawn from this source, how could a new nation form itself into a living unity, by uniting and fusing the various elements of its nature and history? Unity implies a unifying force, a present ability to grasp and dominate the past, without which there can be no nation, but only fragments and reminiscences of national life. The mistake of reactionary Romanticism was to believe that the German nation could now exist simply because it had existed in the past; and to try anachronistically to revive, by the magic of culture, a dead historical world. Yet even so it served the national cause; but only by its present cultural efforts, and not in virtue of the immovable and lifeless object of its contemplation and homesick longings.

Nationality, then, is an affirmative and synthetic force, not unlike that which forms various psychological elements and the manifold experiences of life into the personality of a single individual. The development of the nation and of the individual is regulated by analogous laws and inspired by analogous impulses.

Owing to this affinity, the rise of a nation exhibits all the Liberal characteristics which the spirit of reaction attempted to suppress as incompatible with nationality. Nations, no less than individuals, are creatures of liberty. The political experience of absolutism demonstrates, with nations as with individuals, that compulsion only generates revolt and impels national feeling to assert itself against the oppressor. No violent annexation of foreign territory can subject and absorb the spirit of its inhabitants; even when the work of oppression is most insidious, as in the case of the French Revolutionaries, with their attempt to revive the programme of absolutism by conquering people's minds first and their countries after, it achieves in the end an opposite result to that which it expects; it rouses the nations indeed, but rouses them against the oppressing nation. Such facts, from the beginning of the nineteenth century, threw into strong relief the spontaneous and autonomous consent which forms the basis of the national organism. But it is a peculiar kind of consent, very different from the mere legal and contractual consent on which the State is built according to the eighteenth-century school of natural rights. So lively indeed was the perception of this difference, that the Liberal consciousness frequently opposed the nation to the State, and, in its progress from its early atomistic phase to a more organic phase, was led to transfer to the nation the character and the value which it denied to the State, because the latter, being reduced to a mere legal fiction, could no longer bear their weight.

Attempts were certainly made to interpret this national consent in terms of the old theory of natural rights : and this was the error exactly opposite to that of reactionary Romanticism, because consisting in a one-sided and exclusive emphasis upon will, in its immediate expression, to the detriment of history and tradition. This is the error of what are known as plebiscites, which in fact are nothing but a reminiscence of the old social contract converted into a national contract. Experience has abundantly shown the falsifications, mutilations, and misinterpretations to which plebiscites are liable, when made to serve as the criterion of a declaration of national rights. Not that the idea of an expression of consent is erroneous; what is erroneous is the claim to restrict this expression to an instantaneous and isolated act, often swayed by passion or dictated by external force ; the consent which goes to make a national conscious-ness is, as Renan said, a plebiscite of every day, a silent continuity of action which unites the present to the past in an uninterrupted history.

The fact that Liberalism after the Revolution regarded the nation as prior in origin and value to the State, understood as the outcome of convention and the organ of external legal defence, was a providential means of elevating its conscious-ness of the State itself. The nation, conceived as an auto-nomous organism capable of self-government, contained in itself, at least in embryo, the new national State towards which Liberalism, its merely negative and critical phase left behind, was advancing. In the chief national movements of the nineteenth century, in Germany and in Italy, the nation first arises as a cultural unity, which, as in the case of Ger-many, may even be indifferent to political unity ; but, as its organization progresses, it tends to complete itself and find the seal of its completion in the form of the State.

The growth of the new national States displays in all its vigour the Liberal spirit immanent in their origin. What was a dynastic motive or a motive of State becomes a national motive ; every political act is identified with the people from which it proceeds and whose peculiar character it expresses. The Liberal idea of the State as the self-government of the people is realized in the national State, which finds in the nation underlying it that harmonious consent of racially homogeneous individuals which no abstract constitution could express, and finds there at the same time all the his-torical and traditional elements which confirm this consent and make it permanent, purging it of the inconstant and arbitrary character of an isolated and ephemeral declaration of will. If the forces of conservation and of progress, tradi-tion and reason, are both equally essential to the Liberal State, as we have seen that they are, the national organism may be regarded as an inexhaustible reservoir of both forces, consistently with the synthetic character of its nature.

These Liberal values are most prominent in the political unification of those nations which, like Germany and Italy, rise to a new life in the nineteenth century; but in those which were already organized into States, the revelation of their character through liberty and self-government, as opposed to the old administrative despotism, is no less remarkable. The solidity of their historical fabric was diminished and impaired by the persistence of the old dualism between the prince and the people, and the State stood over against the nation as something external and hostile. Once this distinction was broken down, all the elements of national life, whose political expression was formerly indirect and to some extent feeble, began to develop freely and lent new energy to the political movements which the old dynasties had set on foot but could not bring to a conclusion. It is sufficient to recall the success of Revolutionary France in developing the policy of Louis XIV.

Thus, partly by its elevation to the dignity of a State, partly by vitalizing States already in existence, nationality, in the nineteenth century, formed the true centre of gravity in European politics. The mutual relations between nationalities displayed, at least at first, the Liberal spirit which had inspired their rise. If in the past peoples had been bought and sold like articles of trade, they now began to be treated as subjects of rights, as individualities worthy of recognition and respect. They appeared as higher and more complex incarnations of that human personality which asserted its moral and political significance at the Revolution ; and hence all the principles originally formulated with reference to individuals were now applied by analogy to nations. No nation had the right to invade the sphere of another ; a nation's aspirations towards independence were worthy of encouragement by older nations, as the acts of a nascent personality ; the smaller and poorer nations had an equal right to existence with the greatest.

This did not mean that these demands were everywhere respected ; but only that in the nineteenth century they began to be regarded as moral principles governing political prac-

tice in the same way in which they governed relations between individuals, between whom the proclamation of Liberal
principles does not in fact do away with oppression and
injury, but proclaims the existence of a right and of the duty
to respect it. And the practical significance of these principles, in the sphere of international relations, appeared in the
policy of the European Powers towards Greece, Belgium, and
Italy; in the moral isolation of Austria owing to her contempt of nationality; and in general in the growing consciousness of the limits imposed by the existence of civilized
nations upon expansion and conquest. The division of territories belonging to foreign nations, which was judged by the
eighteenth century as a question in which motives of State
alone were concerned, found itself opposed in the nineteenth
century by a moral judgement capable of translating itself
into political action.

It is on these ethical and Liberal principles that international politics are founded. The principle of non-intervention in the internal affairs of another people is the first
and most elementary recognition of national personality. It
requires a State not only to refrain from acts of intervention,
but also to frustrate attempts at such acts on the part of
others. This is the positive and active side of the negative
principle which regulated the relations between the European Powers during the period when the new national States
were growing up.

The ideal of Liberalism in international affairs is that the
nations should transcend the phase of political rivalry, should
live together in peace, and, by the active and free exchange
of economic and cultural goods, should satisfy each other's
needs and develop in the best way their respective talents.
From this point of view the only justifiable kind of war is the
national war, by which the political unification of a nation
is brought about; once this end is achieved, competitions and
rivalries, though still existing, must be transferred to another
field on which they can be more effectively resolved and
laid to rest. A war intended to settle a commercial conflict
between two nations is madness, because it ends by destroy-

ing not only that for which the parties are contending but more important forms of wealth; the only form which such a conflict can take, given the end in view, is a competition leading to the triumph of the strongest, but stimulating all alike to self-improvement.

The international policy of nineteenth-century Liberalism thus appeared as a great rationalistic simplification of the tangled skein created by motives of dynasty and State in the period of absolute monarchy. It was in fact only a higher stage of the same process of simplification which inspired the new relations of individuals within Society, liberated from the old fetters of custom and compulsion. And indeed the relation which Liberalism is trying to create between nation and nation is precisely a kind of society; not a bureaucratically ordered association, like that which the dominant spirit of democracy tried to create after the Great War, but a society more articulated and more free, growing up spontaneously and organically out of relations subsisting less between governments than between peoples.

No one can fail to recognize that, Utopian though this conception is in part, the nineteenth century did see the growth of an active spirit of international sociability. The relations between peoples became more active and more fertile, the wealth of civilization became the object of wider mutual exchange; the spiritual originality of each nation found, in the new society of nations, an expression more truly its own and at the same time of more universal human significance.

§ 2. NATIONALISM

But there is a point beyond which the principles of liberty and equality, in their extension from the individual to the nation, cannot be applied. Above the individual there is a State, guaranteeing by its force the legal equality and freedom of all; above nations organized into States, there is no higher safe-guarding power. Hence the freedom which with individuals takes the shape of rights, in the case of States undergoes no such transformation, and may be converted by the absence of any superior sanction into arbitrary action and the victory of the stronger. International society, with its liberal and moral convictions, liable as these are to issue in practical sanctions, certainly exercises a restraining influence upon outbreaks of licence; yet the lack of a legal standard, and an authority expressly destined to enforce respect for it, renders the rights of nations precarious and often results in an appeal to the uncertain arbitration of the sword.

Moreover, there is in the personality of a nation something less definite and more questionable than in that of an individual. What nation is entirely self-contained and self-sufficient, and what racial group is wholly unable to live a life of its own, whether through spiritual exhaustion, or through inclusion in a larger national complex, or because it is composed of an inextricable confusion of heterogeneous elements? It is often difficult to decide. But even where it is possible, must it be asserted as an axomatic principle, that the destinies of a great nation, organically formed, must be at the mercy of trivial and fruitless national vanities bent upon dividing it? And where two nations claim a national right over a single district, who ought to act as judge?

The principle of nationality is one of those principles which must be accepted in the main and subject to discussion in detail, in the light of reasons of State. This truth was first realized at the time when Liberalism was at its zenith, and served to moderate Utopian desires and turn the attention of Liberals to more concrete questions. At bottom, the international policy of Liberalism, as summed up in the idea of a society of nations, was the negation of a policy. Hence the classical maxim: 'Let peoples have as many points of contact as possible, and their governments as few as possible.'

But the Liberals, finding themselves in power and confronted with controversial questions, began to feel the need of a policy in the proper sense of the word; and with practice they came to see that its main lines could only be those of the State—the national State, but still the State. This is similar to what we have seen in the case of the internal policy of Liberalism, which began by a negation of all State interference, in the interests of individual freedom, and ended by recognizing that without the State individual freedom vanishes.

But the State has a tradition of its own, a peculiar 'reason' which often overrides a vague and uncertain national feeling. Thus the Liberal policy of the great European States, without ceasing to be guided in the main by the principle of nationality, has by degrees turned back to the historical tasks of the preceding period, and thus imperceptibly inverted the original relation between nation and State. Whereas at first it was the nation which imposed its tendency on the State, it now receives it from the State, and in return only confers a richer nutriment of national energy upon the State's expansion.

But the inversion has not been, and could not be, the work of Liberalism, which confined itself to a prudent compromise between the old policy of State reasons and the new policy of nationalities. The determining influence has been that of other factors. The development of democracy has laid fresh emphasis upon the State, and reduced the importance of nationality by an excessive insistence upon international and humanitarian ideals. The very vitality of the new national States, working along an opposite but converging path, has made them increasingly dissatisfied with their natural boundaries and anxious to expand even to the detriment of other nations. These impulses towards an aggressive policy appeared at first indirectly, through commercial and colonial rivalries, but soon began to affect the relations between the States themselves.

Thus the principle of nationality was wholly overthrown. Each nation erected customs barriers against the rest, and gave every manifestation of its own activity a turn hostile to others; nations conceived and carried out plans of mutual destruction and enslavement. This policy found its theoretical expression in what was called nationalism, a conception which, in its logical development, involves the hegemony of one nation over all the rest, that is, a double negation of the principle of nationality, by denying the nationality both of the subject nations and of the conquering nations, neces-

sarily swamped by the absorption of elements so heterogeneous. In effect, the term nationalism may be replaced by
the more appropriate term imperialism, which expresses precisely the idea of a supra-national State.

In spite of appearances, then, nationalism rests not on the
idea of the nation, but on the idea of the State : that State
which, roused to new life and intenser activity by the acquisition of a rich national content, has ended by subjecting this
content to a form of its own which in the last resort oppresses
and crushes it.

This disastrous result appears not only in the international
policy of nationalism, but also, still more, in internal policy,
which assumes an authoritarian and despotic character in
order to subject the entire nation to the will of a handful of
politicians. Hence the alliance of the various European
nationalisms with the most reactionary parties in their respective countries; and hence their hostility to every Liberal point
of view, whose individualistic atomism they pretend to abhor,
while they really fear its insistence upon a popular consent
which they could never enjoy.

The most typical of these nationalistic tendencies is German nationalism, culminating during the War in the conception of a Central European super-State, and resting upon
the forces of Prussian *Junkertum*. English imperialism has a
character of its own, and shows traces of the Liberal experience acquired during its formation. French nationalism is
a hybrid mixture of legitimist traditions, genuinely national
chauvinism, and a literary pose.

The contrast between the new imperialistic attitude of the
great European States and the old Liberal spirit of nationality
appeared at its sharpest in the Great War, which was a
struggle both for hegemony and for national unification.
But the sequel of the War has not resolved the conflict between the two principles. From this point of view, as from
others which we are now to consider, the crisis of Liberalism
is not yet over.

VI

THE CRISIS OF LIBERALISM

§ 1. THE ECONOMIC ASPECTS OF THE CRISIS

THE account of the development of modern Liberalism given in the first and second parts of the present work has already laid bare the factors of the profound crisis which, beginning in the hour of triumph of the Liberal State, the State which seemed about to satisfy all the demands of freedom, increased constantly though imperceptibly in gravity, till, in our own days, it appears almost irreparable. This crisis has long been concealed by the survival of outward forms and historical institutions created by freedom, veiling an internal decay beneath an unbroken surface, and its whole gravity only appeared when finally the evil reached the surface and destroyed or decomposed certain parts of this also. The alarm which then broke out was the more violent in proportion as the previous confidence had been careless and complete; the first exaggeration, as often, led to the second, its opposite in everything except the insufficiency of its grounds.

We shall here attempt a calm and accurate diagnosis of the case, by the analytical methods of a physician who examines all the limbs, even those which seem least affected by the symptoms of disease; for in the political organism, no less than in the physiological, everything is connected with everything else.

Let us begin with the simplest elements of European Liberalism, which, as we know, are the economic. Here we have distinguished two forms, or rather two general types of Liberal outlook and institutions, the one based chiefly upon land, the other on industry. The first, to which in its most complex historical structure we have alternatively given the name of continental, has its origin in the economic and legal institution of modern or *bourgeois* property, growing up by degrees in the age of the great monarchies, but universalized and codified by the French Revolution. The fundamental principle of this Liberalism is the independence of the free landowner, expressed through constitutional guarantism, local self-government, and unpaid political and administrative functions. Its best historical manifestations are the French constitutionalism of the Restoration and the age of Louis-Philippe, and that of the Right in Italian history. These two currents of Liberalism draw their inspiration from the English Liberalism of the eighteenth century, transformed and purged of its particularism and feudalism by the great *bourgeois* experience of the Revolution.

Now during the second half of the nineteenth century the economic and political independence of the landowners was compromised and undermined by a number of convergent causes. First and foremost, the great development of industry progressively diminished the relative importance of landed property. Granted the protectionistic character generally assumed by continental industrialism, agricultural interests are either sacrificed by tariffs intended to support industry in an artificial and parasitic situation, as in Italy, or else they join hands with industry to impose upon themselves the bond of a common protectionism, as in France and Germany. This second case is equally fatal to the Liberal spirit of the landowners, though they preserve much of their original power by compromise and adaptation. They learn from their rivals and allies, the manufacturers, to consider the State as an instrument which they can control in order to secure their own selfish interests. They lose their character as a disinterested and governing general class; their sense of autonomy and their power of criticism diminish; and the idea of power takes in their minds the place of the idea of freedom.

To this fundamental consideration others may be added, derived from the great progress in agricultural methods effected during the nineteenth century. The industrialization of agriculture, which has proved so beneficial to the economic life of Europe, has from a political point of view lowered the quality of the governing class. The tendency to assimilate the status of land to that of personal property, already displayed by the French Revolution, has been so accelerated by the overpowering influence of industrialism, that land has become entirely detached from the personality of the landlord, with which it was once indissolubly united ; it has consequently lost that peculiar force which it owed to a life spent in constant and unremitting contact with the soil. As Fourier's ideal of joint-stock property in land was progressively realized ; as all the traditional barriers which hindered and retarded the alienation of landed property, the relaxation of regulations concerning the rotation of crops, the precarious character of tenants' rights, and so forth, were by degrees broken down ; land, which in the past had been a force tending to mould character, was drawn into the vortex of modern individualism ; and since, owing to its natural resistance, it could not keep pace with the movement, it has ended by becoming a dead weight. Its great educational value has been for the most part lost ; the landowner has lost his love for his property, owing to the fact that he can at any time convert it into cash that can be otherwise and more profitably invested ; its essential and permanent demands have been subordinated to the momentary interests of a temporary owner; in a word, agriculture has become a minor form of investment for capital, among the least popular because among the slowest to yield a return. Landed property once reduced to the status of a personal possession, its old-established political character has waned, till finally the sense of an unpaid public function inherently bound up with the rights of the landowner has entirely disappeared.

The invasion of agriculture by industrialism has had the further consequence of creating a vast agricultural proletariate, without connexions or interests in a soil whose very fruits do not belong to it ; and has thus fostered crude and ill-considered hopes of socializing and nationalizing land, which have greatly contributed to the precarious condition of property and everything that depends upon it.

Another fundamental cause of the political crisis of the landowning class is bound up with the nature of continental

Liberalism. As we have seen, it regards property as an integral part of human personality; it therefore demands the extension of such rights to an ever-increasing number of individuals. Formally, this principle is unassailable, except at the cost of falling back into the old divisions of estate and denying *a priori* to a majority of human beings the power and the right to rise, by their own labour, to the status of a complete personality. The practical result of this principle has been the democratization of landed property; which, beginning with the French Revolution, has proceeded without intermission to the present day. But, as the soil has been broken up into more and more minute fractions, the political character of the agricultural classes has concurrently lost its distinguishing features. Burke may have been exaggerating when he said that the political influence of land is indissolubly bound up with the existence of great estates; but it is certainly the case that without properties of some size, the owners can possess neither economic independence nor the peculiar *forma mentis* of the landlord. If properties are too small, their owners' minds turn to other preoccupations, professions, or employments, and the cultivation of the land becomes a subsidiary occupation. In this way they lose interest in all essentially agricultural problems, and bring with them into public life an outlook formed by the experiences and demands of their chief occupation. An excessive economic subdivision of the land pulverizes it politically; it becomes less and less able to resist the aggressive forces of industry and finance, acting through great concentrated masses, and usurping, even in mainly agricultural countries, a disproportionate share of public power.

No doubt, this democratization has some good results; above all, the creation of a great class of small landowning cultivators. But up to now this class has done very little to express itself economically and socially; its dispersion over the face of the country, its lack of the spirit of association, its absorption in agricultural work, render it all but deaf to the call of politics. It is a reservoir for the future rather than a force now in action.

It may easily be inferred from the foregoing reflections that agricultural Liberalism, which formerly could rest upon a true governing class, has decayed by degrees, partly through the external pressure of industrialism, partly through the internal crisis of landed property. To-day things have reached the point where, even in agricultural countries, the land is hardly represented at all, at least under its own name, in political assemblies; and instead of bestowing its own peculiar form on public life, it receives from it an indirect and reflected form due to the influence of its own more or less distant offspring, the so-called liberal professions, which, springing up and growing as they have done on the margin of landed property, have ended by inverting the original relation of dependence, and exerting over the land an arbitrary and often unintelligent tyranny.

A different character attaches to the crisis of that industrial Liberalism which has been most conspicuously exemplified in nineteenth-century England, and has thence spread to the continent, and imparted something of its outlook to the classes that control certain exporting industries. Of this form of Liberalism, the policy of free trade is only a partial expression, confined to a single aspect of industrial activity; its ideal centre lies in the personality of the independent *entrepreneur*, who by his initiative and his unremitting and unprejudiced toil broke up the rigid fabric of the medieval artisan system, swept aside the relics of feudalism, and finally created political forms and institutions appropriate to himself.

But the free *entrepreneur* in his turn was a passing figure on the stage of history. He brought about the transformation of small industries into great, and was destined to disappear as soon as his work was complete. With the coming of great industry, isolated individual initiative yielded to the new demand for co-ordination and organization. Competition was replaced by the solidarity of the trust. The individual effort by which single enterprises were capitalized was succeeded by the methodical and mechanical canalization of capital through the banking system. Production and its products became increasingly impersonal; the manufacturer became an employee in a business now extending far beyond his personality.

The formation and the character of great modern joint-stock companies provide inestimable documents of the process by which capitalism and industrialism lose in individual tone what they gain in extension and connexion. The modern company is an authoritarian and bureaucratic State in embryo, with its courts, its hierarchies, and its skilfully designed machinery for distributing over the whole mass the living force accumulated at its centre. And the State itself, the political State *par excellence*, comes to model itself upon the new form of business; it appears as the supreme synthesis of productive forces, the way to which is prepared by the increasingly universal connexions uniting these forces to one another, and destined in its turn to take the part of a distributor in international economic Society. Thus the industrial classes, which formally saw in the State something hostile or at least foreign to their work, come to see in it their strongest ally, able to create prosperity for certain industries out of next to nothing, and to provide them with new markets. They yield themselves willingly to the encroachments of the State's power, which save them the trouble of self-development and self-improvement in order to live, and ensure them a life often degraded to the status of a courtier's, but prosperous and tranquil. The aggressive Liberalism of the past is replaced by nationalism and imperialism, creating lords of finance and industry, lords no less than those of ancient feudalism.

This movement of unification and concentration, proceeding from above, corresponds with a similar movement beginning from below, by the work of industrial democracy; which, opposed though it is to capitalism, is compelled to obey the same synthetic and organic laws, and the same impulse towards the capture and exploitation of the State. If it were necessary to provide a conclusive proof that the class struggle has a strictly social and non-political character, and that the political sphere reunites the elements which are divided in society, it would suffice to reflect on the close affinity which

connects the plutocratic policy of imperialism and nationalism with the democratic policy of Socialism. In both cases
the policy consists in making the State an instrument of
economic exploitation and political dictatorship, and thus
reviving the ancient forms of absolutism, turned to a new end.

Beneath the converging force of these two pressures, exercised from above and from beneath by industrial Society,
Liberal individualism finds itself all but crushed. But even
so there are certain resistances tending not altogether un-
successfully to counteract the pressure and create a more free
environment. Not all industries are equally concerned in the
rigid solidarity of the industrial system ; some of the greatest,
such as the cotton industry in England and the silk industry
in Italy, have a capacity for independent development and
are not only in no way indebted to State protectionism, but
are even impaired by a tariff system which, connecting them
indirectly with industries of a more parasitic kind, neutra-
lizes their natural advantages. For this reason they form a
strong centre of resistance for Liberalism and the tradition of
free trade.

Further, the tendency to unification and centralization
does not act with equal strength in all branches of industrial
activity. On the contrary, it is found that while the production of raw materials, such as steel and coal, becomes more
uniform, that of manufactures properly so called becomes
more diversified and individualized. Hence it is not true that
standardized and centralized great industry absorbs medium
and small industry, whose structure is more individualistic
and its movement more free ; in a certain sense it actually
facilitates its development, by offering it raw or semi-raw
materials upon which it can employ a highly specialized and
differentiated activity. Thus, if on the one hand the centri-
petal tendency of heavy industry destroys the autonomy of
the individual business, on the other hand the centrifugal
force of specialized production reintroduces a rich variety of
industrial organisms, whose importance consists in the autonomy of their initiative and the originality of their various
products. Thus reappears the figure of the free *entrepreneur*,

whose business is closely bound up with his personality and whose success depends on inventive talent, conscientious execution, and the selective function of competition, leading to technical improvements and the adaptation of products to the consumer's taste, rather than on an arbitrary protection by the State, which in this field proves wholly impotent.

But here, too, as in the case of the small and medium land-owning farmer, there is a reservoir of Liberalism for the future, rather than a power now in action. To-day, the economic forces which still dominate political life are those of heavy industry and high finance, in close mutual relation. Specialized manufactures, though representing the great majority of interests and activities in the total mass of production, exert an altogether inadequate influence on the control of public affairs, and are overwhelmed by the centralized industries, which control the most important elements of the political machine: finance, the press, and the government itself.

In conclusion, when we consider the economic situation in all its elements, agricultural and industrial, we find that it presents this paradox: a vast number of potential Liberal forces, diffused throughout the social organism, but unable as yet to find a political expression adequate to their extent, and serving to support an economic and political superstructure in great part parasitic, which suppresses them, impoverishes them, and keeps them prisoner. And this is precisely the most characteristic feature of the crisis affecting the forces of Liberalism: it is not that they are exhausted or destroyed, but that they are suppressed and imprisoned. Their vitality is proved by the very fact that in spite of adverse circumstances they survive, and support not only themselves but the forces which exploit them. Oppressed though they are by the weight of the State, they support this weight by their own strength. Yet they are no helots; subjection and exploitation make them restive; and they have not lost the power of reasserting themselves when the tyranny under which they are labouring becomes still wider and more arbitrary.

§ 2. THE POLITICAL CRISIS

These economic elements in the crisis of Liberalism have an indirect action; they work by modifying the social structure of the middle classes, on which Liberalism is essentially based. During the period when the middle classes were increasing in strength, their central position gave them an advantage, because it enabled them to attract elements both from above and from below, and, once consolidated, to confer stability on the whole fabric. But it became a disadvantage when industrial evolution polarized the interests of Society, and gave rise to a reverse attractive tendency towards the extremes of plutocracy and social democracy. Thus began a slow but constant erosion of the middle classes, whose fragments were thrown by this centrifugal action partly into the proletariate, and partly into the new *bourgeois* aristocracy, leaving the central nucleus reduced both in bulk and in coherence.

The effects of this erosion on the entire moral and political structure of the middle classes have been incalculable. The chief characteristic of their spirit from the time of the French Revolution onward was a profound consciousness of the universality of their social and political function. Sieyès said that the Third Estate was the nation; and this was true, not in the sense that no other classes except the *bourgeoisie* existed, but in the sense that the *bourgeois* forms of economic activity, legal feeling, and political organization, were valid for all classes, offering to each class opportunities of action commensurate with its strength, freedom of competition and opposition, and a guarantee of legality and justice. The Liberalism of the middle classes, at the period of their greatest expansion, expresses precisely this universality, which converts their particularistic quality, as an economic class, into the quality of a political governing class. The true greatness of this Liberalism appeared in the innumerable cases in which the *bourgeoisie* was able to postpone or even to sacrifice its own private interests to the public good, and accept the verdict of freedom even when given against itself.

This universalistic capacity of the middle classes has expressed itself in two main forms, corresponding to the two fundamental types of function which make up the activity of the State : one legal and one political. As we have already seen, the idea of the State of rights, implying in its most elementary significance a single law for all citizens, to whatever class they belong, is characteristic of the nineteenth-century *bourgeoisie*. In the political sphere, this same demand takes the practical form of the parliamentary system, giving all parties an opportunity of undertaking the government of the State, and providing in the opposition a means of ensuring that the governing party for the time being shall govern in the interests of all citizens.

Now the crisis of the middle classes, in its deeper aspect and motive, is a crisis of the legal and political consciousness, a weakening of the two main props of the Liberal régime. Here appears the indirect influence of the economic crisis. Feeling itself threatened by the rise of other classes, the *bourgeoisie* has reacted by opposing to them a class consciousness of its own, no less particularistic than theirs, with the inevitable result that from a general class it becomes a merely economic class. In order to live it has been compelled to lose, or at any rate to impair, what made its life worth living. History shows that as soon as social competition becomes aggressive, as soon as democracy and Socialism become threatening, the Liberal *bourgeoisie* stiffens into an attitude of defence to preserve its own private interests, and uses the power of the State, which is the power of the whole community, to bar the road to its opponents and secure its own conquests.

This is a necessity, not a crime. But once the selfish instinct of conservation has been aroused, it is reinforced by contact with other forms of selfishness, asserting themselves against it. Thus the *bourgeoisie* has felt not only the attack, but the spiritual influence, of its opponents : it has learned to think of the State as an instrument to serve its own ends ; of government as a business committee of the class in power ; and of the legal system as a means of domination. Historical materialism, originally a theory of one contending party, has become an article of belief for all, and has conferred its own character and direction upon the struggle. In this sense it is profoundly true that the nineteenth century saw the triumph of historical materialism. It did see the degradation of all moral, legal, and political values to an economic level, a perversion of all criteria to the ends of selfish and material interests.

This degradation is perceptible without distinction of party throughout the political atmosphere of the last few decades. Economic and social determinism has been regarded as the final and crowning expression of science; progress as a mechanical fact, depending more upon machines than on the consciousness of man; all human activity as something collective, anonymous, impersonal; freedom, responsibility, individuality, as mere academic abstractions. Above all, all institutions and values of a universal character have been profoundly affected by an economic particularism, which has impaired their inner ideality and made it seem the hypocritical cloak of a narrow and selfish reality. Thus the conviction that the legal system, instead of a universal safeguard of social life, was a weapon for holding the masses in subjection was bound to emerge from the sphere of abstract theory into that of practice and express itself in legislative and judicial action. Thus arose a dangerous spirit of partiality, which has corrupted the legal sense of the governing classes and has justified the criticisms and suspicions of their opponents. In our civilized Europe, the law rarely condescends to assert the rights of the poor and the weak; in general, it is the apanage of the rich and powerful. And if the disinherited classes are still allowed a few crumbs of private right, public rights are entirely forbidden them. We need only remember that the most elementary liberties of the majority of citizens are almost everywhere at the mercy of the executive power.

Is it strange then that many people think of right and might as synonymous, and try to assert their own rights by force? This leads to the formation of as many conflicting standards of social life as there are groups of social forces, instead of a single standard. The laws, instead of serving to decide the conflict, become the object of contention; from the safeguard of all parties alike, they become the weapon of a faction. Here lies the real gravity of the degradation of the legal system to an economic level, and at the same time the reason for the bitterness of modern social conflicts, which, precisely because all universal standards have been overthrown, cannot be moderated and controlled by principles belonging to a higher and unchallenged sphere.

This eclipse of legal consciousness has not come about equally everywhere. There are peoples in which the sense of rights is not only livelier and more alert, but has spread from class to class through an uninterrupted tradition, diminishing the shock and friction of their conflict. This is the case with the English people, and to a certain extent the German. Elsewhere a genuine legal tradition has failed to establish itself, and the historical rise of new classes has been marked by sharp revolutionary movements, each dislocating the former legal system, and encouraging the dangerous belief that law is the mere property of a class, and must follow the fortunes of that class. This implies that classes stand to one another not in any permanent legal relation but in a crude state of nature. These experiences and this belief are characteristic of the Latin peoples.

This is one of the most serious aspects of the crisis of Liberalism. Without a higher and universal law, and without the widespread consciousness of this law, there can be no freedom, either for the individual or for the social group, but only servitude and caprice. The lack or weakness of legal sense in a people only becomes manifest in periods of transition, in contact with a hostile and intractable reality. This is why our own age, simply because it is an age of social crisis, is being shaken by a profound legal crisis.

The political crisis is only a further development of the same psychological process which has subverted the legal system of Liberalism, and is due to the same causes. If government is not in the public interest, but in the private interest of classes or of parties degraded into the expression of classes, the goal of political activity can only be the conquest of the State by this or that group. Thus the political conflict, instead of issuing in the conquest of individual and social forces by the State, its strictly Liberal function, assumes a character and end of precisely opposite character : with what a disastrous effect upon all political values, we can see not only by inference, but by observation.

These extreme consequences of the degradation which the political conflict has undergone have been sufficiently illustrated in the foregoing pages. Here we may examine another and commoner case, far removed from this limit, but deducible from the same premisses. When none of the political groups expressing the particularism of social interests has the power and skill to suppress or frustrate the claims of the rest and to conquer the State single-handed, the result is a compromise. The various groups claim a proportional share of the government, as if the State were a piece of private property divisible among individuals. This is the principle underlying coalition governments, which are by degrees taking the place of party governments regulated by the classical system of constitutional opposition.

Coalitionism has been an historical necessity, which no European nation has escaped ; none the less, its influence on their political education has been thoroughly bad. A party government, criticized by an opposition, is a responsible government. It brings out the best elements of the political class expressing itself through the government, and, since the continuance of its power depends upon the quality and success of its work, and because its opponents will one day inevitably succeed it in office, there is some guarantee that the work of governing will be carried out in the interests of all. Further, the conflict of opinions and tendencies throws light on every aspect of the political situation, and discussion assumes a complete and organic character. In such a school political talent is formed and revealed ; abilities are specialized ; and there is a general heightening of political intelligence in the country, which takes an indirect part in the parliamentary struggle by means of the press, political meetings, and elections.

These advantages, in which the principal values of political freedom are summed up, are largely lost in a coalition government; where, since all have a share and an interest in public work, no one is in a position to observe and criticize; indeed, a tendency grows up to forgive each other's faults and to assume a corporate responsibility indistinguishable in effect from universal irresponsibility. The alternation of parties, which brings out the best elements in each, is replaced by a succession of personalities, each asserting a right or at any rate a legitimate claim to a share of office; this leads to the invasion of the political stage by schemers and incompetents, to say no worse, and the inevitable and progressive deterioration of the political class. One might at least suppose that a coalition government, being a compromise between conflicting interests, might last longer and provide a greater continuity of public service; but in practice the opposite is the case, because, given the narrowly personal grounds for the succession of individuals holding office, the impatience with which each awaits his turn precipitates crises, and makes them at once more arbitrary and trivial in their cause and more serious in their effect.

Politics thus become a game, or at best an alchemy, devoid of all seriousness and dignity. To justify rapid changes and to satisfy individual vanities and ambitions, programmes and parties are improvised which need never have existed, but, once existing, lay serious burdens upon the country. And the country is soon convinced that the game is not worth the candle; its healthier and more industrious elements hold aloof from public life, leaving it a prey to professional politicians, who thus form an unedifying society whose smaller members live parasitically on the greater, while the tone of political life as a whole is degraded by the mutual influence of great and small, its centre and circumference.

We said that coalitionism was a necessary evil. It is necessary just because the political consciousness has been degraded into a guardian of economic, or even frankly business, interests. If public life is only a mechanical combination of private interests, it is bound to fall apart into infinitesimal particles whose temporary cohesion can produce only a kind of mud. But, here too, forces of resistance are at work, whose effect is such as to justify a hope that the political crisis of Liberalism is not irreparable.

In England, where party government has taken firm root through an experience extending over centuries, and where the political consciousness has never wholly lost sight of the universality of governmental functions, a process of laborious readjustment is now taking place, due to the appearance of a third party disturbing the traditional two-party system. The first attempt at a solution was to attach no definite function to the third party, which till lately was the Labour Party, and is now the Liberal; the second in numerical strength undertaking by itself the function of constitutional opposition. But this formal solution was only the first step towards a more radical simplification, absorbing the third party into the other two. According to the most fanatical believers in the two-party system, the result is to be the disappearance of the Liberal Party, which is weaker than the others, and whose affinities might permit the transference of its energies in part to the Conservative side, in part to that of Labour. Thus the antithesis between the conservative and progressive forces of society would be reasserted in its simplest and strictest form.

This solution is exaggerated, impracticable, and, if it could be effected, harmful. Apart from the fact that the Liberal Party seems an unconscionable time in dying, it must be observed that the reduction of political forces to two groups and no more, in presence of the serious social conflicts of our age, would result in a ruthless struggle for the control of the State, or in other words a degradation of the political struggle into a social conflict, a subordination of parties to economic classes. As we already know, the great merit of the Liberal State is that the division between its parties cuts across the division of classes, transcends their rigid barriers, and redistributes social forces by means of an independent series of political distinctions; so that the struggle between the classes emerges into political life, which is the life of the State, with its bitterness already tempered and its combatants already prepared for compromise and peace. But if the political world is to repeat in its own parties the divisions of the classes, it can only provide a field for a disastrous reduplication of the social conflict, whose only termination can now be the defeat of one combatant and the dictatorship of the victor. In these circumstances, an intermediate body capable of withstanding social pressure, and of leading the parties back to their normal political function, performs a valuable service.

The tendency of continental peoples is in the opposite direction, towards an indefinite multiplication of small political parties. These parties are modelled upon the particularism of interests, and end by losing their way in a maze of personal rivalries and ambitions. This tendency is as harmful as the other, because it deprives the parties of all ideal content, and all ability to rise to universal views and activities. A better political education, together with direct experience of the irreparable injury inflicted upon public life by the confusion of all political parties in a single government, condemning it to impotence, might result in a beneficent simplification and reduction of numbers. The continent of Europe, owing to the complexity of its social structure and historical traditions, can never imitate the extreme simplicity of the English party system; but it can resist the destructive particularism which is invading its public consciousness, by encouraging in its parties a sense of the universality of their mission, and directing their activity along the main lines of development essential to political life. A degree of coalitionism will always be inevitable; but instead of a static and stagnant union of wholly disparate forces, annihilating criticism and blunting political sensibility in rulers and ruled, there may be partial coalitions, tolerably homogeneous and uniform, into groups like that of the Right, the Left, the Centre, and so forth, each able to function as a single party sufficiently to permit the revival of that interaction between government and opposition which the spirit of Liberalism demands.

This is not an arbitrary supposition of our own ; the political experience of to-day points unmistakably towards some such conclusion. The advantages which it offers are great. A larger grouping of similar political tendencies and policies leads the constituent elements to realize the relations between them and the common function which they are called upon to fulfil ; in this way they modify, correct, and elevate whatever in them was due to narrow selfishness. This process demonstrates that there are good grounds for hoping that the political education of the governing classes may improve ; and guarantees the permanence of those Liberal forms, methods, and institutions, which at the present stage in the history of civilization are the best fruits as yet produced by human genius in the sphere of political relations.

VII

CONCLUSION

THE conclusion of the foregoing analysis is that the crisis of Liberalism, grave and deep-seated as it is, is not so irreparable as it may appear to superficial observers and impatient heirs.

The historian has no gift of prophecy; and we shall abstain from conjecture about the future, halting on its threshold, and leaving to politicians the task of preparing new material for the continuation of this history. As we write the crisis is still in being, and the true conclusion of our work is a perception of the vital struggle in which Liberalism is so deeply involved.

Yet many elements of the future are already in the making; in the very crisis of the disease, the healthy energies of the organism are seen at work. For this reason we may legitimately indulge in a brief final survey, to collect the scattered elements of life that have emerged from our narration and bring them to a focus of hope and encouragement, without transcending the proper sphere of history.

For us, the men of to-day, any confidence in the vitality of the forms and institutions created by Liberalism in the course of its development depends upon the conviction that represents an imperishable value, because identical with the value of that spiritual activity which develops out of itself and draws from itself its laws, its standards, and its destiny. Even if the historical and contingent manifestations of Liberalism must pass away, this fundamental conviction gives us full assurance that freedom can never lose the power of creating for itself new paths, new forms, and new institutions. We see by experience that in every branch of human activity freedom is an essential condition of development and progress. Without freedom, religious faith degenerates into a paralysing and servile submission; science congeals into dogma; art shrivels into imitation; the production of economic wealth declines; and the life of human society sinks to the level of animal society. Freedom is an expansive force, differentiating itself and propagating itself in its effects, to each of which it gives a tone of novelty and originality, which is the tone of the spirit, the distinctive mark of the individual.

But together with this expansive tendency, freedom also displays the opposite tendency to return to its own source, to criticize and reflect upon its own activity. All free action involves the ideal assumption of something opposed to itself, which trains the mind in reflection and criticism, and rouses it to a sense of its own responsibility. Only one who is free is able to render an account of his own acts either to himself or to another; only one who is free can distinguish good and evil, deserve reward and punishment, know sin and repentance, raise the contingency of his own being to the universality of the moral law. Liberty is at once a spur and a check, an advance and a return; the whole life of the spirit issues from it and flows back into it.

From the eternal fountain-head of moral liberty flow, in modern times, the liberties of the individual. Their inner significance far transcends the abstractly individualistic banner under which they were won; indeed, they display a progressive effort on the part of the individual to extend his sphere of action, and to liberate, that is, to spiritualize, an ever-increasing portion of the world of his experience and his labour. In this process, an ever-increasing self is achieving liberty, and with this liberty a prodigiously increased vitality and development—a self which takes the form of consciousness, thought, speech, action, the family, property, association, class, and society; which, in short, becomes coextensive with the whole kingdom of man. Thus civil and social liberties are only the further development of individual liberties, and political liberties are their sequel and their crown. By liberating the State from the ancient bonds of servitude and compulsion, and by making it the highest expression of self-government, the modern individual is merely affirming his own nature in all its fullness.

Arrived at this point, might it not be said that freedom, having now fulfilled its function, and having no higher goal at which to aim, should retire from the stage of history, and give place to passive mechanism and the conservatism of routine?

Such a view would be tenable only if the fruits of liberty could be preserved otherwise than by liberty, and if their preservation were not in reality a perpetual creation. But further, the liberation of the natural world, and of the passive elements in human nature, by the energy of spirit, is very far from complete; it might be described as barely begun. It has been hitherto the privilege of a few, who have completed within themselves, intensively, the entire process of human emancipation; extensively considered, much remains to be done, since the majority of human beings are very far from having achieved a genuinely human level of existence, and a share in the gifts and burdens of a free spiritual life.

From this point of view, all the social and political forms of experience which, in their immediate expression, are inconsistent with Liberalism, may be regarded as indirect elements of liberty; as means, often misguided, yet always useful by way of experiment and *reductio ad absurdum*, for bringing within the orbit of civilization forces languishing or slumbering outside it. We have found a Liberal significance of this kind in the great modern movement of democracy, Socialism, nationalism, and organized religion. This discovery gives some degree of assurance that compulsion and liberty, matter and spirit, do not lie on the same ideal plane, and do not represent two alternatives in a choice which is left to historical contingencies; but that, of these two terms, one is subordinate to the other, and serves only to distinguish rest from movement, the pause from the rhythm, the episode from the drama.

This assurance is confirmed by a summary review of the history which we have already narrated. All the various forms of political Society, arising and developing in the nineteenth century, have been the creatures of liberty. Without freedom of speech, of the press, and of association, neither democracy, nor Socialism, nor nationalism, nor any of their infinite varieties, could have arisen. Their luxuriant growth is a living proof of the power of human freedom to propagate and expand through its products, to create a rich variety of forms, institutions, and attitudes, to intensify the rhythm of historical life. But at the same time, it is also a proof of the lofty impartiality with which the Liberal spirit distributes its gifts, to the enrichment even of those who spurn and deny them. The shadow which breaks the light is itself the creature of light.

But if freedom has produced this rich, conflicting, and tumultuous variety, nothing but freedom can govern the relations between its parts and direct its internal conflicts towards a higher end. This means that the simultaneous presence of discordant social and political formations, far from superseding the method of Liberalism, renders it more appropriate and necessary. It is to the common interest that no original voice should be silenced, that opposing qualities should be moderated by their very opposition, and that the triumph of a doctrine should depend upon its spontaneous ability to assert itself in competition with others, thus contributing to the improvement of these also. Take away freedom, and the struggle degenerates into oppression, caprice on the part of the victor, and servitude on the part of the vanquished; and servitude in its turn nourishes a false and degraded sense of freedom, issuing in the savagery of the revolted slave.

Now, owing to the irresistible operation of civil society itself, the method of Liberalism is beginning by degrees to influence the outlook even of those organizations which seem most resolutely hostile to it. We have seen this tendency at work in Socialism and Catholicism, in which the necessities of political life have triumphed over theoretical bigotry, and have ended by introducing new and transforming elements into the theories themselves. The educational power of the Liberal method lies precisely in the fact that it saps and destroys the sense of dogmatic self-sufficiency and the attitude of suspicion towards views opposed to one's own; thus it opens the mind to new ideas, reveals profound elements of truth in the views of opponents, and creates a belief in the possibility of a higher co-operation in all activities, a hidden harmony in all discords. In this way pride is tempered by humility, and confidence learns to rest not on contingent and transient individuals but on the superior individuality of the spirit which embraces and redeems them all.

The vitality of the Liberal method offers an assurance for the future of a party whose particular function is to safeguard and promote the spirit of liberty in the whole. Clearly, this function cannot be a monopoly; simply because Liberalism, formerly incarnate in a mere fraction, distinguished by privileges of economic and cultural welfare, has spread by degrees through the whole of Society, and has become, through the creation of a Liberal government and State, the virtual possession of all. None the less, there are certain social classes, which by their central position, and their power of mediating and balancing the opposed forces of economic society, are peculiarly called to represent and express the demands of the general body of citizens.

These middle classes have been in recent times, through the causes considered in the preceding chapter, submerged and almost crushed by forces converging upon them from above and from below, gigantically increased by the violence of the Industrial Revolution and the consequent over-emphasis on the function of production. In this way they have lost much of their ability to direct social and political progress, and are now carried along by the current rather than controlling it. The Liberal parties have everywhere suffered a serious reverse; and even if they survive their reverses, it is reasonable to suppose that they will never recover their former prestige; either because new forces have established their right to exist, or because, as we have said, the original motive of Liberalism has become a wider thing than any party programme.

But their power of reviving and shaking off their present decadence is more than a well-grounded hope; it is a fact already beginning to assert itself. We have observed, in our examination of the economic aspects of the Liberal crisis, the increasing growth of new middle classes, equidistant from the great capitalistic *bourgeoisie* and the proletariate, due to the ever-increasing specialization of industrial and agricultural activity, and destined to play a part somewhat analogous to that formerly played by the *bourgeoisie* as a whole in its relation to the aristocracy and the lower classes. These classes have as yet no political expression commensurate with their real importance; but they are bound to find one before long, in order to resist encroachment upon both frontiers of their own province.

The potential forces upon which a reorganized Liberal party might draw are by no means exhausted when we have mentioned the new recruits to Liberalism from the spheres of industry and agriculture. It would be necessary to add both the innumerable branches of the professional and commercial classes and the aristocracy of labour in its more highly specialized forms. All these elements play a mediating and therefore Liberal part in Society; not only as producers of economic goods and services, but also as consumers, in which capacity they are interested in limiting the interference of the great industrial and financial organizations in the economic policy of the State, and promoting internal and international competition. Hitherto our society, well organized in the interest of production, has been very badly organized with reference to consumption; the great mass of consumers has no influence upon public policy comparable to its actual importance. Thus a lack of equilibrium has arisen, harmful in the last resort to production itself, because depriving it of checks and controls, and giving rise to the dangers of overproduction and to crises destructive of wealth. The organization of consumption, so as to restore the equilibrium of the two fundamental activities in the economic world, is one of the most vital Liberal needs of our time.

But the strength of the Liberal party, however widely recruited, can never consist in its numerical strength: in that field it must always be inferior to democracy and Socialism. It should and must consist in quality rather than quantity.

Some Liberals would wish to see the Liberal party elevated into a kind of general staff of the political army. Such a claim is certainly exaggerated; but it is at least reasonable to demand that Liberalism should be one of the 'scientific corps' of the service. It is not every infantry man in the political service who can understand the value of freedom, human personality, and spiritual autonomy; for that, a more highly developed experience and a more highly specialized type of mind are required. For this very reason, a Liberal party is bound to choose its recruits from the middle classes, which are better trained in independent work, have a stronger sense of law, and above all possess that culture which is the ability to live the lives of others in one's own person, to look at oneself with a critical eye, and to understand and realize the dominion of thought over the inferior activities of the mind.

The reconstitution of Liberal parties therefore essentially depends on the cultural task of recalling the middle classes to a sense of the reflective and critical value of their own activity, and a recognition of the universal character of their historical mission. They must recover those political talents which they have so brilliantly exhibited in the past, but which to-day are dormant, smothered beneath the weight of economic technicalities and the encroachments of a mechanical view of Society, which degrade politics into a cash account or a conflict of brute forces.

The revival of Liberalism as a party confers upon governments in their turn a more sincerely Liberal spirit. Party and government, as we have already seen,[1] are not the same thing: in the first the predominant feature is differentiation, in the second the universality of the end. The very phrase 'governing party' symbolizes this relation of species and genus, and thus indicates a degree of political maturity at which the party is capable of grasping the ideal motives of the entire nation. But if a Liberal government has a wider sphere, not necessarily depending on the existence of a Liberal party, it may yet owe to the revival of this party a livelier conscious-

[1] Part II, Chap. I, § 3.

ness of its mission; and to the better preparation of the environment, a further incentive to its activity.

Everything that we have said concerning the necessity of a Liberal method in the relations between individuals and social groups applies even more strongly to governments, as the supreme forces controlling all relations. But it is generally the case, in the world of human affairs, that the most necessary things are also the most difficult things, precisely because this necessity is always a moral necessity. And for governments, the difficulty of being Liberal is due to the immediate opportunities offered them for use of compulsion and force instead of trying the longer way of freedom and consent. Now the employment of force is not in itself incompatible with Liberalism; on the contrary, without force on the part of the government, the liberties of the people cannot be safeguarded. Force is only illiberal when it is illiberally used; when, that is, it is used either with partial motives or in the attempt to enforce with brutal impatience the solution of a problem requiring vital travail. A government requires a profound experience of human nature in order to understand the simple wisdom of *laissez-faire*, and not only curb the ardour which would lead it to govern too much, but cultivate the discretion and tact necessary for invisible and unostentatious work where work is needed.

In our own times, full as they are of divisions, of conflicts, of heterogeneous and conflicting demands, the Liberalism that governments most need consists ultimately in a profound conviction that reasonableness in the long run always defeats its enemies; that in the conflict of opinions and tendencies, the most rational are the fittest to survive; that fictions and falsehoods live no longer than they deserve to live; and that the experience of error and evil is as necessary for peoples as for individuals: a labour from which no one can save them by presenting them with a truth or a good which they cannot understand or value. These maxims are simple, even trite; yet those who obey them are authentic statesmen, and not the mere politicians, professional or amateur, who spring up at every street corner.

We have now traversed once more the various phases
through which our conception of Liberalism passed,[1] and are
in sight of the goal of that development, the Liberal State.
The State is not the government, as the government is not
the party; it is a higher incarnation of the same spirit; it is
the higher unity which includes and dominates all differences.

Our confidence in the vitality of Liberalism rests, in the
last resort, upon the Liberal State. It is the political State *par
excellence*, the πολιτεία of the modern world. Its nature, a
nature strictly dialectical, draws nourishment from all oppositions, from discord no less than concord, dissent no less than
consent. No other political organism which has yet appeared
in the course of history has ever succeeded, with so economical a use of means, in embracing so many divergent and
centrifugal forces, and leaving them the fullest liberty of
action. The modern Liberal State has not only done this, but
it has made these forces elements in its own strength, partly
by drawing them little by little into its own channel, partly by
using their hostile criticism of itself as means to its own self-
improvement.

Is this State now in decay? It certainly appears to have
been exhausted by the gigantic efforts which have been demanded of it, one following another without intermission.
Socialism and nationalism, illiberally employing the liberty
bestowed upon them, first tried to undermine it from within,
and to create an autocratic and dictatorial anti-State. Then
came the European war, with its inevitably illiberal demands, and its waste of those moral energies which are the
great reservoir of Liberalism. Lastly, the economic and social
storm that followed the War burst upon the State before it
had time to recover its balance; the rigid framework that
grew up during the War was shattered before a Liberal reorganization could come about; and the result was a collapse,
of especial gravity in those countries whose historical traditions were least deeply rooted. And yet, even in Italy, the
most sorely tried of all these countries, the Liberal State has
survived and survives: however hostile conditions may be to

----

[1] [As method, party, government, State; cf. p. 357.]

its manifestation, freedom is triumphing over its enemies, reducing them to impotence through the shock of their mutual opposition, and proving once more that on the battle-field of free human competition nothing survives that does not deserve to live.

Thus recent experience affords a proof of the vitality of the Liberal State, hard beset, yet issuing victorious from the battle. Its rivals, the 'technical' State, the 'administrative' State, the 'dictatorial' State, have served only to vindicate once more, by their virtual bankruptcy, the triumph of the 'political' State.

BIBLIOGRAPHY

THE absence of any previous history, whether in whole or in part, of European Liberalism, and also the peculiar nature of the subject, touching as it does every side of modern life, make the compilation of a bibliography very difficult. That which is offered below is almost certain to be at once too long and too short; but my endeavour has been to name the books which will best serve to illustrate the way in which my work came into being, in the hope that when at some future time a tradition of political studies establishes itself, my imperfect outline may be completed and supplemented by other writers.

INTRODUCTION

(*Eighteenth Century*)

The growth of the ' bourgeoisie ' : A. THIERRY, Essai sur la formation du tiers État, Paris, ed. 4, 1864 [Engl. tr., 2 vols., 1855]. CH. NORMAND, La bourgeoisie française au xviie siècle, 1908. CH. DE RIBBE, Les familles et la société en France avant la révolution, Paris, ed. 2, 1874. BARDOUX, La bourgeoisie française, 1908. W. SOMBART, Der Bourgeois (*Zur Geistes-geschichte des modernen Wirtschaftsmenschen*), 1913. Cf. below on the history of capitalism.

The Protestant origins of Liberalism : T. H. GREEN, Four Lectures on the English Revolution (*Works*, iii). TROELTSCH, Die Soziallehre der christlichen Kirchen und Gruppen, Tübingen, 1919. MAX WEBER, Gesammelte Aufsätze zur Religionssoziologie, Tübingen, 1920. GOTHEIN, Reformation und Gegenreformation, ed. 2, 1924. SCHULZE GAEVERNITZ, Britischer Imperialismus und englischer Freihandelspolitik, Leipzig, 1906. RACHFALL, Kalvinismus und Kapitalismus, 1909. F. SCHMIDT, Kapitalismus und Protestantismus (*Preuss. Jahrbücher*, vol. 122). GIO-VANETTI, Il tramonto del liberalismo, Bari, 1917. *Contra* : SCHELL, Der Katolizismus als Prinzip des Fortschrittes, Würzburg, 1897. Also hostile to the spirit of the Reformation: F. C. MONTAGUE, The Limits of Individual Liberty, London, 1885 (Ital. tr., Brunialti's *Bibl. di Scienze politiche*, ser. i, vol. v).

The work of the reformers and jurists : AD. FRANCK, Réformateurs et publicistes de l'Europe (Moyen âge—Renaissance, 1864; dix-septième siècle, 1881; dix-huitième siècle, 1893). A. BARDOUX, Les légistes, leur influence sur la société française, 1877.

Natural Rights : the most important critical works are German:

AHRENS, Das Naturrecht, ed. 6, Wien, 1871, 2 vols. STAHL, Die Philosophie des Rechts auf Geschichtlicher Grundlage, ed. 4, 1870. LASSON, Rechtsphilosophie, 1880. IEHRING, Der Kampf ums Recht, ed. 8, Wien, 1886; Der Zweck im Recht, Leipzig, 2 vols., ed. 2, 1884-6. JELLINEK, Allgemeine Rechtslehre, Berlin, ed. 2, 1905. French: MICHEL, De l'idée de l'État, Paris, ed. 3, 1898. Italian: G. DE MONTEMAYOR, Storia del diritto naturale.

The Industrial Revolution : TOYNBEE, Lectures on the Industrial Revolution in England, London, 1884. W. CUNNINGHAM, The Growth of English Industry and Commerce, 1882; Essay on Western Civilization in its Economic Aspects, 1902. HOBSON, The Evolution of Modern Capitalism, 1894. SCHULZE GAEVERNITZ, La Grande Intrapresa (Bibl. degli Econom., ser. v). BEARD, The Industrial Revolution, 1902. SOMBART, Der Moderne Kapitalismus, 1902. SHADWELL, Industrial Efficiency, 1906. A. DE CILLEULE, La grande Industrie, 1908. BARROW, On Industry. MACGREGOR, The Evolution of Industry (Home University Library).

The development of Agriculture : LAVERGNE, Économie rurale de la France (ed. 4, 1871) and Économie rurale de l'Angleterre (Ital. tr. in Bibl. degli Econ.: both out of date but accurate). For England : J. R. GREEN, History of the English People, London, 1874 (Fr. tr. 1880; Ital. tr. 1884). SCHULZE GAEVERNITZ, Britischer Imperialismus, cit. HALÉVY, Histoire du peuple anglais, vol. i. For France : DE TOCQUEVILLE, L'ancien régime et la révolution, is fundamental and the basis of all later works. For more recent developments : WAGNER, Agrar- und Industriestaat, ed. 2, 1902. FUETER, Weltgeschichte der letzten hundert Jahren, 1921. GIDE and RIST, Histoire des doctrines économiques, ed. 4, 1922.

English political history to the eighteenth century: MACAULAY, History of England from the Accession of James II, 1848-64; Critical and Historical Essays, 1843; Biographical Essays, 1852. J. R. GREEN, op. cit. An interesting historical sketch is given by A. SOREL in vol. i of his great work L'Europe et la révolution. For the economic system of the feudal period : ASHLEY, Introduction to English Economic History and Theory, 1888-93 (Fr. tr. 1900). For the origins of English Liberalism : BOUTMY, La première évolution des classes et la formation du Parlement en Angleterre, in Revue des Deux Mondes, 1885. ACTON, The History of Freedom and other Essays, 1907. Cf. also the various constitutional histories, beginning with that of GUIZOT, quoted below. For the English political system in the eighteenth century, see the good description in GNEIST, Das Rechtsstaat (Ital. tr., vol. 5 of Bibl. di Scienze politiche). Cf. also the various works on English constitutional law, e.g. BROUGHAM, The British Constitution, 1884. BAGEHOT, The English Constitution, 1867 (Fr. tr. 1869). STUBBS, Constitutional History of England, 1878. MAITLAND, Constitutional History of England, 1908. For English thought in the eighteenth century : LESLIE STEPHEN, English Thought in the Eighteenth Century, and general works on the history of philosophy.

The sources of English liberal thought to the eighteenth century : LOCKE, Second Treatise of Civil Government, 1689. HUME, Political Discourses, 1752. PRIESTLEY, An Essay on the First Principles of Government and of the Nature of Political, Civil, and Religious Liberty, 1868. PRICE, Observations on Civil Liberty and the Justice and Policy of the War with America, 1776. BLACKSTONE, Commentaries on the Laws of England, in Four Books, London, 1765 (the first lectures from which the book arose date from 1753). DELOLME, Constitution d'Angleterre, 1787. A. SMITH, An Inquiry into the Nature and Causes of the Wealth of Nations, 1776. (On SMITH, cf. HASBACH, Die allgemeinen Grundlagen der von Fr. Quesnay und Ad. Smith begründeten politischen Oekonomie, in Schmoller, *Staats- und Sozialwissensch. Forschungen*, x. 2, 1890 ; GIDE and RIST, Hist. des doctr. écon., *cit.* ; for English economic literature before SMITH, cf. SCHULZE GAEVERNITZ, La Grande Intrapresa, *cit.*) English thought in the revolutionary period : BURKE, Reflections on the French Revolution, 1790 ; Letter to a Member of the National Assembly, 1791 ; Thoughts on French Affairs, 1791 (cf. MORLEY, Burke, in *English Men of Letters*). *Contra* : T. PAINE, Rights of Man, 1791 (Fr. tr. 1793). MACKIN-TOSH, Vindiciae Galliae. GODWIN, Inquiry concerning Political Justice, 1796. ARTHUR YOUNG, Political Arithmetic, Part I, 1774 ; Part II, 1779 ; Travels in France during the Years 1787, 1788, and 1789, London, 1794.

French political history before the Revolution : besides *opp. citt.*, esp. DE TOCQUEVILLE, cf. LAVISSE and RAMBAUD, Histoire générale du IVᵉ siècle à nos jours, vols. vii, viii, with copious bibliography. A mine of information is TAINE, Les origines de la France contemporaine. Cf. also FAGUET, Le dix-huitième siècle, ed. 19, 1901. J. ROQUIN, L'esprit révolutionnaire avant la révolution.

The French Revolution : The outlook of the historians of the Revolution is illustrated by JANET, La philosophie de la révolution française, 1875. Among more recent histories, A. SOREL, L'Europe et la révolution, *cit.* (in 8 vols. ; deals especially with foreign relations, but contains important references to our subject). AULARD, Histoire politique de la révolution française, Paris, 1901 (important for the study of political forms). SALVEMINI, La rivoluzione francese (to 1792), published by *La Voce*. Collections of *cahiers* are numerous ; for those of Paris, cf. CHASSIN's ed., 1888 ; ED. CHAMPION, La France d'après les cahiers de 1789 ; L'esprit de la révolution.

The Declaration of Rights : JELLINEK, Die Erklärung der Menschen- und Bürgerrechte, ed. 2, 1904. Similar in tendency is BORGEAUD, Établissement et révision des constitutions en Amérique et en Europe, 1893. Cf. also MERRIAM, History of the Theory of Sovereignty since Rousseau, New York, 1900.

Chief sources of pre-Revolutionary French political thought : MONTESQUIEU, Lettres persanes, 1721 ; Considérations sur les causes de la grandeur et de la décadence des Romains, 1734 ; L'Esprit des Lois, 1748. DIDEROT,

D'ALEMBERT, ROUSSEAU, &c., Encyclopédie, 17 vols., 1751-65. D'AR-
GENSON, Considérations sur le gouvernement ancien et présent de la
France, Amsterdam, 1764. VOLTAIRE, Essai sur l'esprit et les mœurs des
nations, 1758; Traité sur la tolérance, 1763; La religion naturelle, 1756;
Dictionnaire philosophique, 1764 (see articles *liberté, égalité, lois,* &c.).
CONDILLAC, Le commerce et le gouvernement considérés relativement
l'un à l'autre, 2 vols., 1776. GRIMM, Correspondance, Paris, 1812-13.
D'HOLBACH, Système social. CONDORCET, Esquisse d'un tableau his-
torique des progrès de l'esprit humain, 1795 (posthumous). ROUSSEAU,
Discours de l'origine et les fondements de l'inégalité parmi les hommes,
1755; Du contrat social, 1762; Gouvernement de la Pologne, &c.
(Œuvres, Hachette, 13 vols., 1865). On ROUSSEAU, cf. the histories of
political theory and MERRIAM, *op. cit.*; also G. DEL VECCHIO, La teoria
del contratto sociale, 1906. The anarchists: MABLY, Entretiens de
Phocion; De la législation ou des principes des lois, 1777. MORELLY,
Code de la nature, 1755. BRISSOT, Recherches philosophiques sur la propriété et sur le vol, 1778. The physiocrats (vols. ii and iii of *Biblioteca
degli Econ.*): QUESNAY, Droit naturel; Analyse du tableau économique
d'un royaume agricole; Dialogues, &c. MARQ. DE MIRABEAU, Philosophie rurale. TURGOT, writings in the volumes quoted, and Œuvres
in course of publication since 1913; ed. G. SCHELLES, Paris (cf. SAY,
Turgot, in *Grands écrivains français*). MERCIER DE LA RIVIÈRE, De l'ordre
naturel et essentiel des sociétés politiques, London, 1767. DUPONT DE
NEMOURS, Correspondance avec J.-B. Say. BAUDEAU, Introduction à la
philosophie économique. *Contra*: GALIANI (cf. this Bibliography, under
Chapter IV). NECKER, La législation et la commerce des grains, 1775.
On the physiocrats see GIDE and RIST, Histoire, *cit.*

    The Revolutionary period: CONDORCET, Les assemblées provinciales,
1788. Sieyès, Essai sur les privilèges, 1788; Qu'est-ce que le Tiers État ?
1789; Reconnaissance et exposition des droits de l'homme et du citoyen,
1789. MIRABEAU, Essai sur le despotisme, 1772; Lettres de cachet et
les prisons d'État, 1782; Dénonciation de l'agiotage (against Necker),
1781; Monarchie prussienne sous Frédéric le Grand, 1787; Discours et
opinions, 3 vols., 1820 (cf. DECRUE, Les idées politiques de M.; ROUSSE,
M.; CAGGESE, M., 1925). MOUNIER, Considérations sur les gouverne-
ments, 1789; Recherches sur les causes qui ont empêché les Français
de devenir libres, 1792. NECKER, Du pouvoir exécutif. LALLY TOLLEN-
DAL, Lettres à Edm. Burke, 1792. SAINT-JUST, Fragments sur les institutions républicaines, in the year III. BABŒUF, Système politique et
social des égaux. BUONARROTI, Conspiration pour l'égalité. For the
innumerable pamphlets, cf. general histories of the Revolution.

I. ENGLAND

General histories: J. McCarthy, A History of Our Own Times to the Election of 1880 (Fr. tr. in 5 vols.; very incomplete work by an Irish nationalist). Very rich in information and sound in judgement is É. Halévy, Histoire du peuple anglais au xixe siècle, 7 vols., of which i–iii are published: i, L'Angleterre au 1815; ii, Du lendemain de Waterloo à la veille du Reform Bill (1815–30); iii, De la crise du Reform Bill à l'avènement de Sir Robert Peel (1830–41).

General works on English Liberalism: Acton, History of Freedom, *cit.* Dunning, History of Political Theories, 3 vols., 1903. Sidgwick, The Development of European Polity, 1903. Hobhouse, Liberalism (*Home University Library*).

The British Constitution, beside works already quoted: E. A. Freeman, Comparative Politics, 1873. Dicey, Introduction to the Study of the Law of the Constitution, ed. 3, 1889. Gneist, Das englische Verwaltungsrecht im Gegenwart (Ital. tr., Il parlamento inglese, 1891) [Engl. tr., The History of the English Constitution, 2 vols., 1886]. Glasson, Histoire du droit et des institutions d'Angleterre. L. Lowell, Government of England, 1908. Sidney Low, Governance of England. Courtenay P. Ilbert, Parliament (*Home University Library*). Cf. also A. Shaw, Municipal Government in England, New York, 1896.

The Land Question in the nineteenth century: R. Faber, Die Entstehung des Agrarschutzes in England, 1888. Shaw-Lefevre, Essays on the English and Irish Land Question [ed. 2, 1881]. R. Wallace, Land Nationalization, its necessity and aims, 1882. Hammond, The Agricultural Labourer in the Nineteenth Century. H. Levy, Entstehung und Rückgang des landwirtsch. Grossbetrieb in England, 1904. The Poor-law: E. Chevalier, La loi des pauvres et la société anglaise, 1895.

English Radicalism: Mill, Utilitarianism, 1862; Autobiography, 1873. Guyau, La morale anglaise contemporaine, ed. 2, 1885. W. Harris, History of the Radical Party in Parliament, 1885. C. B. Roylance Kent, The English Radicals, an Historical Sketch, 1899. Leslie Stephen, The English Utilitarians, 1900. Albee, A History of English Utilitarianism, 1902. Halévy, La Formation du radicalisme philosophique, 3 vols.: i, La Jeunesse de Bentham; ii, L'Évolution de la doctrine utilitaire de 1789 à 1815; iii, La Radicalisme philosophique, Alcan, 1901–4. J. Bardoux, L'Angleterre radicale, 1913. Sources: J. Bentham, Works, ed. Bowring, 11 vols., 1838–43 (Fr. tr., Bruxelles, ed. 3, 1840, 3 vols.). James Mill, contributions to the *Westminster Review* 1844–6; The Church and its Reform, 1836, in *London Review* founded by Molesworth; Fragment on Mackintosh, 1835 (a severe criticism of M.'s Dissertation on the Progress of Ethical Philosophy). Grote, Essentials of Parliamentary Reform, 1831. Macaulay, Works, ed. Mrs. Trevelyan (his sister), 8 vols., 1866: vols. i–iv, the History; v–viii, the Essays. On him : TREVELYAN, Life of Macaulay. On the Radicals : J. MacCUNN, Six Radical Thinkers.

The Economists : MALTHUS, Essay on the Principles of Population, 1798 ; Observations on the Effect of the Corn Laws, Inquiry into the Nature and Progress of Rent, incorporated into Principles of Political Economy (Ital. tr. in *Bibl. degli Econ.*). RICARDO, Principles of Political Economy and Taxation, 1817, and minor essays (cf. *Bibl. degli Econ.*). URE, Philosophy of Manufactures, London, 1835 (extracts in *Bibl. degli Econ.*, ser. ii, vol. iii, pp. 17 *seqq.*). J. S. MILL, Essays on some Unsettled Questions of Political Economy, 1844 ; Principles of Political Economy, 1848 ; political writings, see below. Chief modern work : MARSHALL, Principles of Economics, 1890. For the modern conception of the relation between profits and wages : E. ATKINSON, Distribution of Profits. For the whole school : GIDE and RIST, Histoire, *cit.*

The Manchester School : BASTIAT, Cobden et la Ligue (select speeches by members of the League, with introduction). CAVOUR, Quistione relativa alla legislazione inglese sul commercio dei cereali (in *Bibliothéque universelle*, 1845 ; reprinted in *Scritti*, ed. Zanichelli, 1892). PRENTICE, History of the Free Trade Movement. CUNNINGHAM, Rise and Decline of the Free Trade Movement. FAWCETT, Free Trade. F. W. HIRST, Free Trade and other Fundamental Doctrines of the Manchester School, 1903 (the best selection of writings and speeches). MacCUNN, Six Radical Thinkers, *cit.* COBDEN, Political Writings, 1870 (MORLEY, Life of Cobden, 1881). BRIGHT, Life and Speeches of Bright, ed. Barnett Smith, 2 vols., 1888. THOMPSON, Catechism on the Corn Laws. Cf. also the general histories.

The Religious Movement : Abbé DELISLE, L'Anglicanisme et les sectes dissidentes, 1893. R. P. RAGEY, La Crise religieuse en Angleterre, 1896. OVERTON, The Anglican Revival, London, 1897. SELBIE, Nonconformity, its origins and progress (*Home University Library*). The Oxford Movement : NEWMAN, Tracts for the Times ; Grammar of Assent, 1870 ; Apologia and Correspondence, ed. Anna Mozley, 1882 ; Development of Christian Doctrine, 1845 (Fr. tr. 1905 ; Ital. tr. 1909). MANNING, England and Christendom, 1867 ; The True History of the Vatican Council ; Apologia pro Vita Sua, 1878 (DE PRESSENSÉ, Le card. M., 1897 ; E. S. PURCELL, Life of Card. M., 1896). FROUDE, Short Studies. CHURCH, The Oxford Movement. FAIRBAIRN, Catholicism, Roman and Anglican. THUREAU-DANGIN, La Renaissance catholique en Angleterre, 3 vols., ed. 2, 1899.

The Christian-Socialist and anti-Liberal movement : KINGSLEY, Alton Locke, 1849 ; Cheap Clothes and Nasty, 1850 ; The Message of the Church to Labouring Men, 1851 ; Letters and Memories, ed. 3, 1877. LUDLOW, Christian Socialism and its Opponents. ANON., Tracts on Christian Socialism, 1849 ; The Christian Socialist, 1850–1. More recently KIDD, Social Evolution, 1894, expounds Darwinism in a Christian-Socialist sense.

The Reaction against Free Trade: SISMONDI, Nouveaux principes d'Économie politique, 1820. BURET, De la misère des classes laborieuses en Angleterre et en France, 1842. From a Socialist point of view: OWEN, New View of Society, 1813; The New Moral World; Revolution in the Mind and Practice of the Human Race; Life of Robert Owen, written by himself, 1857 (cf. E. DOLLÉANS, R. Owen, 1905; G. J. HOLYOAKE, History of Co-operation in England, 1906). Much influence has been exercised by the protectionism of the American CAREY, Principles of Social Science (Fr. tr. 1858-9).

The Idealistic Reaction against Utilitarianism: COLERIDGE, On the Constitution of Church and State, 1830 (on his literary work cf. HALL CAINE, Life of C., 1887, in *Great Writers*). CARLYLE, French Revolution, 1837; On Heroes, 1846; Past and Present, 1843; Chartism; Life of John Sterling, 1851 (cf. GARNETT, T. C., 1887; HENSEL, C., Stuttgart, 1901). The social aspect of RUSKIN's work is important: Unto this Last, 1860; Munera Pulveris, 1862-3; Crown of Wild Olive, 1866; Fors Clavigera, 1871-4 (cf. GEDDES, J. R., Economist, 1887; HOBSON, J. R., Social Reformer, ed. 2, 1899; HERKNER, R., als Sozialreformer, 1900). DISRAELI, What is he? 1833; Vindication of the British Constitution, 1835; novels: Coningsby, 1844; Sybil, 1845; Tancred, 1847; Lothair, 1870; Endymion, 1881; speeches: Constitutional Reform, Five Speeches, 1886; Parliamentary Reform, 1867; Conservative Policy of the last Thirty Years, 1870 (cf. BRANDES, Lord Beaconsfield, Berlin, 1879). BARDOUX, Le Mouvement idéaliste et social dans la littérature anglaise contemporaine au xixᵉ siècle.

Later Liberalism: GLADSTONE, The State in its Relations with the Church, 1838; Gleanings of Past Years, 1843-78, 7 vols., London, 1879 (cf. MORLEY, Life of Gladstone, 2 vols., 1905-7). ASHLEY, Life of Viscount Palmerston, 2 vols., 1876. REID, Life of Forster. MILL, On Liberty, 1859 (Ital. tr. 1924); Considerations on Representative Government, 1865; The Subjection of Women, 1869: Autobiography, 1873; Three Essays on Religion, 1874. Against Mill's individualism: J. F. STEPHEN, Liberty, Equality, Fraternity, 1873. H. SPENCER, Principles of Sociology, 1876; Political Institutions, 1882; The Man versus the State, 1884 (Fr. tr. 1888). *Contra*: F. C. MONTAGUE, The Limits of Individual Liberty (Ital. tr. in *Bibl. di Scienze polit.*, ser. i, vol. v, by ORLANDO). T. H. GREEN, Principles of Political Obligation; Liberal Legislation and Freedom of Contract, in Works, vols. ii, iii. Speeches of leading Liberals on current politics (HARCOURT, HARTINGTON, BRIGHT, CHAMBERLAIN), 1879-80.

Modern Liberal writings: MORLEY, *opp. citt.*, and also Compromise; Recollections. ASQUITH, The Paisley Policy, 1920. HIRST, Liberalism and Empire, 1900. HOLLAND, Imperium and Libertas, 1901. RAMSAY MUIR, Liberalism and Industry; The New Liberalism. G. LOWES DICKINSON, Justice and Liberty. L. T. HOBHOUSE, Liberalism (*Home University Library*). HEARNSHAW, National Self-Government. POLLARD,

The Evolution of Parliament, 1920. KEYNES, The Economic Consequences of the Peace, 1919.

Democracy: MAINE, Popular Government, 1886. BRYCE, The American
Commonwealth, 1888 (Ital. tr., *Bibl. sc. polit.*, ser. iii, vol. i). ERSKINE
MAY, Democracy in Europe, 1877 (Ital. tr., *Bibl. sc. polit.*). OSTRO-
GORSKI, La Démocratie et l'organisation des partis politiques, 2 vols.,
1903 (a work of great importance : vol. i on England, vol. ii on America).
HOBHOUSE, Democracy and Reaction, 1904. GOOCH, History of English
Democratic Ideas, 1898 ; The Heart of Europe. On Conservatism :
H. CECIL, Conservatism (*Home University Library*). On Imperialism :
J. K. SEELEY, The Expansion of England, 1883 (Ital. tr., *Bibl. sc. polit.*,
ser. ii, vol. ix). CHAMBERLAIN, Speeches, ed. Boyd, 2 vols., 1914.
C. RHODES, Speeches. Imperialistic literature is very abundant and very
instructive for Liberalism. In English : HOBSON, Psychology of Jingoism,
1901. PERRIS, The Protectionist Peril, 1903. HOBHOUSE, Imperialism,
1905. In French : GAZEAU, L'impérialisme anglais, 1903. DUPLAN,
La Crise anglaise et les idées de Chamberlain, 1903. BERARD, L'Angleterre et l'impérialisme. In German (the most important) : SCHULZE
GAEVERNITZ, Britischer Imperialismus. In Italian : G. DE RUGGIERO,
La formazione dell' Impero britannico (lectures before the Istituto
superiore di commercio, Brescia, 1923). On Socialism : Fabian Essays
on Socialism, ed. SHAW. S. and B. WEBB, History of Trade Unionism ;
Industrial Democracy ; Problems of Modern Industry. Guild Socialism :
HOBSON, National Guilds, ed. 3, 1919. COLE, The World of Labour,
ed. 2, 1915. PENTY, Guilds, Trade, and Agriculture, 1921.

For a larger modern bibliography, cf. the author's L'Impero britannico
dopo la guerra, Florence, Vallecchi, 1921.

II. FRANCE

General Works : LAVISSE and RAMBAUD, Histoire générale, *cit.*, vols. x–
xii. SEIGNOBOS, Histoire politique de l'Europe contemporaine, 1814–96,
ed. 3, 1903. P. JANET, Histoire des sciences politiques, *cit.*, vol. ii,
appendix. MICHEL, L'Idée de l'État. Essai critique sur l'histoire des
théories sociales et politiques depuis la révolution, ed. 3, 1898. LOWELL,
Government and Parties in Continental Europe.

The Reactionaries : SAINT-MARTIN, Des erreurs et de la vérité, 1775 ;
Lettre à un ami, ou Considérations politiques, philosophiques et
religieuses sur la révolution française, in the year III ; Éclair sur l'association humaine, in the year IV. G. DE MAISTRE, Considérations sur la
France, 1796 ; Essai sur le principe générateur des constitutions politiques, 1810 ; Du pape, 1808 ; Les Soirées de St. Pétersbourg, 1821 ;
Mémoires politiques et correspondance diplomatique (collected by
A. BLANC Paris, ed. 2, 1859). COGORDEAU, De Maistre, in *Les grands
écrivains français*. DE BONALD, Théorie du pouvoir politique et religieux
dans la société civile, 1796 ; Législation primitive considérée dans les

derniers temps par les seules lumières de la raison, 3 vols., 1802 ; Essai analytique sur les lois naturelles de l'ordre social, 1816. BALLANCHE, Essai sur les institutions sociales dans leur rapport avec les idées nouvelles, 1818 ; Essai de palingénésie sociale, 1827-8. LAMENNAIS, Réflections sur l'état de l'Église en France pendant le XVIIIᵉ siècle et sur la situation actuelle, ed. 2, 1821 ; Essai sur l'indifférence en matière de religion, 1819 (reprinted 1885) ; La religion dans ses rapports avec l'ordre civil et politique, 1826 ; Des progrès de la révolution et de la guerre contre l'Église, 1829; for works after 1830, see below. Cf. JANET, La philosophie de Lamennais.

The Restoration constitutionalists : COUSIN, Cours d'histoire de philosophie morale au XVIIIᵉ siècle, 1839-40. DESTUTT DE TRACY, Commentaire sur l'esprit des lois, 1811 (America ; 1822 in France). CHATEAUBRIAND, La Monarchie selon la Charte, 1816. MME DE STAËL, Considérations sur la révolution française, 1818. B. CONSTANT, De l'esprit de conquête et d'usurpation, 1814 ; Principes de politique ; Réflections sur les constitutions et les garanties, 1814-18 ; De la responsabilité des ministres ; De la liberté des anciens comparée à celle des modernes ; De la religion. Most of these works were included in Cours de politique constitutionelle, ed. Laboulaye, 1861, 2 vols. De la liberté, &c. (1819), has been translated into Italian, *Bibl. sc. polit.*, vol. v. DAUNOU, Essai sur les garanties individuelles, 1818. DE BARANTE, Vie et opinions de Royer-Collard. SPULLER, Royer-Collard (*Les grands écrivains français*). CH. COMTE and CH. DUNOYER edited Le censeur européen, the chief Liberal review of the Restoration period ; cf. also COMTE, Traité de la législation ; and DUNOYER, De la liberté du travail, 3 vols., 1845 (the nucleus of the work was written and published twenty years earlier). HELLO, Du régime constitutionnel, ed. 2, 1830. GUIZOT, Du gouvernement de la France depuis la Restauration et du Ministère actuel, 1821 ; Des moyens de gouvernement et de l'opposition dans l'état actuel de la France, 1821 ; Histoire du gouvernement représentatif, 1821-2 ; Essai sur l'histoire de France, 1821-4 ; Histoire de la civilisation en Europe ; Histoire de la civilisation en France, 1830 (cf. BARDOUX, Guizot, in *Les grands écrivains français*). A. THIERRY, Œuvres, Bruxelles, 1839. CHERBULIEZ, Théorie des garanties individuelles, 1838. DE BARANTE, Questions constitutionnelles, 1849. RÉMUSAT, Passé et présent. THUREAU-DANGIN, Le parti libéral sous la Restauration, 1876.

Economic and social theories (cf. MICHEL, De l'idée de l'État, *cit.* ; GIDE and RIST, Histoire, *cit.*). The fundamental work for the economies of free trade is J.-B. SAY, Traité d'économie politique, 1803 ; Cours d'économie politique, 1828-30. SAINT-SIMON, Introduction aux travaux scientifiques du XIXᵉ siècle, 1808 ; Système industriel, 1821-2 ; Catéchisme des industriels, 1822 ; Nouveau Christianisme, 1825. Œuvres of SAINT-SIMON and ENFANTIN, 47 vols., Paris, 1865-78. Œuvres choisis, publ. by Lemonnier, Bruxelles, 1878. WEIL, L'école saint-simonienne, 1896. BOISSIER, Saint-Simon (*Les grands écrivains français*). FEDERICI, Saint-

Simon, 1922. FOURIER, Théorie des quatre mouvements, 1808; Théorie de l'unité universelle, 3 vols., 1838 (2nd ed.; first published 1822 under the title Association domestique agricole); Le nouveau monde industriel et sociétaire, 1829 (4th ed., 1848); La fausse industrie, 1835–6, 2 vols.; Œuvres choisis, ed. CH. GIDE, with introd.; cf. BOURGIN, Fourier, 1905. CONSIDÉRANT, Doctrine sociale, 1834–41; Exposition abrégée du système phalanstérien de Fourier (four lectures at Dijon in 1841). SISMONDI, Nouveaux principes d'économie politique ou De la richesse dans ses rapports avec la population, 1820; Étude sur la constitution des peuples libres; Études sur les sciences sociales, 1837. BURET, De la misère des classes laborieuses en Angleterre et en France, 1842. BUCHEZ, Introduction à la science de l'histoire, 1833; Histoire parlementaire de la révolution française, 1833–8; Traité de politique et de la science sociale, 1866. PECQUEUR, Des améliorations matérielles dans leur rapport avec la liberté, 1839; Théorie nouvelle de l'économie sociale et politique, 1842. VIDAL, De la répartition des richesses ou de la justice distributive en économie sociale, 1846; Vivre en travaillant; projets, voies et moyens de réformes sociales, 1848. VILLENEUVE-BARGEMONT, Économie politique chrétienne, 1834 (cf. H. JOLY, Le socialisme chrétien). P. LEROUX, De l'humanité, 1840; Réfutation de l'eclectisme, 1841; De l'Église, 1848; Du christianisme et de ses origines démocratiques, 1848; Projet d'un constitution démocratique et sociale, 1848 (cf. THOMAS, P. Leroux, 1905). L. NAPOLÉON BONAPARTE, Des idées napoléoniennes, 1839; L'idée napoléonienne, 1840; De l'extinction du pauperisme, 1844. L. BLANC, Organisation du travail, 1839; Le socialisme : droit au travail, 1848; Questions d'aujourd'hui et de demain, sér. 1–5; Histoire de dix ans; Histoire de la révolution française, 1847–62. L. STEIN, Geschichte d. soz. Bewegung in Frankreich, 1850. REYBAUD, Études sur les réformateurs ou socialistes modernes, ed. 2, 1856, 2 vols.

Anarchism: CABET, Voyage en Icarie, 1842; Le vrai Christianisme, 1847. PROUDHON, Qu'est-ce que la propriété? 1840; Système des contradictions économiques ou Philosophie de la misère, 1846; Intérêts et principal : Discussion entre Bastiat et Proudhon, 1850; De la capacité politique des classes ouvrières, 1865; &c. Cf. PUECH, Proudhon et l'internationale, 1907. *Contra* : the free-trade anarchism of BASTIAT, Cobden et la Ligue, 1845; Harmonies économiques, 1849.

Liberal Catholicism. L'Avenir, 1830, journal condemned by Gregory XVI in the Encyclical *Mirari vos.* To this movement belong the writings of the later period of LAMENNAIS, Paroles d'un croyant, 1834; Affaires de Rome, 1836–7, 2 vols. (Œuvres, Paris, 1836, 2nd ed., 1844; Œuvres posthumes, 1856). MONTALEMBERT, Des intérêts catholiques au XIXe siècle, 1852; L'Église libre dans l'état libre, 1863. On LACORDAIRE, cf. MONTALEMBERT, Le père L., 1862; Comte d'HAUSSONVILLE, L. (*Les grands écrivains français*). DUPANLOUP, La convention du 15 sept. et l'encyclique du 8 dec. 1865. P. GRATRY, Lettres a Mgr. Dupanloup, 1870. *Contra* : VEUILLOT, L'illusion libérale, 1866. On the whole movement cf. A. LEROY-BEAULIEU, Les catholiques libéraux, l'Église et la Libéralisme de 1830 à nos jours, 1885. On the Protestant side : VINET, Essai sur la manifestation des convictions religieuses et de la séparation de l'Église de l'État, 1842. Cf. SCHERER, Vinet, 1853. QUINET, Œuvres, 1857. On the relation of Church and State : DEBIDOUR, Hist. des rapports de l'Église et de l'État, 1898.

Liberal and democratic writers before 1848 : THIERS, Hist. de la révolution française, 1823-7 ; in 1830, with CARREL and MAGNET, Thiers founded the *Journal national*, in which he published the famous programme of the Liberal party ; Histoire du consulat et de l'Empire, 1840 and following years (cf. J. SIMON, Thiers, Guizot, Rémusat, 1885 ; RÉMUSAT, Thiers, in *Les grands écrivains français*). LAMARTINE, political writings and speeches collected in La France parlementaire, 6 vols., 1865 ; La politique rationnelle, 1831 (cf. DOUMIE, L., in *Les grands écrivains français*). DE TOCQUEVILLE, De la démocratie en Amérique, part i, 1835 ; part ii, 1840 ; L'ancien régime et la révolution, 1856 ; Souvenirs (Œuvres complètes, 1860-5, 9 vols. ; cf. D'EICHTHAL, A. de T. et la démocratie libérale, 1897). DUVERGIER DE HARANNE, Hist. du gouvernement parlementaire en France, 1857. THUREAU-DANGIN, Hist. de la monarchie de juillet, 7 vols.

The Revolution of 1848 : THIERS, De la propriété, 1848. GUIZOT, De la démocratie en France (janvier 1849), 1849. O. BARROT, Mémoires posthumes, 4 vols., 1875-6. DE TOCQUEVILLE, Souvenirs, *cit.* CHEVALIER, Question des travailleurs, 1848. LAMENNAIS, La question du travail, 1848. CONSIDÉRANT, La révolution ou le gouvernement direct du peuple, 1851. *Contra* : BLANC, Le gouvernement direct du peuple par lui-même. PROUDHON, Idée générale de la révolution au XIXe siècle, ed. 2, 1851. L. BLANC, Histoire de la révolution de 1848, 2 vols., 1870. D. STERN, Histoire de la révolution de 1848, 2 vols., 1850 ; ed. 2, 1862. AD. BLANQUI, Les classes ouvrières en France en 1848-9, 1849 ; Les populations rurales de la France (*Journal des Écon.*, 1852). MARX, La lotta di classe in Francia dal 1848 al 1850, preface by ENGELS (in the Italian ed. of MARX's works published by *Avanti*).

Liberalism under the Second Empire : VACHEROT, La démocratie, 1859. LABOULAYE, La liberté antique et la liberté moderne, 1863 ; Le parti libéral, son programme et son avenir, 1863 ; L'État et ses limites, 1868 (Ital. tr., *Bibl. sc. polit.*, ser. i, vol. vii) ; La liberté religieuse : Questions constitutionnelles. PRÉVOST-PARADOL, Essai de politique et de littérature, 1859 ; De gouvernement parlementaire, 1860 ; Nouveaux essais, 1862 ; La France nouvelle, 1868. Duc de BROGLIE, Vues sur le gouvernement de la France. J. SIMON, Le devoir, 1854 ; La liberté, 2 vols., 1859 ; Le travail, ed. 4, 1867 ; La politique radicale, 1868, &c. OLLIVIER, L'Empire libéral, 13 vols., 1897-1908.

Reactionary positivism : A. COMTE, Cours de philosophie positive, 1830-42 ; Système de philosophie positive, 1851-4 ; Appel aux conservateurs, 1855. A more moderate view is taken by his pupil LITTRÉ, Application

de la philosophie positive au gouvernement de la société, 1850 ; Conservation, révolution, positivisme, 1852 (ed. 2, 1879) ; L'Établissement de la
troisième République, 1880.

The school of LE PLAY (La réforme sociale en France, 1864 ; L'Organisation du travail, 1870 ; La constitution essentielle de l'humanité, 1881)
stands by itself. So does GOBINEAU, Essai sur l'inégalité des races
humaines, 1853-5 (2nd ed., 1884). Intermediate between Liberalism
and the democratic worship of the State is DUPONT WHITE, L'individu
et l'État, ed. 2, 1858 ; La centralisation, 1860 ; La liberté politique
considérée dans ses rapports avec l'administration locale, 1864 ; Le
progrès politique, 1868.

Political literature of the Third Republic : DE PARIEU, L'État et ses fonctions, 1871. H. PASSY, Des formes de gouvernement et des lois qui les
régissent. RENAN, Questions contemporaines, 1872 ; La réforme intel-
lectuelle et morale de la France, 1872 ; Qu'est-ce qu'une nation? 1882.
RENOUVIER, La science et la morale, 1869 ; La critique philosophique,
1872-89. FOUILLÉE, L'idée moderne du droit, 1878 ; La science sociale
contemporaine, 1880 ; Critique des systèmes de morale contemporaines,
1883 ; La propriété sociale et la démocratie, 1884. TAINE, Les origines
de la France contemporaine : L'ancien régime, 1875 ; La révolution
(i, 1878 ; ii, 1881 ; iii, 1884) ; Le régime moderne (i, 1891 ; ii, unfinished,
1893). GUYAN, Esquisse d'un morale sans obligation ni sanction, 1885.
SCHERER, La démocratie en France, 1884. MOLINARI, L'évolution
politique et la révolution, 1884 ; Les problèmes de XXᵉ siècle, 1901.
P. LEROY-BEAULIEU, L'État moderne et ses fonctions, 1880 (Ital. tr.,
Bibl. sc. polit., ser. i, vol. vii). A. LEROY-BEAULIEU, La révolution et le
libéralisme, 1890. PRINS (Belgian) La démocratie et le régime parlementaire, 1884 ; L'organisation de la liberté et le devenir social, 1895.
LAVELEYE (Belgian), Le gouvernement dans la démocratie, ed. 2, 1892 ;
De l'avenir des peuples catholiques, 1894. A. DESJARDIN, La liberté
politique dans l'État moderne. DURKHEIM, La division du travail social,
1893. D'EICHTHAL, Souveraineté du peuple et gouvernement, 1895.
L. BOURGEOIS, La solidarité (*Nouvelle Revue*, 1896 ; states a quasi-con-
tractual doctrine related to the social contract as Bourgeois to Rousseau,
and more fully expounded in a series of lectures by various writers,
edited by B., and entitled Essai d'une philosophie de solidarité, 1902).
M. F. BUISSON, La politique radicale. FAGUET, Le libéralisme, 1902.
CHARMONT, La transformation du droit civil. DUGUIT, Le droit social
et le droit individuel. YVES GUYOT, La morale dans la concurrence, &c.
H. MICHEL, L'idée de l'État, *cit.* FONSEGRIVE, Morale et société, 1907.
P. MATTER, La dissolution des assemblées parlementaires. DANOS,
L'autarchie économique et l'évolution du commerce extérieur, 1921.
Cf. also WEILL, Hist. du mouvement social en France, 1852-1902, Paris,
1904. On Guild Socialism : G. SOREL, Les illusions du progrès, 1908 ;
Réflections sur la violence, 1908 (4th ed., 1912) ; Matériaux d'une
théorie du prolétariat, 1919.

III. GERMANY

General Histories: SYBEL, Geschichte der Revolutionszeit: 1789-95, ed. 4, 1877; 1795-1800, ed. 2, 1878-9; Die deutsche Nation und das Kaiserreich, 1862. GERVINUS (Liberal writer), Einleitung in die Geschichte des 19ten Jahrb., 1853 (Fr. tr. 1858); Geschichte des 19ten Jahrb., 1856-66. TREITSCHKE, Deutsche Geschichte in 19ten Jahrh., 5 vols., 1886-95 (down to 1848). FUETER (Swiss), Weltgeschichte der letzten hundert Jahren, 1815-1920, Zürich, 1921. G. KOCH, Beiträge zur Geschichte d. politischen Ideen, 1892-6. I. PETRONE, La fase recentissima della filosofia del diritto in Germania.

The Romantic Period: HAYM, Die romantische Schule, 1870. WALZEL, Deutsche Romantik, 1908. MEINECKE, Weltburgertum und National-staat, ed. 2, 1911. Sources: KANT, Grundlegung zur Metaphysik der Sitten, 1785; Kritik der praktischen Vernunft, 1788; Metaphysische Anfangsgründe der Rechts- und Tugendlehre, 1797; Zum ewigen Frieden. J. FRIES, Philosophische Rechtslehre und Kritik aller positiven Gesetzgebung, 1803. W. von HUMBOLDT, Ideen über Staatsverfassung, durch die neue französische Revolution veranlasst, 1791; Ideen zu einem Versuch die Grenzen des Staats zu bestimmen, 1791-2 (cf. HAYM, H.; KITTEL, W. von Hs. geschichtliche Weltanschauung, 1901; E. SPRANGER, W. von H. und die Humanitätsidee, 1909). F. SCHLEGEL, Versuch über den Begriff des Republikanismus, 1796; Philosophische Vorlesungen aus Jahren 1804 bis 1806, ed. WINDISCHMANN, 1836-7; Ueber die neue Geschichte, Vorlesungen gehalten im Jahre 1810, Wien, 1811 (cf. ROUGE, F. Schl. et la génèse du romanticisme alle-mand, 2 vols., 1904). FICHTE, Beitrag zur Berichtigung der Urtheile des Publikums ueber die franz. Revolution, 1793; Zurückforderung der Denkfreiheit, au die Fürsten Europas, 1794; Vorlesungen ueber die Bestimmung des Gelehrten, 1794; Grundlagen des Naturrechts, 1796; Die geschlossene Handelsstaat, 1800; Reden an die deutsche Nation, 1808. HARDENBERG, memoir on the reorganization of the Prussian state, in vol. xlviii of RANKE's Werke. STEIN, cf. DELBRÜCK, Die Ideen Steins ueber deutsche Verfassung: Erinnerungen, Aufsätze und Reden, and MEYER, Die Reform der Verwaltungsorganisation nach Stein und Hardenberg, 1880. A. MÜLLER, Vorlesungen ueber die Elemente der Staatskunst, 3 vols., 1808. The historical school: HUGO, Lehrbuch des Naturrechts, 1798; SAVIGNY, Vom Beruf unserer Zeit für Gesetzgebung und Rechtswissenschaft, 1814 (3rd ed., 1892); Geschichte des röm. Rechts in Mittelalter, 1815-31; System des heutigen röm. Rechts, 1840 and later (cf. BECKER, Ueber den Streit der historischen und der philosophischen Rechtsschule, 1887; VANNI, I giuristi della scuola storica di Germania nella storia della sociologia e della filosofia positiva, 1885). SCHLEIERMACHER, Ueber den Begriff der verschiedenen Staatsformen, 1814; Lehre vom Staate (posthumous). HALLER (Swiss), Restauration der Staatswissenschaften, 1820–34, 6 vols. (cf. CROCE, Elementi di politica, 1925). HEGEL, Grundlinien der Philosophie des Rechts, 1820 (the additions, which are very important, were extracted from Hotho and Griesholm's notes of subsequent lectures (Ital. tr., MESSINEO, in *Classici della filos. moderna*. Cf. again CROCE, Elementi di politica, *cit.*).

Liberalism before Frankfort : R. von MOHL, Die Geschichte und die Literatur der Staatswissenschaften, 3 vols., 1855. ANCILLON, Ueber Souveränität und Staatsverfassung, 1815. K. G. ZACHARIÄ, Vierzig Bücher vom Staate, 1820–32. K. von ROTTECK, Rechtsprinzipien oder idealer Politik unter hist. begründ. Verhältnissen, 1820; Lehrbuch des Vernunftrechts, 1829–35. ARETIN, Staatsrecht der konstitutionellen Monarchie, 1824. L. HOFFMANN, Die staatbürgerlichen Garantien, ed. 2, 1831. L. BÜCHER, Der Parlamentarismus, 1831. MATTHIAS, Die Idee der Freiheit in Individuum, im Staate und in der Kirche, 1834. EICHHORN, Deutsche Staats- und Rechtsgeschichte, ed. 4, 1843–4. A. MOHL, Ueber das Repräsentativsystem, 1840. AHRENS, Organische Staatslehre, 1850 (incomplete; revised reissue under the title Naturrecht oder Philosophie des Rechts und des Staates, 2 vols., 1870). On the Parliament of Frankfort, cf. the general histories, and memoirs by HAYM (1848–50), DUNKER (1849), LAMBE (1849), HELLER (1849), and others, and correspondence of the GRIMM brothers and of DAHLMANN with GERVINUS.

The theory of political parties : ROHMER (Swiss), Lehre von der politischen Parteien, 1844 (comparing the four parties with the four ages of man). STAHL, Die gegenwartige Parteien in Staat und Kirche, 1863 (by the same : Ueber das monarchische Prinzip, 1845; Die Revolution und die constitutionelle Monarchie, 1848). FRANTZ, Kritik aller Parteien, 1864. BLUNTSCHLI (Swiss), Charakter und Geist der politischen Parteien. TREITSCHKE, Hist. pol. Aufsätze (Parteien und Fraktionen, vol. iii). PEITZIG, Die national-liberal Partei, 1867–92. PAULSEN, Parteipolitik und Moral, 1900. STILLICH, Die politischen Parteien in Deutschland, 1908.

Nationality : A great contribution to the growth of a national political thought as distinct from the humanitarianism of the Romantics was made by RANKE: especially Frankreich und Deutschland, 1832; Ueber die Trennung und Einheit von Deutschland, 1832; Die grossen Mächte, 1833; Politisches Gespräch, 1836; in vols. 49–50 of his Werke, except Die grossen Mächte in vol. 24. The Polit. Gespräch was reprinted with introduction by MEINECKE in 1924. Cf. LENZ, Bismarck und Ranke, Kleine hist. Schriften. For the modern idea of nationality cf. NAUMANN, Volk und Nation, 1888; HENRITT, Nationalität und Recht, 1899; A. KIRCHHOFF, Was ist National? 1902; Verständigung ueber die Begriffe Nation und Nationalität, 1905; MEINECKE, Weltbürgertum und Nationalstaat, *cit.*

The State according to rights : A. MERKEL, Philos. Einleitung in die Rechtswissenschaft, in Holtzendorf's Encyclopaedia. REHM, Geschichte der Staatswissenschaft. GUMPLOWICZ, Gesch. der Staatstheorien, 1905. L. STEIN, System der Staatswissenschaft, 1856. ZACHARIÄ, Deutsches Staats- und Bundesrecht, ed. 3, 1865. LABAND, Staatsrecht des d. Reichs, 3 vols., 1876-82. GNEIST, Der Rechtstaat und die Verwaltungsgeschichte in Deutschland, ed. 2, 1879 (Ital. tr. in vol. v of *Bibl. sc. polit.*). GIERKE, Das deutsche Genossenschaftsrecht, 1868-9; Die Grundbegriffe des Staatsrechts und die neuesten Staatstheorien, 1874; Die Genossenschaftstheorie und die d. Rechtssprechung, 1877. JELLINEK, Gesetz und Verordnung, 1887; Die subjectiven öffentlichen Rechte, Die Erklärung der Menschen- und Bürgerrechte, ed. 2, 1904; Allgemeine Rechtslehre, ed. 2, 1905. Juridico-social works: WAGENER, Entwurf zu einem Programm des Rechtes, 1855; A. MENGER, Das bürgerliche Recht und die besitzlosen Volksklassen, 1890; Ueber die sozialen Aufgaben der Rechtswissenschaft, 1885; Neue Staatslehre, 1903 (Ital. tr., Lo Stato socialista, 1915); R. STAMMLER, Wirtschaft und Recht nach den materialistischen Geschichtsauffassung.

Social theory: nationalist-conservative economists: F. LIST, Das nationale system der politischen Oekonomie, 1841. His pupil DÜHRING, Kursus der National- und Sozialökonomie, 1873. *Contra*: ENGELS, Herrn E. Dührings Umwalzung der Wissenschaft, 1894. Free trade: SCHULZE DELITZSCH, Catechismo di Economia politicale ad uso degli operai tedeschi (Ital. tr., *Bibl. degli Econ.*, ser. iii, vol. ix). *Contra*: LASSALLE, Bastiat-Schulze di Delitzsch Giuliano economico, ossia Capitale e lavoro (Ital. tr., *Bibl. degli Econ.*, ser. iii, vol. ix). Social Liberals: F. A. LANGE, Die Arbeiterfrage, ed. 3, 1875. GLASER, Erhebung des Arbeitsbestandes zur wirtschaftlicher Selbständigkeit, 1865. BRENTANO, Arbeitergilde der Gegenwart; Meine Polemik mit K. Marx, 1890; Ueber Ursachen der heutigen sozialen Noth, 1889. HERKNER, Die soziale Reform als Gebot des wirtschaftlichen Fortschritts, 1891; Die Arbeiterfrage, ed. 5, 1908. SCHULZE GAEVERNITZ, La Grande Intrapresa (Ital. tr., *Bibl. degli Econ.*, ser. iv, part i); Zum sozialen Frieden; Britischer Imperialismus, *cit.* Cf. SIMMEL, Ueber soziale Differenzierung, 1890. On the agricultural classes: Von der GOLZ, Die landliche Arbeitsklasse und der preussische Staat, 1893. WAGNER, Agrar- und Industriestaat, ed. 2, 1902.

Socialism: MEHRING, Gesch. d. deuts. Sozialdemokratie, 1898. ANDLER, Le socialisme d'État en Allemagne, 1897. W. SOMBART, Le socialisme et le mouvement social au xixe siècle, 1898. BERNSTEIN, Zur Gesch. u. Theorie des Sozialismus, 1901.

Christian-Socialist theories: JÖRG (Catholic), Gesch. d. sozialpolitischen Parteien, 1867. GÖHRE, Die evangelischsoziale Bewegung, 1896. ULHORN, Katholizismus und Protestantismus gegenüber der sozialen Frage, 1887. WEBER, Die soziale Organisation des röm. Katholizismus in Deutschland, 1890. TROELTSCH, Politische Etik und Christentum, 1904. GOYAU, L'Allemagne religieuse (Protestantisme-Catholicisme).

Anarchism: MAX STIRNER, Der Einzige und sein Eigentum, 1844.

STAMMLER, Theorie des Anarchismus, 1894. ZENKER, Der Anarchismus, 1895. ELSBACHER, Der Anarchismus, 1900.

The Empire : J. FISCHER (Liberal writer) Preussen am Abschlusse des ersten Hälfte des 19ten Jahrh., 1876. TREITSCHKE, Zehn Jahre deutscher Kämpfe, 1865–70; Hist. politische Aufsätze, 1886–97; Politik, 1899 (Ital. tr., Ruta, 4 vols.) [Engl. tr., 2 vols., 1916]. ONKEN, Kaiser Wilhelm I. E. MARKS, Kaiser Wilhelm I, ed. 3, 1899. LAVISSE, Trois Empereurs d'Allemagne, 1888. LOWELL, Government and Parties in Central Europe, *cit.* BISMARCK, Ausgewählte Reden, 1862–81, Berlin, 1877–81; Pensieri e ricordi (Ital. tr., 2 vols., 1898). Cf. P. MATTER, Bismarck et son temps, 3 vols., 1908. The Kulturkampf: HAM, Der Kulturkampf, 1881. GOYAU, Bismarck et l'Église; Le Culturkampf. BAZIN, L'Allemagne catholique au xixᵉ siècle. KANNEGIESSER, Les catholiques allemands, 1891. The Old Catholic movement of the seventies : BÜHLE, Der Altkathol., 1880. SCHULTE, Der Altkathol., Gesch. seiner Entwicklung, 1887. Imperialistic policy: ADLER, Die imperialistische Sozialpolitik, 1897. DEITZEL, Weltwirtschaft und Volkswirtschaft, 1900. NAUMANN, Demokratie und Kaisertum, ed. 3, 1904.

On the present day, the following may serve as general guides : NAUMANN, Mitteleuropa, 1915 (Ital. tr., 2 vols.) [Engl. tr., 1916]. MAX WEBER, *cit.*, and Nationalstaat und Volkswirtschaft, 1895; Wahlrecht und Demokratie in Deutschland, 1918; Parlament und Regierung in neugeordneten Deutschland, 1918 (Ital. tr., Ruta, 1919). FUETER (Swiss), Weltgeschichte, *cit.* RATHENAU, Der neue Staat, 1919. VIERKANDT, Stetigkeit im Kulturwandel, 1924. MEINECKE, Die Staatsräson, 1925.

IV. ITALY

We shall give a briefer account of Italian political literature, because the number of works that have in any important way influenced the development of political ideas is very restricted. For a larger bibliography the reader may refer to the general works quoted below.

General works : LAVISSE-RAMBAUD, *cit.*, SEIGNOBOS, *cit.*, LOWELL, *cit.* BOLTON KING, History of Italian Unity, 1899 (Fr. tr., 2 vols., 1901). ORIANI, La Cotta politica in Italia (3 vols., published by La Voce). RAULICH, Storia del Risorgimento politico d'Italia, 1815–48, 3 vols., 1920. HARTMANN, Il Risorgimento (Ital. tr., Mazanini, 1924). CROCE, Storia della storiografia italiana nel secolo XIX, 1921. CIASCA, L'origine del Programma per l'opinione nazionale italiana del 1847–8, 1916. SOLMI, Il Risorgimento italiano, 1919. ANZILLOTTI, Gioberti (*Collezione, storica*, published by Vallecchi). ROSI, L'Italia odierna, 1918; Storia contemporanea d'Italia, ed. 2, 1922.

The period of preparation : the southern tradition, CROCE, Storia del Regno di Napoli, 1925. G. DE RUGGIERO, Il pensiero politico meridionale nei secoli XVIII e XIX, 1922. Sources : GIANNONE, Dell' Istoria civile del Regno di Napoli, 1723; Il Triregno, 1895; Vita, ed. Nicolini, 1915;

Dialogue sur le commerce des blés (Il pensiero dell' Abate Galiani, ed. Nicolini, 1909). FILANGIERI, La scienza della legislazione, 1788 and later (Florence, 1864). PAGANO, Saggi politici (Opere, Lugano, 1831). CUOCO, Frammenti di lettere a V. Russo ; Saggio storico (ed. Nicolini) ; Platone in Italia (d'Ajala, 1861) ; articles and essays selected by GENTILE, Scritti pedagogici di V. C., 1909. Northern Italy : CIASCA, *op. cit.*, and L'evoluzione economica della Lombardia dagli inizi del secolo XIX al 1860, 1924. PRATO, La vita economica in Piemonte a mezzo il secolo XVIII, 1908. HAZARD, La révolution française et les lettres italiennes, 1910. ALFIERI, Della tirannide, libri ii, 1777; Del principe e delle lettere, 1786; Misogallo, 1799 (cf. GOBETTI, La filosofia politica di V. Alfieri, 1924). On *Caffè*, L. FERRARI, Del Caffè, periodico milanese, 1899. P. VERRI, Scritti inediti, London, 1825; Storia di Milano, continued by P. Custodi, Florence, 1851 (cf. A. OTTOLINI, P. Verri e i suoi tempi). GIOIA, Dissertazione sul problema, quale dei governi liberi meglio convenga alla felicità d'Italia, 1798 (ed. 3, Lugano, 1833). ROMAGNOSI, Opere, 1842; Scienza delle costituzioni, 1847. FOSCOLO, Prose politiche (Discorso su l'Italia ; Orazione a Bonaparte ; Della servitù d'Italia, discorsi 4 ; Lettera apologetica), 1850.

The movements of 1820-1 : Naples : CROCE, Storia, *cit.*, and Una famiglia di patrioti, 1920. Turin : SANTAROSA, Delle speranze d'Italia (Risorgimento, 1920) ; La rivoluzione piemontese del 1821 (tr. Luzio, 1920). The Moderates : the journal Il Conciliatore, 1818–19. MANZONI, Osservazioni sulla morale cattolica, 1819. ROSMINI, Filosofia della politica (Opere edite ed inedite, xx, 1837) ; La costituzione secondo la giustizia sociale (with appendix on the unity of Italy), 1848. GIOBERTI, Del primato morale e civile degl' Italiani, 1843; Del rinnovamento civile d'Italia (ed. Nicolini, 3 vols. ; cf. ANZILLOTTI, Gioberti, *cit.*). TOMMASEO, Dell' Italia, 1835. BALBO, Delle speranze d'Italia, 1843 ; Della monarchia rappresentativa in Italia, 1857 (incomplete and posthumous). MAMIANI, Scritti politici, 1853. D'AZEGLIO, Scritti politici e letterari, 2 vols., 1872. G. CAPPONI, Scritti editi ed inediti, 1877. LAMBRUSCHINI, Pensieri di un solitario (Barbera, 1887). G. DURANDO, Della nazionalità italiana, 1846. L. TORELLI, Pensieri sull' Italia di un anonimo Lombardo, 1846.

The social and economic movement of 1848 : G. PRATO, Fatti e dottrine economiche alla vigilia di 1848, 1921 ; F. Ferrara a Torino, 1849–59, 1923. Liberalism in Italy : CAVOUR's works, and FERRARA's fine introductions to the *Biblioteca degli Economisti*, 1850 and later. French Socialism and its influence in Italy : PETRUCCELLI, La rivoluzione di Napoli nel 1848 (ed. 2, Torraca, 1912). MONDAINI, I moti politici del 1848, 1902. G. DE RUGGIERO, *op. cit.*

Democrats : G. MAZZINI, Scritti editi ed inediti (author's ed., 1841–81 ; national ed., 1906 and later ; less cumbrous, Scritti : Politica ed Economia, 2 vols., 1898 ; Filosofia, 2 vols., 1902. Cf. R. KING, Mazzini (Ital. tr. 1903) ; SALVEMINI, Il pensiero religioso, politico e sociale di

G. M., 1905; GENTILE, Mazzini e Gioberti). C. CATTANEO, Opere edite ed inedite, 1892 (cf. SALVEMINI, Le più belle pagine di C. C., with introduction, Treves). G. FERRARI, Filosofia della rivoluzione, 1851; Storia delle rivoluzioni d'Italia, 1856 and later; Teoria dei periodi politici, 1874; Histoire de la raison d'État, 1860.

Origins of the Right: BROFFERIO, Storia del Parlamento subalpino, 1866. CAVOUR, Gli Scritti, ed. Zanichelli, 1892; Lettere edite ed inedite, ed. Chiala, 3rd ed., 1903; Discorsi scelti, 1851–61, published L'Esame, edited with introduction by Lely, 1925. TREITSCHKE, Cavour (Ital. tr., Cecchini, 1921). ZANICHELLI, C., 1905. F. RUFFINI, La giovinezza del Conte di C., 2 vols., 1912. R. MURRI, C., 1915. P. MATTER, C. et l'unité italienne, 1922–5.

Religious policy: MINGHETTI, Della libertà religiosa (in Opusc. econ. e letter., 1871); Stato e Chiesa, ed. 2, 1878; Miei ricordi, 1889. BONGHI, La chiesa libera (Nuova Antologia), 1870. Padre CURCI, La nuova Italia e i vecchi zelanti. PIOLA, Della libertà della Chiesa, 1874. G. M. BERTINI, Il Vaticano e lo Stato, 1877. MARIANO, La libertà di coscienza; Cristianesimo, cattolicismo e civiltà, &c. Cf. also QUADROTTA, La chiesa cattolica nella crisi universale, 1921. GANGALE, Rivoluzione protestante, 1925.

Policy and administration: S. SPAVENTA, Dal 1848 al 1861, ed. Croce, ed. 2, 1923; La politica della Destra, ed. Croce, 1901. MINGHETTI, I partiti politici e la loro ingerenza nella giustizia e nell' amministrazione, 1885. Economic and social problems: CORRENTI, Scritti scelti, ed. Massarani, 4 vols., 1891–4. JACINI, Frammenti dell' inchiesta agraria (with other studies, in a volume published by the Ministry of Agriculture, ed. 2, 1883).

Political thought of De Sanctis: Scritti politici (Ferrarelli); Discorsi politici, collected by Croce in *La Critica*, 1914; Storia della letteratura italiana, ed. Croce, vol. ii. Cf. also B. SPAVENTA, Principii di etica, ed. Gentile, 1901. De MEIS, Dopo la laurea, 2 vols., 1868–9.

Nationality: TAPARELLI D'AZEGLIO, Della nazionalità, 1847. PISANELLI, Lo Stato e la Nazione, 1862. MARIANO, L'individuo e lo Stato, 1876. MANCINI, Prelezioni, 1873. ZANICHELLI, Nazione e democrazia, 1885. HOLTZENDORFT, Le principe de nationalité et la littérature italienne (*Revue de droit intern.*, ii. 92). MICELI, Lo Stato e la Nazione, 1890.

The southern question: FORTUNATO, Il Mezzogiorno e lo Stato italiano, 1880–1910, 1911; Questione meridionale e riforma tributaria, 1920. SONNINO and FRANCHETTI, Condizioni economiche e amministrative dell' Italia meridionale, 1875 (reprinted 1925). FRANCHETTI, Condizioni politiche e amministrative della Sicilia, 1877. BRUCCOLERI, La Sicilia d'oggi, 1913. AZIMONTI, Il mezzogiorno agrario quale è, 1921. CIASCA, Il problema della terra, 1921. STURZO, Il mezzogiorno e la politica italiana (in Riforma statale e indirizzi politici, 1923).

Present day: See *Biblioteca di scienze politiche*, ed. BRUNIALTI, whose copious introductions may be consulted for a comprehensive bibliography of political thought in recent decades. As a whole, the level of this literature shows a marked decline. We shall mention only a few works of general interest. P. TURIELLO, Governo e governati in Italia, 2 vols., 1882. F. PAPAFAVA, Dieci anni di vita politica italiana, 2 vols. G. MOSCA, Sulla teoria dei governi e sul governo parlamentare, 1884; Elementi di scienza politica, 1896 (2nd ed., 1923). V. PARETO, Les systèmes socialistes, 1902; Trattato di sociologia generale, 2 vols., 1916. Free trade : EINAUDI, Prediche, 1920; Gli ideali di un economista, 1921. U. RICCI, Protezionisti e liberisti, 1920. For the political aspect of modern philosophical thought, CROCE, Elementi di Politica (cit.), is important; cf. his postilla, Liberalismo, in La Critica, March 1925. Writings by leaders of the Liberal party : GIOLITTI, Memorie della mia vita, 2 vols., 1922. SALANDRA, La politica nazionale e il partito liberale, 1912; Politica e legislazione (essays collected by Fortunato), 1915. ORLANDO, Teoria giuridica della guarentigie della libertà (Bibl. di sc. polit., vol. 5); Principii di diritto costituzionale (Barbera). Liberal democracy : NITTI, Nord e Sud, 1900; Il Capitale straniero in Italia, 1915; L'Europa senza pace, 1921, 2nd ed., 1922; La decadenza dell' Europa, 1922; La tragedia dell' Europa, 1924; La pace, 1925. AMEN-DOLA, Una battaglia liberale, 1924; La democrazia, 1924. Cf. also MICHELS, Il partito politico nella democrazia moderna, ed. 2, 1924.

Liberal Catholicism : L. STURZO, Riforma statale e indirizzi politici, 1924; Popolarismo e fascismo, 1924; La libertà in Italia, 1925 New tendencies in Liberalism : M. MISSIROLI, La monarchia socialista, 1914 (ed. 2, 1923); Il fascismo e la crisi italiana, 1921; Polemica liberale, 1920; Una battaglia perduta, 1925; Il colpo di Stato, 1925. SALVA-TORELLI, Nazionalfascismo, 1923. BURZIO, Politica demiurgica, 1923. N. PAPAFAVA, Fissazioni liberali, 1924. G. PIAZZA, La fiamma bilingue, 1925. Cf. also the Liberal reviews Rivoluzione liberale, Rinascita liberale, Il Caffè, L'Esame, Il Saggiatore. Articles, often of importance, appear in the general Liberal press (Il Corriere della sera, La Stampa, Il Mondo, Il Giornale d'Italia, Il Mattino, &c.).

Socialism : A. LABRIOLA, Saggi intorno a una concezione materialistica della Storia, 1895. CROCE, Materialismo storico ed economia marxistica (Saggi filosofici, vol. iv, ed. 4 : Engl. tr.). TURATI, Trenta anni di critica sociale, 1921. MONDOLFO, Sulle orme di Marx, ed. 3, 1923. LONGS-BARDI, La conferma del Marxismo, 1921. SALVEMINI, Tendenze vecchie e necessità nuove del movimento operaio italiano, 1922.

INDEX